ALSO BY BARRY STRAUSS

The Death of Caesar: The Story of History's Most Famous Assassination

*Masters of Command: Alexander, Hannibal,
Caesar, and the Genius of Leadership*

The Spartacus War

The Trojan War: A New History

*The Battle of Salamis: The Naval Encounter That
Saved Greece—and Western Civilization*

*What If?: The World's Foremost Military Historians
Imagine What Might Have Been* (contributor)

Western Civilization: The Continuing Experiment
(with Thomas F. X. Noble and others)

*War and Democracy: A Comparative Study of the Korean War
and the Peloponnesian War* (with David McCann, coeditor)

Rowing Against the Current: On Learning to Scull at Forty

*Fathers and Sons in Athens: Ideology and Society
in the Era of the Peloponnesian War*

*Hegemonic Rivalry: From Thucydides to the Nuclear
Age* (with Richard Ned Lebow, coeditor)

*The Anatomy of Error: Ancient Military Disasters and Their
Lessons for Modern Strategists* (with Josiah Ober)

*Athens After the Peloponnesian War: Class,
Faction, and Policy, 403–386 BC*

TEN
CAESARS

Roman Emperors

from Augustus to Constantine

BARRY STRAUSS

SIMON & SCHUSTER

NEW YORK   LONDON   TORONTO   SYDNEY   NEW DELHI

Simon & Schuster
1230 Avenue of the Americas
New York, NY 10020

First Simon & Schuster hardcover edition March 2019

SIMON & SCHUSTER and colophon are registered trademarks of Simon & Schuster, Inc.

For information about special discounts for bulk purchases, please contact Simon & Schuster Special Sales at 1-866-506-1949 or business@simonandschuster.com.

The Simon & Schuster Speakers Bureau can bring authors to your live event. For more information or to book an event, contact the Simon & Schuster Speakers Bureau at 1-866-248-3049 or visit our website at www.simonspeakers.com.

Interior design by Ruth Lee-Mui
Maps by Paul J. Pugliese

Manufactured in the United States of America

1   3   5   7   9   10   8   6   4   2

Library of Congress Cataloging-in-Publication Data

Names: Strauss, Barry S., author
Title: Ten Caesars : Roman Emperors from Augustus to Constantine / Barry Strauss.
Description: New York : Simon & Schuster, 2019. | Includes bibliographical references and index.
Identifiers: LCCN 2018036261 | ISBN 9781451668834 (hardback) | ISBN 145166883X
Subjects: LCSH: Emperors—Rome—Biography. | Rome—History—Empire,
30 B.C.–476 A.D. | BISAC: HISTORY / Ancient / Rome. | HISTORY / Europe / Western. | BIOGRAPHY & AUTOBIOGRAPHY / Historical.
Classification: LCC DG274 .S77 2019 | DDC 937/.060922—dc23 LC record available at https://urldefense.proofpoint.com/v2/url?u=https-3A__1ccn.loc.gov_2018036261&d=DwIFAg&c=jGUuvAdBXp_VqQ6t0yah2g&r=zKAnnLSQItsYNuYG0gjF6SYJylpwsS1CuoJqVbpsc2Q&m=oPSVZaPgE2bMcsvD7SxW7JPawGvWyZT6BzwvB-frzdA&s=X4Y4wIRPhPKdfdlaphbcWMhF-dQ96RQ2xyFCdWfHQcE&e=

ISBN 978-1-4516-6883-4
ISBN 978-1-4516-6885-8 (ebook)

To my students

CONTENTS

AUTHOR'S NOTE

Ancient names are generally spelled following the style of the standard reference work, *The Oxford Classical Dictionary*, 4th ed. (Oxford: Oxford University Press, 2012).

Translations from the Greek or Latin are my own, unless otherwise noted.

All dates are AD unless noted otherwise.

CHRONOLOGY OF THE EMPERORS

THE REIGNS

All dates AD unless stated otherwise.

Augustus	27 BC–14 AD
Tiberius	14–37
Nero	54–68
Vespasian	69–79
Trajan	98–117
Hadrian	117–138
Marcus Aurelius	161–180
Septimius Severus	193–211
Diocletian	284–305
Constantine	306–337

TEN CAESARS

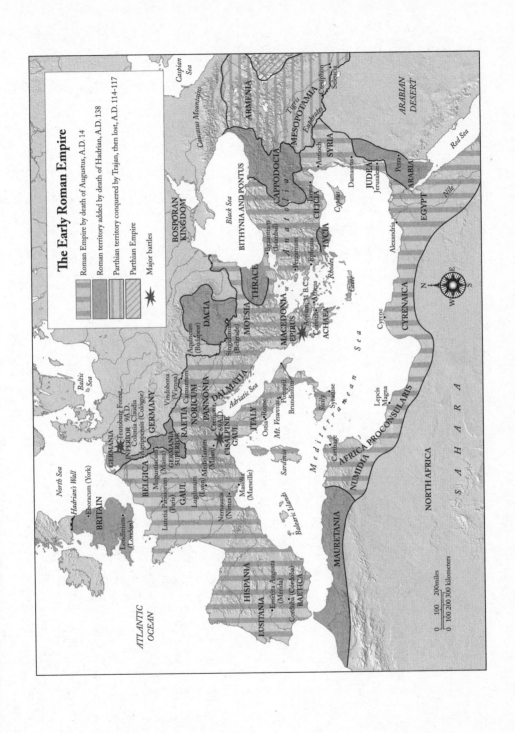

The Early Roman Empire

Roman Empire by death of Augustus, A.D.14
Roman territory added by death of Hadrian, A.D. 138
Parthian territory conquered by Trajan, then lost, A.D. 114-117
Parthian Empire
Major battles

ATLANTIC OCEAN

North Sea

Baltic Sea

BRITAIN
Hadrian's Wall
Eboracum (York)
Londinium (London)

HISPANIA
LUSITANIA
Emerita Augusta (Mérida)
BAETICA
Corduba (Cordoba)

MAURETANIA

NORTH AFRICA

GERMANIA
GERMANIA INFERIOR
Teutoburg Forest, 9 A.D.
Colonia Claudia Agrippensis (Cologne)
BELGICA
GERMANIA SUPERIOR
Moguntiacum (Mainz)
GAUL
Lutetia Parisiorum (Paris)
Lugdunum (Lyon)
Nemausus (Nîmes)
Massilia (Marseille)
Balearic Islands
Sardinia

RAETIA
Vindobona (Vienna)
NORICUM
Carnuntum
PANNONIA
Aquincum (Budapest)
Singidunum (Belgrade)

DACIA

MOESIA

THRACE
Byzantium (Istanbul)

BOSPORAN KINGDOM

Caspian Sea

Caucasus Mountains

ARMENIA

Black Sea

BITHYNIA AND PONTUS

CAPPADOCIA
Anatolia
Pergamum
Ephesus
Tarsus
CILICIA
LYCIA

Rhodes
Crete

MESOPOTAMIA
Tigris
Euphrates
Ctesiphon
Seleucia

SYRIA
Antioch
Damascus
ARABIA
Petra
JUDEA
Jerusalem

ARABIAN DESERT

Red Sea

EGYPT
Alexandria
Nile

CYRENAICA
Cyrene

AFRICA PROCONSULARIS
Lepcis Magna
Carthage
NUMIDIA

SAHARA

CISALPINE GAUL
Cremona, 69 A.D.
Mediolanum (Milan)
ITALY
Ostia Rome
Mt. Vesuvius
Pompeii
Brundisium
Sicily Syracuse

DALMATIA
Adriatic Sea

MACEDONIA
EPIRUS
Actium, 31 B.C.
ACHAEA
Corinth Athens

Mediterranean Sea

N W E S

0 100 200miles
0 100 200 300 kilometers

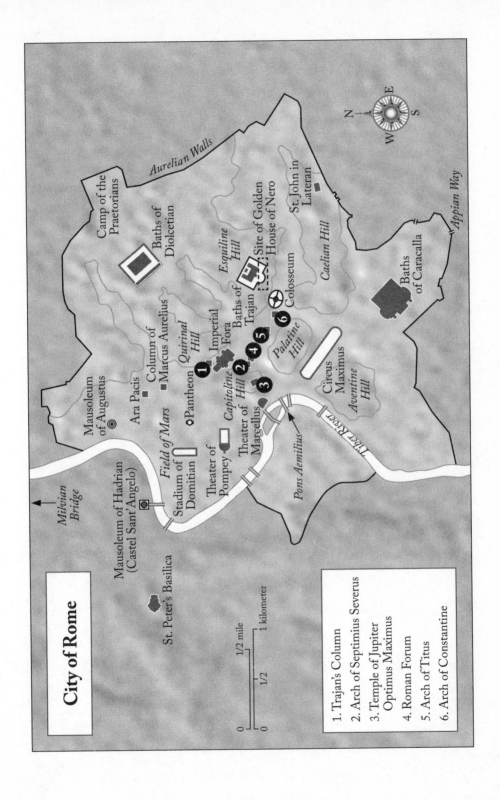

City of Rome

Legend:
1. Trajan's Column
2. Arch of Septimius Severus
3. Temple of Jupiter Optimus Maximus
4. Roman Forum
5. Arch of Titus
6. Arch of Constantine

St. Peter's Basilica

Mausoleum of Hadrian (Castel Sant'Angelo)

Milvian Bridge

Mausoleum of Augustus

Ara Pacis

Column of Marcus Aurelius

Field of Mars

Stadium of Domitian

Theater of Pompey

Pantheon

Quirinal Hill

Capitoline Hill

Theater of Marcellus

Pons Aemilius

Tiber River

Camp of the Praetorians

Baths of Diocletian

Aurelian Walls

Esquiline Hill

Imperial Fora

Baths of Trajan

Site of Golden House of Nero

St. John in Lateran

Colosseum

Caelian Hill

Palatine Hill

Circus Maximus

Aventine Hill

Baths of Caracalla

Appian Way

0   1/2   1 kilometer
0   1/2 mile

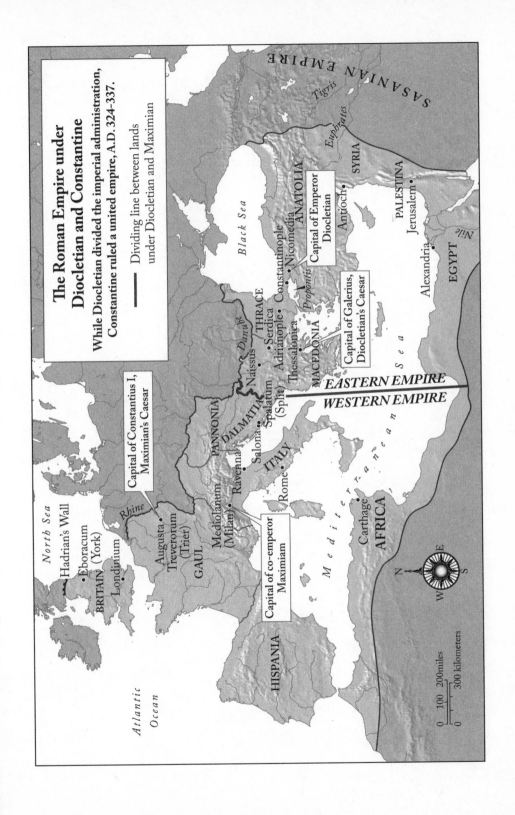

The Roman Empire under Diocletian and Constantine

While Diocletian divided the imperial administration, Constantine ruled a united empire, A.D. 324-337.

—— Dividing line between lands under Diocletian and Maximian

SASANIAN EMPIRE

Tigris

Euphrates

SYRIA

Antioch

PALESTINE

Jerusalem

Nile

EGYPT

Alexandria

ANATOLIA

Capital of Emperor Diocletian

Nicomedia

Constantinople

Propontis

Capital of Galerius, Diocletian's Caesar

Black Sea

THRACE

Serdica

Adrianople

Thessalonica

MACEDONIA

Danube

Naissus

EASTERN EMPIRE

WESTERN EMPIRE

Capital of Constantius I, Maximian's Caesar

PANNONIA

DALMATIA

Spalatum (Split)

Salona

ITALY

Ravenna

Mediolanum (Milan)

Rome

Rhine

Augusta Treverorum (Trier)

GAUL

Capital of co-emperor Maximiam

M e d i t e r r a n e a n   S e a

HISPANIA

AFRICA

Carthage

North Sea

Hadrian's Wall

Eboracum (York)

BRITAIN

Londinium

Atlantic Ocean

N E S W

0   100   200miles
0   300 kilometers

A NIGHT ON THE PALATINE

It is night on the Palatine Hill, a historic height in the heart of Rome. Imagine yourself alone there after the tourists go home and the guards lock the gates. Even during the day, the Palatine is quiet compared with the crowded sites in the valleys below. At night, alone and given an eerie nocturnal run of the place, could you rouse imperial ghosts?

At first sight, the answer might seem to be no. The breezy, leafy hilltop lacks the majesty of the nearby Roman Forum's columns and arches or the spectacle of the Colosseum and its bloodstained arcades. The ruins on the Palatine appear as a confusing jumble of brick and concrete and misnomers. The so-called Hippodrome, or oval-shaped stadium, for example, is really a sunken garden, while the "House of Livia" did not belong to that great lady.

But look more closely. Give rein to your imagination, and you will understand why the Palatine Hill gave us our word *palace*. It was here on the Palatine that Rome's first emperor planted the flag of power and where, for centuries, most of his successors each ruled over fifty million to sixty million people. It began as a modest compound for the ruler and his family and a temple to his patron god. Then it turned into a series of ever-grander *domus*, or "houses." They were palatial estates used not only as homes but also for imperial audiences, councils, embassies, morning salutations, evening banquets, love affairs, old and new religious rituals, conspiracies, and assassinations.

In their day, they bespoke magnificence. Their walls were lined with colored marbles from around the empire. Their columns gleamed with Numidian yellow, Phrygian purple, Egyptian granite, Greek gray, and Italian white. Gilded ceilings rose high over tall windows and heated floors. One banquet room seated thousands while another revolved. Water flowed in fountains and pools fed by the Palatine's own aqueduct. Some rooms looked over the chariot races in the Circus Maximus in the valley to the south, offering a kind of skybox.

Perhaps a modern night visitor to the Palatine could imagine a famous dinner party with the emperor at which one guest said he felt like he was dining with Jupiter in midheaven. Or a less pleasant banquet when the emperor had the walls painted black and the dining couches laid out like tombstones, leaving the terrified guests in fear of their lives—which were spared. Or we might remember the rumor that another emperor turned the palace into a brothel—a salacious but not very credible tale. We might think of the palace steps, where one emperor was first hailed and another announced his abdication. We might think of the grand entrance, where one new emperor's wife proclaimed her resolution not to be corrupted, or the back door, where another emperor slinked home, barely escaping with his life from a food riot in the Forum. Or we might imagine a Senate meeting in a palace hall, with the emperor's mother watching through a curtain. Or the covered passage where a crowd of conspirators murdered a young tyrant. They all happened here.

From the Palatine, the emperors ruled what they called the world, a vast realm stretching at its height from Britain to Iraq. Or at least they tried to rule it. Few excelled at the grueling job. The imperial administration took care of ordinary business, but crises proved a challenge. Many emperors turned out not to be up to the task. A few did extremely well. They brought to bear, in equal measure, ambition, cunning, and cruelty.

They brought family, too. The Roman emperors ran one of history's most successful family businesses and one of its most paradoxical. In order to concentrate power in trusted hands, the imperial family made full use of its members, including women. As a result, mothers, wives, daughters, sisters, and mistresses enjoyed what some might consider a surprising amount of power. But it was sometimes an unhappy family, with forced marriages common and infighting and murder hardly rare. It was, moreover, a family whose definition was loose and flexible. More emperors came to the throne from adoption than by inheriting it from their fathers, and not a few seized power in civil war. It was both the empire's glory and curse that succession was often contested. It opened the door to talent and to violence.

The first emperor, Augustus, set the tone. Adopted by the founder of the family's fortune, his great-uncle and Rome's last dictator, Julius Caesar, Augustus had to fight a civil war in order to prevail. Indeed, his wife, Livia, eventually perhaps the most powerful woman in Roman history, was once a refugee in that war and had run away from the man she eventually married.

The following pages tell the story of ten who ruled. They were Rome's most capable and successful emperors—or, in the case of Nero, at least one of the most titillating, and even he was a great builder. Success was defined variously according to circumstance and talent, but all emperors wanted to exercise political control at home, project military power abroad, preside over prosperity, build up the city of Rome, and enjoy a good relationship with the divine. And every emperor wanted to die in bed and turn over power to his chosen heir.

We begin with the founder, the first emperor, Augustus, and end about 350 years later with the second founder, Constantine, who converted to Christianity and created a new capital in the East, Constantinople (today's Istanbul, Turkey). Roughly halfway in time between the two men came Hadrian, who called himself a second Augustus and who did more than most to make the empire peaceable and to open the elite to outsiders. Alas, Hadrian was also tyrannical and murderous. In that, he was not unusual.

From beginning to end, the Roman emperors resorted to force. They rarely hesitated to have rivals and dissidents killed. They depended on the army, which conquered the empire, defended it, and put down revolt with brutality. Even Marcus Aurelius, a philosopher-emperor who preferred the arts of peace and came to power with no military experience, devoted most of his reign to fighting on the frontier.

No less important, the army made and broke emperors. No emperor could rule without the soldiers' consent. They mattered even more than the Roman Senate, those members of the elite who supplied the leadership class, at least at first. The emperors increasingly relied for administration on nonsenators, even on ex-slaves. The people of Rome also mattered to the emperors, but they were bought off with subsidized food and entertainment—not that life was ever easy for the poor, who made up the vast majority of the empire. Finally, the gods also mattered. Every emperor established peace with the gods, and more than a few introduced new gods while not rejecting the old. Constantine was different not in worshipping a new god but in turning his back on Rome's ancestral deities.

But religion is embedded in culture, and the character of Rome's culture would change mightily with the coming of monarchy. Between them, Augustus and his successor, Tiberius, accomplished a herculean feat. They turned the Roman Empire from conquest to administration. They took power away from the proud, militaristic, quarrelsome nobility and began to transfer it to bureaucrats, who came from less prestigious social classes. They decentered the city of Rome to the benefit first of Italy and then of the provinces.

Augustus's successors added two new provinces to the empire by armed force; but these were minor border adjustments compared with the two previous centuries, when Rome conquered the entire Mediterranean and northwestern Europe. Conquering elites always burn themselves out and become more interested in money and pleasure than in expansion. Every empire declines without exception. However, the Romans did an excellent job of holding onto what they had won.

Behind a façade of sumptuous and extravagant rhetoric lay the heart of a pragmatist. That was the real Rome. The real Rome is found less in the periodic sentences of Cicero or the polished prose of Publius Cornelius

Tacitus than in Tiberius's giving up Germany without a backward glance or in the emperor Vespasian justifying a tax on public toilets with the observation that "money has no smell." New blood and new gods; tough choices and strategic retreats: in order to survive as an empire, the Romans were willing to do whatever it took.

Eventually Rome lost its role as capital. The Western emperor ruled from northern Italy or Germany—and eventually there was a Western emperor as well as an Eastern emperor. Constantine's predecessor, Diocletian, recognized that the empire was too big and its problems too great for one man to manage. Constantine, who carried the full burden, was an exception.

Rome outgrew itself, but that was one of the reasons for its success. Change was built into the very fabric of the system, not that it came easily or without bloodshed. New men rose to the top. The two middle emperors of the book, Trajan and Hadrian, were both born in Hispania, today's Spain. Two generations later, the emperor Septimius Severus came from North Africa. He was of Italian-immigrant descent, as well possibly of mixed African and Middle Eastern ancestry, but not Diocletian or Constantine, both of whom came from the Balkans and had no Italian blood. New women rose, too: Severus's wife came from Syria and Constantine's mother from Asia Minor, today's Turkey.

The lords and ladies of the Palatine proved in time to be more diverse than the empire's founder could have imagined. Their voices are long stilled, many of their names forgotten. In some cases, their statues are lost or the ancients tore them down after revolution or scratched their images off paintings or stone reliefs. Yet we can call up their ghosts from literary texts and inscriptions, from art and archaeology, and from the scientific study of everything from shipwrecks to sewage.

The Romans live, and they do so not only in the imagination of a night on the Palatine.

Augustus, detail of Prima Porta statue.

1

AUGUSTUS

THE FOUNDER

Augustus is an icon, and well he should be. Few historical figures show better what it takes to win at everything. He ended a century of revolution, brought down the Roman Republic, and replaced it with the empire of which he was the first emperor. But Augustus is also a mystery. Fatherless at the age of four, he became one of Rome's top political players by the age of nineteen. How did he do that—and so much more?

How did he overcome an opposition led by the most glamorous team in history, Antony and Cleopatra? How did a frail boy become a successful warlord, and how did he then turn into one of history's most famous promoters of peace? How did he find the perfect number two: a partner to serve as his general and administrator without threatening the boss's power? How did he manage one of the most productive but challenging marriages in history, to the brilliant, talented, and crafty Livia? How did he found a dynasty that lasted a century and an empire that lasted many centuries more?

Toward the end of his long life, Augustus answered some of these questions. On bronze pillars before his mausoleum in Rome, he had a detailed inscription erected that included this statement: "When I had extinguished the flames of civil war, after receiving by universal consent the absolute control of affairs, I transferred the republic from my own control to the will of the senate and the Roman people. For this service on my part I was given the title of Augustus by decree of the senate."

That was the official account. What was the real story? Let us begin with a young boy and follow his career.

ATIA'S BOY

He was born on September 23, 63 BC. We know him as Augustus, but it is customary to call him Octavian when referring to the first thirty-five years of his life. Only then did he take the name Augustus.

His father, Gaius Octavius, came from a family of strivers from a small town south of Rome. Octavius was wealthy and politically aspiring, but he lacked the noble heritage that most Romans, rich or poor, expected in their leaders. By "nobility," the Romans meant a very small group: descendants of the consuls, the Roman government's two annually elected chief magistrates. Octavius married into the nobility by wedding Julius Caesar's niece, the daughter of the future dictator's sister. She opened the doors to power for her husband and their young son. Her name was Atia.

Her marriage began well, with a move to Rome and a rise in the political ranks for her husband. Gaius Octavius seemed headed for the consulship, but he died suddenly in 58 BC on the way home from a trip abroad after a successful stint as a provincial governor. Atia was now a widow and had two children: Octavian and his older sister, Octavia.

To add to the fatherless young Octavian's troubles, at least one of his guardians mismanaged or even plundered his inheritance. Yet the boy not only survived; he thrived. He had three things going for him: his mother, her family, and his own resilience.

Atia is one of history's unsung heroines. True, we don't see her in the round. We don't know what she looked like, for no coin image or sculpture of her appears to have survived. Augustus's now-lost *Memoirs* probably drew the portrait that survives in later Roman writing: of a chaste, old-school mother who exercised strict discipline and kept a close watch on her son's upbringing. The sources reveal a woman who was shrewd, pragmatic, politic, and a relentless booster of her son's career.

Roman mothers had to be boosters. Their husbands often predeceased them, leaving it up to the mother to fend for the children. Roman history is full of forceful mothers who pushed their sons ahead. Latin literature offers the example of the goddess Venus, who drives her son, Aeneas, forward to his divine fate of founding Rome. No wonder Roman men often revered their mothers.

Shortly after being widowed, Atia remarried, this time to another prominent public figure, a slippery character who managed not to commit himself to either side in Rome's Civil War (49–45 BC) and yet still came out on top. Young Octavian might have learned more than a little of the art of deception from his stepfather. But Atia entrusted him to his grandmother Julia, Atia's mother, who raised the boy under her roof during his formative years. Her brother, Julius Caesar, was in the process of conquering Gaul, an ancient country in the area now occupied by France and Belgium, and becoming the first man in Rome. Surely Julia wrote to him about the bright and ambitious youngster in her charge and how he did the family proud.

When Julia died circa 51 BC, Octavian moved to his mother and stepfather's house, but he kept thinking of his famous great-uncle. It is said that Octavian was eager to join Caesar at the front in 46 BC, but Atia, who worried about the boy's health, refused.

While Octavian grew up, Caesar was revolutionizing Rome, which had evolved into a proud, self-governing republic. The people and the elites shared power through institutions such as assemblies, courts, elected officials, and the Senate. That was the theory. In practice, the republic could not hold its own against a conquering general like Caesar and his tens of thousands of loyal soldiers.

When Caesar crossed the Rubicon River and marched from Gaul

into Italy in 49 BC, he inflicted civil war on a country that had already suffered five decades of intermittent civil conflict, with roots in a crisis going back another two generations. Rome, it seems, was trapped in a maze of political, military, social, economic, cultural, and administrative impossibilities.

Only someone who could tame both the city of Rome and its empire could bring peace, order, and stability. Caesar was not that man. He was a conqueror, not a builder. But if Caesar couldn't do it, who could?

Caesar had no legitimate son of his own, although he probably had sired a foreign prince born out of wedlock, Caesarion, son of Cleopatra. Instead, Caesar would choose another relative as his heir. He had several legitimate Roman nephews and great-nephews, but Octavian rose to the top.

Burning with ambition, Octavian was a natural politician: intelligent, charming, communicative, and handsome. Although not a born soldier, he was tenacious, cunning, and brave. He had an iron will. And he had Atia, who surely sang his praises to Caesar at every opportunity. She might have even told him a tale making the rounds that her son's father was not really Gaius Octavius but the god Apollo, who in the form of a snake visited her in a temple, impregnated her, and left a permanent mark on her body. Only the gullible would believe this, but Caesar knew that the masses were gullible, and so he might have been impressed.

Caesar kept promoting his great-nephew. Around 51 BC, at the age of eleven, Octavian gave the funeral oration for his grandmother Julia on the speaker's platform in the Roman Forum. Soon after turning fourteen, Octavian was named to an important religious office at Caesar's request. At seventeen, Octavian marched through Rome in Caesar's triumphs— his victory parades—for his conquests in Gaul and the Civil War. It was 46 BC, and Caesar honored the young man the way a triumphing general would normally honor only his son.

A prominent boy like Octavian had many friends, one of whom became his lifelong right-hand man: Marcus Vipsanius Agrippa. Like Octavian, he came from a prosperous Italian family, although without a connection to the Roman nobility. What Agrippa had in abundance was practical genius.

He was courageous, assertive, and, above all, loyal. To be sure, Octavian had a gift for making men follow him. In Agrippa's case, Octavian went to his great-uncle and got Agrippa's brother freed even though he had fought against Caesar. Agrippa was grateful.

In 45 BC Octavian became sick, and Caesar supposedly even visited his bedside before departing Rome to stamp out a rebellion in Hispania. Octavian faced chronic health problems and endured several major bouts of illness in his life, but until the very end, he always soldiered on. Soon the young man was on his feet again, and he left for the front. His small entourage probably included Agrippa but not Atia. She wanted to join them but Octavian turned her down.

Octavian arrived in Hispania too late for the fighting but reached Caesar after a dangerous trip through hostile country. This earned his uncle's admiration—a quality that only increased during the several months that Caesar spent with the gifted young go-getter. It was Octavian's chance to shine, and he used it well. When Caesar returned to Italy shortly afterward, he made Octavian his main heir and offered him posthumous adoption as his son.

By choosing Octavian as his successor, Caesar surely saw the seed of greatness. Yet when the news of Caesar's choice came out, some found it hard to believe that a seventeen-year-old could persuade the most powerful man in the world to pick him without some underhanded ploy: sex. Octavian's rival Mark Antony later accused the boy of having an affair with Caesar while in Hispania. On the one hand, this was just the kind of slander that Roman politicians dished out. On the other hand, Octavian was as handsome as he was ambitious, and rumor said that when Caesar was a teenager, he himself had gone to bed with a powerful older man. Yet both Caesar and Augustus were ladies' men, so the tale is probably untrue.

When he returned to Rome, Octavian finally moved out but continued to live near his mother and stepfather, supposedly spending most of his time with them. He also continued his education in oratory, philosophy, and literature, in both Latin and Greek—the preferred curriculum of the Roman elite. Although war and revolution interrupted Octavian's studies, he continued to read and to practice delivering speeches daily. At the age of eighteen, he is supposed to have given up sex for a year, which he thought would keep his voice strong. Perhaps it worked because in later years, he had a sweet, distinctive speaking voice unlike Caesar's piercing vocal sound.

Caesar's plan now was a three-year war of conquest in the East. He gave Octavian a big role by naming him, at the age of eighteen, his Master of the Horse, or second in command. Although this was in some ways a ceremonial position, it offered visibility and networking opportunities. The expedition was scheduled to begin in March 44 BC. Around December 45 BC, Octavian left Rome at Caesar's command and, along with Agrippa, crossed the Adriatic Sea to Caesar's military headquarters in what is today Albania. There Octavian made invaluable contacts with legionary commanders.

But the Ides of March changed everything. On that day, March 15, 44 BC, a conspiracy of more than sixty prominent Romans, led by Marcus Brutus, Gaius Cassius Longinus, and Decimus Brutus, assassinated Caesar at a meeting of the Senate.

Suddenly Octavian's closeness to Caesar made him a target. Atia was in Rome when Caesar's will named her to organize his funeral. But her first priority was Octavian, and she immediately sent a messenger to him across the Adriatic. Octavian was considering the possibility of launching an armed revolt at the Adriatic headquarters. Atia disagreed strongly. She knew that Rome was the key, and she urged Octavian to return there. She wrote that "now he had to be a man and consider prudently what he had to do and do it according to fortune and opportunity." After consulting his friends and advisors, Octavian agreed and sailed back to Italy.

What a loss for Octavian Caesar's death was. The man who had stepped in to become Octavian's father, and who had gone out of his way to give him his sense of potential greatness, had been murdered. In a traditional Roman gesture of mourning, Octavian grew a beard. But sorrow was not his only emotion; he also felt fear, anger, and a lust for vengeance. Yet Caesar's death was an opportunity as well as a blow. Octavian was now the head of the family, as well as heir to Rome's dictator. But he had to fight for his inheritance.

MY NAME IS CAESAR

November 44 BC
The Forum, Rome, the plaza that was Rome's civic center

Octavian gave a speech that he later proudly circulated. It was a defining moment. He stretched his right hand out to a statue of Julius Caesar and swore by his hopes of attaining his adoptive father's honors. He had just turned nineteen but had already claimed all the power and glory of Rome's former dictator for life. Men have been sent to mental hospitals for less.

Megalomania it might have been, but after six months of hustling, Octavian was making progress. As Atia advised, he had hurried back to Italy. He was cautious and obedient enough to consult his mother and her husband but too ambitious to accept their advice to proceed slowly—or even, as his stepfather supposedly said, to turn down Caesar's inheritance and retire from public life when he had barely entered it.

Rome was full of enemies. The consul Mark Antony was in charge of the city, and Caesar's assassins were regrouping after a temporary setback. They had little use for Octavian. Neither did Antony. At thirty-nine years old, Antony was in the prime of his life. Son of a noble Roman family, he was a superb general, a cagey politician, and an excellent orator. Strong and handsome, Antony took as his patron deity Hercules—a symbol of responsibility and justice as well as military prowess. Antony looked down on Octavian. As a distant relative and longtime associate of Caesar's, Antony considered himself the slain dictator's rightful successor.

But Octavian was determined. He wanted honor and glory, and he didn't care what they cost. He was ready to fight. He wasn't going to mourn Caesar; he was going to avenge him. No, he was going to *be* him. He began the process of finalizing the adoption that Caesar had offered him in his will. Although we'll continue to call him Octavian, he now called himself

Caesar. He adopted the name as easily as if he had been born to it. Not only that, but he treated it like a talisman of power, as if it already had the weight of centuries behind it. His mother was the first person to address him as Caesar, but she would not be the last.

Octavian was audacious but not impetuous, and violent without being wild. After her own initial doubt and indecision and having shown respect for her husband's position, Atia changed her mind: she decided to give her full support to Octavian's ambition. But she advised cunning and patience, and Octavian now agreed. He moved strategically and showed people only what he wanted them to see. He was mysterious, so it seems appropriate that for a part of his career he sealed documents with the image of a sphinx; later on, he replaced it with his own likeness. (A later emperor called Augustus a "chameleon.") The sources say that Octavian got his sphinx seal from Atia, which brings us back to the god Apollo, his supposed heavenly father, as the Romans associated the sphinx with that deity.

The "sphinx" knew how to tempt people, starting with his stepfather's neighbor in his country villa on the Bay of Naples. This was Rome's greatest living statesman: Marcus Tullius Cicero. Of all the statesmen of the ancient world, none speaks to us more intensely than Cicero. His tongue was eloquently persuasive; his hands wrote ceaselessly; his heart beat for the republic, whose last decades his career spanned. His orations still sparkle, his letters lay bare the political maneuvering of the age, and his philosophical works practically invent Latin political thought.

As a politician, Cicero enjoyed mixed success. He put down a revolt during his term of office as consul, but, along the way, he executed five Roman citizens without benefit of a trial, which later forced him into temporary exile. After vacillating in the Civil War, Cicero received Caesar's pardon and compliments on his literary works, but he found the door to power slammed shut. Following the Ides of March, Cicero came out of retirement and supported the assassins. Now Octavian convinced Cicero that he, Octavian, could restore the liberty that Caesar had curbed.

On the face of it, that seems naïve. Cicero wanted to save the republic from another military dictator like Caesar. Octavian wanted to be that dictator. Had the old man gone soft? No. He knew that Octavian was a risky bet, but he thought it worth taking. Cicero considered Antony older, more experienced, and more dangerous than young Octavian, while Octavian feared no man. So Cicero and Octavian made an alliance of convenience, and then the real question was who would dump whom first and come out on top.

Octavian's youth turned out to be an advantage. Since he had little investment in the old system, he had little inhibition about upending it.

Octavian was determined to push the issue with Antony. Hiding his real plans from his mother, Octavian went to southern Italy and lobbied for support among Julius Caesar's former soldiers. He convinced three thousand veterans to come out of retirement and support him. This private army violated the law, but years later, he boasted of his action, which he rebranded as a way of saving the republic: "At the age of nineteen at my own initiative and private expense I raised an army, by which I set free the republic which had been oppressed by the tyranny of a faction."

The most important part of that army consisted of two veteran legions that Octavian's agents lured away from Antony by offering more money and less discipline. The two legions suddenly gave Octavian the power to compete in a bloody game of maneuver. And they got the Senate's attention.

With an armed showdown against Antony imminent, the Senate turned to Octavian and his legions. His claim of loyalty to the republic rang hollow, but his youth made him seem less threatening to the senators than Antony. In April 43 BC, the two sides clashed in two battles in northern Italy. Antony, a hardened warrior, hurled a charge of cowardice at Octavian, who had never seen combat before. Although Octavian was not a natural warrior, he was capable of courage. At the second battle in 43 BC, for instance, he heroically shouldered the eagle when his legion's eagle bearer suffered a severe wound. In war, as in all else, Octavian displayed self-control. By way of illustration, consider that although he was in the company of soldiers, he drank no more than three glasses of wine at dinner—probably only about nine ounces.

The Senate's armies were victorious and forced Antony to retreat. He crossed the Alps and withdrew to Gaul, but Octavian did not pursue him, as the Senate had wished. Octavian knew better than to trust the senators. When he heard that Cicero had said of him, "The young man should be honored and lifted up—and out," Octavian was angry but probably not surprised. Antony regrouped by winning over the armies of Gaul. Meanwhile, Octavian decided to change course and support Antony.

The Senate was only a temporary ally, useful to confer Octavian legitimacy but hostile to his goal of attaining Caesar's status. Antony made a better partner because he lacked the Senate's attachment to the republic's institutions. Besides, his new armies made Antony too strong for Octavian to defeat. So Octavian turned to Antony.

In the summer of 43 BC, Octavian sent a centurion (captain) to the Senate to demand that it name him consul, the highest office in the state and one customarily unattainable before the age of forty. He didn't care about custom. The senators agreed reluctantly and then reneged, hoping vainly for new troops from abroad. They tried to take hostage Atia and Octavia, who were in the city, but the women fled for safety among the Vestal Virgins. The six Vestals were priestesses of an important state cult and lived in an official residence beside the Roman Forum. In part to protect them, Octavian, ever devoted to his family, hurried to Rome with his legions. He became master of Rome on August 19, 43 BC. Now liberated, Atia and Octavia embraced him.

Sadly, the reunion was brief, as his mother died sometime between August and November. Her husband probably died around the same time. Octavian persuaded the Senate to give Atia a public funeral, if *persuaded* is the right word for someone who won the consulship via military might. A public funeral was a rare honor. In fact, as far as we know, Atia was the first woman in Roman history to receive one. A poet wrote Atia's epitaph. It says:

"Here, stranger, the ashes of Atia, here the mother of Caesar / Is found; so ordained the Roman fathers that is, the Senate."

Atia had been indispensable as Octavian's mother, advocate, and political advisor in his early crises. Even after death, she was recalled in literature. Even as a memory, Atia was a reminder of her son's claim to nobility.

And in Rome, vengeance was a noble virtue, with Romans fearing its outcome but admiring its pursuit. Right after the Ides of March, the Senate had hammered out an amnesty for Caesar's killers. Now Octavian tore it up. He had a law passed that set up a special court that condemned them to death. As a good son, he took Caesar's murder personally.

Octavian invited Antony back to Italy and made peace. In October they met, along with Julius Caesar's old ally Marcus Aemilius Lepidus, and formed a three-man commission with dictatorial powers for five years, later renewed. They had over forty legions. They divided up the western part of the empire among them, while Brutus and Cassius, who had fled Rome after the assassination of Julius Caesar, controlled the East. It was a coup d'état.

Less than two years after returning to Italy, Octavian had maneuvered his way through politics and war, outfoxed his competitors, and become one of the three most powerful men in the Roman Empire—all by the age of twenty.

When Julius Caesar conquered Rome, he followed a policy of clemency, pardoning his enemies. But his assassination suggested that clemency did not pay. Instead, the triumvirs chose proscription: a purge. They marked out around two thousand elite and wealthy Romans for death and confiscated their lands. Most escaped; probably around three hundred were killed. Cicero was the most famous casualty. Antony wanted his archenemy dead. Octavian said later he tried to save Cicero but, if so, he didn't try very hard.

As part of his new alliance with Antony, Octavian married Antony's young stepdaughter, Claudia. Her mother, Antony's wife, Fulvia, was a formidable woman who had outlived two previous husbands—both politicians who died violently.

On January 1, 42 BC, Octavian took his devotion to his father's memory up a notch and had the Senate declare Caesar a god, which allowed

Octavian to call himself the son of a god. A law was passed to build a temple and institute the worship of the deified Julius Caesar. Four years later, in 38 BC, Octavian was acclaimed by his troops as imperator, or victorious general. He now became known as "the victorious general Caesar son of a god."

At age twenty-four, Octavian had achieved great things. His ambition was boundless, his intelligence was keen, his judgment was sure, his work ethic was limitless, and his persuasion was winning. Like any young man, he felt emotion—above all, rage at his adoptive father's murder—but he mastered the art of turning pain into strategy. And strategy, it became clear, was Octavian's specialty. He always thought far ahead. He would have to, to face the trials that awaited.

ANTONY AND CLEOPATRA

The showdown with Brutus and Cassius came outside the Greek city of Philippi in 42 BC. Octavian partnered with Antony, and the latter shone in the two battles that brought victory. Octavian had once again to face the charge of cowardice when, in the first battle, the enemy captured his camp but he had already fled. He said later that he was ill and had a vision warning him of danger. This was probably true, since Octavian faced recurrent medical challenges. But he recovered and issued the bloodthirsty command to cut off the head of Brutus's corpse and send it to Rome to place at the foot of a statue of Julius Caesar as revenge.

Philippi was a tremendous victory for Antony and Octavian, but they still had to bring the Roman world under their control. After pushing aside Lepidus, Octavian and Antony divided the empire, with Antony taking the East and making his base in Athens, while Octavian ruled the West from Rome.

That left Octavian the unpopular task of confiscating civilians' land in Italy to give to veterans. Antony's wife, Fulvia, and his brother, Lucius Antonius, led the charge against him. She made an appearance with Antony's children and his mother before the soldiers in order to keep their loyalty.

(Octavian had recently divorced Claudia, claiming under oath that the marriage had never been consummated. No doubt this angered his former mother-in-law.) Octavian now had to subdue Fulvia. He surrounded her and Lucius and their army in the central Italian town of Perusia (modern Perugia). Fulvia got the backhanded compliment of having her name inscribed on her enemy's sling bullets along with rude references to her body parts. Fulvia wrote to Antony's generals in Gaul to ask them to hurry across the Alps to her aid, but it was too late. Octavian's forces won. If the report is true and not just propaganda, Octavian then massacred a large number of enemy leaders on the altar of the deified Julius—on the Ides of March. Octavian supposedly met every request for mercy with a cold "It's time to die." But he let Fulvia and Lucius go free.

Antony, meanwhile, restored Roman control to the East, which Brutus and Cassius had left in turmoil. But Antony is known for something different during his time in the East: his relationship with Cleopatra, an affair not only of the heart but also of the sword and the purse.

Cleopatra was the most powerful, richest, and most glamorous woman of the era. Queen of Egypt, she was a female ruler in a male world. Like all of her ancestors in the three-century-old Ptolemaic dynasty, she was Greek (or, more precisely, Macedonian), even though she ruled Egypt. She was clever, cunning, educated, and seductive. Cleopatra had great physical presence. She was short and vigorous. She could ride a horse and hunt. She paid enormous attention to her public image. Greco-Roman portrait sculptures made her elegant, while coin portraits showed her as kingly and even slightly masculine.

Cleopatra exuded charisma, and Egypt's capital, Alexandria, was an architectural marvel and a cultural magnet. Whichever man had Cleopatra had access to Egypt's fabled wealth and to the mystique she created in the bedroom. Octavian had Caesar's name, but Antony had Caesar's mistress. In 41 BC Antony and Cleopatra began an affair that produced a set of twins. Nevertheless, with Fulvia having died of a sudden illness, Antony took a new wife: Octavian's sister, Octavia. She was newly widowed herself and understood the way the game was played; the purpose of such a marriage was politics, not love. Yet Octavia seems to have enjoyed Antony's charm. They had two daughters together whom she raised in their house in Athens along with three children from his and her previous marriages. No one seems to have wondered about Antony's ties to Cleopatra.

OCTAVIAN MAKES LOVE AND WAR

In his midtwenties, Octavian faced his greatest crises to date. He fought his most dangerous military campaign by far, and he met the love of his life—a woman who changed him for the better.

Octavian had not yet consolidated power in the West. He had to defeat Sextus Pompey, the last surviving son of Caesar's rival Pompey the Great. Sextus Pompey controlled the seas around Italy with a fleet based in Sicily. Sextus was a cunning and alluring figure who championed the republic and offered asylum to the victims of proscription. Although he blocked grain ships and left Italy hungry, he was popular in a Rome grown weary of purges and property confiscation. Octavian and Antony were forced to make peace with Pompey and recognize his realm. Octavian also acknowledged Sextus's power by marrying Sextus's aunt (by marriage), Scribonia. She was strong and severe—and about ten years older than Octavian.

Then, in 39 BC, Octavian met Livia. The moment could not have been more fraught. At twenty-four, he had just shaved his mourning beard for Caesar after having worn it for five years. Livia Drusilla, to use her full name, was nineteen, noble, bright, and beautiful. Octavian was handsome and rich. True, three years earlier, Octavian had sent Livia running from Italy, just one step ahead of his troops, after she'd supported his enemies Fulvia and Lucius in the war at Perusia. But eventually it was safe for her to come home. Like Octavian, Livia was married. In fact, she was pregnant— and so was Scribonia. Falling in love broke every rule, and that made it irresistible.

For Livia at age nineteen, winning Octavian's heart was as much a coup as winning Caesar's approval had been for Octavian at seventeen. As later events would show, she was Octavian's soulmate, matching him in intelligence and ambition. But Octavian was a politician, and so there was more to the story than the marriage of true minds. Livia offered him a great increase in respectability because she came from the bluest of noble blood. Her forebears occupied a higher rank in the Roman elite than did Scribonia's. Livia's ancestors held Rome's highest offices and were variously prominent as statesmen, generals, orators, and reformers. Scribonia's were less important. Meanwhile, Scribonia annoyed Octavian by complaining about his adultery. She was also outliving her political usefulness, since relations with Sextus Pompey showed signs of souring.

On January 14, 38 BC, Scribonia gave birth to a daughter, Julia. Octavian divorced Scribonia the same day. Around that time, Livia's husband also divorced her. On January 17 Octavian and Livia were married.

Livia was six months' pregnant at the time of the marriage. Three months later, already living in Octavian's house, she gave birth to a son, Drusus, who joined an older brother, the three-year-old Tiberius. People gossiped and said, "The lucky have children in three months," which gained the status of a proverb. It turned out to be especially cruel because Livia would bear only one stillborn child for Octavian. Yet they would remain married for fifty-two years, even though he wanted a dynasty that she could not give him.

Octavian might have divorced Livia, but doing so was dangerous, for she might remarry and create a rival power center. He could have killed her, but that would have sullied his reputation. Maybe Octavian stayed married to Livia because he loved and admired her. Perhaps she proved from the start to be a source of wise advice as well as support. In later years, she was one of the shrewdest politicians in Rome. "He loved and esteemed her to the end without a rival," the historian Suetonius wrote.

The peace agreements with Sextus Pompey did not last. Octavian considered his wily and aggressive opponent too dangerous for peaceful coexistence, so he went back to war. Octavian strained the Italian economy and courted unpopularity in order to build a massive new fleet. He went into battle, and, more than once, he was lucky to escape with his life. But his old comrade Agrippa came to Octavian's rescue as his admiral. Agrippa was a shrewd strategist, brave in battle, and, above all, a superb organizer. With Agrippa in charge, Octavian's fleet was finally able to beat Sextus decisively at sea in 36 BC. Sextus escaped but was soon captured and killed.

SHOWDOWN WITH ANTONY
AND CLEOPATRA

Antony, meanwhile, planned an invasion of Parthia, Rome's rival empire in what is today Iran and Iraq. He wanted men and money from Octavian, but Octavian still had his hands full with Sextus. So, in 37 BC, Antony turned to Cleopatra, who became his supplier and once again his lover—she soon bore him a third child. For one stunning moment, the Roman Empire appeared to be a fool for love, governed at opposite ends of the Mediterranean by two pairs of lovers: Antony and Cleopatra, and Octavian and Livia. And in a perverse twist typical of the hothouse world of the Roman elite, Antony was still married to Octavian's sister, Octavia.

In an even more perverse twist, each couple represented a competing claim to Julius Caesar's legacy. Octavian was Caesar's legally adopted son by Roman law. He had Caesar's name, and he lived in Rome. Antony was Julius Caesar's closest surviving lieutenant. He had Caesar's former mistress, Cleopatra, and lived in a city that Caesar had conquered, Alexandria. And Cleopatra was the mother not only of Antony's children but also of a son who was probably Caesar's love child and now Egypt's king, Ptolemy XV, nicknamed Caesarion. Rome and Alexandria, Caesar and Caesarion: which one would win?

War, not love, answered the question. The situation grew ever tenser between 36 and 32 BC. First, Antony's invasion of Parthian territory ended in military disaster. A second campaign did secure him Armenia, but that was a consolation prize. Meanwhile, Octavian was in firm control of Italy and the Roman West. Antony distributed some of Rome's territories in the East to Cleopatra and their children. He also recognized Caesarion as Julius Caesar's son, which was a slap in the face to Octavian. In 32 BC

Antony made a decisive break with Octavian by divorcing his sister. It is unclear if he formally married Cleopatra.

But Octavian held the upper hand when it came to propaganda, especially after he seized Antony's will from the Vestal Virgins in Rome. The will stated Antony's desire to be buried in Alexandria alongside Cleopatra. Octavian accused his rival of treason, arguing that Antony intended to move the seat of Rome's empire there.

Was that really possible? The East had more money, people, and cities than the West, and beyond it beckoned the lands that Alexander the Great had once ruled, stretching all the way to India. Before Julius Caesar's death, there were rumors that he had planned to move the capital from Rome to Troy (in today's Turkey).

Many eminent senators, however, were unconvinced. For all his flaws, Antony was one of them—a member of the Roman nobility—while Octavian was not. Many senators fled to Antony, but the rest declared war. But it was war on Cleopatra, not Antony. Octavian shrewdly recast the fight as a foreign war and not a civil conflict. "Poor Antony," he said in effect. "An alien queen had unmanned him."

So war it was, with Greece the focus of action. Although Antony had huge resources and great military experience, Octavian was hardened by the struggle against Sextus and buoyed by Livia's support. Octavian's navy, commanded by the faithful and talented Agrippa, slowly cut off the enemy's supplies. Antony and Cleopatra's fleet was under great pressure when it finally faced Octavian's navy off the Actium Peninsula in western Greece. The day of decision was September 2, 31 BC. Actium was a historical turning point. On a likely reconstruction of the battle, Antony and Cleopatra gambled on a master stroke but failed. They then fled the scene, leaving most of their fleet to fend for itself.

Octavian (or, actually, Agrippa), had an enormous victory, which he followed up the next year by invading Egypt, where armed resistance crumbled. Antony and Cleopatra each committed suicide in Alexandria in 30 BC.

The torch was out. The world was duller but calmer. Octavian's patron, Apollo, the god of reason, had defeated Antony's patron, Hercules, the symbol of might. Octavian now stood alone, the master of the Roman Empire. And it would be Roman indeed. Actium kept the center of gravity of the empire in Rome, where it would remain for another three centuries.

Cleopatra was a strategic genius, but she had moved the world through love. She had seduced in succession two of the most powerful men in Rome and had borne their children. She almost brought down the Roman Empire. But she had met her match in Octavian.

Octavian entered Alexandria. He was the new ruler, but he behaved more like a political boss than a conqueror, preferring to make deals with the locals than to crush them.

The victor rode into town in a carriage not with a fierce legionary but with his tutor, a native of Alexandria. Octavian entered the most beautiful public building in the city, the Gymnasium, the very symbol of Greek culture. There he got up on a dais and addressed the people—not in Latin but in Greek. He said that he would spare them for three reasons: the memory of Alexander the Great, the size and beauty of the city, and as a favor to his teacher. The combination of royalty, culture, and cronyism was classic Octavian. Leniency toward a city of perhaps a half million people was incidental! Indeed, Octavian spared the city but not its king. He had Caesarion executed. As Octavian's tutor explained, "Too many Caesars is not a good thing."

Octavian got off a good line himself. After seeing the mummified body of Alexander the Great, he turned down the eager locals who wanted to show him the mummies of the Ptolemies. "I wished to see a king, not corpses," Octavian said. This was vintage Octavian, too: cutting irony and a sense of his own majesty.

Egypt was now a Roman province, and Octavian was its pharaoh. The prestige of the city of both Alexander and Caesar, as well as of Cleopatra, now belonged to him. By force of arms and by the power of persuasion, Octavian showed himself to be Caesar's son.

Yet another execution awaited. On Octavian's order, one Cassius of Parma, a poet and the last survivor among Julius Caesar's assassins, was executed in Athens. Caesar's adopted son finally had the last full measure of revenge. But the entire Roman world had paid for it.

MY NAME IS AUGUSTUS

Having defeated Antony and Cleopatra, Octavian faced another great challenge: stabilizing Rome's political system after a century of war and revolution. And he had to do so in a way that would leave him in charge without exposing himself to the daggers that had brought down Caesar. He began with a name, or, rather, a title.

Augustus was unique and invented for the occasion, although it did recall certain Roman traditions. On January 16, 27 BC, the Roman Senate voted that from now on Octavian would be called Augustus or, more formally, Caesar Augustus.

Three days earlier, on January 13, Augustus had announced that he was stepping down from power, but everyone knew that it was a mere show. He was only thirty-five and had many more years of rule in him. But the careful stage-managing hints at how Augustus, as we will now call him, broke the cycle of war and violence.

Soon Augustus would be everywhere. You couldn't cross the street, go to a dinner party, enter a temple, or handle a coin without hearing his name or seeing his face, or that of his beautiful wife or his adorable children. He had been a man; now Augustus was a brand.

Augustus used his image to promote stability. Coins issued in 27 and 26 BC, for instance, bear a familiar image of his face but with the new names Augustus as well as Caesar. They highlight images of peace and plenty such as laurel wreaths, stalks of grain, and cornucopias. They evoke the gods Apollo and Jupiter. They praise Augustus for saving citizens' lives.

Like Augustus, the women of his family were ubiquitous. Their images appeared on statues, sculpted reliefs, gems, and, less commonly, on coins.

Buildings were dedicated to them. Prayers and sacrifices honored them. Their birthdays were celebrated.

Augustus believed that Rome had to settle down, not just politically but also personally. The personal decadence of the elite bothered him. (As a former bad boy himself, he knew whereof he spoke.) He also fretted over Rome's declining birth rate and the toll that years of civil war had taken on the size of the population.

So Augustus sponsored a program of moral reform. He passed an ambitious series of laws that promoted childbearing and punished the childless and unmarried by limiting their ability to inherit. Romans paid a penalty, in effect, for celibacy. They also paid a price for adultery, as Augustus turned sex with a married woman (other than a man's wife), widow, or unmarried woman into a public crime. Previously these matters were handled within the family. Note that it was not a crime for a husband to have an extramarital affair with a slave, a freedwoman (an ex-slave), or a prostitute. Augustus was serious, and he gave the laws teeth, but that also raised opposition because Rome's upper classes enjoyed their fun. Eventually these restrictions came back to hurt Augustus hard.

THE AUGUSTAN PEACE

Roman civil wars had a well-established pattern: first came the bloodshed, then came the settlement. But it was easier to win the war than to forge the peace, since few generals were as good at making peace as at waging war. Augustus was the exception. The cold-blooded killer grew with the job. He ended a century of civil war and laid the foundations of two hundred years of peace and prosperity—the famous Pax Romana, or Roman Peace. Trade flourished in the Augustan peace. The cheapest way to transport goods was at sea. Thanks to Agrippa's victories, Rome ruled the waves, and piracy virtually disappeared. Rome represented a huge market for grain imports, but many other goods were traded as well. Stability and the security of Roman law encouraged money lending, while a military drawdown took pressure off taxes. In short, conditions were ripe for good times.

Augustus also achieved the ambitious agenda that he had set himself at age nineteen. He had all of the power and glory of Julius Caesar. But it took fifteen years to get it, and it cost a heavy price in blood and treasure. At least Augustus learned something in the process: how to build a lasting and stable peace, something that Caesar had failed to do. Julius Caesar might have ruled the battlefield, but when it came to politics, the son outdid the father.

How did he do it? What, besides a new title, explains his success?

Augustus ruled for a long time. After defeating his rivals at Actium in 31 BC, just short of the age of thirty-two, he led the empire for the next forty-five years, dying in the year 14 at age seventy-six. No one ever ruled the Roman Empire longer than he did. Augustus had the advantage of learning from his predecessors as well as the wisdom of avoiding their mistakes. During his long reign, he experimented with various forms of government and made numerous changes and adjustments. He was nothing if not flexible.

He was immensely rich, having inherited a fortune from Caesar and acquiring more wealth during his career of conquest. Agriculture and mineral resources made Egypt one of the wealthiest places on earth, and Augustus controlled it as his personal possession.

He chose his advisors wisely. None did more to execute Augustus's vision than his old friend Agrippa. Both at home and abroad, Agrippa was a troubleshooter, a manager, a builder, and, when need be, an enforcer. He negotiated with senators and kings and sponsored major infrastructure programs at Rome and in the provinces. Agrippa did not lack personal ambition, but he always put loyalty to Augustus first. The poet Horace called Agrippa "a cunning fox imitating a noble lion," a reference both to his craftiness and his social climbing. Augustus himself would eulogize Agrippa as a man whose virtues everyone acknowledged.

Augustus was Machiavellian centuries before Niccolò Machiavelli, who advised usurpers to start their reigns by putting into effect all the cruel measures that they considered most necessary and then to rule in a way that calmed and enriched the people, to win them over. Doing the opposite—starting soft but becoming increasingly cruel—would be fatal.

Augustus did not start soft. From 43 to 30 BC, he fought, lied, cheated, and trampled on the law. It is estimated that he killed more than a hundred senators. Then, after defeating all his domestic enemies, Augustus dedicated himself to peace at home and limited military expansion against foreign—and never Roman—enemies. Still, however gentle he became, Augustus always remembered that his rule depended on his soldiers.

He satisfied his troops by giving several hundred thousand veterans land, money, or both, settling them in colonies both in Italy and overseas. This was very expensive, and at first Augustus paid for it from war booty. Then, after the year 6, he taxed the rich. He kept a careful eye out for renegade commanders—potential new Caesars, as it were. He reduced the size of the army from more than sixty legions to twenty-eight, yielding a total military (including light infantry and cavalry) of about three hundred thousand men. This reduced taxes but also limited the empire's ability to expand its boundaries. No wonder Augustus negotiated peace with Parthia instead of renewing war.

But he did not stop expansion—far from it. Romans expected their leaders to conquer new territory and thereby demonstrate the favor of the gods. Augustus carried out this responsibility with enthusiasm. As his favored poet Virgil wrote, Rome had a duty to achieve "empire without end." So Augustus won new lands in Hispania, the northern Balkans, and Germany, as well as annexing Egypt. The wealth gained from conquest helped to pay for new projects in Rome.

Although never a natural commander, Augustus fought in campaigns when he could. In later years, he left generalship to others—preferably, trusted members of his family. Perhaps it was then that he got into the habit of writing words of caution to his generals: "Make haste slowly."

He wanted to push eastward and conquer Germany as far as the Elbe

River. But Augustus suffered badly when, in the year 9, Publius Quinctilius Varus lost three legions, or about fifteen thousand men, in Germany's Teutoburg Forest. The disaster reduced the number of the legions
from twenty-eight to twenty-five for a generation. More important in
the long term, it cost Rome control of most of Germany. "Quinctilius
Varus, give me back my legions!" Augustus is supposed to have cried out
at the news, not just once but occasionally for months afterward. Once
again he grew a beard of mourning, though this time for only a few
months.

RESTORING THE REPUBLIC?
OR RENOVATING IT?

Augustus learned from Julius Caesar that power grew from the blade of a
sword. Yet, unless it had the support of an outstretched arm and a willing
heart, power would vanish in the flash of a dagger. Augustus learned that
from Caesar, too.

Through a process of trial and error, Augustus found a way to adapt
traditional Roman constitutional procedures to new circumstances. Never
mind that in doing so, he changed their meaning entirely. It was a pragmatic solution to the problem of one-man rule, and it was very Roman. The
Romans, like all people, sometimes floundered in the face of crisis, but in
the end they displayed the ability to change. Augustus embodied his na-
tion's adaptability.

Augustus asked the Senate to grant him the powers of a people's
tribune—that is, the powers to propose legislation and exercise a veto. The
ten people's tribunes represented the interests of ordinary people. Although
they continued to exist, people's tribunes effectively ceded their clout to
Augustus and his successors. Augustus also asked for supreme military
power in both Rome and the provinces. The Senate agreed, as no doubt it
had to, but it put Augustus's rule on a legal footing.

Augustus's standing in Rome never rested solely on his legal powers,
though. It was also a function of his authority—what the Romans called

auctoritas, which meant not just authority but also prestige, respect, and the ability to inspire awe.

Augustus had the fingertip feel for power that was typically Roman. He understood that successful regimes don't merely crush the opposition but co-opt it. So he granted senators a degree of influence and honor.

By no means, though, did Augustus intend for the Senate to be its old self. It was, as the Roman historian Tacitus put it, a much diminished body; a mere "semblance of the republic." For instance, the new Senate no longer controlled foreign policy, finance, or war. Under the republic, senators had governed provinces, and they still did, but generally only the less important provinces. Augustus kept for himself the key provinces on the frontiers with the main concentration of armies, as well as Egypt. The local authorities there were not senators but Roman knights. Knights were a group of extremely rich men around the empire, almost equal to senators in wealth and far greater in number. Augustus and his successors increasingly made use of knights as military officers and as administrators, much to senators' dismay. Cowed by the memory of those who fell in the civil wars or were evicted in purges, senators all claimed to support the emperor, but many privately mourned the old days.

Augustus never made the mistake of confusing the Roman Empire with the city of Rome. He had only one foot in the old Roman aristocracy himself—as his opponents never let him forget—and in some sense, he saw his primary constituency as the elite of Italy rather than the first families of Rome. And he also looked much further afield. Indeed, after returning from the civil war in 28 BC, Augustus spent another decade outside Italy on a series of military and political trips around the empire, more time abroad than any other emperor until Hadrian ruled, from 117 to 138.

Like Julius Caesar before him, Augustus shifted power away from the city of Rome toward the provinces. He laid the groundwork for what became under his successors an international ruling class. It was something new to the Romans but familiar to us today. We call it globalization.

From one end of the empire to another, from Britain to Iraq, people shared a common culture. Here, *people* means a tiny privileged, wealthy, and educated elite. They all shared a similar education, held common values, and maintained like ambitions. They wore the same clothes, quoted the same literary classics, showed off the same rhetorical skill, boasted the same table manners, and aimed at similar careers. Like today's "Davos elite" they belonged to a rarefied globalized club. Nowadays, a CEO in California's Silicon Valley often has more in common with a CEO in Mumbai than with a garlic farmer down the road in Gilroy. So in ancient times, a Roman estate owner in Gaul had more in common with his counterpart in Syria than with the peasant who lived down the road.

The big losers were the people of the city of Rome: both the old nobility, which had to give up its monopoly of political power, and the ordinary plebeians—the common people—who lost the right to take part in elections. Politics as it had existed in the republic—messy, lively, parochial, cranky, sometimes violent but always free—was gone. It was replaced by order, internationalization, and control; replaced, in short, by the emperor and his helpers. Meanwhile, imperial society was split between a tiny ruling group and a mass of ordinary people.

In theory, Rome was still a republic. Augustus was just a public official exercising enhanced powers at the request of SPQR: senatus populusque Romanus, or the Senate and the Roman people. In practice, Augustus was a monarch, but the founder of the Roman Empire never called himself king, much less emperor, at least not in Rome. He was too cagey for that. Instead, he called himself by a variety of other titles, of which the most important were Caesar, Augustus, Imperator, and Princeps, or First Citizen.

Our word *emperor* comes from the Latin *imperator*, which meant "victorious general." Augustus knew that the spirit of republican liberty—the impulse that had murdered Julius Caesar—still survived. So, having won supreme power, he masked it. In the Greek-speaking East, Augustus was often called king, but not in Rome.

Augustus lived in a house on Rome's Palatine Hill. His successors would build splendid palaces there. In contrast, he lived in relatively modest circumstances, but only relatively so, as his estate did include such features as a temple of Apollo. Previously a neighborhood for wealthy families, the Palatine was on its way to an imperial takeover. It became an exclusive site for the emperor and his courtiers. Still, when Augustus went down from the Palatine to the Forum to attend Senate meetings, he made sure to greet every member by name, without a prompter, and he didn't make them get up from their seats in his presence. Nor did he allow people to call him Lord; it took three hundred years until one of his successors took that title.

Augustus managed change not by the language of revolution but by the language of reform and renewal. In 27 BC he proclaimed "the transfer of the state to the free disposal of the Senate and the people." He used language that suggested that he had restored the republic, but it could also mean simply that he had restored constitutional government or that he had renovated the republic—and not that he had restored the system as it was before Julius Caesar.

CITY OF MARBLE

Augustus turned the common people of Rome from feisty political actors into pampered spectators. And he completed the transformation of their city from a lean, mean, fighting machine into a spectacular stage set of an imperial capital.

Julius Caesar had already given Rome a new forum. Augustus went further and practically rebranded Rome's cityscape with his and his family's name. In the late 30s BC, before he was thirty-five, he began building his mausoleum. A grandiose dynastic tomb for Augustus and his extended family, it was the tallest building in the city. It consisted of an artificial hill sitting on a white marble foundation, and was covered with evergreens and crowned by a bronze statue of Augustus. The exterior was decorated with the loot of battle, rendering it a war memorial and trophy as well as a tomb. The massive ruins are still visible today in the Campo Marzio neighborhood of central Rome.

In 29 BC Augustus dedicated a temple to the deified Julius Caesar. Located on the edge of the Roman Forum, on the site of Caesar's cremation, it was his shrine. In addition, Augustus gave Rome a new forum, the Forum of Augustus, complete with a Temple of Mars the Avenger—the avenger of Julius Caesar, that is—and a statue gallery of famous Romans. Augustus paid for the new forum with the spoils of war, which gave the project added prestige in Roman eyes. He also built a victory arch, a sundial, and a stunning new altar of peace. His family members built or renovated temples, aqueducts, baths, theaters, parks, and covered porches. On his deathbed, Augustus would say, "I found a Rome of bricks; I leave to you one of marble." It was meant to be a metaphor for the empire's strength, but it was literally true of much of the city.

Poets and historians under Augustus coined the idea of Rome as the Eternal City. It was a vivid metaphor of the lasting power that Augustus hoped his new regime would have. Although the empire is long gone, that name for the city has survived.

Augustus paid careful attention to the poor people of Rome, who, in the past, had been the source of riot and revolution. He made grain distribution to the poor more efficient and instituted public works programs. To keep order in the streets, Augustus created Rome's first police force and also stationed his own personal guard on the edge of town. Called the Praetorians or Praetorian Guard, the name used for a Roman general's bodyguard, the Guard would play a crucial role in future imperial politics.

Nor was Augustus all stick and no carrot. He made celebration a theme of his regime, undoubtedly on the principle that if people behaved as if they were happy, then they really would be happy. In 29 BC, after returning from Egypt, he staged a magnificent triumph to dramatize the end of the civil wars. As an impresario, Augustus outdid all earlier Roman leaders by staging bigger, better, and more frequent games and shows. His "Secular" or New Era Games in 17 BC were a two-week spectacular of sports, theater, music, animal sacrifices, eating, and drinking. Whenever Augustus

attended a game or show, he made sure the crowd saw him watching carefully, and he let people know that he loved a good show. When he appeared
in public, he tried to look the part of leader. For example, because he was
of only average height for a Roman male, at five foot seven, he wore lifts in
his shoes to look taller.

BETWEEN A ROCK STAR AND A SAINT

Augustus put religion at his service to sell his regime. Conquering bodies was not enough for him; he wanted people's souls as well. He brought
sacred monarchy to Rome, borrowing the basic ideas from the great Greek
kingdoms of the East where Cleopatra and her fellow rulers had long been
worshiped in one form or another. But he shrewdly gave Greek kingship a
Roman accent.

Augustus founded the emperor cult that recognized him as the son of
a god (Julius Caesar) in Rome and a divine being elsewhere. In the ancient
world, having the status of a god was something like a cross between being
a rock star and a saint today. Neither Greeks nor Gauls minded giving Augustus that status, but it offended republican ideas of equality, so he came
close to accepting divine honors in Rome without actually doing so. He put
up a colossal statue of the Guardian Spirit of Augustus (Genius Augusti)
in his new forum, and it resembled him without actually being him. Meanwhile, the East had a popular cult of Rome and Augustus, while Gaul and
Germany were centers of emperor worship.

Grassroots organizations sprang up in many cities of the Western Empire to spread the word about Augustus and honor him. Most of the members of these groups were freedmen (ex-slaves), showing how Augustus's
message expanded beyond the citizen class. Meanwhile, men whose careers
he had promoted, regardless of their rank, employed themes of Augustan
art and architecture in their tombs and gravestones.

Even Rome conceded that there was something divine about Augustus. After reorganizing the city of Rome into 265 districts, he paid for a

new crossroads shrine in each of them, and as a result he was worshipped at those shrines alongside the gods. In a sign of local initiative, people in Rome, as elsewhere, started pouring wine as an offering to the emperor at every banquet, public and private.

The Roman father was a priest as well as the head of his household. He was responsible for the family maintaining a proper relationship with the gods. As chief priest, or pontifex maximus, the emperor did the same for all of Rome. Augustus set the pattern: religion was the emperor's responsibility, and many a later emperor launched a major religious reform.

The reign of Augustus was a classic moment in the history of the world. It was one of the most creative and enduring eras of Western political history, yielding basic political concepts such as emperor, prince, and palace. The very term Augustan Age means a period of peace, prosperity, and cultural flowering under an enlightened and orderly political patron. Writers such as the poets Virgil, Horace, and Ovid, as well as the historian Livy, flourished. Augustus was an educated man who appreciated literature.

THE FAMILY BUSINESS

Augustus ran his regime like a family business. He kept the circle closed and turned to a trusted group of reliable men and women related to him by blood or marriage. Family branding also humanized the process of communicating to the world outside. Everybody loves family dramas, but few people like the details of road building or grain procurement.

The role of family in Roman politics was not new. A few proud aristocratic houses had always dominated Roman politics in every period of the republic. What was new was that from now on, only one house, the Julian clan, would rule. That was a tall order for one family, so it was only logical that Augustus increased its resources, both male and female. He brought Agrippa, his most trusted lieutenant, into the family by marrying Agrippa to his daughter, Julia. Augustus eventually adopted their sons. He also increased Agrippa's powers to the point that he was in effect Augustus's deputy and a potential heir.

Women loomed large in Augustus's family business. Across the stage of the late republic stepped some of the most powerful women of ancient history. And then came Livia, the mightiest of them all. Yet she was neither flamboyant nor lascivious, at least not after, as a pregnant nineteen-year-old, she left her husband for Octavian. For the rest of her life she put on a mask of modesty and simplicity, like the man she married, and worked her will behind the scenes.

The new Livia made an effort to present herself as the ideal Roman wife and mother; the picture of domesticity. She never overtly interfered in politics or her husband's public business. She played her part in the regime's ongoing effort to differentiate itself from the excesses of the late republic.

But Livia had extraordinary influence, with only Augustus's sister, Octavia, as a near rival. Augustus had both women made inviolable (sacrosanct) like the people's tribunes, freed from male guardianship and honored in statues. Each woman controlled enormous wealth, ran a huge household, and even sponsored public buildings. But Livia was closer to Augustus and lived much longer than Octavia, who died in 11 BC.

Centuries later, in the Middle Ages, a notorious love affair would attest to Livia's lasting prestige. The French theologian Peter Abelard seduced his brilliant student Heloise d'Argenteuil. Although the relationship cost them both, she had no regrets. Heloise once defiantly wrote to Abelard that she would rather be his whore than Augustus's empress. Heloise chose her figure of wifely privilege well.

Livia's great-grandson, the emperor Caligula, called her "Ulysses in a stola," that is, a model of cunning in the long, free-flowing linen robe that was the traditional dress of a Roman woman, and thus the image of modesty. She and Augustus, the master strategist, Carl von Clausewitz in a toga, made an incomparable couple.

One of the secrets of Augustus's success was a certain androgyny, or so it appears to a modern eye looking at the many portrait statues that show him young and ageless, with a sweet face, even when wearing a soldier's armor. Augustus was both a man's man and the greatest friend that elite Roman women had ever had. At times, it seems almost as if he were playing to them as to a constituency in modern politics. No Roman woman had the vote, of course, but elite women enjoyed enormous wealth and even political power.

Livia was one of Augustus's most trusted advisors. She was his traveling partner around the empire in spite of the previous Roman male practice to leave the wife at home while on business abroad. Other elite women also began traveling with their husbands on business abroad and sometimes took part in their decisions. When discussing important matters with Livia, Augustus wrote memoranda in advance and read them from a notebook in order to get things just right. For her part, Livia saved her husband's letters, kept them in a shrine, and pulled them out when needed after his death.

Hostile and sometimes brilliant literary tradition made Livia into a witch. She was, it was claimed, a poisoner who murdered one by one the males of Augustus's line as well as her grandson and finally Augustus himself—all so that her son by her previous husband, Tiberius, could inherit the empire and she could be the power behind the throne. Although it makes for delicious novels and television dramas, that is myth. Strong women were part of Roman culture, but so was misogyny. A powerful female often attracted slander, none more so than Livia.

She was subordinate to her husband but carved her own place in the public sphere. Her image was a very distant second to Augustus's in the Roman public eye, and yet she made the most of it. An art historian describes her as "the first woman in the history of the West to be depicted systematically in portraits." Livia copied and popularized a new hairstyle, a *nodus*, or forehead roll, first worn by her sister-in-law, Octavia. Livia helped the new style overtake Cleopatra's tightly braided coiffure in popularity in the Roman world.

Livia certainly knew how to use publicity; for example, making public a miracle that supposedly took place not long before her marriage to Octavian. She was returning to her estate north of Rome when an eagle is said to have dropped into her lap a white hen holding a laurel sprig in its beak. Considering this a great omen, Livia decided to raise the bird and to plant the laurel sprig. The bird had so many chicks that the villa became known as the "Hen Roost." The laurel flourished, and Augustus began the practice, continued by his successors, of carrying a branch from the grove in which it stood when celebrating his triumphs.

Livia depicted the miracle in the famous *Painted Garden*, a painting that covered the walls of an underground chamber of the Hen Roost villa, a room probably used for dining in the heat of summer. A powerful woman, Livia may well have played up the miracle to increase her authority. At least one later historian in ancient times, Cassius Dio, saw it that way when stating: "Livia was destined to hold in her lap even Caesar's power and to dominate him in everything."

PLANNING FOR THE SUCCESSION

Like any good family businessman, Augustus thought long term and planned for the succession. His own experience as Julius Caesar's heir underlined the need for such thinking. Augustus made plans, but he found it harder to build a dynasty than to defeat his fiercest warrior or shrewdest political foe.

Livia gave Augustus only one stillborn child. Her two sons from her first marriage, Tiberius and Drusus, grew up to be excellent soldiers, and while Augustus made full use of them, he had other plans for his succession.

If a family is a business, then its members have to set their personal wishes and desires aside for the sake of the firm. That takes its toll, and more than one person was scarred by Augustus's dynastic needs. No one paid a higher price than Julia, his only biological child. She was the product of divorce, since her father divorced her mother, Scribonia, the day of Julia's birth. Scribonia never remarried, and Julia was raised in the home of her father and stepmother, Livia.

In spite of her difficult background, Julia grew up to be bright and witty. She was popular with the public, who saw in her a kind and gentle spirit. She was also conceited and proud of her unique status as Augustus's blood. Unfortunately for her, she was also his broodmare.

Augustus married Julia first to the ambitious young son of his sister, Octavia. But when he died before the couple had any children, Augustus next married the eighteen-year-old Julia to Agrippa—making his advisor divorce his wife first. He and Julia proceeded to have three boys and two girls together. In 17 BC a happy Augustus adopted the two oldest boys, his grandsons Gaius, three, and Lucius, an infant. Soon he began grooming them as his successors.

About a decade later, Augustus showed off his family on the Ara Pacis Augustae, the Altar of Augustan Peace. A white marble structure originally painted in vivid colors, it is one of the most famous and beautiful monuments of the ancient world. Dedicated in 9 BC, the altar is carved in exquisite relief with scenes of fertility and sacrifice while highlighting the imperial household marching in a stately procession. It shows Rome's first family as Augustus wanted them to be seen: patriotic, dignified, and united, as well as a living symbol of peace, prosperity, and piety. The reality was quite different.

Agrippa is depicted among the family members, although he'd died in 12 BC at the age of fifty-one. Augustus honored him by delivering the funeral oration and burying Agrippa's ashes in the mausoleum of Augustus. Meanwhile, Julia was a widow again.

Augustus now married her to Livia's son Tiberius. But the marriage failed, and Tiberius went into self-imposed exile on the Greek island of Rhodes. Julia traveled with a smart set, and she took a series of lovers, apparently not her first. When Augustus complained about her spending too much time around young men, Julia supposedly told him not to worry because she would soon make old men of them. When asked on another occasion how she managed to conduct love affairs while bearing children who resembled her husband, Julia supposedly replied that she only took on passengers when the ship was full (that is, when she was already pregnant).

Today we might see such behavior as a response to the tremendous pressure that her father put on Julia for an heir. Augustus found her behavior embarrassing, but there was worse still to come.

THE FATHER OF HIS COUNTRY—
AND OF JULIA

In 2 BC the Senate and people voted in a new title for Augustus: Father of His Country. He was sixty years old. It was a great honor, voted before only to Julius Caesar and, informally, to Cicero. It capped his program of putting the Julian family at the center of the Roman state. It was also a bitter irony, for later the same year, Augustus was forced to confront the evidence of his daughter's betrayal.

Julia and her young men hurt Augustus politically. Various sources claimed that she behaved scandalously with them in public but we can't rely on such gossipy and misogynistic tales. What is certain is that one of her lovers was Iullus, Mark Antony's surviving son (by Fulvia). The thought that Julia might want to divorce Tiberius and marry Antony's son threatened to give Augustus's old rival a victory from beyond the grave.

Augustus responded with the steel of a paterfamilias and the chill of a potentate. He had most of Julia's lovers exiled; he condemned Iullus to kill himself. As for Julia, Augustus brutally divorced her in Tiberius's name (without consulting Tiberius) and exiled her to a small and barren island off the Italian coast—today, ironically, a resort. Her mother, Scribonia, Augustus's ex-wife, loyally followed Julia into exile. Augustus's behavior could be cruel now that Julia had produced sons to serve as heirs. She was dispensable.

Five years later, in the year 3, Augustus allowed Julia to return to the Italian mainland but only to an out-of-the-way southern Italian city.

Tragedy followed her. Her son Lucius died of an illness in the year 2, and her son Gaius died two years later of a war wound. Their deaths deprived Augustus of his planned successors. As for Julia, she did not suffer an official erasure of memory, unlike other Romans who fell from grace, but the image makers of the empire seem to have gotten the message about her status. She was honored with many statues and inscriptions until her fall in 2 BC, after which that stopped. The complete silence is a backhanded compliment of sorts to Roman women, who were barely noticed as individuals outside the household before the end of the republic.

Augustus encountered many great women in his life, but the three closest to him were his mother, Atia, who raised him; his wife Livia, who inspired him; and his daughter, Julia, who betrayed him.

THE END

Augustus regrouped. In the year 4, he adopted two more sons. One was Agrippa Postumus, the sixteen-year-old son of Agrippa and Julia. Augustus had not adopted him before, allowing the boy to carry on Agrippa's family name, but now he needed him, so Postumus became a Caesar. The other was Livia's surviving son, Tiberius, who had returned to Rome from Rhodes. Livia's younger son, Drusus, had died earlier in an accident in Germany. Tiberius was a mature man of forty-five, while Postumus was only sixteen. As it turned out, Postumus was also hopeless; he had a strong body but a weak mind. Augustus had ice in his veins when it came to the survival of his regime. So even though Postumus was his biological grandson, Augustus rescinded the adoption and, as he had done with his mother, sent the boy into exile. That left Tiberius. He had no biological connection to Augustus, but he was capable, experienced, and could keep the dynasty going.

When Julius Caesar had adopted Octavian years earlier, he set an unintentional precedent and laid the groundwork for the empire's future success. Romans were relatively relaxed about adoption compared with modern people and used it frequently as a way to continue a family's name. While they preferred to adopt a blood relative and to adopt an adult rather than a child, they didn't insist on either. Because the emperor was free to adopt a son rather than having to pass power on to his birth child, he had flexibility in choosing a successor. The upshot was to open the succession to talent.

At the time he sent Postumus into exile, Augustus was sixty-six. He began to make serious plans for imperial transition. When he adopted Tiberius, Augustus also gave him a share of his legal powers. In addition, he used Tiberius as he had once used Agrippa—to command his armies. Augustus sent Tiberius to hold the violent frontiers in Central Europe and the Balkans, where Tiberius spent most of the time between the years 6 and 12 in a series of hard-fought wars and revolts.

The emperor could be in only one place at a time, but he needed to be everywhere. Ruling a great empire in an era of primitive technology and communications raised great practical difficulties. It would have been safer to keep the ruler's heir in Rome, but Augustus couldn't spare him; Tiberius was an experienced general and the only man Augustus trusted. Tiberius finally returned to Rome in the year 12. After celebrating a triumph, he gained the power to govern the provinces jointly with Augustus. Tiberius was now all but equal to the *princeps*.

In these years, Augustus put the final touch on his record. He left a will and instructions for his funeral as well as a detailed record of his achievements to be inscribed on bronze columns and set up in front of his mausoleum. The original is long gone, but copies in Latin and Greek were set up around the empire, and one complete version survives in Ankara, Turkey.

The Latin title at the head of the Ankara text fits the bill of Roman heroism: *Res Gestae Divi Augusti*, or "Exploits of the Deified Augustus." There was nothing antiheroic about Augustus; like Julius Caesar before him, Augustus was declared a god after his death. "A copy of the military exploits of the deified Augustus through which he subjected the whole world to the rule of the Roman people" is how the inscription begins.

Victory is a key theme of the document. Augustus stated that he put out the flames of civil war, rid the sea of pirates, and brought peace to the provinces. Mercy is a related theme, as Augustus noted that he spared all citizens who sued him for a pardon.

The document left much out, though, such as the murders, betrayals, dishonesty, and cruelty, as well as the excesses of the imperial court. Nowhere does Augustus state that he ended the free institutions of the Roman Republic and replaced them with the benevolent despotism of the Caesars. Finally, in keeping with the masculine tone of a record of military exploits, Augustus mentioned not one woman, although he did refer to several goddesses. In short, his official version of his achievements is a work of propaganda that bends and twists the truth. One thing, however, was clear and accurate about the *Res Gestae*: it was a text for the empire and not just Rome.

Fittingly, Augustus ended his political career outside of Rome, as he had begun it, on a mission for the empire. In 44 BC, when he got the news of Julius Caesar's assassination, he was just across the Adriatic Sea and opposite the last station of the Appian Way, the road that led south from Rome. When he died fifty-eight years later, Augustus was still looking eastward. Now long past his fighting prime, he still prioritized the empire. He escorted his son and heir, Tiberius, down the Appian Way on the road to the Adriatic, which Tiberius planned to cross in order to handle the latest crisis in a zone of continual conflict. As often as he could on his travels, Augustus brought Livia with him.

Augustus combined work with a holiday in his favorite place: the island of Capreae (modern Capri). He had already begun to feel ill. After crossing back to the mainland and participating in a ceremony in Naples, Augustus escorted Tiberius farther south on a journey of about four days. Then he turned back and felt so sick that he had to stop in the city of Nola, where he stayed in his family's villa. A message was sent to Tiberius to hurry back; in one version of the story, he reached his adoptive father in time for a last conference.

Augustus died in Nola on August 19, 14, just over a month short of his seventy-seventh birthday. Imperial mythmakers surely left their mark on the public details of Augustus's last day.

For what it is worth, his friends are supposed to have reached his bedside. Augustus asked them if they thought he had concluded the "mime" of life appropriately—that is, had he spoken like a comic actor at the end of the show. He added, "If the play has anything of merit, clap and send us out joyfully." Then he dismissed them, and soon he was kissing Livia. His last words were supposedly "Livia, live mindful of our marriage and farewell."

The man who had remade the world should have left it with a crash of thunder. Yet if the stories are true, Augustus concluded his life quietly with wit and modesty. The man who had ended the wars of the republic and then created the Roman Empire and the Roman peace also ended his life with recognition of how much he owed his mate. Cold blooded to the end, perhaps Augustus really did say good-bye to his omnipotence with gestures of humility.

People noticed the irony that Augustus died in the very same room where his biological father, Gaius Octavius, had died long before. But if Augustus thought of any man at the end, it was probably Julius Caesar.

Caesar and Augustus were two sides of the coin of Roman genius. Caesar was the god of battle who poured his talent and his ego into two literary classics. Augustus was the Machiavellian statesman who forged his power in blood and iron, and then went on to build a structure of peace and wealth that survived his passing for two hundred years. Caesar was a peacock; Augustus was a sphinx. Caesar fell under a hail of daggers in the Senate; Augustus died in his bed with a last kiss from his wife. Augustus started out as young murderer and ended up as father of his country. If his mother, Atia, and his great-uncle Caesar gave him his start, Augustus owed his mature achievement to two people: his friend Agrippa, and his wife Livia.

Augustus invented the concept of the *princeps*, the man we call emperor. His successors took him as a model. Augustus was a conqueror, a legislator, a builder, and a priest. Although he exercised supreme power, he hid it behind existing offices, misleading titles, invocations of the republic, charismatic authority, and a degree of deference to the Senate.

Caesar's death left Rome a generation of civil war. Would Augustus's death bequeath peace? The worries piled up. In his last years, Augustus made careful plans to transfer power, but who would obey a dead man? Was his adopted son and successor Tiberius really up to the job? Would Agrippa Postumus or Julia be freed and serve as a rallying point for opposition? Would republican sentiment burst back up to the surface in the Senate?

These questions surely troubled many minds in Rome, none more than that shrewdest of political operators, Livia. In public, the widow devoted herself to grieving. After Augustus's cremation in Rome, for example, she stayed on the spot for five days with an honor guard of the most distinguished knights. Then she had his ashes collected and placed in his tomb.

But in private, as she began a year of mourning for her late husband, Livia surely worked tirelessly behind the scenes. What schemes, speeches, and bloodshed would smooth the path for Rome's new ruler—her son?

Tiberius, marble seated figure.

2

TIBERIUS

THE TYRANT

On the seventeenth of September in the year 14, Tiberius Julius Caesar, adopted son and heir of Augustus, rose and addressed the Roman Senate. His adoptive father had been dead a month. After an emotional public funeral, the Senate voted for what the Romans called "consecration": they voted to declare Augustus a god. Dealing with Augustus's legacy in heaven was the easy part. Things on earth were harder.

We call him emperor, but to his contemporaries Augustus was Princeps, First Citizen, a vague and unstable position. There was no guarantee that his system wouldn't collapse at his death. After all, Rome did not have a written constitution. Some senators dreamed of restoring their old glory and power in the days before Julius Caesar, while others wanted to replace Tiberius as leader.

Yet most senators wanted to ask Tiberius to take on the full powers of Augustus. The trick for them was not to seem too subservient; Tiberius wanted to accept but without seeming too eager. That was probably not difficult. Despite Livia's ambitions for her son, Tiberius did not aspire to supreme political power.

Tiberius was a professional soldier, and he might have yearned for an easier time and for the bluff and straightforward atmosphere of the camp. He might have thought back to an occasion on Rome's northern front about ten years earlier, when he returned to the field on Augustus's order after a long absence. According to one source, Tiberius's old soldiers were thrilled to have him back again. Some men, the source says, had tears in their eyes at the sight of Tiberius, and others wanted to touch him. They remembered service with him on various campaigns and in various theaters of war. They said things such as "Is it really you that we see, Commander?" and "Have we received you safely back among us?"

Maybe Tiberius wished for a purely military career, but what faced him now was the most difficult political job in his world and stepping into the shoes of a god. Tiberius might not have wanted it, but the empire was his duty, and Tiberius was devoted to a fault. So he rose and addressed the senators.

Tiberius said that Augustus's job was too big for anyone else to handle and that it should be divided into three parts: Rome and Italy, the legions, and the provinces. He didn't mean it, of course, but an overeager senator missed the point. He said it was a good idea, and he asked Tiberius which of the three parts he preferred to have. Tiberius, appearing composed if perhaps really taken aback, replied elegantly. He was good at hiding what he felt when he had to. He said that the same man couldn't both divide and choose. The senator backed off, but it was too late. (Tiberius remembered the man's slight and avenged it years later with imprisonment and death by starvation.) Meanwhile, most senators begged Tiberius to take full power.

Finally, and only after hesitation, Tiberius accepted. And he left himself a way out, promising to stay in office, as he said, "Until I reach the point that it seems fair to you to give me a little respite in my old age." Considering that he was already fifty-five he knew that old age wasn't far off. Another reason to hesitate was Tiberius's knowledge of the dangers of the job. At least, he often described it as "holding a wolf by the ears." Still, however diffident Tiberius was, he took power and continued Rome's government in more or less the form Augustus had left it. That, in and of itself, was a major achievement.

Tiberius had no easy role to play. Not only did he have to manage expectations after his great predecessor, but also he had to do so in the full knowledge that he wasn't Augustus's first choice as successor. Besides, Augustus had bequeathed him a nearly impossible job. Tiberius followed Augustus the way John Adams followed George Washington or the way Tim Cook followed Steve Jobs. In each case, the second man was more effective than he was popular or charismatic.

Conqueror and peacemaker, the emperor was also builder and demolisher; benefactor and judge; head of his family and Father of the Fatherland; tribune of the people and First Man in the Senate; most authoritative of the Romans and champion of the provinces; manager and magnetic leader; showman and symbol of severity; priest and commander; sacrosanct in Rome and king in the East—and even god. Every emperor had to work out an arrangement with the elites that mattered: with the army, the Senate, the imperial court, and the provincial notables. The urban plebeians of Rome mattered too, but their power was much less than it had been under the republic. Augustus managed to pull it off, but only after a civil war and a process of political trial and error and thanks only to a long, long reign. Even a political virtuoso like him did not find the job easy.

His successors had trouble balancing the various and contradictory demands on the emperor. Nor did any of them reign as long as Augustus, who held unrivaled power in the Roman world for forty-five years.

Whereas Augustus adored the mix of force and fraud by which he ruled, Tiberius was a manager and a pragmatist who cut things down to size and made them work—even at the price of repression at home and retrenchment abroad.

As much as Augustus may have identified with the sphinx, Tiberius was the true man of mystery. His guarded personality confounded contemporaries and sometimes baffles today's historians. Yet Tiberius had a truly consequential reign and proved to be a transformational leader. He cemented Augustus's monarchy in place but not Augustus's foreign policy. After centuries of expansion, Tiberius put on the brakes. Nor did any peacetime emperor ever do more damage to the old Roman nobility than

Tiberius did. The man who started out as a friend of the Senate ended up as a tyrant in its eyes.

EARLY CAREER

Tiberius was born in Rome on November 16, 42 BC, the son of Tiberius Claudius Nero and Livia Drusilla. They passed on to Tiberius a hereditary attachment to the Roman Republic. But the republic of the Senate and the Roman people was dying, crushed by the invincible armies of Octavian and Antony. In 42 BC no one could guess that Octavian, later Augustus, would play a key role in Tiberius's life. The two men came from different heritages.

Augustus had only one foot in the Roman nobility. Tiberius, by contrast, came from blue blood. Both of his parents claimed descent from the ancient patrician house of the Claudians, a family that had held Rome's highest offices for centuries from the start of the republic and had built the Appian Way, Rome's first great road. The Claudians had a sense of duty but also a feeling of entitlement and a tendency toward arrogance.

Tiberius's father and grandfather each fought against Octavian at various times. A firm supporter of the republic, Tiberius's grandfather committed suicide after going into battle on the losing side at Philippi. Tiberius's father had more flexible principles. First he served Caesar in the Civil War, but then he found Caesar's monarchical ways unbearable. After Caesar's assassination, he voted for the Senate to honor the killers. (The Senate declined to do so.) Then after fighting Octavian, he fled Italy and Sicily in turn to take refuge in Greece. Tiberius was just a toddler then, but he and his mother Livia joined in the flight. Later, they returned to Italy, where Livia married Octavian.

Octavian was one of the most powerful men in the world. If Tiberius's father objected to Octavian stealing his wife, he was in no position to stop him. So when Octavian and Livia were married in January 38 BC, Tiberius's father was present at the wedding and gave away Livia "just as a father would." She was pregnant at the time and soon gave birth to Tiberius's younger brother, Drusus. Their father raised Tiberius and Drusus for the next five years. No doubt he introduced them to the proud traditions of the Claudian family. The Claudians, champions of the nobility, considered the Roman people a distant second. When he died in 33 BC, Tiberius's father left Octavian as guardian to the two boys, who were now raised by Octavian and Livia. Although he was only nine, Tiberius delivered the eulogy at his father's funeral—presumably someone else wrote it.

Tiberius and Drusus grew up in their stepfather's house under the same roof as their stepsister, Augustus's daughter, Julia. Augustus raised all three children to play a part in his regime, but he gave pride of place to Julia and her progeny, his blood relations. Livia, meanwhile, always the powerbroker, had great expectations for her own two sons.

A Roman woman who sought political power had no choice but to act through a man. Husbands could be influenced, as could lovers, fathers, and brothers, but the strongest male-female emotional tie in Rome was that of mother and son. Livia behaved accordingly. She advanced her boys both assiduously and patiently. Tough and unyielding herself, Livia raised Tiberius and Drusus to be hard men, which served them well in adversity but won few popularity contests.

The brothers developed a lifelong closeness. Julia and Tiberius, however, had a more complicated bond. He was dutiful, while she was wild; and he had an awkward relationship with Augustus, while she was daddy's girl (at first). Raised as stepbrother and stepsister, they suddenly found themselves having to start all over as adults.

Julia and Livia each had a great impact on Tiberius's life. So, ironically, would three other women related to Augustus by blood or marriage. A man's man and the scion of his own proud noble house, Tiberius found that much of his career revolved around the women of his stepfather's family. As a man who thought that women should not be allowed to rise too high, he could not have liked it. He "considered an exalted rank for a woman to be a diminution of his own," wrote the Roman historian Tacitus.

Raised to be a soldier and statesman, Tiberius was also trained in the Greek and Latin classics. He was a skilled orator, poet, and wine connoisseur. He was knowledgeable in Roman law. He had an interest in philosophy and a passion for astrology. In short, Tiberius was military but educated and literate.

He is said to have been tall and strong. Both his coins and the literary sources depict a handsome man, but he was supposedly so stiff and stern that he came off as unpleasant or arrogant. Augustus allegedly quipped on his deathbed that Tiberius would crunch Rome in his tough and obstinate jaws.

Beneath the toughness, perhaps there lay mental scars. An early life as a refugee, a broken home, a change of households, the loss of a father, a stepfather who considered other young men more promising than him, and an overbearing mother—Tiberius suffered through quite a lot in his boyhood. Throughout his life, he had a reputation for insincerity, yet perhaps he found that he needed to hide his true feelings in order to survive.

THE RISE TO POWER

Tiberius traveled a long, glorious, but bitter road to power. Practically from the time he took on the toga of manhood at the age of fifteen in 27 BC, he was active in public affairs. After holding his first military and political offices, he married Vipsania, the daughter of Agrippa, Augustus's right-hand man and son-in-law. Vipsania was the third important woman in Tiberius's life with a close connection to the ruler. She did not come from an old noble family, but Tiberius loved her, and they enjoyed a happy home life with their son, Drusus the Younger. That is, when Tiberius was home.

After serving as a judicial official known as a praetor in 16 BC, Tiberius spent the next decade continually campaigning north of Italy in an attempt to bring Rome's borders to the Danube and Elbe Rivers. He fought in the dark, cold, poor, and unglamorous parts of the empire, the ancient equivalents of today's Switzerland, Germany, Austria, Serbia, and Hungary. Between 12 and 9 BC, Tiberius led the hard fighting that conquered Pannonia, an area lying south and west of the Danube. Tiberius proved to be a popular commander, hard drinking and risk averse but also someone who little by little expanded Rome's borders. Meanwhile, Drusus led Rome's armies in Germany all the way eastward to the Elbe.

Then Tiberius's personal life turned upside down. When Agrippa died in 12 BC, Augustus needed someone new to serve as administrator and to guard the interests of the young princes Gaius and Lucius Caesar, Augustus's two adopted sons. He turned to a mature and responsible man: Tiberius. Livia, not one to let sentiment get in the way of a good career move, probably encouraged Augustus's decision, and she certainly smiled on it. Augustus now forced Tiberius to end his happy marriage, divorce Vipsania, and marry Julia, his stepsister.

Tiberius got along with Julia at first. Although he loved his first wife, marriage to Julia represented a promotion within the imperial family. Julia was attractive, witty, and helpful, and she was certainly a known quantity. She traveled to northern Italy to be nearer Tiberius fighting across the Alps. She bore him a son.

But their infant son died, and their interests diverged. Julia wanted to promote the careers of her sons by Agrippa, while Tiberius had his own career and his own son, Drusus the Younger. Tiberius considered himself a champion of the nobles, while Julia arguably had populist tendencies. More important, Tiberius thought little of women in politics, and Julia had no intention of staying home. Tiberius also missed Vipsania. The story goes that Tiberius was so upset when he once happened to see his ex-wife on the streets of Rome that it was arranged for them never to cross paths again.

When his brother suffered a severe injury in Germany in 9 BC after a riding accident, Tiberius made the long and difficult trip from Pannonia to see him. He reached Drusus just before he died. Tiberius followed his brother's body to Rome—all the way on foot. If it was a nod to Augustus's promotion of family values, it might also have expressed sincere grief at the loss of the last link to Tiberius's father. Drusus earned the posthumous name Germanicus—conqueror of Germany—and passed it on to his descendants.

In 6 BC Augustus decided to send Tiberius on a new mission to the East. But Tiberius shocked him by announcing his plan to retire to Rhodes instead, a beautiful Greek island far from the center of power. He said that he was exhausted and in need of rest and that he didn't want to stand in the way of Augustus's grandsons—and Julia's sons—Gaius and Lucius, who were about to come of age and who were being groomed as Augustus's successors. Others said that Tiberius wanted to get away from Julia, but his dislike for her was more than just personal. Tiberius might well have feared that Gaius and Lucius would eventually have him executed. Sure enough, Gaius soon displayed his hostility to Tiberius, and perhaps Tiberius had seen it coming. Gossip added an additional reason for Tiberius's retreat to Rhodes: supposedly he wanted to indulge his sex life there in a way he couldn't at Rome, as if Rhodes were some ancient Las Vegas.

Tiberius enjoyed Rhodes, from its exquisite landscape to the company of a Greek scholar and astrologer whom he met there, and perhaps because of its illicit pleasures. Eventually Tiberius wanted to return to Rome, but Augustus forced him to wait until the year 2, when Tiberius took up a quiet residence in town. He brought the scholar-astrologer back with him and made him a Roman citizen.

RETURN TO ROME

Tiberius's future looked dim in 6 BC, when he left for Rhodes. Ten years later, he was named Augustus's successor. What happened? Julia had gotten tired of waiting for power. She committed serial adultery and plotted against her father but was caught. In 2 BC she faced disgrace and exile, and Augustus required Tiberius to divorce her. Her sons continued in favor, but they were both dead by the year 4. Gossip, as usual, blamed Livia, saying she had arranged for Gaius and Lucius to be poisoned so that Tiberius could come back to power. Yet each died on a mission abroad, far from Livia's power base in Rome: Lucius succumbed to an illness; Gaius, to the lingering effects of a battle wound. Ancient conditions were often fragile and risky, and we can only wonder at Augustus's willingness to risk their lives overseas. And Livia was probably not unhappy to see the obstacles to her sons' elevation die.

Augustus solved his succession crisis by adopting Tiberius as his son.

He was not the emperor's first or second or even third choice, but Augustus was a realist. Besides, as will become clear, he added a sting to his gift.

In spite of their past disagreements, Tiberius was Rome's most experienced general. Augustus also gave Tiberius tribunician power along with a grant of overriding authority (*imperium maius*). He said that he was adopting Tiberius for the good of the republic, a comment that was surely meant to strengthen Tiberius's position rather than insult him. Although Augustus also adopted his youngest grandson, Agrippa Postumus, the boy was only sixteen and no threat at the time to Tiberius, a senior statesman aged forty-six. Augustus had no other grandchildren.

Soon afterward, Augustus sent Tiberius back to the northern front. A pro-Tiberius source praises Tiberius as a wise, prudent, authoritative, and moderate general who was considerate of his men's lives. Certainly, Tiberius was successful. First he campaigned in Germany, where he matched his brother's achievement of reaching the Elbe River with Roman arms. Then, in the year 6, he hurried back to Pannonia, where a major revolt was under way, this time including the neighboring region of Dalmatia (roughly, the coastal region of Croatia).

In three years of hard fighting, Tiberius put down one of the more serious revolts Rome had faced. He showed himself to be a cool practitioner of what would now be called counterinsurgency. It was a pacification campaign that the Romans won as much by cutting off the enemy from food and supplies as by engaging in battle.

Then, in the year 9, came the General Varus disaster in Germany and the loss of three Roman legions. Augustus sent Tiberius back to Germany over the next two years, where he engaged in the slow, patient, inglorious work of reorganizing the surviving legions and punishing Rome's enemies across the Rhine River.

Back in Rome in the year 12, Tiberius celebrated a long-delayed triumph for the reconquest of Pannonia. His powers were extended and made equal to those of Augustus. A coin from the year 13 shows Augustus on one side and Tiberius on the other, as if the Roman world were preparing for the inevitable transfer of power.

THE SUCCESSION

In some ways, Augustus arranged for the smoothest and most peaceful transition imaginable. When he died, Tiberius had the good fortune to be at his bedside or at least to show up soon enough afterward that people could say he was there. It is likely that Augustus himself gave the cold-blooded order to have Agrippa Postumus executed upon his own death, in order to remove a potential rival to the new ruler. After all, Augustus had earlier established the principle that "too many Caesars is not a good thing."

But in other ways, Augustus tied Tiberius's hands. Livia was now seventy years old but still vigorous, and Augustus left her strong tools. He assured Livia's position by adopting her in his will—as his daughter!—which made her a member of the Julian family. After his death, the Senate approved the adoption. As far as we know, no one asked whether Livia was now also the adoptive sister of her son Tiberius, who had already been adopted by Augustus.

No less important, Augustus's will renamed Livia as Julia Augusta. This was an unprecedented distinction, and no one knew precisely what it meant. Livia, Tiberius, and the Senate would have to work that out. Yet clearly Augustus intended his wife to maintain considerable authority. The prestigious title of Julia Augusta placed her in Rome's first family and left her only two letters away (*a* versus *us*) from the supreme position in the state. It was a way, in effect, of continuing Augustus's power beyond the grave and of tempering Tiberius.

Nor was that the end of Livia's authority. She was also the first priestess of the deified Augustus's cult. This was no small thing because no woman held a major priesthood in Rome, aside from the Vestal Virgins. With Livia's new office also came the right to have a bodyguard whenever she carried out her new religious duties, another sign of her importance. Many other honors followed, from a seat in the theater with the Vestal Virgins, to the several cities named after her. A province in the East erected a temple in honor of Tiberius, Livia, and the Senate. Sculpture and inscriptions began to connect Livia with Ceres, goddess of fertility and abundance, something only hinted at under Augustus.

Livia was one of the richest people in the empire, and, unlike most Roman women, she received complete control of her property. Augustus bequeathed Livia one-third of his estate, while he gave the other two-thirds to Tiberius. She owned property both in Italy and in several provinces East and West. As a woman, Livia couldn't be a senator, but she received senators in her home, where a huge staff waited on them. All in all, she employed over a thousand people.

Time spent with Livia sometimes paid off down the road. Her household included a man who would end up as commander of the Praetorian Guard under a later emperor. Among her court favorites was someone who would later go on to become Rome's first emperor from outside the dynastic circle: the first not descended from either Augustus or Livia.

Livia served as a bridge between the reigns of her husband and her son. Tiberius surely both appreciated the continuity and resented it. While he allowed his mother to amass honors and to exercise certain powers, he also imposed limits. For example, early in his reign, the Senate wanted to give her the unprecedented title Mother of Her Country, but Tiberius vetoed it, along with other senatorial suggestions such as officially calling him Son of Julia and renaming the month of October as Livius. Tiberius preferred the title of Son of a God, which he had by virtue of Augustus's deification.

To understand Tiberius, we have to understand Livia. No Roman woman had ever matched her position of wealth and honor. Not only was she the living link to the founder of the dynasty, but also she was de facto First Lady, since Tiberius was divorced and without a mistress. She was also the most knowledgeable political veteran in Rome. And she was a daily reminder to the proud Tiberius of someone who exceeded what he considered the proper role of a woman. One imagines that if ever someone called him the Son of the Augusta, he surely winced—and yet whenever he faced a knotty political problem, he may well have asked his mother for advice.

From time to time, Livia threw around her weight in Roman public life: advancing a friend here, granting special privileges to an ally there, now dedicating statues in her name and Tiberius's, now inviting senators to a reception in her home. Tiberius generally accepted these things and even worked behind the scenes to present a united front. That was especially true in the early part of his reign, but as time went by, he grew less patient with his mother.

One person whom Tiberius did not consult was his ex-wife, Julia. Augustus had commuted her exile from an island off the Italian coast to the southern Italian city of Regium, but she still lived under what amounted to house arrest. Within six months of Tiberius's becoming emperor in the year 14, she was dead of malnutrition. It was said that Julia gave up and starved herself to death, perhaps in grief over the execution of her son Agrippa Postumus or perhaps just in desperation at the thought of her ex-husband in power.

When Tiberius became *princeps*, he was a mature man and in some ways one of the best-prepared emperors that Rome would ever have. But he was hardly the youngest. At fifty-five, Tiberius was done with leading armies and traveling abroad. Although he followed Augustus's lead in this—he too had begun to stay put at that age—Tiberius nonetheless came in for unfair criticism for his supposed lack of courage and enterprise.

TIBERIUS AND THE SENATE

Tiberius was fundamentally an oligarch. Unlike Augustus, who enjoyed popularity with Rome's ordinary people, this emperor was aloof and reserved. He had little time for funding public works and less for attending the games.

Although Tiberius never knew the old republic, his family heritage gave him a stake in the Senate, and in his first years, he showed it respect. He attended senate meetings regularly. He acknowledged the senators' freedom of speech, listened politely, and tried to be discreet in injecting his own opinion. He rejected titles such as Master or Father of the Fatherland. As he often said, "I am master of the slaves, imperator of the soldiers, and chief of the rest." He once told the Senate that he considered himself its servant and one who looked on the senators as "kind, just, and indulgent masters."

But few believed him. To claim to be the First Citizen while really being the king, as in the case of Augustus, you had to be a political magician.

Augustus paid attention to the Senate and flattered its members while really manipulating them.

Tiberius was no magician. He gave the senators freedom and expected to get cooperation in return. Instead, the result was a mix of servility and conspiracy. Most senators lacked the courage to speak freely before him. When, at the start of his reign, Tiberius promised the Senate to share power, one senator replied that "the body of the republic is one and must be ruled by one mind"—that is, the First Citizen. Tiberius scorned such sentiments. He supposedly once left a Senate meeting muttering in Greek, "Men fit to be slaves!"

The emperor's personality did not help. Tiberius lacked the affability and thoughtfulness that a Roman noble was supposed to show toward his friends. Julius Caesar, for example, could be described as "easy" in his relations with his friends, whereas Tiberius could be described as such only in his fluency in Greek.

He was insincere and often cruel and an unreliable judge of character, sometimes dangerously so. He was austere to the point of bad taste; for instance, he attended Senate meetings rather than visiting his dying son or mourning him afterward. Tiberius had such a strong contempt for honors that he left people nervous and uncertain of how to treat him.

But he had many virtues as well. Tiberius was realistic, prudent, moderate, sober, and thrifty. He was modest enough to turn down a request for a temple to himself and his mother, stating instead that his real temples would be in people's hearts. He did insist on building a grander residence on the Palatine Hill than Augustus had. Still, Tiberius was frugal enough to die leaving a surplus in the Treasury.

After his divorce from Julia, Tiberius never remarried, nor is he known to have had a long-term mistress. One imagines a lonely man, the Citizen Kane of Roman emperors. Yet Tiberius was not simple. A later historian put it well: "Tiberius possessed a great many virtues and a great many vices, and followed each set in turn as if the other did not exist."

After a relatively quiet half dozen years of rule, Tiberius allowed his enemies to be put on trial for the crime of *maiestas*: diminishing the majesty of the Roman people, the emperor, or his family. It was a vague and dangerous charge that almost guaranteed abuse. Senators accused one another of treason. That rarely happened under Augustus, who paid close enough attention to the Senate, but Tiberius let them turn on one another.

Although the trial took place in the Senate, defendants did not relish the venue. Unlike a regular courtroom, the Senate had few rules to protect the accused. In the end, dozens of senators were victims of these trials and lost their lives. The result chilled the freedom of the hundreds of senators who escaped. Most considered Tiberius dishonest and cruel.

If Tiberius behaved tyrannically, he was certainly provoked, not that it justifies his response. Hostility was always bubbling below the surface of the nobility. It came out in little ways again and again. When, for example, an elderly noble widow died at the end of the year 22, she showed what she thought of Tiberius by leaving him out of her will—a gesture that few others of her class dared to follow. Tiberius let it pass with only one act in response. He refused to let her family display the wax masks of her late husband or half brother among the ancestral greats depicted in the funeral procession. She was the widow of Cassius and the half sister of Brutus, two of the leaders of the conspiracy that assassinated Julius Caesar, Tiberius's adoptive grandfather, in 44 BC. Even after sixty-six years, some wounds still festered.

THE HOUSE OF AUGUSTUS

Tiberius made a good manager, but Augustus had wanted more: he had wanted a hero. He found one in Tiberius's nephew, the dashing and charismatic general Germanicus (15 BC to the year 19), son of Tiberius's late brother, Drusus. At the time, Tiberius had his own son, Drusus the Younger, but Germanicus now came before him as heir. Since Germanicus was married to Augustus's granddaughter, the adoption guaranteed that Augustus's bloodline would eventually return to power. Conveniently for Livia, Germanicus was her grandson, so her bloodline would hold power, starting with her son, Tiberius. The grim emperor and his magnetic nephew did not get along, with disastrous results for the imperial family.

Germanicus was an icon of Tiberius's early years as emperor. At the age of twenty-eight, he commanded Rome's armies on the Rhine. Augustus sent him there in the year 13, and placed him in charge of Rome's eight legions. The Roman people loved Germanicus; his wife, Agrippina the Elder, granddaughter of the divine Augustus; and their six surviving children. (Three others died young.) The sources say that Germanicus was easygoing, accessible, modest, and charming, all of which won him a following among both senators and ordinary folk in Rome and the provinces. Coins and busts show a handsome young man with an aquiline nose, a prominent chin, and curly locks of hair. He was as literate as he was warlike, killing an enemy in hand-to-hand combat and writing poetry in Greek. Portraits show Agrippina the Elder as a serious woman with a classical profile and long, braided hair.

When Augustus died in the year 14, the legions of Germany mutinied and wanted Germanicus instead of Tiberius to be emperor. With the help of his capable wife, Germanicus put down the mutiny and restored loyalty to Tiberius. Then in the year 16 Tiberius recalled Germanicus from the Rhine, where, in spite of his name ("conqueror of Germany"), the general had won battles but did not extend the empire. His standout success was recapturing legionary standards lost by Varus and burying the still-exposed dead men's bones.

Back in Rome, Germanicus celebrated a triumph that exaggerated his achievements and magnified the adulation of the crowd. All eyes were on him as he rode in a chariot with five of his children. His friends and supporters were ever ready to polish his image. Even Germanicus's previous, failed expedition to the North Sea received an epic poem trumpeting his boldness.

Next, Tiberius sent Germanicus to the East with a broad portfolio, but the young man pushed for even more power. He and Agrippina clashed with the governor of Syria, Gnaeus Calpurnius Piso, and his wife, Plancina, who had joined them on his mission. Both were nobles and not easily intimidated.

Soon Germanicus left for Egypt, which he visited without Tiberius's permission, even though no senator was allowed to enter the province without it. In Alexandria, Germanicus received a hero's welcome. He owed his popularity in part to his ancestry: through his mother, Antonia the Younger, Germanicus was the grandson of Mark Antony (and Octavia). His generosity also won him acclaim, because Germanicus helped people by putting state-owned grain on sale during a food shortage. The cheering was so great that Germanicus had to ask the Alexandrians to tone it down. He said that only Tiberius and Livia were worthy of such acclamation.

When he fell sick in Syria, Germanicus blamed poison and he allegedly suspected Piso and Plancina. He died on October 10, 19, aged thirty-three. In the uproar afterward, Piso was recalled to Rome and forced to stand trial before the Senate. He was convicted of lesser crimes than murder, but he committed suicide before the sentencing. Plancina was also forced back to Rome, but she was saved by the powerful protection of Livia, who had Tiberius intercede on her behalf and arrange her acquittal. Many in Rome pointed a finger at a jealous Tiberius, with Livia supposedly behind him as the real cause of Germanicus's death. Distant and elitist as they were, they could not match Germanicus's popularity. That they resented it seems likely—they were only human, but murder is another matter. Incidentally, Plancina outlived Livia only to find her protection gone, so Plancina, like her husband, committed suicide.

Even in death, Germanicus was the public's darling. The sources speak of a universal outpouring of grief, as if everyone felt he or she had lost one of his own. A poet wrote at the time: "I, Hades, declare, 'Germanicus is not mine; he's of the stars.'"

His ashes were laid to rest in the mausoleum of Augustus on a day when torches blazed around the monument and the raucous city for once knew only silence broken by cries of grief.

Germanicus's death robbed Rome of a hero and Tiberius of a successor. At the age of sixty, he surely felt pressure to find the next emperor. Germanicus had three sons, but they were too young. Tiberius's thirty-two-year-old son, Drusus, was an experienced soldier and statesman but also a playboy. Besides, Augustus had clearly meant for Germanicus and his descendants to rule. So Tiberius named Drusus the Younger as the emperor-in-waiting, with the understanding that he would pass the throne to one of Germanicus's sons. Unfortunately, a family feud got in the way; that, and the craftiness of an ambitious outsider who took advantage of an old man.

But before turning to the blood and thunder that ended Tiberius's reign, consider for a moment the way he took charge of Rome's foreign policy and changed it forever. That was the legacy of Tiberius's best years.

THE IMPERIAL ARMY

Like General George Washington or General Dwight D. Eisenhower, Tiberius was a soldier to the core who preferred to keep his sword in its sheath once he became chief executive. He wrenched the military system out of the pattern that Augustus had established, and he gave the army what would be its new and lasting main task: to defend the Roman peace.

The army was the greatest institution in the empire, but it was no mere military machine. For most people, it was the only ladder of social mobility. It was also a tool of assimilation. The army made provincial subjects into citizens, and it mixed together people from one end of the Mediterranean to the other and from Britain to Iraq. The word *people*, and not *men*, is used advisedly, because in military camps and in communities that grew up around them, there were women and children who, along with soldiers and civilian men, were shaped and influenced by the Roman military. This was the case even though Roman soldiers were not allowed by law to marry, which was a big source of discontent. Many of them formed common-law marriages anyhow.

The Roman Imperial Army had about three hundred thousand men in Tiberius's day and later rose to roughly five hundred thousand at its peak in the second century. Professional and well paid, it was also very well outfitted, highly disciplined, and large.

The military consisted of three main groups: the legions, auxiliaries, and others (rowers and sailors; tribal units on the edges of the empire; and the city of Rome's guards, paramilitary police, and firemen).

Legionaries were heavy infantrymen and the pride of the Roman military. They served for twenty-five years. In addition to their annual salary, the men received a cash bonus upon retirement. Emperors were also expected to give additional cash bonuses from time to time—if they knew what was good for them. After all, the army put the Caesars in power, and the army could unseat them.

Legionaries were generally Roman citizens, but they rarely came from Rome or even Italy. Increasingly, Italians lost interest in military service, since they were now successful farmers enjoying peace and prosperity. Recruits came from other areas such as southern Gaul and Hispania and the provinces along the Danube.

There were twenty-five legions under Tiberius, three fewer than before Varus's defeat in Germany in the year 9. Not long after Tiberius, the number of legions would go back to twenty-eight, and then, over the next century and a half, it reached thirty and finally a high of thirty-three. The total number of legionaries varied between about 130,000 and 170,000 men.

Auxilliaries, which fought alongside the legions, were composed of noncitizens. They were paid at a lower rate than legionaries, tended to be poorer and less literate, and, frankly, were more likely to have to fight and die in the thick of battle. They served in locally recruited units that were equipped and trained according to local customs. Starting around the year 50, auxiliaries received citizenship after twenty-five years of service. As proof, they received a folding bronze tablet called a diploma.

Special forces were kept in Rome. The Praetorian Guard, about several thousand strong, served as an elite unit to support and protect the emperor. Another 1,500 or so soldiers were deployed as the city's police force. Approximately another 3,000 soldiers made up Rome's fire fighters. Unlike the rest of the army, soldiers in Rome were, in the main, Italians.

The navy had two bases in Italy, one on the Bay of Naples and the other on the Adriatic. Rome also had warships on the Rhine and Danube.

One last part of the Roman military consisted of tribesmen who lived on both sides of the frontier on the empire's edges. They served in semi-irregular units.

As impressive as the Roman army was, it included few men who'd ever set foot in Rome. That did not rob the military of a sense of purpose, but it did tend to make pay and conditions of service loom ever larger in the men's minds. After all, if they weren't fighting for hearth and home, they might as well be fighting for money.

Another problem was the army's combat edge. It is easier to inspire troops who are marching off to war than those who are sitting on garrison duty. Maintaining discipline became ever more important for the imperial army—and more difficult.

One day, far in the future, Rome's soft and comfortable peacetime army would offer a tempting target to hard men on the other side of the frontier. But not in Tiberius's era.

"A PRINCE UNINTERESTED IN EXTENDING THE EMPIRE"

Germanicus wanted to win back Germany east of the Rhine, but Tiberius, a realist, disagreed. For all the talk of "empire without end" under Augustus, he knew better. Tiberius was, as Tacitus described him in the quotation above, uninterested in expansion, or at least in armed expansion. The new policy marked a dramatic change. For nearly three hundred years, men who conquered new territory had dominated Roman politics. Not anymore; not if Tiberius had his way. And there were sound and sensible reasons for the emperor to prevail.

Rome had just enough troops to patrol the border: about three hundred thousand men. The military was the government's largest expense, typically accounting for more than half the annual budget, according to very rough scholarly estimates. A modern state, even a military power such as the United States, typically devotes less of its budget to the military and more to social welfare programs.

Rome's economy was relatively poor and inelastic compared with later empires. Its ability to bear a greater military burden was limited. Nor did Germany offer enough riches to make it gleam in a would-be-conqueror's eye. It presented only a defensible border—the Elbe-Danube line—and the prospect of glory. The levelheaded Tiberius had enough glory. Many in the Roman elite believed that Rome had already conquered the best part of the world, and the rest might not have seemed worth the effort.

More conquest required more soldiers. That would be not only expensive but also dangerous, since their numbers would increase the chance of rebellion. Besides, conscription was unpopular. And who would lead any invasion? The emperors did not want any of their generals to get the credit for major conquests.

People did not realize it at the time, but 16 was a watershed year in the history of the empire. By recalling Germanicus, Tiberius ended Rome's last serious attempt to win back the territory between the Rhine and the Elbe. The only exception was the Rhineland, a narrow strip of land east of the Rhine, which Rome controlled for centuries.

Years of hard fighting in northern Europe taught Tiberius the bitter truth about wars of conquest. He lacked Augustus's desire to conquer the world. Always cunning, Tiberius reported to the Senate that Augustus on his deathbed told him not to expand the empire. So major a policy change needed the prestige of Augustus, and Tiberius was wise to invoke him, but it's doubtful that his predecessor really said it. If he did, and if Tiberius really did see him before the old man died, then it was a deathbed conversion. Everything that Augustus did while emperor shows him to have been a full-blooded imperialist. Tiberius deserves credit for having conceived the new policy and putting it into effect.

Tiberius was a pragmatist, and he was not alone, but deep in the Roman heart, there still beat a desire for military glory. So some emperors continued to fight wars of conquest, especially those few who were able field commanders and, unlike Tiberius, were still young enough to engage in arduous campaigns. Those men waged major wars that added the new provinces of Britain and Dacia to the empire. They also engaged in a long and fruitless generations-long contest with the Parthians and their successors. But they were the exception. Most of Rome's emperors followed Tiberius's new imperial policy.

It would be hard to overestimate the consequences of Tiberius's transformation. True, he built on foundations laid by Augustus and Julius Caesar. But Tiberius took them further to a logical if sometimes harsh conclusion—and he wasted little effort sugarcoating the truth. The result was a fundamental alteration in the character of Rome. Romans continued to debate his policies and some disagreed, but Rome changed as follows:

An empire in search of new lands to conquer needs ambitious generals to lead military campaigns as well as dynamic politicians to guide diplomacy. It needs free and open debate to hammer out strategies, and eloquent orators to persuade the people to follow and serve in the army. A settled empire, by contrast, needs garrison commanders to maintain discipline and suppress revolt, and it needs bureaucrats, managers, and tax collectors. It does not require the Roman people to play any civic role at all, not even as soldiers, since there were plenty of men in Italy and the provinces who were ready to serve.

Nor did Rome need senators as leaders of the political system. The new Rome left senators, at best, as advisors to the emperor and, at worst, as dissidents who needed to be silenced. Augustus had reduced the senatorial elite's sense of purpose; Tiberius cut it further. Some rebelled and paid with their lives, but most turned docile. They began to look inward, seeking the consolation of philosophy or of pleasure.

RULE BY THE PRAETORIAN GUARD

Tiberius began his reign with warmth toward the Senate and ended it with hostility. Such a turn of events seems almost inevitable, given the new reality of power, the unwillingness of proud Roman nobles to surrender without a fight, and the brusque and no-nonsense personality of the emperor. For much of his reign, and particularly between the years 26 and 31, his chief advisor and partner in his struggle with the nobility was Lucius Aelius Sejanus. Tacitus calls Sejanus daring, wicked, and crafty, and blames him for bringing out the worst in Tiberius. But the truth lies hidden, and it is also possible that Sejanus was doing his master's bidding.

Like Augustus's right-hand man Agrippa, Sejanus came from an equestrian family; a prominent one with ties to various senators. Like Agrippa,

Sejanus was capable and ambitious and indispensable to his master. Also like Agrippa, Sejanus wanted a share of the emperor's power. Sejanus did well under Augustus, and he was first cocommander of the Praetorian Guard under Tiberius and then sole commander: a position known as Praetorian prefect.

Sejanus used that position to reach the heights of power. A man in his late thirties at the time of Tiberius's rise to power, he won the emperor's trust. One by one, Tiberius's other advisors disappeared, leaving Sejanus in an unrivaled position. The sudden and unexpected death of his son, Drusus the Younger, in the year 23 was a harsh blow to Tiberius. Once again the emperor's plans for the succession were in ruins.

The noble ladies of Rome found Sejanus charming. One of his conquests was Tiberius's daughter-in-law, Livilla, who became his lover. Sejanus's bitter wife claimed later that Livilla poisoned her husband, Drusus the Younger, at Sejanus's behest. There was corroborating evidence, but it was obtained by torture. Although the Romans accepted torture-derived evidence, we recognize it as worthless. In any case, by the time the information was produced, Sejanus was no longer alive to defend himself.

Earlier, when Sejanus was still on the rise, he convinced Tiberius to construct a barracks for the Praetorian Guard on the outskirts of Rome. This imposing place covered more than forty acres. It had the standard, rectangular shape of a Roman army camp but with more massive fortifications than usual. A high concrete-and-brick wall, topped by ramparts and punctuated by gates with towers, surrounded the camp. Much of it can still be seen today, not far from Rome's central train station.

The site was known as the Praetorian Camp. An elite unit, about several thousand men strong, the Guard provided security for the emperor. They were highly paid professionals. Augustus created the Praetorian Guard, but, clever politician that he was, he kept it outside Rome, in nearby towns, so as not to offend the Senate. Tiberius dropped the pretense. First he brought the Guard into the city, housed in various places, and then he began building the permanent camp.

Gathering the Guard together in one strategic place made it easier to instill discipline and impose fear. No doubt it contributed to the Guard's esprit de corps, and this might have been the moment when the Guard adopted its famous scorpion symbol. The scorpion was Tiberius's birth sign, and the emperor was addicted to astrology, while the venomous stinger suggested the Guard's malign power.

The more efficient the Praetorian Guard, the less free the people of Rome. The same could be said for Sejanus's power, which increased in tandem with a decline in political liberty. In the year 26, chance raised Sejanus's stock higher. Tiberius owned a villa in and around a cave at a picturesque spot on the coast south of Rome. He was dining there when rocks at the cave entrance suddenly tumbled down and crushed some attendants. Panic followed, but a calm Sejanus used his own body to shield the emperor. After this, Tiberius trusted the Guard commander more than ever and considered him a selfless advisor.

The cave still exists at modern Sperlonga and offers numerous signs of ancient luxury, from fishponds and bedrooms, to exquisite statuary. Considering the executions carried out by Sejanus and Tiberius, a visitor might think of the cave as the place where tyranny was born.

Shortly afterward, Tiberius left Rome for good. The island of Capreae in the Bay of Naples was Augustus's favorite getaway. Tiberius went one better and made the island his home. In the year 26, at the age of sixtyeight, he retired there. Although much of his power flowed into Sejanus's hands, Tiberius continued as emperor. He kept on making decisions and ordering executions, simply ceasing to go to Rome. He spent most of his last ten years in a luxurious island villa, the Villa of Jupiter (Villa Iovis) about 170 miles from the capital.

The relocation was shocking because it showed the truth of the later saying "Rome is where the emperor is." The statement refers to a ruler 150 years later, but it was already true in Tiberius's day.

It was shocking, too, because it showed that Tiberius's policy of respecting the Senate had ended. If he was no longer in Rome, then he could no longer attend Senate meetings. After trying to revive the Senate's power, the emperor in effect declared the experiment a failure.

But Tiberius's withdrawal from Rome was also not shocking, because it followed in the footsteps of his predecessors. Julius Caesar spent only brief periods in Rome—less than a year, all told—during the eventful final fifteen years of his life. And Augustus spent much of his time as emperor outside Rome. True, they were away on essential business, either waging war, conducting diplomacy, or inspecting the provinces. Yet Caesar and Augustus each enjoyed reliable channels of information. Not so Tiberius. Sejanus controlled the flow of information to the island and decided what Tiberius did and didn't need to know. The gatekeeper took over the role of decision-maker.

It seems unlikely that Tiberius left Rome to escape his mother, Livia, as some said, although he may have had his fill of that very strong personality. They quarreled once over her repeated insistence that he appoint an un-qualified person to a prestigious position on a panel of judges. Tiberius fi-nally agreed but criticized her in public. Livia then drove Tiberius over the edge by pulling out old letters from Augustus that she had kept for safe-keeping in a shrine, letters that called Tiberius grim and stubborn. Tiberius was too disciplined to respond emotionally to such a low blow. Besides, he enjoyed his revenge cold.

Three years after Tiberius withdrew to Capreae, in the year 29, Livia died. Tiberius did not return to Rome for her funeral and burial in the mausoleum of Augustus. It was a contrast to his dash across northern Europe years earlier to reach the side of his mortally injured brother and his quick return to Rome in the year 22 at the news that his mother was ill. Nor did Tiberius make Livia a goddess after her death as she had wished and as the Senate decreed. She got what she wanted eventually but not until a later reign. The Senate also voted to honor Livia with a triumphal arch, which would have been the first ever for a woman, but Tiberius made sure it was never built.

Yet no one could deny the importance of Livia's role. As her ashes were laid to rest, the monumental nature of her achievement lived on. When she was born eighty-seven years earlier, the proud nobles of the Senate still felt entitled to guide the fate of empire. When she died, she guided that nobility on behalf of the empire. She could honestly consider herself the bringer of a new order; a woman who had served both as wife and mother of the First Citizen; someone who was a member in good standing of the Claudian clan but who was also Julia Augusta; and a woman who had both renovated the republic and buried it. Rome had known powerful women before but never one to match Livia.

Tiberius, now in his seventies, continued to carry out some public business, particularly provincial administration. When some governors wrote and asked to increase provincial taxation, the emperor replied, "A good shepherd shears his flock; he does not flay them." But when it came to the politics of the capital and especially the imperial family, he was far too trusting of Sejanus.

Tiberius's astrologer accompanied him to Capreae. The historian Suetonius is full of juicy stories about Tiberius's sexual misdeeds on the island. The "old goat," as people are said to have called him, supposedly went after women as well as children of both sexes. His debaucheries are said to have included orgies, threesomes, pedophilia, and the murder of someone who refused him. He supposedly trained little boys to chase him when he was swimming and to get between his legs and lick and nibble him—he called them his "minnows." Reports like this may have contributed to Tiberius's low public standing in Rome, but Roman history is full of salacious rumors, and we should be skeptical. In reality, stargazing and fortune-telling are probably as risqué as Tiberius got on the island. Meanwhile, things heated up in the capital.

The pace of treason trials against Tiberius's enemies now picked up. How much of what followed was the emperor's doing and how much was Sejanus's is hard to say. For example, a historian was indicted for saying that Brutus and Cassius were "the last of the Romans." A bitter enemy of Sejanus, he was forced to commit suicide.

Sejanus convinced Tiberius that Germanicus's widow, the proud and assertive Agrippina the Elder, was plotting against him. The charge might even have been true, because Augustus's granddaughter, and the fourth member of his family to shape Tiberius's life, truly hated the emperor. She was, wrote Tacitus, "so eager to rule that she cast aside women's flaws for the masculine world of public business." Proud and popular, she considered

Tiberius an interloper to the true heirs. Bad relations between the two escalated.

They quarreled over the prosecution of Agrippina's friend and cousin. When a furious Agrippina accused Tiberius of a veiled attack on her, he replied with a Greek quotation asking her if she felt entitled to reign. Not long afterward, Agrippina asked for Tiberius's approval to remarry. He kept silent, which was in effect to say no. In later years, he accused her of adultery. Finally, when she was seated next to Tiberius at a dinner party, Agrippina refused to touch some apples that he passed to her—as if to imply that he wanted to poison her. Tiberius complained about this to Livia, who was also there. He never invited Agrippina to dinner again.

Finally, in the year 29, shortly after Livia's death, Tiberius accused Agrippina of planning to take refuge at the statue of Augustus and with the army. He had her arrested and got the Senate to exile her from Italy to an offshore island, the same place where Augustus once banished the wretched Julia. Four years later, Agrippina died. The official story is that she went on a hunger strike, but there was also a rumor that she was starved to death. Like Julia, she shared Augustus's blood but came to a terrible end after turning on his heir.

Nor did her sons thrive under Tiberius. Instead of passing the throne to one of them, as originally planned, the emperor imprisoned the two older boys. Neither survived. Only their younger brother, Gaius, who was only seventeen, was left alone.

Sejanus became ever more powerful, and by the year 31, he had convinced Tiberius to make him nearly his equal in legal authority. The septuagenarian emperor, meanwhile, paid less and less attention to matters in Rome. He is supposed to have said, in reference to his unpopularity in the Senate, "Let them hate me, as long as they respect me."

The emperor withdrew his long opposition to a marriage between Sejanus and Livilla, the widow of Tiberius's son. Everything seemed ready for Sejanus to be named heir to the throne. Having gotten rid of Agrippina and her grown sons, he was ready to step out from the shadows and seize power. Enter doom.

If the sources can be trusted, it was now that one final woman in Augustus's family who saved Tiberius: his sister-in-law, Antonia the Younger. Antonia was the complete imperial woman. She was the daughter of Octavia and Mark Antony, niece of Augustus, widow of Tiberius's brother, Drusus, mother of Germanicus, and grandmother of his and Agrippina's surviving children. She was said to be as beautiful as Venus and so gentle that she wouldn't so much as spit. She was also the model of wifely loyalty. After the death of her husband in 9 BC, she remained a widow and decided to keep living in the house of her mother-in-law, Livia. There she raised her own three children and, after Livia's death, her grandchildren. In addition, she supervised a circle of young foreign princes who were hostages in Rome. She also helped manage her extensive estates. All the while, she kept a finger in politics.

In the year 31 Antonia made her boldest political move. She took the risk of writing to Tiberius and informing him that Sejanus was planning a conspiracy against him. The letter succeeded in convincing the emperor that Sejanus intended to murder Agrippina and Germanicus's surviving son. Then he would put Tiberius's young grandson on the throne and wield the real power in Rome.

That was enough for Tiberius. He already had his suspicions of his all-powerful minister, and the letter sealed them. On October 18, 31, the emperor had another letter read in the Senate, with Sejanus present. This was a scathing denunciation of Sejanus, written by Tiberius himself. As cunning as he was, Sejanus didn't see it coming. Shocked and unprepared, he was guilty of a fatal error: underestimating Tiberius. The senators, meanwhile, jumped to their master's voice. They had Sejanus immediately taken out and executed, as were his young children. He did not receive a trial or even a formal charge, depriving him of the rights of a Roman citizen. Then his corpse was mutilated and thrown into the Tiber. His supporters were hauled into court. And it was all because a woman of the imperial household had set the wheels in motion.

Sejanus's name was erased from official records, and all images of him were destroyed—so effectively that no securely identified figure of this once-famous man has survived. Someone declared an enemy of the state by the Senate usually had his or her memory erased. Details differed from case to case. Although sometimes called *damnatio memoriae*—"condemnation of memory"—that is not an ancient term but one invented later.

Before striking at Sejanus, Tiberius took the precaution of coordinating with the chief of Rome's fire brigade (a military organization), Quintus Sutorius Macro. Afterward, Tiberius named him the new commander of the Praetorian Guard. That was no help for the Senate. In fact, Macro carried out even more treason trials than did Sejanus. Tiberius ordered the execution of everyone in prison on suspicion of supporting his former advisor. Their corpses were left first to rot and then were dumped into the Tiber. The emperor and his two Praetorian prefects destroyed most of what little independence was left in the old nobility of Rome.

Tiberius survived, but at a price. He had to recognize that Sejanus had tricked him. Worse still, Tiberius knew that he had trusted the man who possibly ordered the murder of Tiberius's own son. No wonder the emperor spent his last years in bitterness.

GERMANICUS'S REVENGE

Tiberius was responsible for the death of two of Agrippina the Elder's sons by Germanicus, but he saved the third son, Gaius, and brought him to Capreae. The emperor had a grandson through his biological son, Drusus the Younger, and he left open the question of which young man would succeed him. Tiberius surely preferred his own grandson, but Gaius had the popularity of Germanicus and the blood of Augustus.

The sources say that Tiberius sensed Gaius's bad character and even liked it, since it would make Tiberius look good in retrospect and hurt his enemies in the Senate. Tiberius supposedly saw Gaius as a viper. "When I am dead, let fire overwhelm the earth," Tiberius supposedly said. Good stories, but they arouse skepticism.

Yet the student of history pauses at the thought of the cynical old emperor and the corrupt and spoiled young prince together on a beautiful island in the Mediterranean. As they passed the fate of the world between their hands, perhaps they shared lessons in political realism that each had learned at the knees of Livia—Tiberius's mother and Gaius's great-grandmother. She raised Gaius in her own house after the death of his mother. Perhaps Tiberius noticed that not only was Livia gone now, but also so were nearly all the other women of Augustus's extended family who'd so influenced Tiberius's life: beautiful and scheming Julia, loyal Vipsania, and vengeful Agrippina. Bold, generous Antonia was still alive, but she outlasted Tiberius by less than seven weeks. For all intents and purposes, the imperial family boiled down to the old goat and the young viper.

On March 16, 37, when Gaius was twenty-four and his great-uncle Tiberius was seventy-eight, the old emperor finally died. Some said that Gaius had Tiberius poisoned or starved or smothered with a pillow. Others attributed the deed to Macro, commander of the Praetorian Guard. The troops hailed Gaius as emperor, and the Senate followed two days later. Gaius is better known today by his childhood nickname, Caligula—"little soldier's boots," after the miniature uniform that his parents dressed him in when, as a boy, he lived with them in a military camp in Germany. The son of Germanicus, the great-grandson of the divine Augustus, and descended from Mark Antony as well, Caligula practically overflowed with geneological greatness. So Germanicus exacted a kind of revenge on Tiberius in the end.

Tiberius would not be remembered fondly. People in Rome were so happy with the news of his death that they ran about crying, "To the Tiber with Tiberius!" Caligula declined to deify his predecessor, making Tiberius one of the few emperors in the principate's first two centuries to be denied that honor.

Yet Tiberius was one of Rome's most successful emperors if judged by policy results: abroad, he secured the borders of the empire; while at home, he permanently subordinated the Senate. He reversed Augustus's imperialism and stopped any serious domestic opposition to his rule. He continued the conditions that promoted trade and prosperity. Above all, Tiberius ensured that the principate would continue. The Caesars would go on ruling Rome. Not, however, without problems ahead.

Augustus started his reign with violence and ended with persuasion and benevolence. He thus followed Machiavelli's rule for a successful prince. Tiberius, by contrast, did exactly the reverse, starting mild and ending severe and violent.

Tacitus portrayed Tiberius as a sly and gloomy tyrant, but most scholars today consider this judgment exaggerated. Certainly it leaves out Tiberius's many positive qualities. Yet there is no denying the ferocity that he inflicted on Rome's nobility; no gainsaying the barracks of the Praetorian Guard that now broached Rome's new political reality. With them Tiberius "riveted the fetters of his country," as British historian Edward Gibbon wrote in the eighteenth century. There is a case to be made for Tiberius as an enlightened despot, and his character was surely more complex than Tacitus allows. Yet we can't deny the label of tyrant to the man who persecuted his political opponents on vague charges of treason and drove them to their deaths.

As a result, Tiberius lifted the veil from Roman monarchy. All that was missing to turn Rome into an autocracy without enlightenment was a megalomaniac. As it happened, he was just over the horizon; in fact, two of them were. The big test facing the political system that Augustus had built would soon become whether it could remove a bad emperor without causing chaos.

Tiberius considered himself strong and masculine, and he had the military record to prove it. Yet women played a big role in his career: from his savior, Antonia; to his estranged wife and stepsister, Julia; to his rival and adoptive daughter-in-law, Agrippina; and, above all, to his mother, Livia. She was the most powerful woman Rome had ever known. Tiberius was in love once, with his first wife, Vipsania, but this most guarded of rulers has left no portrait of their marriage.

The clashes between Tiberius, on the one hand, and Livia, Julia, and Agrippina, on the other hand, personify the sea change going on in Roman life. Assertive manliness, supported by women on the home front, won Rome its empire. Yet now the point was to defend the empire, not to expand it. Strength and prowess were less important than intelligence and calculation. Only societal prejudice and the rigors of childbirth kept women from competing on an equal footing.

Yet that left men in search of redefinition. Tiberius may have thought that he solved the problem of heroic leadership and the sense of mission it gave to the empire, but, in fact, he merely left it to return in a new form. After Tiberius, the wheel turned again back to charisma. For the next three generations of emperors after him, the Roman government was all about Germanicus: first an autocratic version (his son, Caligula); then a lame version (his brother, Claudius); and then a bacchanalia (his grandson, Nero). Then, at last, Rome returned to a second Tiberius, as it were—a soldier-emperor, but this time one with much more popular appeal—Vespasian, the builder of the Colosseum.

The more the emperors succeeded in making the empire about peace, the less edgy and dangerous they rendered the Roman army. The more the emperors made Roman government an autocracy, the less energetic, strong, and efficacious they rendered individual Romans, especially elite Romans. A republic made up of potential Caesars could not stand, but a republic made up of sheep and voluptuaries could not defend itself.

Tiberius was a transformational leader but not a charismatic one. How ironic it is, then, that the greatest religious revolution in Western history began during his reign: the mission of Jesus Christ. After preaching the Gospel in Galilee, Jesus of Nazareth was crucified in Jerusalem circa the year 30. His followers hailed him as the Messiah—in Greek, the "Christ." They believed in his resurrection and came to see his mission as the start of a new religion, Christianity. Tiberius knew nothing of this, of course, as he sat in the Villa of Jupiter on faraway Capreae.

Bust of Nero.

3

NERO

THE ENTERTAINER

On the night of July 18–19, 64, fifty years after the death of Augustus, a fire broke out in Rome. It started in the shops at one end of the Circus Maximus. Winds sent it roaring down the circus, then through adjacent valleys and up the hills. People fled, many losing everything, and gangs of looters soon prowled the streets.

Fires in Rome were frequent and hard to put out. The city was a firetrap, full of narrow winding lanes and houses that were made mostly of mud-brick with wooden beams or wooden lattices daubed with clay. Brick and marble building materials were the exception, not the rule. Homes often shared party walls, and few homeowners kept firefighting equipment on hand. Rome's oppressive summer heat and frequent droughts made it easy for fires to roar out of control. Augustus gave Rome its first fire brigade, but it was small and relied on buckets that had to be refilled from aqueducts. In the summer, water levels were often low, due to rich malefactors siphoning off water for use in their stately homes. Tearing down buildings as a firebreak was the best way to put out a big blaze.

This blaze, the worst in the capital's history, raged for five days. Only on the sixth day did crews pull down enough buildings to stop the flames, but then the conflagration started up again elsewhere. By the time it was finally done, the Great Fire burned three of Rome's fourteen districts to the ground, left only a few damaged buildings standing in seven others, and spared only four districts. The loss of life was considerable.

When the fire began, the emperor Nero was in his seaside villa south of Rome. Unlike previous rulers faced with tragedy, he didn't hurry back to town. In fact, he delayed his return until his own palace was in danger from the flames. The great new House of Passage, as he called the palace, crossed over a valley and linked two of Rome's hills. It burned on one of them but was still standing on the other. It was there that Nero set up his command post in the beleaguered city.

Next comes one of the most famous scenes in ancient history. The historian Tacitus states: "A rumor had gone forth everywhere that, at the very time when the city was in flames, the emperor appeared on a private stage and sang of the destruction of Troy, comparing present misfortunes with the calamities of antiquity."

This is, of course, the basis for the modern expression "Nero fiddled while Rome burned."

Nero could not literally have played the fiddle, since the instrument was not invented until the Middle Ages. Singing was his passion, especially to the accompaniment of a stringed instrument called a lyre, an art form that was as quintessentially Greek then as the classical guitar today is quintessentially Spanish. Now twenty-six, Nero had already given public performances in Rome, to the disgust of conservatives, who saw him making a spectacle of himself in a manner beneath the dignity of the Roman nobility. So the story of his performing while Rome blazed is plausible if not proven.

That his subject was allegedly the burning of Troy adds piquancy, since Romans believed that refugees from Troy had founded their city. In addition, Nero and his ancestor Augustus both traced their ancestry to the Trojan leader Aeneas—a tale told in that superlative work of Latin literature, Virgil's epic poem *The Aeneid*, which was in turn based on Greek models.

So a song about Troy to the sound of the lyre suggested aristocratic love of all things Greek. And if Nero's blood flowed from Rome's beginning, maybe his song announced its end.

But did Nero "fiddle" in the other sense of the word? That is, did he do nothing while Rome burned? He was certainly guilty of delaying his return to the suffering city until his own personal interests were threatened. Then he made amends by opening public buildings and parks to the dispossessed, bringing food into Rome from nearby cities, and slashing the price of grain. The tale of his singing outweighed these gestures in some minds. Anger grew when, after the fire, Nero confiscated much of downtown Rome to build an enormous new palace. So, as far as the Roman people were concerned, not only did Nero fiddle while Rome burned, but also he turned a profit on the catastrophe. Perhaps this was the source of another, even deadlier rumor about Nero: that he didn't only ignore the fire but also actually *caused* it in order to advance his private agenda.

The Great Fire of Rome took only one week of Nero's many years in power, but it defines his reign in both real and symbolic terms. The fire opened the way for a new city of Rome and a new age in Roman building that left its mark on Roman culture as well as on world civilization. And Nero himself was like a fire that cleared out the old senatorial elite and blazed the trail for a new ruling class from the provinces.

Nero was a master of manipulating symbols such as the fire, so there is something appropriate about the attention it gets in history, but there is also something misleading. Before the fire, Nero was wildly popular with the Roman people. They doubted him afterward, but Nero worked hard to win them back. The Great Fire was a bad show. Nero knew that because he lived and died by his showmanship. So after the fire, he put on another bizarre and ghastly show that turned prisoners into human torches—better box office, as he no doubt reasoned.

Nero is a paradox. In some ways, he was the worst of emperors: cruel, murderous, immoral, unmilitary, and ultimately poison in most of the provinces. Yet in other respects, he was a success: well liked, a builder, benefactor, peacemaker, and entertainer of the people. Nero was both mad autocrat and brilliant populist.

Few emperors are as infamous or as famous as Nero. No emperor's story is as encrusted with myth and misperception. Yet even the most sober examination leaves us with a ruler who would have horrified Augustus, his great-great-grandfather. Nero's rule raises the question of whether the monarchy that Augustus founded and Tiberius honed could even continue.

How had things reached this point? For the answer, consider the two emperors who followed Tiberius and preceded Nero.

THE HOUSE OF GERMANICUS

Caligula aroused high hopes when he replaced Tiberius. He was young, son of the beloved Germanicus, and great-grandson of the divine Augustus. He spent part of his youth in the home of his great-grandmother, Livia, a good teacher of the art of ruling if ever there was one. He even delivered her funeral oration when she died in the year 29. He was seventeen at the time.

Unfortunately, Caligula soon disappointed. It would have taken epic self-control to come through his upbringing well adjusted, and Caligula was no hero. He inherited Livia's cunning and ruthlessness but without her restraint or decorum. He proved to be autocratic, cynical, and murderous to his elite rivals.

Caligula's decadence is legendary, delicious, and, alas for historical accuracy, vastly exaggerated by hostile later sources. Such tidbits as a short-lived marriage to one of his sisters and incest with the others or stabling his favorite horse in marble and ivory while planning to make the beast a consul—these are unlikely to be true.

Still, Caligula was clever and fluent and vicious in his wit. So perhaps he really did boast to his horrified, aristocratic grandmother Antonia that he could treat anyone as he pleased. Maybe he, in fact, summed up the extravagance of his court by saying a man ought either to be frugal or be Caesar. And maybe, just maybe, it is true that when the crowd at the races cheered for the team that he opposed, he said, "If only the Roman people had but one neck!"

We are on firmer ground in saying Caligula earned popularity with the people by sponsoring games and entertainments, unlike the stingy Tiberius. Meanwhile, he executed numerous senators. He seems to have seen himself as an absolute monarch and demanded deification while still alive. One sign of this desire to be a god: he built a new and grander palace and extended it to the podium of a temple.

Caligula accumulated so much power that his actions gave birth to several plots against him—until, finally, one succeeded. In the year 41, a conspiracy of senators and the Praetorian Guard killed the emperor. It was a throwback to the assassination of Julius Caesar eighty-five years earlier but with a new twist: Caesar's assassins had left his wife alone, but Caligula's killers also slaughtered the emperor's wife and daughter. The chief conspirator was an officer of the guards. Caligula supposedly used to subject the man to sexual taunts and then make him kiss Caligula's hand with the middle finger extended. It seems that finally the guardsman had endured enough. Caligula had ruled for less than four years. After his death, his images were pulled down and his name erased from inscriptions.

His successor, Claudius (Tiberius Claudius Nero Germanicus), who ruled from 41 to 54, was Germanicus's younger brother, and so, Augustus's grandnephew. Still, Claudius was an unlikely emperor. He was born with a limp, trembling, and a speech defect due possibly to cerebral palsy. He was passed over for high office by Augustus and Tiberius and allowed to become a historian instead. Caligula finally made Claudius consul at the start of his reign but then spent the rest of it insulting and humiliating him.

On the day of Caligula's assassination, a Praetorian found Claudius in the palace and brought him to the guards' barracks. There he was saluted as emperor while the Senate was debating restoring the republic. The senators quickly reversed course and approved Claudius—the first but not the last ruler to be chosen by the Praetorian Guard. Talk of the republic was, manifestly, just talk. Meanwhile, the Guard showed once again that behind the brick-and-concrete walls of its fortress lay power to compete with that of the Senate in its marble-columned halls.

Claudius proved to be a good emperor when it came to opening the door to the provincial elites. He granted citizenship to many men from the provinces and persuaded the Senate to allow more of Gaul's elite to enter its ranks. He broke with Tiberius's peace policy and had his generals conquer Britain, which Caesar had invaded but never settled.

Claudius had little interest in sharing power with the Senate. Under his rule, government came under the control of the palace, particularly his two powerful wives and his freedmen. The new emperor was fifty years old and had little experience in government and none in the military. But he had spent his life in the palace and had observed things carefully. And the palace was an important place because, like all monarchs, the Roman emperor stood at the center of a court. Wives, relatives, bodyguards, flatterers, and, increasingly, freedmen and even slaves had the emperor's ear. Senators rarely did. In fact, some senators knew the palace only as the place where they were forced to stand trial behind closed doors.

To administer the empire, Claudius relied on powerful freedmen. Senators complained bitterly about government by ex-slaves—and Greeks to boot—but the emperors found them indispensable as bureaucrats. Nowadays we might praise Claudius's power shift from privileged Romans to striving Greeks come up from slavery. This, along with the increasing authority of imperial women, might seem like praiseworthy diversity. We would also note that while emperors came and went, the bureaucrats provided continuity. But the Romans thought differently, particularly the elite senators who wrote the history books.

At the start of his reign, Claudius was married to his third wife, a noblewoman named Messalina, who bore him a son and a daughter. A statue shows her in a formal robe, carefully coiffed and serene, cradling her infant son, who reaches out to her. It is a far cry from the many more modern works of art that claim she was domineering, unfaithful, cruel, and murderous. But she eventually betrayed Claudius by marrying a rival behind his back.

The sources are full of stories about Messalina's sexuality. "Augusta the

whore,"—or Female Wolf-Dog, to use her supposed professional name—
she worked secretly all night in a brothel and even outdid a prostitute in
an all-night sex competition. None of these stories is credible. All probably
derive from the propaganda of the victorious faction that replaced the emperor's wife after her fall. Messalina fought hard, but she was no monster.
If she betrayed her husband for another man, it was because she no longer
trusted Claudius to put her and their children first. But Messalina didn't
move fast enough. When a rival discovered her adultery, he exposed it to
Claudius, which led to her execution. Afterward, her image was removed
from monuments and her name erased from inscriptions.

With Messalina's death in the year 48, the emperor was a widower.
Claudius needed a new wife. Enter Nero and his mother.

YOUNG NERO

Nero's mother, Agrippina the Younger (hereafter, Agrippina) was one of
the most eligible noblewomen in Rome. She had the magic of her father's
name, Germanicus, and of the descent of her mother, Agrippina the Elder,
from the divine Augustus. She also numbered Livia and Mark Antony
among her ancestors. Her pedigree persuaded Claudius to marry her, even
though she was his niece, and hence the marriage was technically incestuous. The Senate had to pass a special decree to permit it.

A statue of Agrippina shows a woman with delicate features. She has
a small mouth, a slightly turned-up nose, and a pronounced chin. Her hair
is carefully arranged into ringlets in the style of the day. The statue shows
her as a priestess, with head veiled. Other statues and coins associate Agrippina with fertility goddesses, even more explicitly than Livia was associated
with them. But Agrippina was no saint. She was a tough lady. First she
witnessed the near destruction of her family and then watched her brother
Caligula's sudden triumph followed by tyranny. After being implicated in a
plot against Caligula, possibly involving adultery on her part, she was sent
into exile. Since returning, Agrippina had regrouped and planned to use
Claudius to achieve her ambition: making her son emperor with her as the

power behind the throne. She published a memoir, now lost, which might be the source of the detail that she had an extra canine tooth on her right upper jaw, which was a sign of good luck for the Romans but which surely also symbolized aggression.

The ancient literary sources are hostile to Agrippina, as they are to all women in politics. They depict her as a scheming, power-hungry, incestuous murderer. Visual images, on the other hand—coins, sculpture, and cameos—show a dignified, attractive woman who is a symbol of motherhood and dynasty. The truth probably lies somewhere in between.

Agrippina was a fierce competitor who unhesitatingly had rivals executed. But other leading Romans behaved similarly. In seeking power for Nero, Agrippina was selfish, but she was also public spirited. She knew that he represented the only chance to continue the house of Augustus and Germanicus, and she believed that the dynasty represented the best hope for Rome and the empire.

When she married Claudius, Agrippina saw herself not just as his wife but also as his coruler. She was named Augusta, a title that no wife of a reigning emperor had held before. She sometimes joined Claudius while he was conducting public business and sat on a separate tribunal, in a power play that shocked contemporaries. She collected friends and banished enemies. Above all, she cleared a path to the throne for her son.

Nero was the product of Agrippina's first marriage. He was born December 15, 37, in a seaside town south of Rome. He was named Lucius Domitius Ahenobarbus ("bronze beard"), after his father, Gnaeus Domitius Ahenobarbus. The family were diehard republicans, with noble ancestors going back centuries. They were known for generalship, arrogance, and cruelty as well as for racing chariots and also for sponsoring an indecent theatrical production. Nero's father supposedly said of their young son, "It is impossible for any good man to be sprung from me and this woman."

He would not find out, however, as he died when Nero was three. Like Augustus, Nero lost his father at an early age and was raised by his mother (except for a few months with a paternal aunt). Like Augustus's mother,

Atia, Agrippina worked tirelessly to advance Nero's career but she would pay a severe price for her success.

Nero was eleven when his mother married Claudius. Within a year, she had convinced Claudius to adopt Nero, who dropped his previous name and became Nero Claudius Caesar Drusus Germanicus. Nero was older than Claudius's own son, which meant that he now stood first in the inheritance. Claudius also betrothed his daughter, Octavia, to Nero and decided to put Agrippina's son ahead of his own.

Claudius was now about sixty. Was he just an old man fooled by his new, young wife? Perhaps. Or possibly he thought his dynasty stood a better chance of surviving through the heirs of his daughter and of Nero—heir of Germanicus, the divine Augustus, and Mark Antony—than through his son by the disgraced Messalina. In any case, Agrippina did not hold back. She lined up friends at court and got enemies dismissed. Her most important move was to persuade Claudius to hire a new Praetorian prefect who was solidly in her camp. He was Sextus Afranius Burrus, a Roman knight from Gaul. He had once worked in Livia's household. Not only was Burrus a loyal supporter of Agrippina but also so were many of the officers under his command—men she had handpicked.

For Nero's tutor, Agrippina chose Lucius Annaeus Seneca. He came from a wealthy, influential, and highly literary Roman family from Hispania. His father was a famous writer of rhetoric and history, while his mother studied philosophy. Seneca went to Rome and rose in law and politics while also proving to be a brilliant man of letters. He was an orator, philosopher, essayist, and playwright. But he made enemies.

Caligula had called Seneca "sand without lime"—in other words, flaccid cement—and came close to having him executed. After Caligula's death, Seneca returned the favor by writing that the object of Caligula's whole life was to change a free state into a Persian despotism. Seneca judged Caligula to be bloodthirsty.

Messalina, too, disliked Seneca. She accused him of committing adultery with Caligula's youngest sister. Both lovers were convicted and exiled, but only Seneca survived. After eight years of exile on the island of Corsica, he found himself recalled to Rome by Agrippina.

In 54, five years after he married Agrippina, Claudius decided to advance the career of his biological son, Britannicus, who had turned thirteen. Then, before Claudius could make a move, he died suddenly. People naturally suspected poisoning by Agrippina, but the truth about his death is unrecoverable today. He might have died from a poisonous (but not poisoned) mushroom or from natural causes. In any case, Agrippina was prepared to put her son on center stage. The Praetorians hailed Nero as emperor, and he rewarded them with a big cash payout. The Senate tamely voted Nero the necessary powers and rewarded Agrippina with honors. The new era had begun.

NERO THE GOOD

At first, Rome welcomed the handsome new emperor. After the old and doddering Claudius, here was youth and vigor. Besides, Nero had even bluer blood. With him, the dynasty of Augustus was back in power. And Nero was fashionable—was he ever!

He had blue-gray eyes, light-blond hair, and, we are told, a face that had regular but not especially pleasing features. True, at just short of his seventeenth birthday, Nero was young, but young leaders sometimes succeed. Augustus was only nineteen when he entered politics and shot to the top ranks, while Alexander the Great ascended to the throne at just age twenty. A ruler with intelligence, talent, good advisors, and a good character shaped by a fine upbringing can succeed in spite of youth. Nero had excellent advisors. Nobody knew the ins and outs of court better than Agrippina, while Burrus guaranteed the support of the Praetorians. Nero's tutor Seneca took on a new role as the emperor's counselor, and he argued that *clementia*, or mercy, should be the hallmark of the new ruler's reign. Burrus offered the model of a severe military man, while Seneca contributed eloquence and dignity.

In a speech to the Senate, the new emperor promised to stop the abuses of the past and to restore its power. This was a modest concession rather than a major change, but it was real. For roughly the first five years of his reign, guided by Seneca and Burrus and coaxed by Agrippina, Nero kept his promises and shared power with the senators. He abolished closed-door trials and restrained the power of his freedmen.

So far, so good, but there were inherent problems in the situation, beginning with Nero's character. He was insecure and vain. He wanted to be popular, and he tolerated no rivals. As one source put it, "He was carried away above all by popularity, and he was jealous of everyone who in any way stirred the feeling of the common people."

When Nero didn't get his way, he lashed out in vengeance. A fatherless child, raised in an atmosphere of conspiracy and blood by a stage-door mother, the new emperor was understandably wounded. He was the product of one of history's most dysfunctional families. Now all Rome would pay a price.

Agrippina was determined to exercise power. At the beginning of Nero's reign, she had her own German bodyguards, her own unit of the Praetorian Guard, and two official attendants (lictors) to accompany her in public. (Livia had had only one.) Young Nero accepted all this at first. The password that he gave the Praetorians was "the best mother" (*optima mater*), a favorable reference to Agrippina. Nero agreed to hold Senate meetings in the palace (not unprecedented) so that Agrippina could watch through a curtain (definitely unprecedented). On coins, she was depicted facing Nero, as if she were coruler. But Agrippina soon ran into obstacles. Roman public opinion would not tolerate a woman overtly exercising too much power. Meanwhile, the teenage Nero hated being criticized by his mother for not watching his spending. He retaliated by publicly stopping Agrippina from joining him on the tribunal to hear a foreign embassy; he did it tactfully, with Seneca's help, but a rebuke is still a rebuke. Agrippina, it was said, was fuming: she could give her son the empire but not bear him ruling it.

Nero's Rome is known as an era of wit. It started immediately after Claudius's death. Seneca referred not to Claudius's "deification" but to his "pumpkinification," an obscure joke in a savage satire attacking the late emperor. Seneca's brother said that Claudius had been raised to heaven by a hook, the way Roman executioners dragged the bodies of their victims to the Tiber. Finally, Nero supposedly said that mushrooms are the food of the gods, since Claudius had died after eating mushrooms and was then deified. Agrippina was surely not amused by the way her late husband was now mocked.

Nero's marriage with Claudius's daughter was unhappy. He fell in love with a freedwoman from Asia Minor and was smitten, even talking about marrying her. Agrippina, horrified, let her son know it, but he wouldn't budge. He strengthened his position by getting rid of a powerful freedman who was Agrippina's strongest ally at court.

Agrippina supposedly retaliated by threatening Nero. She pointed out how many other descendants of the divine Augustus there were in Rome, not to mention Claudius's son. Still, she would not have seriously considered driving Nero from the throne. Then in the year 55, Claudius's son took sick suddenly at a court banquet and died shortly afterward. The evidence suggests natural causes, but many people at the time believed that he had been poisoned on Nero's order.

For the next four years, Agrippina was shut out of power, although she tried to work her way back. During this period, Nero made it a habit to go on nocturnal escapades with friends in the streets of Rome. They visited taverns and brothels in search of fun and trouble, such as brawls and breaking and entering. He was dressed in slave's clothes and a wig to avoid being recognized. Bad as it was, such behavior was not unusual for young Roman aristocrats, and most people were willing to wink at it. They were less forgiving, though, when Nero encouraged fights in the theater. To restore order, actors were banished and soldiers were called in.

By the year 59, when he was twenty-one, Nero was ready to settle down, but first he decided to get rid of his mother. Love, power, and control each played a part in his motivation. It is plausible that Agrippina flirted with Nero in a highly inappropriate manner. That the two actually committed incest, as rumor had it, is less believable, but it can't be ruled out. What is clear is that once again she expressed disapproval of his love life, this time over his new infatuation.

Poppaea Sabina was a woman fit for a king. She was wealthy, intelligent, and ambitious. Her family came from Pompeii, where they owned at least five houses, including two grand ones. Poppaea was probably born there. She independentally owned brickworks in the vicinity as well as a stylish seaside villa.

Poppaea's father, a Roman knight named Titus Ollius, was on his way up in Roman government when he was executed after Sejanus's fall for his support of the deposed schemer. Afterward, Poppaea took the name of her maternal grandfather, Gaius Poppaeus Sabinus, a consul and successful provincial governor, so as not to be tarred with her father's brush. She married twice. Her first husband was a Praetorian prefect, and they had a son. After divorcing him, she married Marcus Salvius Otho, a consul's son and a member of Rome's smart set. When she caught Nero's eye, he sent Otho off to govern Lusitania (roughly, Portugal), even though the man was only twenty-six and inexperienced.

Poppaea was broad-minded enough to take an interest in Judaism, although she displayed no interest in conversion. In any case, she did Jews no favor by pushing the appointment of Gessius Florus as governor of Judea, husband of one of her friends. Florus's misgovernment provoked the great Jewish revolt in the year 66. It took Rome seven years to repacify Judea, and only at a great cost in blood and destruction for both sides.

Poppaea was one of the great beauties of the day. No wonder she has been played in films by actresses Claudette Colbert and Brigitte Bardot. Nero wrote a poem about Poppaea's amber hair. She is said to have bathed daily in the milk of five hundred asses to preserve her skin and even inspired in her day a line of cosmetics named after her. She was six years older than Nero and married, but so was he. Nero was deeply in love with her. Some claim that she urged him to kill Agrippina.

Entirely aside from his love life, Nero might have feared Agrippina's continuing influence with the Praetorian Guard, although that hardly justifies murder. But consciously and deliberately, Nero chose to kill his mother.

Poison was out of the question—too suspect after the sudden deaths of Claudius and his son, and, besides, Agrippina took enough antidotes to protect her. The Praetorian Guard was unreliable, so Nero turned to an ally in the Roman navy. On a spring night in the Bay of Naples, a plot unfolded. First Nero invited his mother to a banquet at his villa on the bay in order to settle past differences and to soften her up. Then he planned to drown her in a specially constructed collapsing boat. So the story goes; more likely a warship deliberately rammed her boat. In any case, Agrippina fell into the sea and was injured but survived and was brought back to shore.

Terrified of Agrippina's revenge, Nero turned to Burrus but he refused to help. The Praetorian Guard, he said, would not injure the daughter of Germanicus. So Nero went back to the navy and sent a detachment of marines after Agrippina. He claimed to have discovered that she was trying to kill him.

When the troops reached Agrippina, she refused to believe their announcement that they were there to execute her on Nero's orders. Her son wouldn't do that, she insisted. Then they hit her, and she realized the truth. The story goes that she bared her belly, pointed to the womb that bore Nero, and told the men to strike there. If Agrippina did, in fact, say that, it is unlikely that she admitted her own failings as a mother that had made Nero into the fiend that he was.

Nero's freedman and head of the major naval base nearby killed Agrippina. Nero said afterward that this day had given him rule of the empire, but later he hated the man for killing his mother because, as the historian Tacitus said, "we look on accomplices in evil deeds with a kind of reproach." Wanting to get rid of the man, Nero first used him to give false testimony in another matter and then sent him off to a comfortable exile.

In later years, when he performed roles in Greek tragedy, Nero included in his repertory both a man who slept with his mother and a man who killed his mother. The choice might indicate, as the sources claim, that he felt remorse for his crime. If so, he didn't show it at the time. Nero announced that he had foiled a plot by Agrippina to kill him. Seneca even wrote a letter to the Senate vouching for that cover story. Whatever they really thought, most people accepted Nero's excuse. Days of thanksgiving were proclaimed for his safety, and sacrifices were made upon his safe return to Rome from the Bay of Naples.

ARTIST

Other men were emperors; Nero was a star. A celebrity, he broke all the rules, which made him immortal.

Nero took the business of government seriously, but he considered himself first and foremost an artist. Singing was his forte, but he had wide interests. Nero issued coins that are probably the most exquisite in the entire history of Roman currency. He sponsored beautiful buildings. Whether or not he deserves credit, Latin literature flourished during his reign. Seneca wrote philosophical dialogues and letters as well as tragedies. His nephew Lucan wrote the *Pharsalia*, an epic poem about the civil war between Gnaeus Pompey and Julius Caesar. The writer Petronius published the *Satyricon*, a darkly comic novel about the decadence of the Roman elite.

Augustus understood that one of the emperor's many tasks was to entertain the public, but for Nero it became *the* task. If he were alive today, he would rate as a genius in public relations; a communications giant.

Putting on games was serious business for the emperor. It spoke to his personal interests, but also reflects his political priorities. Every emperor knew that part of the job was serving the people of Rome. Nero did so by entertaining them in the grand style, but he considered entertainment to be educational as well. As he saw it, he was elevating Roman society by introducing elements of Greek culture that ordinary people could understand such as singing, acting, and exercising.

Besides, Nero did not restrict his benevolence to games and shows. He made a major effort to distribute grain and also gave various cash gifts to the public. Still, the games were an efficient way to reach the people. The Circus Maximus, used for horse racing, the amphitheater, and Rome's three great theaters collectively held more than two hundred thousand people, or one-fifth of the city's total population.

Games, races, and shows were special occasions with their own rules and rituals. Spectators sat in sections according to their rank, with senators and knights in front. These events were the only times and places where the Roman people felt free to express their opinion to the emperor.

The Roman elite loved and hated the games. They found them immoral and seditious, yet irresistible. For all the sanctions against it, senators and knights began performing in public. Nero was the first emperor to do so, and his taste for chariot racing was indeed unusual for Roman nobles. Some nobles abhorred his behavior, while others approved, but the common people cheered heartily and applauded their emperor the performer. Not to leave things to chance, Nero organized his own supporters, consisting of thousands of young men, to lead the applause.

In their number, novelty, and production values, Nero's games and shows outdid anything that Rome had seen before. Refreshments were subsidized, and the audience received gifts—often extravagant gifts, including jewels, horses, slaves, and houses, making Nero at least the equal of any modern television game show host. The emperor's main innovation was introducing Greek games to Rome. Chariot racing, gladiatorial bouts, and boxing matches were the common fare in Roman games, but Nero wanted more. Like many elite Romans, he was educated in Greek culture, but he was unusual in the extent to which he admired all things Greek. He knew that Greek games included running, wrestling, the long jump, and throwing discus and javelin as well as boxing and horse races; many events were performed in the nude. They also included musical contests. Nero's new games combined music, athletic and equestrian events, and took place every five years. They were called—what else?—Neronia.

Nero loved singing, accompanying himself on the lyre, as well as racing chariots. He practiced wrestling and might have been planning to compete eventually. Was Nero a good singer? He was not without creative talent. Copies of his poetry, in his own handwriting, including erasures, survived him by decades, and a later observer judged them to be good. As for singing, the sources differ, but it's probably safe to say that his limited talent was improved by training. As a chariot racer, he was game and bold. In addition to singing and playing the lyre, Nero enjoyed performing in tragedy, where he played roles ranging from Hercules and Oedipus, to a woman giving birth. For the latter part, he wore a mask resembling the face of his late wife. In his later years, he also took up solo ballet, which the Romans called pantomime.

Nero was famous for the elaborate parties he threw for the public during the annual celebration of the Saturnalia, the Roman winter festival in December. The festivities featured costumed banquets on boats on artificial lakes in Rome, performances by the emperor, plentiful participation by nobles both male and female, and an abundance of roses—and of prostitutes.

Before Agrippina's death, Nero sang and raced in private. Right after her death in the year 59, he performed and competed before the people in what were technically invitation-only private events. Finally, in 64 he performed in public, first in Naples and then in Rome.

In 66 Nero went to Achaea, the Roman province of Greece. His purpose was to compete in the five great games, from Actium to Olympia. Normally they took place in different years, but Nero ordered them to be bunched up for his visit. It was the first time in the eight hundred-year history of the Olympic Games that they were held off schedule. Nero took part in four different types of contests: he sang and accompanied himself on the lyre; he acted in tragedies; he raced chariots; and he joined in the contest of heralds. To no one's surprise, he was declared the winner of every event in which he competed. That included a race in a ten-horse chariot, a demanding and dangerous event in which Nero fell and almost got run over. Yet he returned to the race and won.

Unlike Augustus, who led armies and toured provinces, Nero made only this one trip beyond Italy. The visit to Achaea was as self-indulgent as it was unusual. As one who fancied himself a performer, Nero naturally focused on the stage. And his greatest stage was Rome. So, like an old-school Hollywood mogul who never left California, Nero stayed close to home. Except for Achaea, the provinces suffered. He treated them like a bank when the government needed money, and eventually they revolted.

A major revolt in Judea broke out in 66 during Nero's stay in Achaea. When he got the news Nero sent one of the few generals whom he still trusted to put it down. It was a wise choice but Nero might have avoided the revolt in the first place by choosing a better governor. In Judea and elsewhere he appointed too many unqualified men as governors; they provoked the revolt in Judea as well as an earlier rebellion in Britain. Fortunately, Nero's generals suppressed the British revolt. Turning to the East, they also worked out a compromise peace with Parthia over Rome's former client state of Armenia, and Nero wisely called it a victory.

Yet Nero faced mounting problems upon his return to Italy. He spent too much time as a performer and not enough time as a ruler. The Senate plotted; a major revolt against him broke out in the West, and Nero responded by consulting his voice coach. His efforts to regain control were feeble and vain. Nero didn't fiddle while Rome burned, but he certainly played while he should have ruled.

TYRANT

Seneca and Burrus wanted Nero to rule as a Civilis Princeps—a Courteous or Civil Prince—showing respect to the Senate and paying at least lip service to the old constitutional forms of the republic. Not that either man was a republican. Seneca, for example, wrote that only the goodness of the ruler protected liberty; the Senate no longer had the power to do so. But after Agrippina's death, Nero's goodness was no longer a given. Seneca and Burrus increasingly lost influence. In the year 62 Burrus died, probably of natural causes. Seneca retired.

That year was a turning point in the reign. A new Praetorian prefect was appointed and encouraged Nero's worst impulses, apparently with Poppaea's support. Soon Nero would be sending a prominent man into exile merely for recognizing one of Caesar's murderers in his family tree.

Nero was far less tolerant of people who wrote or said anything critical of him. He brought back the charge of treason that he had promised not to use. In 62, for the first time, he executed his enemies in the Senate. When the prefect convinced Nero to order the execution of two men of noble lineage, the emperor is supposed to have joked as each man's head was brought to him. One, he said, was prematurely gray. When he saw the other's head, he said, "Why, Nero, did you fear a man with such a big nose?"

That same year, Nero finally divorced Claudius's daughter. He was waiting to get rid of prominent political opponents before daring to turn on such an esteemed figure. He falsely accused his ex-wife of adultery, banished her to a barren island off the southern Italian coast, and finally had her executed. Her wedding day had been her funeral, the historian Tacitus later commented.

Not long afterward, the emperor finally married Poppaea. He remained calm when the daughter she bore him died as an infant, but in the year 65, Nero finally lost his temper with Poppaea. It is said that he kicked her, even though she was pregnant again. She died. It was said that she had prayed to die young, before she lost her good looks, and so she got her wish.

It's hard to believe that even Nero could have wanted such a terrible outcome to his misbehavior. As usual, though, he put on a show. He gave Poppaea a public funeral, where he burned a vast quantity of Arabian incense. Her body was stuffed with spices and embalmed and deposited in the mausoleum of Augustus. She was deified and a shrine erected to her. All of this amounted to no small expense for the Roman state. Within a year of Poppaea's death, Nero married a Roman noblewoman, after first forcing her husband to commit suicide on a trumped-up charge of conspiracy while the man served as consul.

As Nero became more abusive and ruthless, a rebellion against his tyrannical behavior grew. A year after the fire, in the year 65, Nero discovered a major conspiracy to depose and replace him, led by a prominent senator. At least forty-one people are known to have taken part, including nineteen senators. Few senators wanted to abolish the monarchy; they simply wanted to tame it. Not many imagined going back to the republic. They wanted the rule of law and freedom of speech, more power and dignity for the Senate, and more freedom of action for the magistrates, all under the rule of an enlightened prince.

The Senate had been happy to work with Nero at first, but eventually it became clear that cooperation with him was impossible. It was one thing for a senator, or any Roman, to surrender his independence in return for peace and security, as under Tiberius. It was another to surrender his honor and dignity in the service of something shameful. One of the conspirators, an officer of the Praetorian Guard, probably spoke for many when he said of Nero, "No soldier was more loyal to you while you deserved to be loved. I began to hate you when you became the murderer of your mother and your wife, a charioteer, an actor, and an arsonist."

The most famous casualty of Nero's counterattack on the conspirators was his former mentor, Seneca. Although he was probably not guilty, Seneca was ordered to commit suicide. He slit his wrists, choosing the common Roman manner of killing oneself, but the bleeding was slow and painful. Finally, after an extended audience with friends, Seneca suffocated himself in the steam of a hot bath. Like Agrippina, he was a victim of the monster that he had helped to create.

Romans had mixed feelings about suicide. They approved of it when it was deliberate, as in the case of a response to dishonor or an act of self-sacrifice. They condemned it when it was an impulsive act. They also judged suicide on the method by which it was carried out. They condemned hanging oneself or jumping from a height, for example, as cowardly, but they admired someone who took his or her life with a weapon, and so most people admired Seneca.

Seneca had one thing in common with the conspirators: like almost all of them, he was a follower of Stoic philosophy. A centuries-old Greek philosophical school, Stoicism became the favored philosophy of the Roman elite. It was pragmatic and public spirited while also consistent with old-fashioned Roman values. The Stoics emphasized the four cardinal virtues of justice, courage, temperance, and practical wisdom. Stoics taught austerity and self-control. Since Romans traditionally prided themselves on seriousness, simplicity, and strictness, since they valued public service and practical wisdom, and since they prized honor and pursued courage, they found Stoicism compatible.

Although some Stoics wanted to return to the old republic, most accepted monarchy. But they insisted that the ruler be moderate, wise, law-abiding, and gentle. They had no use for tyranny. Naturally they clashed with Nero.

The most influential Roman Stoic of the age, Musonius Rufus, managed to suffer nothing worse than exile in the year 65, while others lost their lives, but it was Musonius's second exile under Nero, and he would later be exiled a third time by another emperor before finally returning to Rome. Although he wrote nothing that we know of, his lectures were famous, recorded by others, and quoted often. His wit and wisdom earned him the title of the "Roman Socrates." For instance, he used to say that applause was for flute players, not philosophers; the most admirable philosopher, he said, was the one whose lectures elicited silence, not words. Musonius cast a giant shadow and influenced several generations of the empire's most prominent politicians, philosophers, and military commanders.

Nero was not done with bloodletting. In the year 67 he ordered the death of his best general, Gnaeus Domitius Corbulo. He was talented and popular, so Nero distrusted him. Besides, Corbulo's son-in-law had participated in a conspiracy against Nero. So, on the emperor's command, Corbulo fell on his sword. His last word was the Greek *Axios!* "You deserved it!"—a term used in athletic games to hail a victor. It seems like bitter irony, and some think Corbulo meant that he was a fool for not killing Nero when he had the chance.

If Nero felt safer after Corbulo's death, he was wrong. The killing sent a message to his other commanders that they might be next. Indeed, Nero also executed two brothers who had ably commanded on the German frontier. Sooner or later, one of Nero's generals would decide to strike first.

PERSECUTOR

After the Great Fire, Nero put on a private show in his gardens. To deflect blame for starting the blaze, he accused an unpopular and relatively new religious sect: Christians.

Christianity was now about thirty-five years old. It began in Judea and Galilee with the life and death of Jesus of Nazareth. Jesus's mission in Galilee attracted large numbers of followers through his emphasis on the values of goodness, humility, charity, and prayer. He electrified them with the notion that the Kingdom of God, which many prayed for, was already beginning to arrive. Eventually Jesus went to the capital city of Jerusalem, where his enthusiastic crowds alarmed both the Jewish and Roman authorities. He was executed by crucifixion around the year 30 during the reign of Tiberius.

Galvanized by the conviction that Jesus had risen from the dead, his adherents spread the new faith, first in Palestine and then around the Mediterranean world. Early churches were communities of faith and charity, havens in an often-hostile world. As a result of missionary work, a small Christian community developed in Rome itself.

Authorities sneered at Christians and perhaps feared them. Romans distrusted innovation and suspected people who assembled for a purpose that the authorities neither knew of nor controlled. Elite writers active several generations later referred to early Christians as "a class of men of a new and pernicious superstition" and "a class hated for their disgraceful acts." There might have been a Christian community near where Rome's Great Fire started. It is possible that some Christians stated openly after the fire that Rome had been punished for its sins. Hence, Christians made good scapegoats for a crime of which they were surely innocent.

According to Tacitus, Nero punished those guilty not only of starting the fire—a crime to which they had supposedly confessed—but also guilty more simply of "hatred of the human race." Ever the impresario, Nero turned their execution into a ghastly show. The scene was apparently his private estate across the Tiber River in the Vatican territory, which included a circus. Romans liked to enact scenes from myth, which may be why some of the victims wore animal skins and were torn apart by dogs, in a dramatization of the myth in which a hunter was turned into a stag and killed by his enraged hounds. Others were crucified or burned to death at night like living torches. Nero himself was present and dressed like a charioteer. He went from the chariot to the crowd, where he mingled with the spectators. Tacitus sneers that his presence merely inspired sympathy for the victims. According to Christian tradition, two of the apostles or early missionaries of the church, Saints Peter and Paul, were among the victims of the persecution following the Great Fire. That, however, cannot be proven.

Why did Nero persecute Christians? They were a convenient target, available and unpopular. But perhaps on some level, Nero recognized them as a deeper threat. Like him, they represented a powerful response to a crisis in Roman culture. By Nero's day, monarchy was dulling the edge of Roman manhood. In the republic, liberty and militarism loomed large in Roman culture, but free elections and freewheeling conquerors were now both things of the past. Largely deprived of prior outlets in the Forum or on the battlefield, Romans began to look inward. The writings of Seneca bear eloquent witness to the development. Nero's Rome was rich, as no one knew better than he did. Yet beneath the opulence lay emptiness. Seneca and the Stoics understood inner peace as a solution.

Nero, of course, offered a different solution. He delivered ever more numerous, more spectacular, more shocking, and more outrageous entertainments. Yet neither food nor drink nor sex could speak to the soul's needs as religion could. Perhaps Nero saw in Christians a challenge that he couldn't defeat, and so he tried to destroy them.

CONCRETE

Familiar words sum up Nero: *art, luxury, irresponsibility,* and *tyranny,* but a less dramatic but equally revealing word must be added: *concrete.* It was a key legacy.

Roman concrete was a mixture of volcanic sand, high-grade lime, and various fist-sized pieces of rubble (stone or broken bricks). It was versatile, flexible, and cheap. Despite its inanimate, porous looks, concrete was the pixie dust of an architectural revolution. It allowed Rome to break free from the posts and lintels of Greek-inspired architecture and to create something all its own. Concrete made possible the vaults and domes that became emblems of Roman imperial architecture. What the marble pillar was to Greece, the concrete dome was to Rome.

And not just to Rome. The stately dome became the symbol of power and glory afterward and has remained so ever since, in both secular and religious settings, with periodic changes and improvements. From the Romans, the dome passed to the Byzantines, and they in turn transmitted it on to Western Christendom and to such secular settings as the United States Capitol. The Byzantine dome, along with Persian domes, also influenced Islamic architecture. It all goes back to Nero.

His most masterful use of concrete is found in a small and sophisticated room. Today it lies buried under one of Rome's hills, but originally it stood out in the open on the hillside, a monument to architectural achievement. The concrete room was octagonal in shape and had a domed ceiling with a "bull's-eye" opening for light. Along with the suite of rooms around it, it represents an architectural revolution. It was the jewel in the crown of Nero's new construction program after the Great Fire; a series of measures that widened streets, outlawed party walls, and monitored the water level in aqueducts, among other things.

First, Nero cleared out 250 acres of prime real estate in the center of Rome for a new palace. It was called the Golden House (Domus Aurea), but it was actually a complex of structures. Working with the best architects and engineers, Nero created something that was elegant, opulent, radical, and greatly influential. On a more mundane level, the concrete vaults that he favored were more fireproof than timber roofs.

The Golden House climbed the hills overlooking the valley where the Colosseum (built later) now stands. The key features were an artificial lake in the valley, a huge vestibule on the hill to the west of the Colosseum high enough to hold a 120-foot-high bronze statue of Nero, a splendid fountain house on the hill to the southeast, and a palace and probably also more public baths on the hill to the northeast. The palace offered innovative architecture decorated with sophisticated wall paintings and mosaics. It was as impressive as any stage set, with views of valley and hills. The domed, octagonal room stood here.

When he built the Golden House, Nero proclaimed that now at last he could live like a human being. He surely planned to share that new lifestyle with the inhabitants of the city, inviting them from time to time to events on the lake or to stroll in the park. Tacitus said, perhaps in reference to the palace, that Nero treated the whole city as if it were his house.

DEATH

Fantasy and decadence marked Nero's last years. Although many considered him a disgrace, Rome's wounded honor did not bring down Nero. Only when he made people fear for their property and their lives did they take action. Nero's building projects, lavish games, and generous gifts to the people and the soldiers were expensive, as were the costs of rebuilding after the Great Fire, and the wars in Armenia, Britain, and Judea. In response, Nero inflated the currency. The silver content in Roman coins decreased by about 10 percent, but it was not enough. Someone had to pay. Although the common people of Rome largely adored Nero even after the Great Fire, his trip to Achaea for a year and a half, much of the time devoted to an artistic tour, was an act of bravura and incompetence, especially with discontent brewing among influential elites. Meanwhile, the emperor made time to do something to disgust his opponents. Still mourning Poppaea, he found a young male freedman who resembled her. He made the young man dress like her. Then he had him castrated and, finally, during his tour of Greece, Nero married him. Earlier, as part of a festival in Rome, Nero had married another freedman. In modern terms, Nero was primarily heterosexual, and all the while he remained married to his third wife. One or both of his marriages to young men was probably a parody, yet they shocked the public nevertheless.

In his last years, Nero turned down a proposal to have Rome build a temple to his divinity because it was not merely bad form but bad luck to worship the emperor as a god while he was still alive. He was happy, however, to change the name of the month April to Neroneus, and he planned on renaming Rome as Neropolis, Nero City in Greek, which was a triple insult to Roman traditionalists. Neropolis took the city named for Romulus, the legendary figure who Romans believed to have founded their city in 753 BC, and replaced it with something foreign, arrogant, and revolutionary.

By now, Nero, the not-quite-god, had deteriorated physically. He had a thick neck, protruding belly, and thin legs, whose bad effects were accentuated by his average height. No more was Nero the young prince.

By the end of his reign, Nero lost the support of the Roman establishment. One province, Judea, was in revolt. Other provinces were angry at having to pay for Nero's expenditures. His generals no longer trusted an emperor who rewarded success with execution. When generals fear, soldiers march. In spring 68 bad news came from the west: a rebellion of Gallic peoples led by a Gallic noble who served Rome as governor of Gallia Lugdunensis (central and western France). Although loyal troops from Germany put down the revolt, news of additional trouble soon followed. The governor of Hispania Tarraconensis (roughly, Mediterranean Spain) was acclaimed as emperor by his troops. He cautiously left the matter up to the Senate to decide. He was Servius Sulpicius Galba, a wealthy and eminent Roman noble. Galba had the connections, the reputation, and the troops for a serious rebellion. Among other things, he had been one of Livia's court favorites in earlier years.

Nero seems to have retreated into fantasy at the end. He talked about winning back Gaul by going there and singing to the troops. Then he spoke of moving to Alexandria and becoming a professional singer. On June 8 the Senate declared him a public enemy. The Praetorian Guard deserted him.

Nero fled Rome. The next day, June 9, abandoned by all but his most dogged loyalists, Nero committed suicide just outside the city. As he prepared to take his life, the man who had once supervised the rebuilding of

Rome ordered around a few companions to prepare a funeral pyre and dig a hole in the ground to bury his ashes. He is supposed to have said at the end, "What an artist perishes in me!" If he did actually utter these words, they might not mean what they seem. The Latin word for *artist* can also mean "artisan." Perhaps what Nero really meant was not that he was still a great artist but, rather, that the once-great artist was now reduced to giving directions to menials.

If so, he needn't have worried, as his ashes were removed by his faithful nurse and taken to a more dignified location—although not to the one an emperor would have wished. Nero was the first and only member of the imperial family to be denied burial in the mausoleum of Augustus. His cremated remains were placed instead in a tomb in the crypt of his birth father's family on the Pincian Hill outside the city walls. Nero came into office to applause and left unwelcome in his dynasty's tomb.

Meanwhile, Galba heard that Nero was dead and that both the Senate and the Praetorians had declared him emperor. He now marched on Rome. He would reign for seven months.

THE FALL OF THE HOUSE OF CAESAR

Nero did quite respectably at some of the aspects of his job. He won the support of the common people. He was a great builder. He was a superb impresario. He presided over a cultural renaissance. He loved Greece and won the support of the Greek East. It should also be remembered that for about the first five years of his reign, he had the support of the Senate as well.

Where did Nero fail? By appointing an incompetent governor, he caused a major revolt in Judea. By confiscating property, he stirred up revolt in the Western provinces. By persecuting and executing elite enemies, and by embarrassing himself in the eyes of the elite through his personal behavior, he stirred up conspiracy and revolt.

Nero was the most cultivated and cruelest emperor Rome had seen, and one of the last members of the old Roman nobility to serve as emperor.

After Nero, and with the exception of Galba's brief reign, it would be nearly two hundred years before another member of the Roman nobility served as emperor.

Nero's predecessors, aristocrats all, were more martial and sometimes madder, but none was more magnificent. None would match his exhibitionism.

Nero's suicide threatened the future of Roman monarchy. Augustus had saved Rome by subjecting it to the rule of one man. Every emperor since had either been Augustus's biological descendant, his grandnephew, or his adopted son. Augustus staked his rule on his family. The principate would stand or fall on family values, and Augustus was confident that it would stand. He was too optimistic.

Unlike Nero, Galba was not descended from Augustus, but no male descendants of the empire's founder were left. Knowing that he had no direct heirs and frightened by potential rivals, Nero had killed them all.

None of the members of Augustus's family matched his success. Tiberius lacked not just charisma but charm and the common touch. Germanicus, his nephew and heir, had all those, but he lacked Tiberius's common sense, and he died before he could rule. The three members of Germanicus's family who followed Tiberius on the throne were unprepared. Caligula, Claudius, and Nero lacked significant administrative experience before ruling nor had any of them commanded an army. The pressures of dynastic life turned them into megalomaniacs, spendthrifts, and killers of the Roman nobility who hastened the decline of the Senate.

Nero's body was in the grave, but his soul went marching on down the centuries of imperial Rome. Augustus earlier tamed the old warrior republic and rededicated it to the twin propositions of empire and peace. Yet he left unanswered the question of what to do with Rome's restless conquering spirit. Nero offered an answer: he would rededicate it to pleasure. But he was too impractical and too imperious to see the limits of his power or to bother about the matter of who would pay the price. Nor did he reckon with the continuing appeal of honor in the Roman heart. The elite really weren't willing to tolerate a charioteer, actor, and arsonist as their ruler, especially not when he'd also murdered his mother and his wife.

Few of Nero's successors proved willing to try the patience of their contemporaries as Nero had, and if they did, the attempt proved quickly fatal. Yet when it came to elevating the importance of entertainment, there was a little Nero in every one of Rome's future emperors.

Rome faced an urgent problem: Could the empire continue without the House of Caesar? Rome without Caesar—after a century of peace since the Battle of Actium, the city shuddered at the thought.

Vespasian on a silver denarius.

4

VESPASIAN

THE COMMONER

The year 67 found the Roman army in a hard fight to retake the rebel province of Judea. Leading the legions was one of the empire's most experienced
generals, Titus Flavius Vespasianus, one of the conquerors of Britain. Vespasian, as we know him today, was every inch a soldier, riding on horseback
among the cavalry in the army's marching column, mixing with the men,
and paying attention to their safety and well-being while driving them forward. When one of the defenders on a city wall in Galilee hit Vespasian in
the sole of his foot with an arrow, the legions shuddered. But it was just a
flesh wound, and the fifty-seven-year-old general got up to show the men
that he was fine, which spurred them to fight harder. He was slow, steady,
and unflappable. He was, says one writer, the equal of the great generals of
old in everything but his greed. And, as we will see, that criticism might just
have been an aristocrat's sneer.

In November 67 Vespasian was under assault inside the walls of Gamla,
a fortified rebel town on a precipitous ridge above the Sea of Galilee. The
Romans had broken into Gamla only to run afoul of tottering houses and
treacherous terrain. As the general in command, Vespasian fought in the

thick of things. Ordering his men to link shields in a protective formation, he and they withdrew calmly and did not turn their backs until they were safely outside the walls. He then went on to regroup and, on a later day, conquer the town. This was the hardy warrior to whom Nero entrusted his army.

Vespasian was ready to begin the siege of Jerusalem in summer 68 when word came of Nero's death. He broke off operations until instructions came from the new government. But before the Roman war machine started up again, the world turned upside down several times, and when it stopped, Vespasian stood on top.

Nero was forced into suicide by a defiant Senate and an increasingly mutinous military. All agreed on the need for change, but when it came to the new emperor—or to deciding whether there should even be an emperor—the only consensus was that the sword would have the final say.

After a century, the Augustan peace was over. The new reality was war, and it raged from Gaul and Germany to Judea and Italy itself. It was an era of pitched battle, sacks, sieges, and street fighting. Two of the empire's most revered shrines, the Jewish Second Temple in Jerusalem and, in Rome, the pagan Temple of Capitoline Jupiter the Best and the Greatest, were reduced to ruins. As if to put an exclamation mark on the age, not long after peace was restored, Italy suffered the most dramatic natural disaster in its history.

The year 69 was the Year of Four Emperors. After Nero's suicide on June 9, 68, four men in turn seized the throne. Three of them came and went quickly: Galba (December 24, 68, to January 15, 69), Otho (January 15 to April 16, 69), and Aulus Vitellius (April 16 to December 22, 69). Only the fourth, Vespasian, made his claim stick. He founded a new dynasty.

And it was something new indeed in Roman eyes. All the previous emperors had been named in Rome, three of those four were chosen in the provinces: Galba in Hispania, Vitellius in Germania, and Vespasian in Egypt. They were also the first emperors to be chosen by their legions. When the Spanish legions decided on Galba, wrote the historian Tacitus, "the secret of empire was now divulged, that an emperor could be made elsewhere than in Rome."

Romans expected their rulers to have the prestige that came with noble birth. They all did, in one way or another, until Vespasian. He was Rome's first nonnoble ruler. The first commoner on the Palatine Hill. The first plebeian emperor. The sources are full of stories about how earthy and practical he was. According to one anecdote, when the commander of a cavalry unit came to see him drenched with perfume, Vespasian said that he would rather that the officer smelled of garlic; in other words, he preferred his officers manly and uncouth to soft and cultured.

Vespasian had no direct ancestors in the Senate. He was what the Romans called a "new man" (novus homo). To the Romans, unlike us, "new and improved" was an oxymoron; they preferred "old and time tested." The road to the palace would be hard for a new man, yet Vespasian decided to take it.

UP FROM SABINE COUNTRY

The rivers of the Sabine country northeast of Rome flow through lush green fields and woods. They empty into the Tiber and add to the surge downstream that, in spring and fall, often used to flood the low-lying areas of the city before the modern embankments were built. You never knew what the river might bring to Rome from the Sabine highlands, and on November 17, 9, it brought a baby who would grow up to be emperor.

He was born Titus Flavius Vespasianus in a hamlet near the Sabine city of Reate (modern Rieti). Vespasian was rooted in the soil and common sense of rural Italy. The Sabine country was a land of ox plows and mule carts, of the tinkling of goat bells and the chirping of cicadas, of hot summer afternoons and icy cold spring water. It seemed so quintessentially Italian that Lake Cutiliae, not far from Reate, was called "the navel of Italy."

According to tradition, the Sabines were early rivals of Rome who quickly became allies. Legend speaks of the "rape"—that is, abduction—of the Sabine women by the early Romans, a largely male group in need of wives. When the Sabine men went to war, the women supposedly made peace between their fathers and brothers and their new husbands. Vespasian, too, would be a peacemaker, though of a different sort.

Vespasian's family, known as the Flavians, consisted of upwardly mobile Italians. They first made a breakthrough to big money during the civil wars of the late republic. His father was a tax collector in Asia Minor and a moneylender in Gaul. Vespasian inherited his father's interest in finance, and it would prove handy to him as emperor. But it was the women of the family who seem to have inspired big ambitions in Vespasian and his older brother, Flavius Sabinus (literally, "the Sabine").

Knowing that Romans set great store by their mothers, perhaps Vespasian played up this angle in public. For example, as emperor, he made a point of visiting his grandparents' estate. The story went that his grandmother had raised young Vespasian there while his father was in Asia Minor.

Vespasian's mother, Vespasia, was, they said, a key figure of his adolescence. She was the daughter of a military officer and Roman knight. More important, her brother was a Roman senator, and she wanted her two sons to follow suit. Her older son, Flavius Sabinus, eagerly became quaestor and thus automatically a senator, but his brother, Vespasian, held back. At first, he wanted to go into finance like his father, but eventually he changed his mind. The story goes that Vespasia drove him to it by insulting him rather than asking him; she called Vespasian his brother's *anteambulo*: the slave that walked before his master to clear the way.

Whether maternal abuse really changed his mind or not, Vespasian decided to follow in his brother's footsteps. Around the year 35, when he was about twenty-five, Vespasian, too, was elected quaestor, and so began his career as a Roman senator. Having chosen his course, he drove forward with the single-mindedness of a Sabine muleteer whipping his animal up a narrow mountain path. He was a strong and healthy young man, well built and vigorous but not handsome. Blunt, earthy, and plebeian, he had the face of a bulldog and the bearing of a soldier.

It was during the last years of the reign of Tiberius. As a man on the make in imperial Rome, Vespasian didn't hesitate to do what he had to do to get ahead. He sucked up to the tyrannical Caligula and took his side against the Senate. Nor did he complain when Caligula ordered his soldiers to cover Vespasian's toga with mud (possibly a euphemism for something worse) for having failed to keep the alleys clean even though it was Vespasian's job as a public official.

In the year 39 Vespasian convinced the Senate to deny burial to a man convicted of conspiracy against Caligula. This won Vespasian a dinner invitation from the emperor but at a price: Vespasian also earned the undying hatred of Agrippina. In spite of being Caligula's sister, she was a coconspirator and possibly the convicted man's lover.

THE SLAVE WHO LOVED ME

Vespasian married an undistinguished woman, perhaps when he was still thinking of a career in finance, since senators usually married up. His wife, Flavia Domitilla, had been abandoned at birth and then taken in and raised as a slave before her birth father successfully sued on her behalf to establish her freedom. She and Vespasian had two sons, Titus (born in 39) and Domitian (born in 51), and a daughter, also named Flavia Domitilla (born around 45).

Meanwhile, Vespasian made a shrewd career move by taking up with one of the more powerful women in the imperial court, Antonia Caenis. The affair began probably in the mid-thirties, when he was in his late twenties; Caenis was at least two years older than him. She was hardly a kinswoman of the emperor—in fact, she started life as a slave. Her name suggests a Greek origin; perhaps from the city of Histria on the western coast of the Euxine Sea (today's Black Sea), which she is known to have visited. No description of her looks survives, but her brains and ambition shine through. She was highly talented: bright and bold, with a photographic memory. Perhaps there is something of her in the so-called *Seated Agrippina* statue in the National Archaeological Museum of Naples. The head, evidently from the Flavian period, to judge by its hair, shows a dignified, serious, and strong-looking woman.

She came to the attention of one of the most powerful women in Rome: Antonia the Younger, daughter of Octavia and Mark Antony, wife of Emperor Tiberius's brother, mother of the great Germanicus and the emperor Claudius, and grandmother of the emperor Caligula. Antonia was honored late in life with the title of Augusta. Caenis served as her personal secretary. If later tradition is accurate, Antonia relied on Caenis in the very risky business of revealing to Emperor Tiberius the conspiracy against him by Sejanus. Antonia and Caenis succeeded and Tiberius put down the plot. Caenis was rewarded: by the time of Antonia's death on May 1, 37, if not earlier, she freed Caenis, which made Caenis what the Romans called a *liberta*, or freedwoman.

Although Vespasian eventually suspended the affair with Caenis, she probably continued to help his career with friends in high places, almost all of them connected to Antonia and Claudius. One such friend was Lucius Vitellius the Elder, father of the later emperor. A very successful diplomat and general, Vitellius was the consummate survivor. He managed to be a power broker under three emperors, to die of natural causes, and to earn a state funeral. A footnote to Vitellius's career: he removed the hugely unpopular governor of Judea, Pontius Pilate—the same Pilate who had condemned Jesus. As for Vespasian, Vitellius helped him become consul in the year 51.

More doors opened to Vespasian at court when Antonia's son Claudius became emperor in the year 41, and his secretary, a freedman, became one of the most influential men in the empire. The freedman favored Vespasian, and we have to wonder if Caenis introduced them. At any rate, he got Vespasian command of a legion, which was perfect timing for an ambitious young man, what with Claudius about to embark on an expedition to conquer Britain. In the end, the conquest took decades and saw many setbacks, but Claudius achieved some real success. So did Vespasian, distinguishing himself as one of four legionary commanders in the campaign of 43.

Vespasian immersed himself in the world of the legions. From the *praetorium* (the general's headquarters) to the battlefield, and from the enemy's walls to his ruined cities, that world was hierarchical, rigorous, unforgiving, and loud. It was a sphere of trumpets and shouts; of the thud of pick-axes and shovels digging trenches; of horses' hoofbeats and the rhythmic, pounding feet of men marching, shoulder to shoulder, six abreast; of the rap of spear against shield, the clang of swords, and the hissing of arrows; of the rush of catapult stones and the shrieks and groans when they found their targets; of howls and applause, eloquence and pleas; the buzzing of flies and the rasp of vultures around corpses after a battle.

Vespasian conquered much of southwestern Britain during four years of operations across the thick vegetation and deep mud of rolling hills and mist-filled valleys. He fought thirty battles, some of them combined land-sea campaigns, took twenty hilltop forts, and subdued two tribes. "It was the beginning of his coming good fortune," wrote the historian Tacitus, adding, "fate came to know Vespasian."

Rome came to know him too. Only members of the emperor's family were allowed to celebrate a triumph, but Vespasian won the next best thing: "triumphal honors"—that is, the right to wear triumphal dress in public, and have a bronze statue erected in the Forum of Augustus and another in his own home. He won two priesthoods as well and, as mentioned, a consulship in the year 51.

Meanwhile, Vespasian's brother, Sabinus, was even more successful. After serving, too, as a commander in Britain, he landed a provincial governorship in the Balkans and then was appointed prefect of the city of Rome, a post he held for eleven years, making him the pride of the family. Vespasian had to wait until 63 for a provincial governorship, in North Africa, and afterward he came home honest but broke. Rumor said that he went into the transport business, which involved the mules for which his hometown of Reate was famous—a profitable activity but one below a senator's dignity.

Perhaps Vespasian suffered for having backed the wrong man in high places. During Claudius's reign, Vespasian was influential enough to have his son Titus raised in the palace with Britannicus, the son of Claudius, where they were taught the same subjects by the same masters. But Claudius took Agrippina as his second wife, and her enmity toward Vespasian made Titus's position dangerous. Titus was reclining on a dining couch at Britannicus's side at what turned out to be Britannicus's last meal: he died shortly afterwards. Rumor said it was poison and also that Titus took some of the poison too and got sick, but the rumor is unverifiable. It's clear that Titus survived. Meanwhile, Vespasian was too good a politician to be kept out of power for long.

THE REVOLT OF JUDEA

The last years of Nero's reign proved bloody for the Roman nobility. The discovery of conspiracies led to executions and enforced suicides of famous politicians, generals, and intellectuals. But Vespasian and his family prospered. Agrippina was gone, murdered at Nero's behest, so she no longer stood in Vespasian's way. In later years, he claimed to have opposed Nero's tyranny. He let it be known, for instance, that the emperor refused to admit him to his company after Vespasian had fallen asleep at one of Nero's performances. But Vespasian was too ambitious for real opposition. Instead, he broke ties with senators opposed to Nero. Meanwhile, Titus divorced his wife, niece of an elderly senator who was accused of treason against Nero and forced to commit suicide.

Nero rewarded such loyalty. When the province of Judea revolted in the year 66, Nero appointed Vespasian commander of three legions to put down the revolt. He also allowed him to appoint the twenty-six-year-old Titus to command of one of the legions, despite Titus's low rank and the rarity of such father-son combinations. An ambitious and successful general might march on Rome, something to worry about, but Nero considered Vespasian safe because the Sabine muleteer lacked the right pedigree to be emperor.

Judea had simmered for decades under oppressive Roman rule, with its high taxes and customs duties, an army garrisoned in Jerusalem, and favoritism toward the non-Jewish communities in the land. Various Roman insults to the Temple in Jerusalem created the impression of Rome as a "kingdom of arrogance." Poor Jews resented the pro-Roman Jewish upper classes, and they had more than one Robin Hood waiting for his moment.

It came when the Roman governor took a large sum of silver from the temple, probably to cover taxes owed. Insurgents now rose up. They stopped offering sacrifices for the welfare of the Roman people and the emperor, crushed the Roman garrison in Jerusalem, defeated a relief army under the governor of Syria, and declared independence. The country was ablaze with clashes between Jews and non-Jews. That is when Nero sent in Vespasian.

Building on his experience in Britain, the commander methodically captured the fortified cities of Galilee's hill country in 67 and the next year began the drive for Jerusalem by taking the surrounding strongholds one by one. And so he began the tough military campaign with which this chapter began; the road that led to Jerusalem until Nero's suicide brought Rome's drive to a standstill.

Among the tens of thousands of prisoners taken by Vespasian in Galilee was the rebel-appointed Jewish governor of the province, Joseph ben Matthias. He was destined to be brought to Rome and executed, but he found a way out. He prophesied to Vespasian that he would be emperor. When in turn the legions indeed proclaimed Vespasian emperor, Joseph was freed from his chains. Although some Romans considered Joseph a Jewish spy, Vespasian and Titus found him useful. After the war, he ended up in Rome living in the palace under their protection, became a Roman citizen named Flavius Josephus, and wrote a detailed history of the revolt that survives today.

THE MAKING OF THE ROMAN EMPEROR, 69

Nero committed suicide in June, and Galba, the new emperor, reached Rome in October 68. Galba went on to disappoint nearly everyone. About seventy years old, he was an aging aristocrat whose political skills were as low grade as his lineage was exalted. He offended the Senate, proved stingy with the soldiers and the people, and chose the wrong friends and enemies.

"By common consent, he would have been a capable ruler—if he had never ruled," was the historian Tacitus's acid verdict.

On January 2, 69, the legions of the Lower Rhine (southern Netherlands and Germany's northern Rhineland) rebelled and named as emperor their commander, Vitellius, son of the Roman powerbroker we met earlier. He'd been appointed by Galba. Then came January 15, 69, a busy day in Rome. The Praetorian Guard named Otho emperor, Galba was murdered in the Forum, and the Senate confirmed Otho's new title, all in one day. Three months later, on April 14, troops led by Vitellius's allies defeated Otho's army in northern Italy. Otho committed suicide, and Vitellius entered Rome in mid-July. Meanwhile, Vespasian prepared to move.

Although he had taken the oath to Galba, Vespasian did not trust him after Galba fired Vespasian's brother Sabinus as prefect of Rome. In December 68 Vespasian rushed Titus off to the capital to work things out, even though it meant a dangerous winter sailing. Then, just weeks later, while in Corinth, on his way to Rome, Titus got the news of Galba's death. He called together his friends for a meeting, and they decided to return to Judea. Titus reached Vespasian in February. It was then that Vespasian decided to go for the throne.

In Roman eyes, he lacked authority, reputation, grandeur. He wasn't even the most distinguished member of his family—that honor went to his brother. But Vespasian must have believed in himself. Perhaps he took to heart various omens and dreams or the prophecies by Josephus and others that he was destined to rule. Nor was Vespasian unduly sentimental about past ties. He rejected Vitellius as emperor, thus turning on the son of his former patron. But Vitellius, unlike Vespasian, did not have three hardened legions racking up victories in Judea. Vespasian might not have been the noblest man in the empire, but his army could make him the First Man in Rome.

Flavian propaganda said that Vespasian's soldiers came up with the idea of naming him emperor and forced him into it. But the truth was the other way around: Vespasian and a few powerful allies, including his legionary commanders, set the agenda, and the troops followed. A military man, Vespasian never forgot the support of the army, and he repaid it generously, but he also watched for news from Rome. Sabinus, reinstated as prefect by Otho and still in that position under Vitellius, represented a vital source. Caenis surely continued to have her ears to the ground in Rome and no doubt fed information to Vespasian as well. Besides them and Titus, Vespasian's most important supporters in were a gay man, a white-collar criminal, and a family of Romanized Jews. They included the most glamorous and powerful Eastern queen since Cleopatra.

MUCIANUS

The gay man was Gaius Licinius Mucianus, governor of Syria. Like Vespasian, Mucianus had a distinguished public career. Tacitus says that Vespasian was a born soldier but greedy, while Mucianus was generous, a superb orator, and a cunning politician, but "his private life had a bad reputation." That is probably a polite way of saying that Mucianus was not only homosexual, something Romans tolerated, but a passive partner, something they did not. Speaking privately to a friend, Vespasian once dismissed Mucianus with a cutting remark about his "notorious unchastity," grumbling, "I at least am a man."

In spite of such obloquy, Mucianus might have pushed his own candidacy for emperor. He was governor of Syria, after all, and controlled four legions, while Vespasian only had three. But he supported Vespasian, the most experienced general in the Roman army, with triumphal honors to his name for his success in Britain, and a reputation for vigilance, thrift, and good sense. Mucianus himself made these points in a speech that Tacitus attributes to him. Vespasian currently commanded an army that was actively fighting and winning in Judea, a campaign in which he added to his reputation for manliness, as the Romans saw it. More important, his men loved him for winning and for paying them well and promoting them rapidly. Mucianus could content himself with exercising enormous power behind the scenes. Or perhaps he never really wanted the burdens and dangers of office. Tacitus thought that Mucianus "was a man who would find it easier to transfer the imperial power to another than to hold it for himself."

And then there was Titus, who played key roles both with the public and with Mucianus. Like Vespasian, Titus was a good commander who earned the love of his troops, but he had a touch of class that his father lacked because the boy had grown up in the imperial court. Although he was short and paunchy, he was handsome, strong, intelligent, a gifted linguist, and even a decent poet and singer. Titus also had a rare ability to earn practically everyone's affection. Although passionate about women, he kept a troupe of pretty boys and eunuchs around him, at least at one point in Rome, which raised eyebrows. Never mind, he was, said the biographer Suetonius, "the darling and delight of the human race." He was, in short, a golden boy.

By putting Titus front and center, with his younger son, Domitian, waiting in the wings, Vespasian played to his strengths and minimized a weakness: his age, sixty-one. That might have worried an empire grown weary of brief reigns. Vespasian proposed a package deal, as if to say to Rome: "Accept me as emperor, and you will get the stability of a dynasty." Not a single previous Roman emperor had succeeded in leaving the throne to his birth son.

Titus served as the broker between Vespasian and Mucianus. "By his character and manner of living, Titus was qualified for attracting even a man of Mucianus's habits," writes Tacitus. No need to bother becoming emperor, said Mucianus, when an Emperor Mucianus would only adopt Titus as his successor—and Titus would follow Vespasian soon enough.

A FAMILY OF ROMANIZED JEWS

As for the family of Romanized Jews, it may seem surprising that Vespasian and Titus, of all people, should have had prominent Jewish supporters. After all, between them, they conquered rebellious Judea, sacked Jerusalem, destroyed the temple, and enslaved, deported, and killed massive numbers of Jews. Rabbinic sources remember Titus as "an evil man, son of an evil man." Yet many Jews had opposed the rebellion. They hated Rome but considered the rebellion doomed and didn't want any part of it. Other Jews, especially among the upper classes, feared their own poor fellow Jews more than they feared the legions, and so were pro-Roman. Titus inherited Jewish friends, some of whom knew Vespasian back in the days of Claudius and Antonia.

One of them was Tiberius Julius Alexander, a Roman citizen and member of a prominent Jewish family of Alexandria. His distinguished military and political careers included a stint as governor of Judea. As governor of Egypt since the year 66, he controlled Rome's wealthiest province and its breadbasket. Annual grain shipments from the fertile Nile Valley fed Rome. Tiberius Alexander had two legions at his disposal. Like Mucianus, he had the potential to be a kingmaker; perhaps even more so because of his influential former sister-in-law, Julia Berenice, and her brother, Marcus Julius Agrippa, like him, prominent Jews and Roman citizens.

The two were descended from the infamous King Herod, their great-grandfather. He had ruled Judea, but then the Romans annexed Judea and made it a Roman province. Julius Agrippa had to settle for a smaller kingdom located in today's northern Israel and Lebanon, along with jurisdiction over the Temple in Jerusalem. He became a friend of Titus and was with him on the mission to Galba in 68 and 69. But his sister proved even more important.

Berenice was briefly married to Tiberius Alexander's brother, but the bridegroom died soon after the wedding. Although she moved on—she married two Eastern kings, both of who died—the two families remained connected. Eventually Berenice served as the partner in rule of her bachelor brother, King Julius Agrippa. He gave her a magnificent diamond, which spurred attention—and fed malicious rumors of incest.

Berenice was ambitious and politically savvy. She was also patriotic but pragmatic. In the year 66 she witnessed Roman atrocities in Jerusalem first-hand and tried to stop them at great personal risk. But she and Julius Agrippa were dead set against revolt from invincible Rome. They tried to talk the Jewish public out of it—Julius Agrippa with a speech; both of them with tears—but in vain. The mob burned their palaces and helped themselves to a (small) part of their treasure. Agrippa and Berenice hewed to Rome and, in particular, to the commander of its legions in Judea and his son.

Berenice and Titus probably met in the year 67, when he and Vespasian were gathering their forces. Agrippa and three other client kings in the region supplied troops to help the Romans. Berenice's beauty and charm won Titus's heart, while her wealth, deployed strategically, won Vespasian's gratitude. She was approximately eleven years older than Titus, but the age difference did not deter him. Indeed, although she was around thirty-nine when they met, she was, says Tacitus, in the prime of her beauty, and she made the twenty-eight-year-old Titus burn with youthful desire.

EGYPT

By early 69, it became clear that Judea wasn't the only place that Vespasian and his talented son could rule: Rome itself beckoned. So Agrippa and Berenice threw their support behind Vespasian's bid for the throne, as did Berenice's former brother-in-law, Tiberius Alexander. On July 1, 69, he had the legions of Egypt swear an oath of loyalty to Vespasian.

It was the first open sign of rebellion against Vitellius, but it was also a revolution in a system. The son of a tax collector from the Sabine hills was hailed as the ruler of the world; the successor of Augustus was proclaimed in the city of Antony and Cleopatra; the shouts of the soldiers in their red woolen cloaks in Alexandria replaced the orderly deliberation of the senators in their purple-bordered togas in Rome. A few days later, the legions of Judea and Syria followed their brothers in Egypt. It took another five months until December for the Senate to recognize Vespasian, and sticklers were annoyed in later years when he marked July 1 as the anniversary of his reign.

Having claimed the empire, Vespasian now had to take it from Vitellius. Vespasian said he hoped to win without bloodshed, by pressuring Rome through shutting off the Egyptian grain supply. But he sent an army to Italy. Yet, despite his military skill, Vespasian did not join it; he stayed in Egypt instead. Meanwhile, he gave Titus the job of finishing the war against the rebels in Judea.

Egypt was strategically important, and it was safely removed from the struggle in Italy. In Egypt Vespasian bided his time and demonstrated a hitherto unknown royal touch. In Alexandria, while seated on his tribunal, he supposedly healed two members of the common people—one blind and one lame—a sign of his new divine gift. Along with omens and portents from Italy, Greece, and Judea, it was great propaganda.

The decision to remain in Egypt was also vintage Vespasian. For all his veneer of unrefined simplicity, he was a master manipulator. He was, one imagines, one of those leaders who likes to be underestimated, as he knew that it made him more dangerous. In fact, he was as strategic as Ulysses, the wily hero of Homer's *Odyssey*.

On his path up, Vespasian was second to none when it came to flattering the boss. And for all his air of being an accidental man, he burned with ambition. He might not have planned all his life to be emperor, but when the opportunity arose, he was ready to seize it. Like Augustus, Vespasian had a talent for getting others to work for him. Caenis, Mucianus, Sabinus, Tiberius Alexander, Julius Agrippa, Berenice—they were all part of a pattern. Nor did Titus break the mold. It might seem as if Vespasian sought the throne merely as a career booster for his son, but it was Vespasian who became emperor. Titus worked for him.

ANTONIUS PRIMUS, CRIMINAL AND CONQUEROR

While he stayed in Egypt, Vespasian sent Mucianus westward with the Syrian legions. They had a mighty force to hurl against Vitellius and his troops, but Mucianus didn't launch the blow. Marcus Antonius Primus beat him to it.

A man of about fifty, Primus came from the city of Tolosa (modern Toulouse) in Gaul. He rose in Roman politics, but in the year 61 he was convicted of forging a will and expelled from the Senate. Then, in 68, he was rewarded for his support of Galba with reinstatement as a senator and command of a legion in Pannonia. Bold and decisive, in 69 the convicted criminal switched to Vespasian. Tacitus describes Primus memorably: "He was brave in battle, ready of speech, dexterous in bringing odium upon other men, powerful amidst civil strife and rebellion, rapacious, prodigal, the worst of citizens in peace, but in war, no contemptible ally."

Primus almost singlehandedly talked the Danubian legions into supporting Vespasian. They marched boldly into Italy, where they seized the key city of Aquileia and then crushed Vitellius's legions in a battle outside Cremona. Afterward, they sacked Cremona itself: a four-day rampage of Roman soldiers killing Roman civilians that came as a shock and a disgrace to the empire.

Meanwhile in Rome, Sabinus negotiated an agreement for Vitellius to abdicate. Peace was at hand, but some of Vitellius's troops refused. They forced Sabinus and his son and grandsons to seek refuge on the Capitoline Hill, high above the Roman Forum. Vespasian's younger son, Domitian, was with them. Vitellius's forces took the hill. Sabinus's family, including Domitian, escaped, but Sabinus was captured. After dragging him to Vitellius, the soldiers brutally murdered him. During the course of the fighting, the Temple of Capitoline Jupiter the Best and the Greatest burned down. It was an ill omen, because the temple was the religious center of the Roman state and because Jupiter was closely associated with the emperor.

The very next day, December 20, Primus and his legions entered Rome. After heavy fighting, they took the city. Vitellius was dragged through the streets, tortured, and killed.

VESPASIAN IN ROME

Domitian took the title of Caesar and moved into the palace, but real control in Rome belonged to Primus. Then Mucianus entered the city and took charge. He didn't dare attack the popular Primus directly, but Mucianus was nothing if not devious. He removed the two legions closest to Primus and his allies, convinced Primus to take a governorship in Hispania, and wrote to Vespasian to turn him against Primus. In due course, Primus retired to his hometown of Tolosa.

It took nearly a year, until October 70, for Vespasian to reach Rome. Until then, Mucianus ran the government, behaving "more like the emperor's colleague than his agent," says Tacitus. He continued to receive recognition and office—triumphal honors for his role in the civil war and two consulships (in 70 and 72)—but power passed into Vespasian's hands. The Senate granted Vespasian the same high offices and the same title as his predecessors: Imperator Caesar Augustus. Their decision sealed what the brief reigns of Galba, Otho, and Vitellius suggested but never got the chance to prove: that the imperial office was highly transferable. The ever-practical Romans solved the problem of legitimacy neatly by simply giving the imperial title to the strongest man, regardless of a blood or adoptive connection to the founder of the empire.

Meanwhile, they granted the appellation of Caesar to Titus and Domitian. For the first time, *Caesar* was used to designate an heir. As for Mucianus, he fades from the historical record. It seems that he retired from public life because he had time to publish his letters, speeches, and memoirs of his years in the East. He died around the year 75.

For eighteen months, from the death of Nero to the victory of Vespasian, the Roman world endured a period of uncertainty, battle, sacks, devastation, and revolt. It was a heavy price to pay, but much less than Rome suffered in fifteen years of war and revolution during Augustus's rise to power. If Vespasian could restore peace, then one might even say that, flaws and all, the system worked.

Compared with the rulers of other empires, most Roman emperors enjoyed only short tenures in office. Although that led to instability, it also let talent from outside the ruling family reach the throne. In order to succeed, a new emperor had to satisfy several key constituencies.

Vespasian wanted to consolidate power and pass it on to his sons, to reestablish the army and the Treasury after years of luxury and war, and to enjoy life with the woman he loved. First, though, he had to sell himself to the Senate and the people of Rome.

It wouldn't be by his looks. By now, Vespasian was balding and given to gout. His face showed determination that could also be taken as a strained expression, as if, as one wit put it, he suffered from constipation.

Nor would Vespasian sell himself by his eloquence. He was no Cicero, although he did have a wicked sense of humor and the timing of a stand-up comic. When, for example, an ex-consul, Lucius Mestrius Florus, corrected his pronunciation of *plostra* to *plaustra*, Vespasian greeted Florus the next day as "Flaurus." In Greek, *phlauros* means "vile"—a pun that would not be lost on Florus, who was friends with Plutarch, the eminent Greek writer.

Nor would Vespasian succeed by divine right. In the provinces, from Iberia to Armenia, he assiduously promoted the worship of himself as a god, but in Rome and Italy, he was just a man. So he was limited in his ability in the capital to use religion as a feature to make his rule attractive.

No, Vespasian would sell himself as Augustus had done, by pageantry and building, all the while crafting an image and rebranding Rome in his family's name. Like Augustus, he denied the reality of civil war, presenting himself and his family as conquerors of foreign enemies of the Roman people. And he did it with a flair for communication that matched Rome's best.

Vespasian didn't abandon Nero's policy of spectacle and pageantry. Instead, he doubled down on it, but with one big difference. Vespasian behaved with dignity and simplicity, and he treated the Senate with relative respect. The emperor did not play the lyre or race chariots in public, nor did he leave himself open to charges of arson or matricide. Vespasian was more dignified than Nero, but he offered no better solution to the crisis of the Roman soul than his predecessor did.

Yet Vespasian did offer one major innovation. The great commoner brought a new class to power: a group of wealthy and ambitious men like himself who came from Italy or the provinces. He greatly expanded the imperial elite, with consequences for many years to come.

THE SELLING OF THE EMPEROR

In spring 70 Titus besieged Jerusalem. The Jews had an inspiring and effective leader in Simon Bar Giora. A former partisan who built an army, he promised freedom for the slaves and a reckoning for the rich. He issued coins with the messianic legend REDEMPTION OF ZION.

Yet in spite of fierce resistance, Jerusalem fell to Titus in late summer

70. Bar Giora and a small group of followers tried to escape through underground tunnels, but even with the help of stonecutters, they failed. In the end, Bar Giora emerged where the Temple of Jerusalem had stood. A leading Roman officer took his surrender. Bar Giora was wearing a white tunic and the purple cloak of a king—or the Messiah.

Only the fortress of Masada—steep, arid, and remote—remained in the hands of the rebels, to fall finally in 73 or 74 after a massive Roman siege. As Vespasian's coins depicted, Judea was defeated. The coins show Judea as a mourning woman seated beneath a palm tree, with a bearded man standing nearby, hands tied behind his back. In Rome, the new emperor had the doors of the Temple of Janus closed to signify peace, as Augustus did after Actium and Nero after the settlement with Parthia over Armenia.

In June 71, after Titus's return to Rome, he and Vespasian celebrated a joint triumph over conquered Judea. Like earlier rulers, they knew how to put on a show: a splendid sight attracting a standing-room-only crowd. Father and son dressed in the tradition of conquering generals, wearing reddish-purple togas and bay-leaf-wreath crowns.

Vespasian began the day by greeting his soldiers and demonstrating his ability to work a crowd. To quote Josephus:

> Now a tribunal had been erected before the Portico of Octavia, and ivory chairs had been set upon it, when Titus and Vespasian came and sat down upon them. Whereupon the soldiery made an acclamation of joy to them immediately, and all gave them attestations of their valor; while they were themselves without their arms, and only in their silken garments, and crowned with laurel: then Vespasian accepted these shouts of theirs; but while they were still disposed to go on in such acclamations, he gave them a signal of silence. And when everybody entirely held their peace, he stood up, and covering the greatest part of his head with his cloak, he put up the accustomed solemn prayers; the like prayers did Titus put up also; after which prayers Vespasian made a short speech to all the people, and then sent away the soldiers to a breakfast prepared for them by the emperors.

The victory parade included floats illustrating the cities conquered along with, wherever possible, the actual enemy leaders who had commanded them. Soldiers and senators, sacrificial animals, and hundreds of tall, healthy prisoners all marched in the procession. The prize captives were Simon Bar Giora and another key leader of the revolt, and they were whipped along the way. Among the spoils displayed were a table and menorah from the temple, both made of gold. Vespasian and Titus rode in chariots—the emperor first—with Domitian on a splendid horse. After Bar Giora was executed (the other leader suffered life imprisonment), there were sacrifices on the Capitoline Hill and then banquets all over the city.

Vespasian made it his first order of business to restore the Temple of Capitoline Jupiter, which had been destroyed in the fighting of December 69. He wanted to show that he had the gods on his side. So when it came time to lay the foundation stone of the new temple, he was the first to help clear the debris. The emperor carried out a load of soil from the site on his head.

It was an important gesture of Roman renewal, but Judea, not Jupiter, burned most brightly in the Flavians' minds. They commemorated their victory in not one but two triumphal arches, the carved reliefs of one of which, the Arch of Titus, are still visible today. A prominent part of the sculptural program was the menorah or seven-branched candelabra from the temple. On the Arch of Titus the menorah now looks colorless. But recent scientific study shows that it was originally painted a rich yellow, representing the gold of the actual menorah. The other arch was destroyed in the Middle Ages, but the inscription, which was recorded, praised Titus for the feat of conquering the Jewish people and destroying Jerusalem, both at his father's orders. Archaeologists recently discovered parts of this second arch in Rome at the edge of the Circus Maximus.

But that was just the beginning of the Flavians' plan to stamp their victory over the Jews on Rome's urban space. Another prominent feature was the Temple of Peace. Vespasian did not choose the name lightly. Like Augustus, who built an Altar of Peace, Vespasian knew from personal experience that only by the grace of the gods had Rome achieved a hard-won peace. Like the forums of Caesar and Augustus, Vespasian's construction was a centrally located public square, with colonnades all around and a temple on one side. It was magnificently decorated with a combination of new construction as well as building parts and art works from Nero's Golden House. It also housed the golden vessels from the Temple, which were probably looted by Alaric, King of the Visigoths, when he sacked Rome in 410. Although recent excavations have brought much of the complex to light, it is hard to appreciate its grandeur today because a large part now lies under the massive road that Fascist premier Benito Mussolini drove through the heart of ancient Rome, the Street of the Imperial Forums, in the 1930s.

But the most visible part of Vespasian's program is also the most famous building in Rome: the Colosseum. The workforce probably included both skilled and unskilled laborers, both free and slave, with captives from the Jewish War likely among them. An inscription says that the building was financed by "the general's share of the booty," probably a reference to the Jewish War. Like Augustus, Vespasian seems to have financed a major building project in Rome with the spoils of war, which boosted his public standing.

Nowadays we think of the Colosseum as typically Roman, but at the time, it was an innovation. Although many Italian cities boasted stone amphitheaters, Rome had preferred to put up temporary wooden stands for gladiatorial games—a holdover from the republican-era fear of crowds. There was once a small, partially stone amphitheater in Rome, but it burned down in the Great Fire of 64. Vespasian ordered a breathtaking replacement that would seat about fifty thousand spectators, making it one of the largest amphitheaters ever built. Construction began during his reign, but it was not completed and opened until a year after his death.

In antiquity, the Colosseum was known as the Flavian Amphitheater. The Colosseum received its current name in the Middle Ages from a colossal bronze statue of Nero, rising an estimated 115 feet that stood beside it.

The name first appears in a saying of the seven hundreds: "While the Colosseum stands, Rome shall stand; when the Colosseum falls, Rome shall fall; when Rome falls, the world shall fall."

Colosseum or Flavian Amphitheater—what's in a name? In this case, plenty, because "Flavian Amphitheater" made the building as iconic and as personal as the city of Alexandria (named for Alexander the Great), the Forum of Julius Caesar, the mausoleum of Augustus, and, in modern times, Victoria Falls, the Eiffel Tower, and Hoover Dam. And the building leapt into the heart of Roman consciousness because the new amphitheater was an arena not just for sports but also for politics. As a means of communication, it was as revolutionary as Facebook or Twitter. From its dedication in 80 on, everyone with power attended the games there, to see and be seen. People sat in order of rank, with emperor, senators, and Roman knights at the front and ordinary people at the back. The crowd alternately cheered the emperor or cried and shouted for their favorite causes. In its own way, the Flavian Amphitheater rivaled the Forum or the Senate House—and it was branded with the name of the new first family in town.

Ironically, Vespasian did not like gladiatorial shows, perhaps because he had seen enough of war. But he knew that the Roman people loved their games. Vespasian sited his amphitheater on land seized by Nero after the Great Fire for his lavish Golden House. The new emperor had most of the Golden House torn down. The Colosseum rose on the site of the Golden House's artificial lake.

Although Vespasian cultivated a lowbrow image, he was the first emperor to establish chairs in Latin and Greek rhetoric. He knew a prestige move when he saw one, and he understood the value of an educated ruling class. The first holder of the Latin chair was Marcus Fabius Quintilianus—Quintilian—the Roman world's most important student of rhetoric. Among his many sayings are "No man can be an orator unless he is a good man," and "It is feeling and force of imagination that make us eloquent." He advised aspiring orators to study history for facts and precedents but not for a model of how to persuade judge and jury, since the purpose of history is to tell a good story and not to prove a case. Since Quintilian later influenced such figures as the early Christian thinker Saint Augustine, the Italian Renaissance poet Petrarch, the Protestant reformer Martin Luther, and also possibly the great composer Johann Sebastian Bach and the liberal philosopher John Stuart Mill, the world owes much to Vespasian's patronage.

LIKE FATHER, LIKE SON

From the first, Vespasian made it clear that his sons, especially his older son, Titus, would be his partners in rule. Like Domitian, Titus took the title of Caesar, but that was just the beginning. Among his many other honors and offices, he shared seven of the eight consulships while Vespasian was emperor. Vespasian also appointed Titus Praetorian prefect, which made him something like the director of the FBI but with a lot more leeway. Titus prided himself on being an expert forger; an odd but no doubt useful skill for the chief of security. Titus was all but co-emperor, and, in particular, he served as his father's enforcer.

Titus took charge of putting down alleged conspirators. When two prominent senators, formerly supporters of Vespasian, were suspected of plotting a coup, Titus had one of them tried and convicted in the Senate, after which the condemned man slit his own throat with a razor. Titus ordered the other conspirator murdered in the palace—after the man got up from dinner with Vespasian.

Then there was the problem of Helvidius Priscus. A staunch defender of the Senate, Helvidius apparently took issue with Titus's role as Vespasian's intended heir. According to one account, Helvidius reduced Vespasian to tears at a senate meeting, with Vespasian saying as he left, "Either my son will succeed me or no one at all will." Helvidius was dangerous because he belonged to the circle of high-minded Stoic philosophers who stood up to what they saw as imperial tyranny. Nero had already exiled him and forced his father-in-law to slit his wrists. Helvidius's wife, Fannia, supported her husband and followed him into a second exile imposed by Vespasian. Eventually Vespasian had Helvidius executed. Fannia lived on and neither forgave nor forgot. Years later, she sponsored a biography of Helvidius that criticized Vespasian. As a result, its author, a senator, was executed, and Fannia was exiled.

Tabloid-type headlines stand out, but by and large, Vespasian and Titus enjoyed good relations with the Senate. The emperor showed respect by attending Senate meetings in person or, when his health prevented that, by sending one of his sons. More important, Vespasian elevated to the Senate his legionary commanders and other important supporters in the East. That made the body more favorably disposed to him, and it added a new source of talent to the Roman aristocracy that had been depleted by luxury and oppression. Its most wide-ranging result, though, was to create a new Roman elite; one with staying power. Roman citizens from Spain and southern Gaul now became senators, consuls, provincial governors, priests, and patricians; their sons and grandsons would rise even higher.

Consider one of Vespasian's lieutenants in the East. Marcus Ulpius Traianus came from Hispania, where his ancestors had migrated from Italy centuries earlier. An ambitious man, Traianus entered the Senate under Claudius and then served as one of Vespasian's legionary commanders in Judea. After becoming emperor, Vespasian kept on promoting Traianus, giving him, among other things, a consulship, important provincial governorships, and the so-called triumphal ornaments—the highest military honor now available outside the imperial family. Fast forward thirty years after Vespasian became emperor, and Traianus's son ascended to the throne himself. He was the emperor Trajan. Two of his successors, Antoninus Pius and Marcus Aurelius, also came from families promoted by Vespasian. The emperor did nothing less than open the Roman ruling class to the leaders of the provinces.

MONEY HAS NO SMELL

Nero drained the Treasury, and civil war took whatever was left while sowing destruction and ruin. Rebuilding Rome's finances was Vespasian's most urgent job besides founding a dynasty. He needed to raise taxes and cut spending, and he did both well. Financial management came naturally to him, given his father's career in tax collecting and money lending—a striking contrast with Vespasian's aristocratic predecessors. The result was that he gained a reputation for greed. Jokes of the day made him into something of an ancient Jack Benny, that mid-twentieth-century miser of the American airwaves. But the truth is that Vespasian was just a wise manager of the national Treasury. He displayed "prudence rather than avarice," to quote one ancient judgment.

We can only piece together the shape of Vespasian's various financial policies. Some of the details that we know are that he renewed harbor taxes, the 5 percent tax on the value of freed slaves, the 1 percent tax on auction sales, the 5 percent inheritance tax on bequests to other than close relatives, the 4 percent tax on slave sales to finance the night watchmen of Rome, and customs duties between Gaul and Iberia. He converted the annual tax that Jews used to send to the Temple in Jerusalem into a fund for rebuilding and maintaining Rome's Temple of Capitoline Jupiter (and ultimately for other purposes), and he extended it from males only to women, children, and slaves. It was a humiliating poll tax on Jews that would last for centuries. Vespasian cracked down on squatters on public land and made them pay for it or see it sold. He increased taxes throughout the provinces and sold imperial property in Alexandria and Asia Minor and taxed the owners. New censuses in Italy and the provinces made the tax collectors' job easier. Meanwhile, Vespasian was frugal with government resources; for example, he reduced the size of diplomatic missions.

None of this made him popular, but, as usual, Vespasian tried to share the bad press. Mucianus, for instance, did yeoman's service of confiscation and taxation, thereby relieving the emperor of some of the blame. Mucianus was known for calling money "the sinews of sovereignty."

A delightful story survives about Vespasian's fiscal policy. When Titus blamed him for the indignity of levying a tax on the use of public latrines, Vespasian replied that money has no smell.

"THE GOOD FORTUNE AND GOOD DISCIPLINE OF EIGHT HUNDRED YEARS"

In 68 and 69, Roman legions and their commanders in Gaul, Germany, Judea, Syria, Egypt, the Balkans, and Italy had violated their oaths by turning on the emperor Nero and his three successors, creating four new emperors in turn. They fought major battles in Gaul, Germany, and Italy, sacked Cremona, and subjected the city of Rome to a reign of terror. On the Lower Rhine, the tribes were in active revolt against Roman rule after Vespasian became emperor and they had allies in Gaul. In earlier times, the Roman army built the empire using "the good fortune and good discipline of eight hundred years," as one general put it when facing down the rebels. In two years, the army had almost destroyed everything, and then Vespasian put the empire back together.

The new emperor's actions consisted of repression, reform, reorganization, and restraint. Vespasian sent a massive army under Petialis Cerealis, his former son-in-law (the widower of Vespasian's late daughter, Domitilla) that put down the revolt on the Rhine in the year 70. In Germany, which had seen heavy fighting, some legions were disbanded and new ones formed—with men and commanders trusted by Vespasian, and new traditions established with loyalty to him and his family in mind. Elsewhere, replacement soldiers were added as needed, and loyal veterans were discharged and settled on land. Likewise, various auxiliary corps were dissolved and replaced.

But the bigger story is what Vespasian didn't do. He didn't expand the size of the army. Its strength remained, as under Nero, around three hundred thousand men. Nor did Vespasian give the army a regular political role, although the army had made him emperor. He returned the legions to their camps and left political power in the hands of civilians in Rome: his friends, his family, and the Senate. In short, Vespasian kept Augustus's political system intact.

It is indicative of Vespasian's emphasis on military discipline that he reduced the donative (the regular gift to the soldiers) to 25 denarii per head. An anecdote is indicative. When the soldiers of the fleet, based in Italy, demanded that the emperor pay for the shoes for their courier duty between the Bay of Naples and Rome, Vespasian replied that, in the future, they should go barefoot. He made it clear that he, and not the soldiers, was in charge.

Vespasian moved some military units from the interior to the borders. Knowing the prestige accorded to extending the empire, he ordered his generals to conquer a bit more territory in Britain and along the Rhine. But a man whose theme was consolidation wouldn't be expected to make major changes in the size of the empire, and Vespasian didn't.

THE EMPEROR'S CONCUBINE

After his wife Flavia Domitilla's death at some point before Vespasian was named emperor in the year 69—we don't know just when she died—he renewed his affair with Caenis. She was at least sixty-two by the time he became emperor, so Caenis was no trophy wife. Presumably Vespasian chose her because he loved her. He now took her as his concubine—that is to say, his de facto or common-law wife because, as a member of the senatorial order, Vespasian could not marry a freedwoman like Caenis. Roman society was used to de facto marriage as a way of coping with various legal prohibitions and restrictions. But let us not underestimate how astonishing it was that the Roman emperor should live openly with a freedwoman— and a Greek—as if she were his wife.

In any case, Vespasian cherished Caenis and treated her as all but an empress. Ironically, the ex-slave whose bed he shared and who had served Antonia the Augusta (daughter of Mark Antony and mother of the emperor Claudius) was the closest he came to the glamor of the House of Caesar. Caenis felt so secure as a member of the family that once, when returning to Rome from a visit abroad, she offered her cheek to Vespasian's son Domitian to kiss. But, snob that he was, Domitian rebuffed her and gave his hand instead.

With Caenis's intelligence and knowledge of how Rome worked, it would be no surprise if she had advised Vespasian on his rise to imperial power. Once he became emperor, Caenis is said to have sold access and offices, including governorships, generalships, and priesthoods as well as pardons. She was, in short, a fixer. These stories can't be verified, but they have the ring of truth—as does the charge that some of the money she earned made its way to Vespasian. In any case, Caenis became a very wealthy woman.

The former slave herself owned slaves and eventually freed some of them, who then took her name. She had a villa and extensive grounds in the suburbs of Rome, with running water piped in—a rare luxury—and opulent baths. After her death, the estate passed to the emperor, and the Baths of Caenis were eventually opened to the public and maintained by one of the emperor's freedmen.

Caenis died around the year 75, at perhaps age sixty-eight. No one ever replaced her in Vespasian's affection. Instead, he occupied himself with a series of mistresses. Caenis's funerary monument, found near her villa, survives to this day. It's not unusual to come across the tombstone of a former Roman slave; in fact, freedmen put up most of the surviving funerary monuments of imperial Rome. Gravestones were status symbols, and who had a greater need than ex-slaves to proclaim, carved in stone, that they had made it? Caenis's monument did the job nicely.

It was an impressive altar-shaped tombstone; a common type of upscale grave monument, always featuring an inscription on the front and sometimes boasting decorations on the sides and back. Caenis's altar was heavy, massive, elaborate, and luxurious: a large piece carved of a single block of Cararra marble, the same material that would be used for Trajan's Column and the Pantheon and, during the Renaissance, for Michelangelo's *David*. The altar stands about four feet high, with a base a little over two feet by about three feet.

The epitaph, on the front, states that one Aglaus, probably the overseer of Caenis's estate, put up the monument in his name and that of his three children. He dedicated it to the memory of "Antonia Caenis, Freedwoman of the Augusta, the best of patrons." Although the epitaph

associates Caenis with one of Rome's most powerful women, it discreetly
says nothing of her role as Vespasian's concubine. But carved reliefs on
three sides of the altar contain reminders that an emperor loved her. They
include cupids and swans—the bird that pulled Venus's chariot—as well
as laurels, a symbol of the emperors. *Swan* was *cygnus* in Latin and *kuknos*
in Greek, so there may also be a pun on the name of Caenis (*Kainis* in
Greek).

Around the time of Caenis's death, Queen Berenice came to Rome,
accompanied by her brother, Julius Agrippa. He was appointed to a prae-
torship, while she moved into the palace with Titus. Whether Caenis had
opposed the presence of Titus's mistress, we have no idea. Yet it is remarkable that the two men who ruled Rome, father and son, each lived in succession in Rome with a common-law wife from the East. Each man took
a walk on the wild side, but the rough-hewn Vespasian slummed it while
the genteel Titus preferred the comfort of a royal bed. Together they were
a world apart from Augustus and Livia.

Titus and Berenice were in love. People said that she expected to
marry him—or even that he promised it—and she behaved as if she were
his wife. She certainly had influence. On one occasion, Vespasian invited
her to sit on the imperial council in a case involving her own interests,
with no less than the great Quintilian as her lawyer. Berenice, in short,
stood near the summit of power. The Roman people, however, wouldn't
have it. To some, she was another Cleopatra—an Eastern queen who
bewitched a Roman man—while to others, she represented the Jewish
enemy whose revolt cost Rome so much blood and treasure. Two philosophers denounced Titus and Berenice in the theater. Titus had one
flogged and the other beheaded. Yet he still had to send Berenice away.
The lovers would not rule Rome.

"METHINKS I'M BECOMING A GOD"

Vespasian followed a regular daily regimen in his last years. He awakened
before daylight and read correspondence and summaries while still in bed;

rose and greeted his friends while dressing and putting on his own shoes, dispensing with the "shoe man," a slave most emperors used; went riding; came home for a midday rest with one of his several mistresses; and then went for a bath and dinner. The freedmen living in the palace knew that the emperor was in his best mood during this last part of the day, so they waited until then to pounce with their requests.

In spring 79 Vespasian took ill while traveling south of Rome. He went to his usual summer place on a lake in the Sabine hills north of Rome, near his birthplace, hoping to recover. Its waters were said to have curative powers, but if so, in this case they failed. As the end drew near, Vespasian made two pungent remarks. "Methinks I'm becoming a god," he said, referring to the deification that a successful emperor could expect in Italy after his death. Then, at the end, stricken with a terrible bout of diarrhea, he struggled to get up, saying, "An emperor should die on his feet." And die he did, in the arms of those helping him. It was June 24, 79, and Vespasian was sixty-nine years old.

The funeral was held in Rome. There a leading actor got in one last joke about Vespasian's cheapness. At the funerals of Roman nobles, it was customary for someone to imitate the deceased, down to copying his gait and gestures, wearing his clothes and putting on a beeswax mask made during the dead person's lifetime. A star actor whose stage name was Favor performed this service during Vespasian's funeral. When he asked the officials how much the funeral cost, he pretended that the reply was the astronomical sum of ten million sesterces. So, still imitating Vespasian, he said, "Give me a hundred thousand and throw me into the Tiber!"

After a delay of six months—we don't know why—the Senate declared Vespasian a god. By the standards of the Romans, he deserved it. Not the most famous of Rome's emperors, Vespasian is easy to dismiss because of his rough facial features, his coarse sense of humor, and the modern meaning of his name: *vespasienne* in French and *vespasiano* in Italian mean "public urinal." Yet he was one of Rome's best emperors.

Of all the princes before him, Vespasian alone changed for the better after taking office, writes Tacitus. He ascended to power by means of rebellion, violence, and manipulation during Rome's most terrible year in a century. The legions and not the Senate made him emperor, and they chose him because of his prowess as a general. Yet this man of war brought peace to Rome. Vespasian was that rarest of things: a soldier-statesman.

Vespasian's achievement was nothing less than keeping the empire alive. He showed that there would still be Caesars even without the blood of the Caesars (or in the case of Tiberius, of Caesar's wife) running through their veins. If Vespasian did nothing else, that would have been achievement enough. But he racked up other accomplishments as well: in rebuilding the city, he gave Rome its most iconic monument and changed the culture of politics. He offered stability and sound finance after the go-go years under Nero and the curse of civil war. He created a new ruling class that would govern the empire for the next century. Vespasian opened Rome to new talent, not least in himself, the son of a tax collector from the Sabine country.

Once again Rome demonstrated the ability to remake itself. In his own modest way, Vespasian put into effect a revolution that emphasized continuity while bringing change as dramatic as the difference between Nero's Golden House and the Flavian Amphitheater that replaced it; or between the Lady Antonia the Augusta and her former slave, Caenis; or, for that matter, between the blue-blooded Nero and the Sabine muleteer Vespasian.

Vespasian's success illustrates Rome's flexibility, adaptability, and creativity. But it also demonstrates the empire's cruelty. His most famous building was a place for men to kill one another as entertainment for tens of thousands of spectators. He came to power through civil war after a bloody and ruinous year of four emperors. In addition to the death and destruction in that conflict, there were the casualties Vespasian caused in Britain and Judea (where he had Titus finish his work). According to Josephus,

1.1 million Jews died in the siege of Jerusalem, and 97,000 Jews were taken prisoner in the entire war with Rome. The first figure is a vast exaggeration, but the truth was probably appalling enough. The second figure is likely to be roughly accurate.

The Romans were destroyers as well as builders, and Vespasian and Titus engaged in one of history's most momentous acts of destruction by burning down the temple and sacking Jerusalem. It was an act of calculated terror aimed at ending Jewish political resistance. It was neither genocidal nor especially anti-Semitic. Jews dispersed outside Israel (in what is called the Diaspora), including Rome, were unharmed, except for the new tax. Jewish communal life continued in the Land of Israel outside Jerusalem. Vespasian personally allowed rabbis to turn the city of Yavneh (in what is today central Israel) into a theological and cultural center. It was there that the foundations were laid for what would become modern Judaism. Meanwhile, the destruction of the temple and Jerusalem tended to widen the gulf between Jewish Christians and Gentile Christians. After the year 70 the early Church moved further away from its Jewish roots.

Upon Vespasian's death, Titus became emperor. Perhaps because he knew his reputation as his father's hatchet man, Titus went on a charm offensive. He wooed the Senate by promising never to kill any senator, but he had to make an additional concession to public opinion. Titus had to send the much-hated Berenice, his queen, from Rome at once, "against his will and hers," according to Suetonius.

So Titus was lonely, but he was popular. Yet his rule was neither long nor easy. Italy suffered a series of major disasters during his reign: a fire in Rome, a plague, and the eruption of Mount Vesuvius in October 79, which destroyed the cities of Pompeii and Herculaneum. It was the worst volcanic eruption in Italy's recorded history. Titus cleverly turned these calamities to his political advantage by responding with kind words and material relief. He moved efficiently and rapidly to rebuild after the fire, and he provided financial aid to the stricken region around the volcano. He died on September 13, 81, after a brief illness, just short of forty-two.

Power now passed to Titus's younger brother, Domitian. He, too, was a Flavian, but, as we shall see, he quickly veered off the smooth trail that his father had blazed.

Bust of Trajan.

5

TRAJAN

THE BEST PRINCE

On the night of December 13, 115, an earthquake struck Antioch. At the time, located in Syria, Antioch was the third largest city in the Roman world, with an estimated population of about a half million people. Only Alexandria and Rome were bigger. The quake was felt all over the Near East and generated a tsunami that reached Judea, but the earthquake hit Antioch hardest of all. It began there with a bellowing roar. The ground shook, and trees and buildings went up in the air and came crashing down, raising an almost impenetrable cloud of dust. With an estimated magnitude of a ferocious 7.3 or 7.5, the quake destroyed much of the town and caused a loss of life made worse by the recent influx of soldiers and civilians. They thronged what had become in effect a temporary capital because the emperor was there. Imperator Caesar Nerva Traianus Divi Nervae filius Augustus, or, as we call him, Trajan, was wintering in Antioch between military campaigns.

The quake killed one of the consuls, who was also in Antioch. Trajan was luckier: he managed to escape from a damaged building by climbing out a window, suffering only minor injuries. He proceeded to live outdoors in the city's hippodrome for the next few days while the aftershocks continued to rumble. For a man who compared himself to Hercules and Jupiter, it was a humiliating turn of events. To soften the blow, Trajan let it be known that a being of superhuman stature had led him to safety. Still, it was a far cry from the official art that showed Jupiter lending his thunderbolt to Trajan as his divinely chosen deputy on earth.

Trajan thrived on drama as long as it put him on center stage. Despite all the devastation, an earthquake had elements that Trajan liked: violence, divine intervention, and the opportunity for him to display his benevolence, protection, and humanity to a suffering world and hence win more popularity among the people who loved him. He was, after all, the Father of the Fatherland—a title granted him by the Senate. Almost immediately, he put the process of rebuilding Antioch into effect. And Trajan was one of the greatest builders Rome would know.

The glimpse of Trajan climbing out of the rubble is a precious one for no ancient biography of him survives. Aside from brief references in ancient histories we have only oratory, architecture, and art—official opinion—and it closes around him like a legionary unit going into a tortoise formation and covering itself with its shields. These sources reveal little of the man. They show us Trajan as he wanted to be seen; and, like most emperors, he wanted the public to see the marble façade that he worked hard to erect and not the brick and concrete behind it.

The public did not object. In fact, the Senate and people rewarded him with the title of the Best Prince, sounding to modern ears almost as if he were in some kind of Academy Award competition with his predecessors. Later Roman tradition looked back on Trajan as one of Rome's greatest emperors. By the mid–third century, people welcomed each new emperor with the wish that he be "luckier than Augustus, better than Trajan."

Yet upon closer look, the real Trajan begins to emerge in all his talent and paradox. He was a much more cunning and complicated man than appears in the image of dull perfection that he put forth. Despite his claim of being the man in charge, he depended on the powerful women in his household as much as any emperor did.

He wasn't born to the imperial family, nor did he come to power during a civil war. He was an outsider who worked his way in, a shrewdly political general who knew how to survive in a tyranny, and a leader who quietly made himself indispensable. The story of Trajan's rise to power begins in the days of his predecessor, Domitian.

DOMITIAN

After Titus's short reign, his brother, Domitian, replaced him in the year 81. Titus had a seventeen-year-old daughter, Julia Flavia, but the Romans never considered the possibility of a ruling empress.

A talented and hardworking administrator, Domitian was arrogant. He put on the airs of a king and married a glamorous and imperious woman. The Senate, used to rugged Vespasian and charming Titus, took it hard. Domitian allegedly began one letter, issued in the name of his officials, with the statement "Our Master and Our God orders that this be done." Far from showing an interest in Senate meetings, he often conducted public business from his estate outside Rome. Senators were angry; informers stirred the pot; conspiracies arose and were put down forcefully. We know the names of fourteen senators who were executed, including twelve ex-consuls. Domitian also twice expelled philosophers from Rome, including many Stoics, a group whose philosophy many senators found congenial.

The Senate eventually got its revenge by poisoning Domitian's reputation in the history books. One of many hostile anecdotes has him sitting alone in his room every day for hours, catching flies and stabbing them with a stylus. Depending on the version of the story, it portrays the man as bored, cruel, obsessive, and tyrannical.

The irony is that Domitian offered good government in many ways. During his fifteen-year-rule, he showed himself to be a responsible financial steward, a fair-minded administrator of the provinces, and an able manager of border and defense policy. He gained popularity for his shows, banquets, and cancellation of debts. His gladiatorial games included such crowd-pleasers as night fights by torchlight and bouts between women gladiators.

He was a great builder, too, whose projects included a new hippodrome, the outline of which is still seen today in Rome's Piazza Navona. Domitian completed the Colosseum as well. Both benefited the public, but Domitian's grandest project was a monument to his own ego rivaling Nero's Golden House: an immense new palace on the Palatine Hill.

Tall and handsome when young, Domitian grew into a man with a fleshy face and a prominent nose like his father, as well as a wrinkled brow and a potbelly. Portrait busts give him a full head of curly hair, but, in fact, he was bald and sensitive about it. But he had a beautiful if highhanded wife.

She was Domitia, the daughter of Nero's talented but ill-starred general Gnaeus Domitius Corbulo. A smitten Domitian persuaded her to divorce her husband and marry him. She looks serenely lovely in a portrait bust, with a smooth-skinned face underneath a mountain of hair. She has tightly wound ringlets rising in a bouffant. But there were problems. Domitia bore Domitian two or three sons, but they all died very young. She had an affair with an actor, which caused Domitian to separate from her and to have the actor executed. Later, Domitian took her back, after his niece Julia Flavia had served as his companion. People gossiped that they were having an affair, especially after Domitian executed Julia's husband for treason. When Julia died a few years later, in 91, rumor said that it was a botched abortion and that Domitian was the father. He in turn calmly had her deified.

TRAJAN'S EARLY RISE

Trajan's father, Marcus Ulpius Traianus, who was born in Hispania, served Vespasian as a legionary commander. Afterward, Traianus rose very high in Roman public life. Traianus's wife—Trajan's mother—was probably a certain Marcia, possibly from a prominent Italian senatorial family. They had two children, Trajan and his sister, Ulpia Marciana. They lived in a rich agricultural region of Hispania known for its olives, but the life of a gentleman farmer interested neither father nor son. For them, it was Rome or nothing. And Rome was willing to give them a chance.

One of the strengths of the empire was its ability to co-opt the wealthy elite of the provinces. First it offered them citizenship, if they weren't Roman citizens already, as Trajan's family was. Then it gave them a seat in the Senate. Finally it made them emperor. Trajan was the first man from the provinces to become emperor.

He was born around the year 53. One of the few things we can surmise about Trajan's youth is that he admired his father. Years later, when emperor, Trajan deified his father, an exceptional honor. Trajan was about sixteen years old when Vespasian became emperor. By then, Trajan might well have lived in Rome because an ambitious father from the provinces would want his son to finish his education in the imperial city. Trajan was never much of a student, but he certainly knew how to network. Rome had a Spanish community, and Trajan need not have felt alone. One has to wonder if, beneath Trajan's proud exterior as a grownup, there remained a boy from the provinces who wanted to show the Romans that he could outdo them both at home and abroad.

Trajan served as a colonel (military tribune) for several years, including a period under his father in Syria around the year 75 and then some time on the Rhine. He did a longer stint than usual as colonel, and, if we can trust an obsequious source, he threw himself into his work. It was probably not long after this that Trajan took a wife, since elite Roman men usually married in their early twenties. His father probably arranged the alliance with Pompeia Plotina.

Like Trajan, Plotina came from a provincial family. Her home was in southern Gaul, in the city of Nemausus (Nîmes). No details survive about her family but it was no doubt wealthy and prominent because Trajan would not have settled for less. We don't know when Plotina was born, but, since wives in the Roman elite were typically about ten years younger than their husbands, we might estimate her birth year as 65. A shrewd, capable, educated woman, Plotina would play a major role as her husband's supporter. Some said she was his manipulator.

In 89 Trajan had command of a legion in the sleepy backwater of northern Hispania when a rebellion broke out against Emperor Domitian on the German frontier. It was Trajan's big chance. He marched rapidly to Germany in Domitian's defense. Although the revolt failed before Trajan got there, he impressed the emperor with his efficiency. As a reward, he received an ordinary consulship and probably the governorship of Upper Germania and a senior command on the Danube front, where he won a victory.

The emperor got on well with soldiers like Trajan. At home, among civilians, he flaunted his power and baited his enemies. After Domitian executed his cousin in 95, a man whose sons he had adopted as heirs, nobody felt safe anymore. Although not known for his wit, Domitian got off a few bon mots, including the observation that no one believes in a conspiracy against an emperor until it has succeeded.

In his case, one finally did. On September 19, 96, a small group of conspirators stabbed Domitian to death in his bedroom. The two Praetorian prefects were aware of the plot. His old childhood nurse cremated Domitian's body, and his ashes were buried in secret in the Temple of the Flavians in Rome. The Senate condemned his memory, and therefore most statues of him were destroyed, and his name was erased from inscriptions—but not from Domitia's memory. She survived her husband by about thirty-five years, living in great wealth, and referred to herself proudly as Domitian's wife. That casts doubt on the rumor that she helped the men who killed him—unless, of course, she had a change of heart later.

NERVA

The Senate moved quickly to name one of its own as Domitian's successor. Marcus Cocceius Nerva was an experienced politician from an old and distinguished family. Twice consul, he was a courtier and a survivor who got along with Nero, Vespasian, and Domitian. He seemed like a safe pair of hands.

Nerva pleased the Senate by releasing prisoners, making amends for past treason trials, and ruling out future ones. He appealed to the people through grain and land distribution and by carrying out various other welfare programs. According to the historian Tacitus, Nerva managed to combine what had seemed incompatible: liberty and imperial power.

But the army had liked Domitian and was not impressed. One army nearly mutinied upon his death, and another was in the hands of an unreliable provincial governor. In the year 97 the Praetorian Guard decided the time was right for revenge on Domitian's assassins. Mutinying, they besieged Nerva in his palace and forced him against his will to give up the culprits, whom they executed, torturing one of them first. Then they forced Nerva to thank them in public.

Realizing his weakness, Nerva conferred with his council of advisors and decided not to abdicate. Instead, he chose a successor. He was in his sixties, widowed and childless, so he turned to an outsider. Having made his decision, he went to the speaker's platform in the Roman Forum and proclaimed in a loud voice, "May good success attend the Roman Senate and people and myself. I hereby adopt Marcus Ulpius Nerva Trajan."

The most likely other candidate belonged to a faction opposed to Nerva. Trajan was politically friendly and the son of a famous father with an impressive personal record to boot. Last but not least, he had a number of legions ready to march on Rome at his command, so choosing him protected the peace.

Nerva's choice was an exercise in Roman pragmatism. Without any fuss or bother, he broke two barriers. For the first time, an emperor adopted a son who was related to him neither by blood nor by marriage. And, for the first time, he nominated a successor from outside Italy.

But in a deeper sense, Trajan represented continuity because the army was the real driver of change. As usual, the army was the most egalitarian and innovative force in Roman society.

Nerva sent Trajan a diamond ring as a sign of his adoption, along with a letter that asked, in an elegant and roundabout way, for revenge on the Praetorians who had humiliated him. He also gave Trajan the titles of Caesar and Imperator, marking him as his chosen successor. Meanwhile, Nerva

ensured Trajan's constitutional position as his successor by calling together
the Senate to endow him with both power and authority.

Nerva died within three or four months, in January 98, and Trajan became emperor. He quickly avenged his predecessor by executing the leaders
of the Praetorians' revolt against him. Never mind that the revolt had led
to Trajan's elevation: emperorship was family, and when it came to family,
honor was everything. And so Trajan avenged his adoptive father. He had
Nerva deified as well and buried in the mausoleum of Augustus, making
him the last emperor to enjoy that honor.

TRAJAN SHOWS HOW TO BE AN EMPEROR

Domitian pleased the army but not the Senate. Nerva pleased the Senate
but not the army. Trajan showed from the very start that he was the man to
gratify both, while also making the people happy. He garnered impressively
widespread support.

Trajan stayed in the north until late 99, building up the army's strength
on the Rhine and Danube frontiers against the Germanic tribes. When
he finally entered Rome, he did so with a shrewd show of public relations.
Instead of riding on a litter or chariot, he walked. He greeted the assembled
senators and knights warmly and sacrificed to Jupiter on the Capitoline
before finally going up to the imperial residence on the Palatine Hill.

Plotina captured the spirit of the new regime when she first entered the
palace. Turning to face the crowd, she said, "I enter here as the same kind of
woman as I would like to be when I depart." She could hardly have struck
a more different tone from the haughty Domitia.

In his forties when he became emperor, Trajan was in the prime of life,
strong physically and mentally, and full of energy and plans. His portrait
busts, of which many survive, have the determined look of an aging ath-
lete. His hair is arranged carefully in a style reminiscent of Augustus. His
features are regular and could be called classical except for thin, tightly
pressed lips. A modern detractor said that Trajan looked stupid and was
believed to be honest. Some of the statues do have dull expressions, yet the

man depicted in Trajan's coin portraits appears no less shrewd than other emperors.

Trajan's mission was clear. He had to demonstrate that he was worthy of power, with the good qualities of Augustus and Vespasian and none of the bad qualities of Nero or Domitian. He would show that he was a statesman, a conqueror, a benefactor, and a builder, favored by the gods, and endowed with a model and obedient family. He had no intention of surrendering a drop of Domitian's power but planned to rule with a smooth tongue and an open hand. Trajan was no republican. "Everything is under the authority of one man" is how one contemporary described Trajan's rule.

Perhaps the word that best sums up Trajan's rule is *paternalistic*. He was not the first emperor to accept the title of Father of the Fatherland (*pater patriae*) from the Senate, but, more than most, he tried to be as benevolent as he was severe.

Although a military man, Trajan had the qualities of a good politician. He was affable, even-tempered, and untroubled by personal attacks. He never forgot that he had three constituencies to please—the Senate, the people, and the army—and he delivered to each of them.

Senate. When he became emperor, Trajan sent the Senate a handwritten letter promising not to execute or disenfranchise any good man, and he followed up with oaths then and later. He was as good as his word in this and executed no senators. He also kept his hands off their money. He treated the Senate with respect and dignity. Behind the scenes, Trajan concentrated power in his hands but he did so with tact and a light touch. A flattering speech claims that unlike the tyrant Domitian, Trajan respected a Roman's freedom to speak freely; even to criticize him. This is no doubt an exaggeration, but Trajan surely relaxed the mood. He banished professional informers, the terror of the elite in Domitian's last years.

For all his pretension to divinity, Trajan could be warm and approachable. He had a habit of taking three others into his carriage and even of entering citizens' houses without a guard and enjoying himself. When friends accused him of being too accessible, he said that he behaved toward private citizens the way he had wanted emperors to behave toward him. Trajan enjoyed playing the role of host. We hear, for example, of how he invited his imperial council to his country villa north of Rome for a series of working sessions and entertained them every evening. A senator describes being charmed by the relative informality and simplicity of the dinner parties, by the recitations or conversation, and by the beauty of the place.

People. That pales in importance compared with the "hospitality" that Trajan offered to the poor of Italy. Trajan expanded a system begun by Nerva that offered subsidies to poor children in Italian towns; probably several hundred thousand boys and girls. The arrangement was complicated and limited, but it offered significant help. It also highlighted Italy's privileged status in the empire, since the benefit did not extend to the provinces. Other welfare measures included extending the distribution of grain and making generous cash disbursements from war booty. Trajan also remitted taxes after he filled the Treasury with loot acquired from foreign conquest.

Trajan lavished resources on games and races. As one ancient writer observed, Trajan knew that the Roman people were interested in only two things: "grain and spectacles." It wasn't far from a poet's complaint about "bread and circuses" or an orator's observation that people wanted only "plenty of bread and a seat at the chariot races."

Army. Trajan had a passion for soldiering. He loved the military life, or what one contemporary called "the camps, bugles, and trumpets, sweat and dust and heat of the sun." Trajan was styled a military man of the old school but wiser and kinder.

Trajan cared deeply about the troops, whom he referred to as "my excellent and most loyal fellow soldiers." He ordered special rules to make it easier for soldiers to make wills, and he founded veterans' colonies on the Rhine and Danube frontiers and in North Africa. He campaigned in person and paid special attention to the soldiers. Trajan ate in the military mess. He shared his men's hardships, marching on foot and fording rivers with the rank and file. When bandages gave out during one of his battles, he is said to have had his own clothing cut into strips to serve. He honored his fallen soldiers with an altar and an annual ceremony.

Like Augustus, Trajan had a gift for friendship. He was closest to Licinius Sura, who was his Agrippa. Like Trajan, Sura came from Hispania. A leading statesman and military commander under Domitian, Sura had supported Trajan's rise to the throne. Afterward, Sura was rewarded with high office and a position by Trajan's side in wartime. Sura used his wealth to serve as a patron of the arts and to build a public gymnasium in Rome. Apparently, he did nothing to hide his close friendship with the emperor, which incited jealousy and slander.

As a show of support for Sura, Trajan went to his friend's house uninvited and without a bodyguard. He let Sura's physician apply ointment to his eyes and allowed Sura's barber to shave him, followed by a bath and dinner. The next day, Trajan told his jealous courtiers, "If Sura had desired to kill me, he would have killed me yesterday." After Sura died circa 108, Trajan gave him outsized honors: a state funeral, a statue, and public baths in Sura's name.

The new emperor was no intellectual, but he did not lack intelligence. Two of his passions were wine and boys, but he held his liquor, and he did not force himself on any lover. We hear of affairs with various imperial page boys, with an actor and a dancer, and even, according to gossip, with Nerva and Sura. Two of his other passions were vanity and war, and in these he was not as moderate.

TRAJAN'S IMPERIAL WOMEN

Trajan presented his family as the First Family, Roman style. Like Vespasian and Nerva, he came to the throne without any blood tie to a previous emperor. So he had to work harder to seem legitimate. One way was to show his family as a return to the pristine Roman ideal of simplicity and obedience. Sure, the Flavians talked about restoring family values after Nero's bacchanalia, but they brought Caenis, Berenice, and Domitia. Nerva was a widower. Finally, with Trajan, Rome would see virtue restored to the imperial house.

When he ascended to the throne in the year 98 Trajan was childless, but he had a large family nonetheless. Although he appeared to embody Roman masculinity, his palace was a feminine place; he shared it with his wife, Pompeia Plotina, his widowed sister, Ulpia Marciana, and her widowed daughter, Salonia Matidia, and Salonia Matidia's daughters, Mindia Matidia and Vibia Sabina. He wanted the world to see them as virtuous, helpful, and obedient. Imperial propagandists did the job.

Official art portrayed Trajan's women as regal and austere. They all have styled but never luxuriant hair; they all have downturned mouths and steady gazes. Plotina's portrait busts show a calm, noble, and impeccably coiffed woman. Marciana is rigid and commanding. Her hair is carefully braided in a tight coil. She lacks the bravura, the riot of curls in portraits of Flavian women such as Domitia. Coin portraits are similarly restrained. Domesticity is a theme. Plotina appears with symbols of house and home and of Chastity—the latter a goddess to whom she had an altar erected. Marciana is seen with her daughter and two granddaughters. The several busts of Salonia Matidia depict a stately and imperturbable-looking woman with an aquiline nose and probing eyes. Her long and almost masculine-looking face bears a resemblance to her uncle Trajan, which might have been the artist's intention.

Official discourse is even more tightly wound. In 100 a newly appointed consul named Gaius Plinius Caecilius Secundus, known as Pliny the Younger, delivered a speech in praise of Trajan to the Senate and later published it. The *Panegyricus*, as it is called, lavishes praise, and Pliny's successful career afterward shows that Trajan approved. In addition to serving on Trajan's council and being elected one of the augurs, who were religious officials, Pliny was appointed governor of the important province of Bithynia and Pontus (northwestern Turkey).

In his speech, Pliny specifically mentions the women in Trajan's family. He points out that many distinguished men have been embarrassed by a poor choice of wife or by weakness in not divorcing one, because people believe that a bad husband cannot be a good citizen. But Trajan's wife is a model of chastity and Rome's ancient virtues. Plotina is modest, moderate, and devoted to her husband. Like Trajan, she prefers silence to having a fuss made over her, and she follows his example of walking on foot "as much as her gender allows." Above all, she is content to seek no greater glory than her obedience. It is all a tribute, says Pliny, to the way Trajan had trained Plotina.

Pliny also praises Marciana for being a good sister and behaving with the same candor and simplicity as Trajan. While noting cattily that rivalry can arise between women in close proximity, he praises the two imperial ladies for getting along without rancor or disagreement. He also applauds their modesty for refusing the title of Augusta that the Senate had wished to award them. Declining the title was another way of striking a difference with Domitia and the previous regime.

Official art creates a similar scene of harmony between the two imperial sisters-in-law. For instance, the names of Marciana and Plotina are inscribed on an arch erected at the new harbor built by Trajan in the Italian port city of Ancona, and statues of the two might have once decorated the top, alongside the emperor. Reality, of course, was probably messier.

We should not believe for a minute that either Plotina, Marciana, or Matidia was as obedient and retiring as Pliny or imperial art suggests. Just as Augustus's *Res Gestae* falsely portrayed his regime as a men's club, so did Trajan's official art and literature undervalue imperial women. Each of them was a wealthy property owner with numerous slaves and freedmen. Plotina's property was probably the most important, including an estate in central Italy with a flourishing brickyard—run by a woman, no less! Her freedmen included officials in the imperial bureaucracy.

In addition to having financial resources of their own, Trajan's imperial women had prestige. Each of them eventually did take the title of Augusta: Plotina and Marciana in 105, Matidia in 112. It strains credulity to believe that they never exercised power or influence, and, indeed, the sources show that they did. Plotina was an educated person with an interest in literature, philosophy, and perhaps also music and math. Ambitious writers were eager to have her read their work; a student of music and math seems to have dedicated a book to her, and she took a personal interest in a philosophical school in Athens.

Certain ancient sources claim that Plotina intervened in politics. Although some scholars reject this as gossip, she did nothing that other emperors' wives hadn't done before. Thus Plotina lobbied senators and Trajan himself on behalf of the Jewish community of Alexandria in its quarrel with the Greek community there. She traveled with Trajan on important missions abroad, including during wartime—although naturally she stayed far from the front. Plotina upbraided Trajan about corrupt administrators who were extorting money from their provinces by making false accusations. She warned him that they were hurting his reputation, so the emperor stopped their abuses and returned the money they had taken. Afterward, Trajan called the Treasury the spleen because when it was enlarged, it got in the way of other organs. Most important, as we shall see, Plotina played a big role in choosing her husband's successor.

We might imagine a reference to Plotina's active role in the work of a Greek politician and orator of the day. Dio Chrysostom (born circa 40; died sometime after 115) wrote a series of speeches, titled collectively *On Kingship*, and he may have delivered the third one before Trajan in 104. The two men enjoyed a warm relationship, at least according to one story about the brainy Greek and the blunt Emperor, in which Trajan supposedly told Dio, "I have no idea what you are talking about, but I love you as myself." In one of his speeches in *On Kingship*, the smooth-talking Dio says that a good king regards his wife "not merely as the partner of his bed and affections, but also as his helpmate in his counsel and action, and indeed in his whole life." If this refers to Plotina, Dio gives her a much greater role than

Pliny does. In any case, Dio offers a counterpoint to Pliny's notion of the silent and obedient wife.

Later generations looked back fondly on Plotina. Even an ancient writer who is sometimes critical of Plotina considers her behavior throughout Trajan's reign to have been above reproach.

When his sister, Marciana, died in 112, Trajan asked the Senate to deify her, and it agreed. No emperor's sister had ever received such an honor before. It was another way of legitimizing Trajan's rule while also potentially widening the base of his support. It allowed him to reach out to the women of the empire, as the tombstone of one wealthy Italian lady shows.

Her elaborate, altar-shaped tombstone once stood in an Italian hill town two hundred miles north of Rome. Cetrania Severina, who lived in Sarsina in the second century, was a priestess of the cult of the deified Marciana. In her day, Roman women could not vote or hold political office, but they could be priests—and by serving in a leadership role in the imperial cult, Cetrania reached one of the highest of priesthoods. Her husband, who survived her and put up the monument, refers to her as a "woman of the highest moral integrity," using the same word, *sanctissima* ("most morally pure"), that Pliny uses in a letter to describe Plotina. It looks like a case of a local trying to show that he had made it by imitating the elite.

Cetrania lived in a period in which a woman could control her property, and, like Plotina, the priestess had extensive holdings. It was enough for Cetrania to set up a foundation, and a detailed inscription on the stone records the terms. In exchange for a hefty annual gift of olive oil on her birthday, the town's major craft guilds would carry out yearly rites in her memory. Cetrania appealed to the good faith, or *fides*, in Latin, of the guildsmen to uphold their end of the bargain. That same word also sums up the ties of loyalty that bound elites together around the empire. By honoring the memory of the emperor Trajan's sister, a prominent local woman showed that her town kept faith with Rome. She also demonstrated the important role a woman could play in holding together the empire.

THE MAN WHO WOULD BE HERCULES

When it came to his public image, Trajan was not subtle. He presented himself as almost a demigod; the representative of the gods on earth. He claimed to have a divine mission to bring victory, virtue, and benevolence to the Roman world. Arrogant as this sounds, it was an improvement upon Domitian's claim to be lord and master. Trajan, in fact, embraced the role that the philosophers urged in vain on earlier emperors: to be a moderate king. Unlike Domitian or Vespasian, he did not expel philosophers from Rome. Instead, Trajan, and Nerva, too, before him, made friends with them.

Trajan's two divine points of reference were Hercules, the greatest ancient hero, and Jupiter, the king of the gods and the father of the human race. Unlike Domitian, who was devoted to the goddess Minerva, Trajan gave her little attention. That allowed him to mark his difference from his predecessor and to brand himself as a man's man.

Hercules sometimes appears as a rogue or bully in ancient myth, but more often he is a symbol of virtue: a virile and courageous person who labors selflessly and fearlessly for the common good. This was how many ancient philosophers saw him. The Romans, too, warmed to this image, and none more so than Trajan. According to Roman mythology, Hercules came to Rome on his way back to Greece from Hispania, where he had completed his tenth labor on an island off the coast. As a native of Hispania and a soldier, Trajan took to the comparison. Hercules was popular in Trajan's hometown, and he often had the demigod depicted on his coins. A new legion, the Second Trajan, took Hercules as its symbol. Pliny says that, like Hercules, Trajan was called from Hispania to do dauntless labors for a lesser man who was king—in Trajan's case, Domitian. And he compares Trajan's hardy body to that of a son of a god.

Jupiter was the king of the gods for the Romans; they called him the Best and Greatest (*optimus maximus*). Trajan adopted a similar status, as literature and art both show.

In *Panegyricus* in 100, Pliny praises the emperor for dispensing justice with calm reason, like a god. Then he compares Trajan to Jupiter. The father of the world no longer has to trouble himself with affairs on earth because he gave Trajan the power to stand in for him in regard to the whole human race. A sculpted relief on the Arch of Trajan in central Italy has much the same message. It depicts Jupiter giving his thunderbolt to Trajan, as if to say that he ruled the empire by divine authority and with all-but Olympian power. Meanwhile, Trajan's coins recognized him as "the Best Prince" (*optimus princeps*).

Although Trajan didn't accept the title of Optimus at first, he did so in time. Jupiter and Hercules were his two reference points in his self-presentation. So was a third symbol of power, Alexander the Great. The famous conqueror traced his ancestry to Hercules and claimed that his father was no less than Jupiter himself. Trajan compared himself to Alexander and said that he aimed to emulate his conquests. It's hard to say whether Trajan was serious about the comparison or whether he aimed merely at flattering Greeks by referring to their famous ancestor.

TRAJAN AND THE CHRISTIANS

Pliny served as governor of the rich and populous province of Bithynia and Pontus in Asia Minor from 110 to 113. Later, he published his correspondence with Trajan from this period. The letters show how decentralized Roman government was, with much leeway given to provincial governors. Sometimes, however, the emperor had to step in. Consider a famous exchange between Pliny and Trajan on the treatment of Christians.

Pliny's letter shows the extent of Christianity's spread in the Greek East. He wrote that he was faced, for the first time in his career, with a large Christian minority, urban and rural, young and old, male and female, free and slave. After receiving a series of denunciations, some anonymous, he was forced to investigate. The Roman public, overwhelmingly pagan and long suspicious of Christians as criminals, was riled up, and Pliny's job as governor was to calm them down. But just what was he supposed to do? The government in Rome considered Christians suspect, but it had no general policy toward them. It left the matter up to local initiative.

From the Roman point of view, Christians were dangerous in many ways. The Romans considered their own religion—time honored, state sponsored, and carried out in public—to be the very foundation of their civilization. By participating in festivals and sacrifices, every person helped earn Rome security and prosperity. Christians broke the rules. They didn't worship the gods, and they didn't offer sacrifices for the emperor, which made them atheists in Roman eyes. A man who wasn't god-fearing was not just a potential lawbreaker but also a threat to the very fabric of society; someone who might anger the gods against the whole community.

But one could also consider Christians *too* religious—guilty of unreasonable and excessive fear of the gods, which the Romans considered to be superstition. Jews were similarly considered atheists, but the Romans tolerated them because of the antiquity of Judaism. Christianity was relatively new, and Rome was suspicious of novelty. The Latin term for revolution was "new things" (*res novae*).

Then too, Christians gathered in private associations, and Roman history taught that where there was association, there was sedition. Indeed, following Trajan's instructions, Pliny had banned religious fraternities in his province.

All that was true, and yet it was equally true that Christians generally kept the peace and minded their own business. So Pliny trod cautiously. He explained that he interrogated accused Christians at least three times. If they proved their innocence by denouncing Christ and worshipping a statue of the emperor with prayer, incense, and wine, he let them go. If they refused, he executed them. As he explained, Christian or not, they deserved to be punished for stubbornness and arrogance.

Class and status mattered, as the letter shows. If stubborn Christians were Roman citizens, Pliny did not execute them. Instead, he signed an order to have them transferred to Rome, since, as citizens, they had a right to a trial there. Slaves, of course, stood at the other end of the social scale.

Pliny explained that, in order to find out what was really happening at Christian meetings, he tortured two female slaves "who were called deaconesses." He didn't believe what Christians said in their defense: that they merely sang hymns, swore oaths to be honest and true and not to commit theft or adultery, and then shared a meal. He expected to discover a conspiracy to commit crime but instead found merely "depraved and immoderate superstition." Of course, Pliny was wrong. The sweetness, sociability, and support of Christian rituals contributed mightily to the new religion's success.

Pliny wrote to the emperor, as he did for anything about which he was in doubt. Had he behaved properly in regard to the Christians? In his response, Trajan praised Pliny for behaving just as he should have. The emperor called for a defensive policy rather than an aggressive one. Christians should not be sought out, but those who were accused should be tested one by one. Every case was different; there was no fixed standard. Even those who were proven guilty should be given a chance to repent "by worshipping our gods" and thereby earn a pardon. Finally, charges had to be signed. There was no place for anonymously posted accusations. They were a bad precedent and "not in the spirit of our era."

By our standards, the Romans under Pliny and Trajan were persecutors. However, by Roman norms, they were tough but humane. Trajan mapped out a middle ground for the future treatment of Christians. Unwittingly, he gave Christianity freedom to grow.

THE CONQUEST OF DACIA

Trajan spent almost half his reign away from Rome on campaign. Considering his love of war, he surely didn't complain. His great success came in Dacia, roughly, modern Romania.

Throughout its history, Rome always looked with worry at the rise of potential threats. Dacia, ruled by a determined and warlike king, had forced Domitian into a compromise. The sources refer to King Decebalus as a shrewd warrior, expert both in ambushes and pitched battle, a master of timing, and an astute manager of victory as well as defeat. Decebalus was defiant, rich, and in the process of building up a network of anti-Roman allies. In doing so, he was violating his agreement with Domitian. Trajan, for his part, was a warrior. He decided to attack.

The Romans invaded Dacia in 101, with Trajan in the lead. It was a major expedition involving perhaps a third of the Roman army. The war required hard fighting, major engineering feats, and prodigies of communications and diplomacy. A year later, after the Romans had destroyed Dacian villages and defeated the enemy in battle, Decebalus agreed to make peace. Hoping to manage the situation, Trajan let him keep his throne. The emperor returned to Rome, celebrated a triumph, and received the title Dacicus.

The joy was premature, though, as King Decebalus was soon on the rise again. So Trajan invaded Dacia again in 105, this time raising two new legions. Hard mountain fighting preceded the conquest of Decebalus's capital. The king fled and, facing capture, committed suicide. His head was brought to Trajan, who in turn had it displayed to the army and sent it to Rome, where it was thrown down the side of the Capitoline Hill.

Although Trajan tactfully sent regular reports from the field to the Senate, just as a republican-era general would have done, he saw the yearlong war as a grand and glorious achievement on his part. Few details survive in the sources, but one writer summarizes the war thus: "In the course of the campaign, he himself performed many deeds of good generalship and bravery, and his troops ran many risks and displayed great prowess on his behalf."

A sculpted relief shows the emperor as he might have liked to see himself, on horseback in the midst of battle. He is wearing full armor, his cape billowing in the wind as he rides boldly into the enemy, who are fighting on foot. In real life, Trajan's guards would have protected him, but the image of splendid combat is how the war was remembered.

Whereas Domitian had to accept a compromise in Dacia, Trajan conquered it, annihilated its ruling class, and opened the country to colonization by Roman veterans. The destruction of the Dacian elite was so complete that although Dacia remained a Roman province for only two hundred years, Romanians today speak a language derived from Latin.

Dacia was a rich country, and the war proved immensely profitable to Rome. Trajan found Decebalus's hidden treasure: an estimated 360,000 pounds of gold and 730,000 pounds of silver. It was one of antiquity's largest treasures, and there was more to come, since the country also had gold mines for Rome to exploit.

Trajan wrote *Dacica*, an account of the Dacian wars. Only one sentence survives, and it is as terse as Caesar: "From Berzobim, we then proceeded to Azi." But the sentence lacks Caesar's egotism. While Caesar refers to himself in his writings as "he," Trajan uses "we," showing fellowship with his fellow soldiers. Always a lavish impresario, Caesar might have approved of the victory games for Dacia that Trajan put on in Rome. They lasted 123 days, during which ten thousand gladiators fought and eleven thousand animals, both wild and tame, were slaughtered.

Trajan resembled Caesar in another way as well, being the greatest conqueror to rule Rome since the days of the dictator. Neither Augustus, who conquered Egypt, nor Claudius, who conquered Britain, was a warrior. Tiberius and Vespasian were great soldiers, but only before they became emperor. For all the talk of expanding the empire, most emperors found it exorbitant and destabilizing. Trajan was the exception.

Unlike Caesar, fortunately, Trajan knew how to moderate his arrogance and to mollify the Senate. He won additional favor by spending the treasure he had conquered on behalf of the Roman people.

THE BUILDER

Trajan was a great builder—by some measures, the greatest of all the emperors. A later emperor called him "a creeper that grows on walls" because his name was inscribed on so many buildings. This was partly a dig at Trajan for taking credit for projects begun by his predecessors—a fair criticism but outweighed by the emperor's new works. He sponsored such engineering feats as a great bridge across the Danube (in what is today Romania) to attack Dacia, with a wooden roadway supported by twenty masonry piers. He reduced travel time on the Appian Way by building a shorter route in southern Italy, known as Trajan's Way. He built new ports for several Italian cities, including Rome. His most famous projects were in the capital itself: Trajan's Column, at ninety-eight feet high a skyscraping tower for its day, with an innovative spiral relief illustrating Trajan's conquest of Dacia; the Baths of Trajan, the first of the great imperial baths and the model for those that followed; Trajan's Forum, including a basilica, the largest and most ambitious of the imperial forums. War spoils from Dacia financed the new forum, thereby giving Trajan bragging rights.

Like Augustus, Trajan increased the amount of marble in Rome, in pavements and columns, for example. But by Trajan's day, brick was the most important material in Roman construction, followed by concrete. Construction was big business, making a few people rich and employing from 4 percent to 6 percent of the total population of Rome in the boom years of the first two centuries AD.

When it came to construction, Trajan's greatest collaborator was Apollodorus of Damascus. As his name and birthplace indicate, he was Greek. Apollodorus was primarily a military engineer. He built the bridge over the Danube and wrote a book on how to conduct a siege. He is most famous, though, for Trajan's Forum. He might possibly also have been the architect of Trajan's Baths.

Trajan's Forum dropped the usual temple-in-a-square arrangement for an almost square plan, perhaps recalling a military camp. It marked an unusual combination of a large Greek-style open square with a Roman roofed public building, or basilica. Elements of Near Eastern architecture can be found here, too. The variety in design symbolized the immense size of the empire, as did the presence of diverse, colored marble and granite columns from East and West. So did the scale of the project: for example, the open square alone was about twice the size of an American football field, and, in a sign of luxury, it was paved in white marble. Statues of captive Dacians lined the roofs, making the forum a kind of victory monument. They were useful as symbols of Trajan's success, Rome's power, and the ever-present threat of foreign foes; better to have people think about that than about any problems at home. There were three arches and two libraries flanking Trajan's Column. At the northern end of the forum stood an imposing temple.

Trajan's building projects were about as subtle as Hercules clubbing a mountain in two as myth said he did to create the Strait of Gibraltar, known to the ancients as the Pillars of Hercules. Trajan's engineers sliced off part of a mountain in order to bring a road near Rome closer to the sea. Meanwhile, they demolished part of the Quirinal Hill in order to build Trajan's Forum, and then they had to erect a new, multitiered structure (today's Trajan's Markets, a complex of shops and offices) to support the remaining hillside. To build his baths, Trajan filled in the only remaining part of Nero's Golden House, a wing on the Esquiline Hill, and sank foundation walls into the once-magnificent halls. It was wasteful but eloquent in its message. Not only was Trajan rich enough to bury a perfectly good building but also selfless enough to deny himself a magnificent palace and devote the space to the Roman people instead.

Trajan's projects advertised him. They all bore his name, including the new aqueduct to meet Rome's increased water needs caused by his baths: the Aqua Traiana, or Trajan's Aqueduct. Romans entered his forum through a monumental gateway that was probably topped with a statue of Trajan in a six-horse chariot. Inside the forum stood a statue of Trajan on horseback, and other statues of him appeared in every corner of the complex. Meanwhile, Trajan's Column told the story of the conquest of Dacia via a sculpted frieze in 155 scenes. It wound its way up the shaft like some giant scroll. Trajan himself appears more than sixty times in the column's scenes. But nothing promoted Trajan as baldly as the imposing temple that rose at the end of the complex. In all likelihood, Trajan declined to name the building as it went up because the Romans would not tolerate a living emperor erecting a temple to his own divinity. Yet that was just what he was doing. It would be dedicated after his death as the Temple of the Deified

Trajan, with a colossal statue inside of seated Trajan as Olympian Zeus or Jupiter. The entire forum was a gigantic propaganda project to Rome's power and the emperor's glory.

NEMESIS IN THE EAST

Around the same time as it was conquering Dacia, Rome annexed what it called Arabia (roughly, modern Jordan, the Sinai Peninsula and the northwestern Arabian Peninsula). With the addition of these two new provinces, the Roman Empire reached its maximum geographical expansion. But Trajan wanted more.

Perhaps because he wanted to equal Alexander, who conquered Iran, or perhaps because he wanted to outdo Caesar and Mark Antony, who failed to do so, or perhaps simply because he saw no greater rival state on the horizon, Trajan made war on Parthia. The pretext was a disagreement over Armenia, long a buffer state between the two empires. Rome claimed a veto power over Armenia, but the Parthians had chosen Armenia's most recent king. Yet when the Parthians backed off, Trajan refused to take yes for an answer. He wanted his war because he wanted glory.

Trajan set off on a major expedition to the East. Plotina and Matidia traveled with him as far as Antioch in 114. Trajan and the army proceeded to take control of Armenia and then conquered all of Mesopotamia (roughly, Iraq) up to the Persian Gulf. The Parthians were distracted by civil strife. In some ways, the hardest opposition that Trajan faced was the December 115 earthquake in Antioch with which this chapter began. The Romans declared Armenia and Mesopotamia to be new provinces.

When he reached the Persian Gulf, Trajan looked eastward wistfully toward India and Alexander's farthest conquests. He was forced to admit that he was too old to emulate his hero. He said: "I should certainly have crossed over to the Indi, too, if I were still young." Nevertheless, he wrote the Senate that he had advanced farther than Alexander. They in turn declared him Parthicus and said that he could celebrate a triumph for as many nations as he pleased, since he had written to them about more triumphs than they could follow.

The Parthians regrouped, however. They stirred up rebellion in Mesopotamia and attacked Roman supply lines as far north as Armenia. At the same time, Jewish communities rose in revolt in the Eastern provinces outside of Judea and in Mesopotamia. It was a major rebellion, the product of discontent over bigotry and taxation, as well as support for Parthia, and Trajan had to send troops and seasoned commanders to suppress it. Trajan managed to reestablish control in Mesopotamia and started home. Roman rule in the East was fragile, though.

On the way back north, the emperor aimed for one last victory by trying to take the wealthy caravan city of Hatra (in northern Iraq) by assault. Trajan himself took part in the cavalry attack, with nearly fatal results, as one report states. Although he had taken off his purple cloak to escape recognition, "the enemy, seeing his majestic gray head and his august countenance, suspected his identity, shot at him, and killed a cavalryman in his escort." It was a major effort for a man over the age of sixty, and it shows how much the emperor loved battle.

It proved impossible for Rome to hold its new territories. By the time Trajan returned to Antioch in 117, he had effectively lost all his Eastern conquests. Parthia had reestablished control. For Rome, the war proved bloody, expensive, and fruitless. As it turned out, Dacia and not Parthia was Rome's last major conquest.

THE FIVE GOOD EMPERORS?

Put off by his warmongering and his Jupiter complex, we may find it hard to warm to Trajan, in spite of his generosity and political good sense. And yet Trajan's approach worked. Following in the footsteps of Nerva, he brought the empire a century of relative peace and prosperity. After the murder of Domitian in 96, no Roman emperor was assassinated for nearly a century. After Trajan's death, Rome engaged in no foreign wars for forty years. Trajan's political touch was so sure, his investment in the welfare of the people of Italy so deep, and his building projects so impressive that both his title as Optimus and his appeal to later ages are understandable.

Trajan was the second of the so-called Five Good Emperors. Besides Nerva (who reigned from 96 to 98) and Trajan (98 to 117), they are Hadrian (117 to 138), Antoninus Pius (138 to 161), and Marcus Aurelius (161 to 180). It is generally thought that the empire enjoyed its zenith under them.

Historian Edward Gibbon made a famous comment about that era in his great work *The History of the Decline and Fall of the Roman Empire*: "If a man were called upon to fix that period in the history of the world during which the condition of the human race was most happy and prosperous, he would, without hesitation, name that which elapsed from the deaths of Domitian to the accession of Commodus."

Although that is certainly not true today, Gibbon wrote it in 1776, and back then he had a point. It is estimated that in the second century of our era, the empire's gross domestic product and per capita gross domestic product were comparable to those of Europe in 1600. Even more impressive, the figures for the city of Rome are comparable to those of cities in the Netherlands in 1600. For all the problems in compiling good statistics from the ancient world, these figures enjoy a wide consensus of support among scholars.

Rome also enjoyed a favorable climate. What scholars refer to as the Roman Climate Optimum, a period of warm, wet, and stable conditions, stretched across the Mediterranean world. It was ideal for farmers and for consumers too.

The empire had a market economy in grain and land. Banks provided a flexible source of credit. Although slavery flourished, emancipation was permitted, and many slaves worked their way to freedom. Not only did the empire reach its maximum geographical extension in this era, but the population peaked at 50 million to 70 million people, Rome's biggest building boom took place, and it was an explosive era of artistic production. Agriculture, mining, and manufacturing all prospered. Peace and good roads and harbors promoted trade and communication.

Nonetheless, all was not rosy. Mortality rates were high, and public health was poor. Romans suffered from poor nutrition and disease. For women, death in childbirth was a real possibility. Life expectancy at birth for members of the senatorial class was thirty and about twenty-five for others. Infant mortality was sky-high, with about one-third of newborns dead by the age of twenty-eight months.

There was great inequality of wealth. There were only six hundred senators, and they were all superrich. There were an estimated two thousand knights (equestrians) in Rome and thirty thousand across the empire, all wealthy. Then came two other well-to-do groups: large landowners and town councilors, followed by shopkeepers, traders, money changers, artisans, doctors, teachers and other members of the professions, followed by minor municipal officials. Aside from a small group of free wage earners, most people were peasants, which is to say, poor but free farmers. Slaves possibly made up between 15 percent and 20 percent of the Roman population. There was no progressive taxation and no property tax in Italy until the end of the third century. The rich got richer, with the state run for their benefit, and the poor masses had no choice but to go along.

Inhabitants of the city of Rome enjoyed some special privileges, but conditions in Rome were often difficult. Romans received free grain and eventually free oil; wine was subsidized. The public baths were discounted for citizens. Meanwhile, well-connected people higher in the social scale benefited from *sportulae*: "freebies" from the rich, such as payments to followers for daily visits to patrons. Followers showed their respect by these visits and also by attending their patron in public, which demonstrated his prestige. The Roman poor also benefited from free theatrical shows, chariot races, gladiatorial combats, and animal-slaughtering shows. But the city of Rome suffered from overcrowding in high-rise tenement blocks, which spread disease and worsened fires.

Rome was bursting with energy and people. It had an estimated population of one million. The city barely resembled the small and homogeneous community of centuries before. It was no longer a place where everyone spoke the same language and worshipped the same gods. Although Latin was the language of administration in Rome, you were as likely to hear Aramaic, Celtic, Egyptian, German, Hebrew, and, above all, Greek.

City life flourished throughout the empire in the second century. From Londinium (London) to Berytus (Beirut, Lebanon), cities founded or refounded by Rome came into their own. Some were originally veterans' colonies, some were army camps that grew into towns, and some were natural market hubs or religious centers. City planning followed Roman patterns, sometimes adjacent to native ones. A Roman might find himself standing in a familiar-looking forum or Senate House in Gaul or Asia Minor or strolling to the column-lined intersection of a town's main east-west and north-south streets. A slight detour might lead to the winding lanes and local architecture of native homes and temples.

It was a great age of cities. Ambitious local elites often had a country estate, but they centered their lives on their townhouse, just as elites did in Rome. They aimed at serving on a local town council, modeled on the Roman Senate. They strove for Roman citizenship, a privilege that the emperors awarded to ever-increasing numbers of prominent people in the provinces.

The age of the Five Good Emperors overflows with material evidence of the lives of ordinary Romans. From the laced-up sandals of a priestess to the plain leather shoes of a carpenter, from the calloused hands of a hunter to the trim fingernails of a goddess, from the grip of a poet on his scroll to a horseman's hold on his reins, from the ecstasy of a dancer to the lowered eyes of parents grieving the loss of a child, ancient art offers thousands of glimpses of ordinary life in the Roman Empire. We have children's dolls and surgeons' scalpels, helmets and hunting horns, polished mirrors and glass perfume jars, slave collars and shrouds, bottle molds and brick stamps, drinking cups and water pipes, playing dice and slingshot projectiles. These humble remains remind us how little Trajan's victory monuments reveal about the world in which most Romans lived.

A DEATH IN TRAJANOPOLIS

As he faced defeat in the East, Trajan's health failed. A bronze bust that some identify as the emperor in his later years shows sunken cheeks, a prominent nose, a furrowed brow, and something of a haunted look in his eyes, as if he knew the end was near. In 117 he is reported to have suffered a stroke, leaving him partially paralyzed. The cause was surely either genetics or hard living, but Trajan was convinced it was poison. It wouldn't be surprising if he were a bitter man at the end, having seen his successes in Parthia fade like flowers in his hand. Although poison cannot explain Trajan's long decline, it is not inconceivable that someone finally gave him poison to finish off the failing emperor.

Plotina and Matidia persuaded Trajan to go home to Rome. No previous emperor had died outside Italy, and no one wanted Trajan to be the first. So he and his party sailed from Antioch's port. After two or three days, however, his condition was so bad that they had to put into the nearest harbor, Selinus, in a rugged region known as "Rough Cilicia" (today Turkey's southwestern Mediterranean coast). It was described by an ancient writer as a zone whose "coast is narrow and has no level ground, or scarcely any; and, besides that, it lies at the foot of the Taurus Mountains, which affords a poor livelihood." Its main claim to fame was as a former pirates' nest.

There was no glory here: no palace and no battlefield. Clearly incapacitated by paralysis and, as Cassius Dio notes, edema (severe swelling caused by fluid retention), the emperor died here, approximately sixty-three years old, on August 8, 117. Selinus was renamed Trajanopolis, Trajan City. Trajanopolis acquired new buildings, in particular, a two-story monument-plus-temple to Trajan, but it never became a city worthy of Trajan's grandiose ambition.

Trajan's remains would be brought back to Antioch for cremation. They then made the long journey home to Rome. After the honor of a triumphal parade, they were placed in an urn at the base of Trajan's Column. Although burial within the city of Rome was prohibited, a unique exception was made for the man dubbed by the Senate as Rome's best ruler.

Perhaps. Or perhaps Trajan was a magnificent and Machiavellian anachronism who provided surprisingly good government when he wasn't chasing vainglory. A rare conqueror-emperor, Trajan was no intellectual, but he more than made up for it in practical wisdom. He combined cunning with self-control. He concentrated power in his hands, but he gave the senators their dignity and spared their lives. He gratified the people while not forgetting to reward the legions. He promoted the image of patriarchy, which might have been a relief after the antics of his predecessors, but his wife probably wielded considerable power. Although he took credit for his vast public works, they served the public and not merely his ego. He promoted trade and communication. Warrior though he was, Trajan laid the groundwork for Rome's greatest era of peace and prosperity.

Yet that prosperity was not shared equally. Most people—tens of millions—lived in poverty, while millions more were enslaved and lived in chains. Things were slightly better for the free population of Italy and especially of Rome. Most people could be grateful at least for the Roman peace, considering how bloody the history of the ancient world often was.

Yet Trajan also annihilated tens of thousands of people in Dacia and all but destroyed its language and culture. He willfully waged a war of aggression against the Parthians in the East that ended in utter failure. And then there was the matter of the succession.

Trajan's philosophy of governance was that Rome could have it all. He could expand the empire, go on a spree of building and infrastructure improvement, start a new welfare program in Italy, and satisfy the Senate, the people, and the army all at the same time. And Rome could do all this without busting the budget or exhausting its resources. His successor would revisit these conclusions.

Who would Rome's new ruler be? Few matters were more important to resolve. Trajan had not done so, although he had made moves in that direction. He finally settled things on his deathbed. Or did he? Uncertainty about that contributed to violence that stained the next reign from the start—the reign of another Roman of Spanish descent, Trajan's distant cousin Hadrian.

Bust of Hadrian.

6

HADRIAN
THE GREEK

Before he died in out-of-the-way Selinus, Trajan adopted his distant cousin Hadrian. So the official story went, but Trajan's past behavior left doubt in some minds. For years, Trajan had promoted Hadrian to ever higher offices. He also allowed him to marry into the imperial family, but he showed a certain hesitation as well, perhaps because of policy differences. He neither adopted Hadrian nor gave him the honors of previous imperial heirs.

Some people claimed that on his deathbed Trajan said nothing about adoption and that the whole affair was stage-managed by two people: Hadrian's champion Plotina, who was Trajan's wife, and Hadrian's former guardian Publius Acilius Attianus, who was Praetorian prefect. They were both with Trajan at the end. One source notes with suspicion that Plotina signed Trajan's letters to the Senate naming Hadrian as his son and heir, even though she had never signed any previous letter by the emperor. Another source claims that Plotina smuggled in an actor to impersonate Trajan and declare, in a weak voice, his decision to adopt Hadrian—without letting people know that Trajan was already dead.

Then there is this odd detail: A chance discovery of a gravestone shows that two days after Trajan's death, his wine taster, a young freedman, died at age twenty-eight. Of course, a natural death is possible—he and Trajan might each have died of the same virus, for example—but we might wonder whether the young man was killed or committed suicide because he knew too much. That it took twelve years to bring his ashes to Rome also incites suspicion, as if someone wanted to keep his memory quiet.

Was there fire behind this smoke or is it just coincidence and another case of Roman prejudice against a strong woman? We'll never know. What is clear is that Rome had a vigorous and talented new ruler.

Hadrian was tall, well built, strong, and fit. Portrait busts show an intelligent and commanding person, with an oval-shaped face with rounded cheeks, an aquiline nose, large ears, and eyes that were "full of light and bright," as a contemporary described them. In those days, he had a full but neatly trimmed beard and a full head of hair that he kept carefully curled.

Hadrian's beard was not just a fashion statement but also a cultural and political sign. Elite Roman men normally went clean shaven; Greek men grew a beard. By not shaving, Hadrian signaled his love of Greek culture and his policy of elevating the eastern, Greek-speaking part of the empire.

The wonder was that he stood still long enough for the very large number of images of him that survive—more than of any other emperor. Always, it seemed, Hadrian was on horseback or aboard ship, always moving from one end of the empire to another, from Britain to Syria and nearly every province in between, visiting more places than any other emperor. He made a point of meeting ordinary people—"pressing the flesh," as the saying goes, in the manner of a modern democratic politician. Everywhere he went, he mingled with the troops, sharing their simple food and eating, like them, outdoors. To set an example, he went without a hat, "alike amid German snows and under scorching Egyptian suns," and he once marched twenty miles in armor to encourage his soldiers. For recreation, he tested his prowess in his favorite pastime, hunting. He was so skilled that once he pulled off the feat of killing a boar with a single blow.

Hadrian was one of the most important and most fascinating of Rome's emperors. No one ever made a greater effort for peace or took a stronger stand against imperial expansion. No one ever paid more personal attention to the provinces. No other emperor was a more committed student of the classics or a better poet or architect—and he was a sculptor and painter to boot. And yet no one ever outmatched Hadrian for paradox. To one ancient writer, "He was, in the same person, austere and genial, dignified and playful, dilatory and quick to act, stingy and generous, deceitful and straightforward, cruel and merciful, and always in all things changeable."

He was a Roman who loved Greece but is best remembered in Italy and Britain—and by Jews, whose culture he tried to destroy and whose annals curse his memory. He was a man's man who owed his success to the women who loved him, but he gave his heart to an adolescent boy.

THE IRRESISTIBLE RISE OF PUBLIUS AELIUS HADRIANUS

The story begins in hope and ambition. Hadrian was born on January 24, 76. Named Publius Aelius Hadrianus after his father, he was born in Rome, where his father's career had brought the family, but their home was Hispania. They came from a city grown rich on its olive oil exports. A prominent family who numbered a senator among their ancestors, they traced their roots to an early settler, a Roman soldier from the northeastern Italian city of Hadria. Hence the name Hadrian.

Rome under Vespasian, who ruled when Hadrian was born, was increasingly friendly to talented elite men from the provinces, and Hadrian's father was one of them. Aelius Hadrianus Afer was a senator, and served as praetor and possibly a legionary commander, a member of a provincial governor's staff, or even governor himself. Hadrian's mother, Domitia Paulina, another Spaniard, came from a seaport on Hispania's Atlantic coast, from a family that probably traced its ancestry back to Phoenician colonists. Hadrian also had a sister, Paulina.

Hadrian Senior died when Hadrian was ten, leaving the boy fatherless, like young Augustus. Since Roman women married younger than Roman men, we might guess that Domitia was still alive. If so, she presumably looked out for her son, as Atia once looked out for the young Augustus. Another resemblance between the two men is certain, because like Augustus, young Hadrian received access to powerful men in Rome. He had two guardians, both with roots in his hometown. One was Acilius Attianus, a Roman knight who would become commander of the Praetorian Guard. The other was Hadrian's father's cousin, an up-and-coming soldier and statesman: the future emperor Trajan. Since Trajan was busy at the time as a commanding officer, Attianus took charge of Hadrian's upbringing. Except for two visits as a teenager to inspect the family property in Hispania, Hadrian was brought up entirely in Rome.

Highly intelligent, with a prodigious memory, Hadrian was an excellent student. The main curriculum item in the schooling of elite Roman youth was the Greek and Latin classics. Hadrian took to Greece's language and literature with passion. Certainly he had plenty of exposure to Greek, since the Rome of his day had a very large Greek population. In fact, Rome rivaled Alexandria as the largest Greek city in the world. Hadrian was Greek even in his taste in sports: he adored hunting, an elite Greek activity but not beloved of Romans.

It all earned him the nickname of Graeculus: "the little Greek." It wasn't a compliment. Elite Romans admired and resented Greece's cultural superiority. Sometimes they compensated by recalling Rome's power over Greece. Hadrian's guardian Trajan was not unusual in his prejudiced comment that "the little Greeks are fond of their gymnasia." He disapproved of Hadrian's hunting.

Luckily for Hadrian, Trajan's wife, Plotina, felt otherwise. Like Hadrian, she was an enthusiastic Hellenist. Indeed, the two had much in common. They were both intelligent and educated, both students of philosophy, both in Trajan's orbit, and—a cynic might say—both loved Hadrian. Hadrian's not inconsiderable self-love aside, Plotina adored her husband's bright, young ward.

Although Plotina was probably closer in age to Hadrian than to Trajan, who was twenty-two years older than Hadrian, she served as a sort of surrogate mother. She certainly looked out for his interests at crucial points in his career, beginning with his education. Plotina arranged for Hadrian to study with one of the best teachers in Rome.

Plotina was a student of Epicurean philosophy, a system of thought developed in Athens centuries earlier and that still had a school there in Hadrian's day. Today an Epicurean is someone devoted to pleasure, especially to sensual and luxurious pleasure, but ancient Epicureans believed in limiting desires. They were materialists who considered religion to be superstition and reason to be the best guide. They preferred good company to gourmet food, and they valued working behind the scenes over being in the public eye. "Live unknown" was their motto, and friendship was their goal. Many elite Romans were Epicureans, including politicians who found the philosophy consoling even if they rejected its quietism.

For Plotina, as for Hadrian, "Greekness" was not merely a fashion statement. Although the Romans owed their empire to force, Hadrian understood that the pen was mightier than the sword—and that the greater pen belonged to the Greeks. He recognized, with the poet Horace, that "conquered Greece took captive her savage conqueror and brought her arts in rustic Latium." He believed that Greece still had deep wisdom to impart. Several of the Greek philosophical schools of his day seem to have influenced him, including Epicureanism, and he once met with the great Stoic philosopher Epictetus.

Hadrian took the life of the mind more seriously than any previous emperor had. After the proudly unintellectual Trajan and the aggressively plebeian Vespasian, it was a big change. Intellectualism undergirded the singular vision that Hadrian brought to the job. It also made him the greatest Roman friend that Greece ever had.

Hadrian entered public life at age eighteen and rose swiftly. First came minor positions in the city of Rome, then assignment as a junior officer (military tribune), first in central Europe and then in the Balkans. He was in a far-off Balkan region on the Euxine Sea when news came in late 97 that the emperor Nerva had adopted Trajan as his son and successor. At the time, Trajan was in command in Upper Germania. Hadrian was chosen to bring his army's congratulations to his guardian—now heir to the throne.

As a reward, he was transferred from the far-off Euxine Sea to a more central location on the Rhine, while remaining a junior officer. By serving three terms as junior officer rather than the senatorial norm of two, Hadrian grew especially knowledgeable about the military.

Soon afterward, in early 98, news came that Nerva was dead and Trajan was declared emperor. Hadrian seized the moment and hurried northward to inform Trajan in person, a distance of about 110 miles. Along the way, his carriage broke down, but he continued on foot and managed to break the good news to Trajan. So the story goes, and it includes the claim that one Servianus sabotaged Hadrian's carriage. Skepticism is called for, since the story might well go back to Hadrian himself, and, in later years, Hadrian and Servianus were at daggers drawn. Strangely, the two men were brothers-in-law.

Lucius Julius Ursus Servianus was married to Hadrian's sister, Paulina. It was a match of access and ambition, since Paulina, like Hadrian, was Trajan's cousin, and Servianus, a governor and former consul, was headed for Trajan's inner circle. It's not surprising that two determined men such as Servianus and Hadrian clashed.

Hadrian was Trajan's closest living male relative, and once the childless Trajan became emperor, Hadrian had an inside track to succeed him. It was no sure thing, however. Ever since Augustus had passed over his grandson Agrippa Postumus for his stepson Tiberius, it was clear that even a close relative had to earn the job. And earn it Hadrian did, by displaying political, military, and administrative skills. But that was not all.

The rise of Hadrian was a triumph of the arts of the courtier. He beguiled the imperial women closest to Trajan, impressed his former guardian Attianus—now prefect of the Praetorian Guard, as well as Trajan's right-hand man Sura, among others.

Hadrian's closest ally as always was Plotina, now wife of the emperor. She persuaded Trajan to give Vibia Sabina to Hadrian as a bride. The marriage moved Hadrian closer to Trajan, since Sabina was his sister Marciana's granddaughter and so was Trajan's grandniece. Sabina came from a family of wealth and influence. She personally owned slaves in Hispania as well as in Rome and elsewhere in Italy. Both her mother, Salonia Matidia, and her grandmother, Marciana, lived in the imperial household and were among Trajan's closest confidants.

The up-and-coming Hadrian and the well-positioned Sabina married in 100. Hadrian adored his mother-in-law, Matidia. Hadrian was twenty-four; Sabina, a girl of fourteen or fifteen. The age gap of ten years between husband and wife was typical for Rome. Rome's minimum age of marriage for a young woman was twelve and for a young man, fourteen. Although women tended to marry in their late teens and men in their late twenties, the senatorial elite and especially the imperial family often married early. An ambitious man like Hadrian was surely eager to wed a woman as eligible as Sabina.

Hadrian might have found much to like in his bride as she grew into a woman. Admittedly, imperial portrait sculpture is idealized and propagandistic. Still, it is unlikely to represent sheer fantasy, since its subjects wanted to be recognized when seen. The various busts and full-length statues of Sabina display an even-featured, pleasant-looking face, a delicate neck, and a classical nose. There is a gentle air about her. Her hair is thick, wavy, and brushed back from a central part, in a Greek style that surely appealed to Hadrian and perhaps to her as well.

Sabina is the rare Roman woman to have left writing. Admittedly, it is brief: just a postscript to four short poems composed by her traveling companion. Yet that companion was a Greek woman and an intellectual, suggesting that Sabina shared interests with Hadrian or at least made an effort to do so. The writing also shows that Sabina shared her husband's pride in their own status and achievements.

Still, theirs was a dynastic marriage, not a love match, and the bridal couple had their differences. The marriage was childless. Hadrian preferred young men. Rumor said the couple disliked each other; that they had sex but Sabina took precautions to prevent pregnancy; that Hadrian found her irritable and short tempered and wished that he were a private citizen so he could divorce her. But rumors are just rumors, and it is not unknown for political spouses to work together even if they don't get along in bed. Despite the alleged bad blood between Sabina and Hadrian, there is also evidence of cooperation and harmony, and Hadrian rewarded his wife with honors. Still, Sabina's role could not have been entirely easy.

Hadrian had the opportunity to advance his career in Trajan's wars in Dacia in 101–102 and 105–106. In the first campaign, Trajan took Hadrian with him as a high-ranking staff member. Hadrian spent a year at the front, an experience from which only one detail survives: that Hadrian came to share Trajan's hard-drinking wine habits, and Trajan rewarded him for this.

Hadrian served again in Trajan's second Dacian campaign in 105–106, this time as a legionary commander. He received military decorations for both campaigns. Although other men played bigger roles in Rome's victory, Hadrian received a symbolic gift from Trajan: a diamond that Trajan had received from the previous emperor, Nerva. It seemed like an omen of success, and Hadrian set great store by omens. Although a student of philosophy, he had a lifelong interest in magic and astrology.

Hadrian continued to rise quickly under Trajan but not as quickly as the ambitious young man would have liked. From 106 to 108, he was governor of Lower Pannonia. In May 108 he was named suffect (substitute) consul at age thirty-two, which was early for a nonpatrician. The story goes that Hadrian now learned from one of Trajan's closest advisors, Sura, that the emperor was going to adopt him. Sura died soon afterward, so the truth of this tale is unknown. In any case, Trajan did not adopt Hadrian, although he did make him his speechwriter.

It was a trusted position but not enough to keep Hadrian in Rome. By 112, if not earlier, he was living in Athens, presumably with Trajan's permission. The emperor might have considered it useful to have the talented young man as his eyes and ears in the Greek east—and perhaps a relief, too, to have this aspirant to power out of his hair. Athens was small compared with Rome, but its cultural heritage still cast a giant shadow. Between the Parthenon, the philosophers, and the poetry, Hadrian was enchanted. The city's elite invited him to become an Athenian citizen, and, shortly after, he was elected chief magistrate.

This stay in Athens might have been the moment when Hadrian made his well-known contribution to Roman fashion: his beard. He set a precedent, and for the next century and a half, his successors as emperor followed suit.

His hirsute young cousin might have surprised Trajan as he passed through Athens on the way to a vast new war in the East. Much of his court came with him, including Plotina and Matidia.

Like Caesar and Mark Antony, Trajan set his sights on war with Parthia. The previous chapter has already told the story of the campaign. Suffice it to add a reference to reports that Plotina used her influence to get Hadrian a position on Trajan's staff during the war. But apparently Hadrian exercised little power before becoming governor of Syria in 117, another job that he is said to have owed to Plotina. It was supposedly her influence as well that allowed him to be named consul a second time, to serve in the year 118.

The smart money was on Hadrian succeeding Trajan, especially when the second consulship was announced. Rumor said that Hadrian was bribing Trajan's freedmen and courting Trajan's influential boyfriends. And yet the emperor neither adopted Hadrian nor honored him with the title of Caesar or with the powers that Tiberius, Titus, and Trajan himself all had when they were made heir. Nor over the years did Trajan ever make Hadrian one of his top generals. Perhaps the reason was Hadrian's lack of enthusiasm for military conquest. Unlike Trajan, Hadrian did not want to expand the empire. That might have made Trajan hesitate to name him as his successor. The severe old Roman also likely distrusted his former ward's Hellenism.

There was a rumor that Trajan planned to name another man his heir or that he would turn the decision over to the Senate. Some even said that the great admirer of Alexander intended to leave the succession "to the strongest," as the Macedonian did when he died in 323 BC, but since Alexander's decision resulted in fifty years of civil war, it seems unlikely that Trajan wanted to follow that precedent. And then the crisis came.

THE SUCCESSION CRISIS

As we have seen, some challenged the report that Trajan adopted Hadrian on his deathbed. But Hadrian had a powerful response, the legions of the

East, whose support he obtained immediately after he moved smartly to give them a double bonus. He later apologized to the Senate for taking the throne without its consent, but the state, he said, could not be left without an emperor. Meanwhile, like Vespasian, another emperor who took power by force, he counted the day of his acclamation by the army as the start of his reign: August 11, 117.

Meanwhile, the new rule began with a gangland-style series of assassinations of Trajan's ex-marshals. Some were rivals for imperial power, while others were not happy with the defensive military policies that Hadrian had in mind. In Rome, Hadrian's former guardian, Attianus, claimed to have found a four-man conspiracy against the new emperor. They were men of great substance: ex-consuls of the Roman state, including one of Trajan's closest associates and another man who was admired by Plutarch. They were killed without trial, and the Senate was forced to approve. Many senators never forgave their new ruler for what became known as "the Affair of the Four Ex-Consuls," but few failed to fear him. As for Attianus, Hadrian promoted him to the Senate, which meant giving up his job as Praetorian prefect, a position reserved for Roman knights.

For all his love of philosophy, the arts, and astrology, Hadrian was ruthless, violent, and unafraid of murder. Yet he was also a politician, and he knew to mend fences. In Rome, Hadrian gave cash to the plebeians, burned the records of overdue taxes, put on splendid gladiatorial games, and started a big building program.

But Hadrian did not believe in constitutional government. Gibbon sums him up nicely by saying, "He was by turns an excellent prince, a ridiculous sophist, and a jealous tyrant."

PEACE AND CONSTRUCTION PROJECTS

Few emperors came to office with as much vision and self-confidence as Hadrian. He wanted nothing less than to be a transformative leader. He came to see himself—eventually, if not at first—as a second Augustus. Indeed, in time he called himself Hadrian Augustus, preferring it to his full name, Imperator Caesar Traianus Hadrianus Augustus. He considered himself a second founder of the empire.

Actually, he was a second Tiberius. By reversing Trajan's policy of expansion, he restored the largely defensive strategy of Tiberius. If Hadrian was more of a humanist than Tiberius, he did not shy away from Tiberius's quarrels with the Senate and, from time to time, his tyranny.

Hadrian faced revolts east and west at the start of his reign: in Dacia, on the Danube, in Mauretania (Morocco), and Britain. He responded by firmness in some areas and pullback in others. He ordered an immediate withdrawal from the little territory that was left of Trajan's conquests in the Parthian Empire, and he made peace with the Parthian king. He also gave up the eastern part of Dacia. As a precautionary measure to stop invaders, Hadrian even had the superstructure of Trajan's great bridge across the Danube dismantled.

Surrendering territory seemed un-Roman, and many senators opposed it fiercely. Indeed, disagreement with the new policy and not a conspiracy was probably the real reason the Four Ex-Consuls paid with their lives. But Hadrian insisted. In his judgment, the empire was exhausted after Trajan's wars of expansion. Furthermore, he seems to have recognized the advantages of rearmament: militarily, economically, and morally.

Though the emperor did have his opponents, most members of the Roman elite probably agreed with Hadrian. There was no longer the same incentive to fight wars to conquer new territory. In fact, there was a disincentive, since emperors feared and sometimes executed victorious generals. It was no longer necessary to have major military experience in order to forge a successful public career or be a senator. One contemporary writer probably spoke for many when he wrote, "within my own time the emperor Hadrian . . . was extremely religious in the respect he paid to the deity and contributed very much to the happiness of his various subjects. He never voluntarily entered upon a war."

For Trajan, Rome was a superpower, and it had to act like one. For Hadrian, Rome was a commonwealth; more like the European Union than the United States, Russia, or China. Hadrian wanted a new empire

in which provincial elites participated in government as equals. He earned
their loyalty by extending Roman citizenship to city councilors around the
empire—a boon previously limited to magistrates.

As far as Hadrian was concerned, those elites would speak Latin in
the West and Greek in the East. But what of the other native elites in the
empire? What of Arabs, Celts, Dacians, Egyptians, Germans, Jews, Maure-
tanians, Numidians, Phoenicians, Syrians, and others? They would have to
assimilate or be left out. Hadrian said to them, in effect, "You don't have the
right to be free; you have the right to be Roman—or Greek." Greek was the
dominant language in the eastern half of the empire. Its sound was music to
the ears of Hadrian, "the little Greek," and he intended to favor it.

Hadrian focused on the eastern half of the empire for most of his reign.
That reflected not merely his personal preference but also the realities of
power. Rome had the military force and the political organization, but the
East had the manpower, the wealth, the cities, the culture, and the intellectual and spiritual depth. The West outside Italy was comparatively under-
developed and backward, boasting few great cities. The greatest exception
was Carthage, located across the Mediterranean Sea, on the northern coast
of Africa. Destroyed in the Third Punic War in 146 BC, Carthage was
rebuilt as a Roman colony by Augustus in accordance with the plan of Julius Caesar. By Hadrian's day, Carthage was the second city of the western
Mediteranean. Yet the empire's urban center was in the East, and to some,
that region represented Rome's future. Hadrian had no doubt of that.

Both Julius Caesar and Mark Antony were tempted to move the capital
of the empire eastward, either to Alexandria or even Troy. Hadrian turned
his eyes to Athens. He loved all Greek cities, but he preferred Athens,
where he spent more time than any other place in the Greek world. He was
initiated into the so-called Mysteries, the city's most solemn and exclusive
religious ritual. It was a secret ceremony offering hope of life after death.

Hadrian built up Athens to a degree not seen since the Golden Age of
Pericles more than five hundred years earlier. He sponsored a building boom
there, and he made Athens the center of a new Panhellenic League of Greek
cities. Visitors to Athens today can still see such signs of Hadrian's construction

projects in the remains of a library; a cistern—now a public square but once part of a new water supply system—the massive columns of the Temple of Olympian Zeus, which was the largest temple in Greece; and a combination marble arch and gate that led to a new quarter of town labeled Hadrian's City. But Athens was only a small part of Hadrian's construction program.

A TEMPLE AND A VILLA

Hadrian might be more famous today as a place name than as a person. He is probably best known for Hadrian's Wall in England and Hadrian's villa in Italy, and those are just the most familiar examples. The city of Rome boasts Hadrian's tomb, also known as Castel Sant'Angelo. Moving on to Hadrian's building projects that don't bear his name, Rome also once contained the massive Temple of Venus and Rome, which amateur architect Hadrian designed himself, to the disgust of Trajan's master architect Apollodorus, who criticized it in writing. Hadrian was so angry that when Apollodorus died shortly afterward, it was rumored that the emperor had ordered him executed. But neither the tomb nor the temple was Hadrian's most important building.

Augustus left his mark on the Field of Mars, an area located between the old core of the city and the bend of the Tiber River. Hadrian emphasized his claim to be the new Augustus by rebranding the area. He rebuilt an important but damaged structure there—the temple to all the gods, the Pantheon—originally constructed by Augustus's right-hand man, Agrippa. The result is not only the best-preserved edifice to survive from classical antiquity but also one of the most beautiful buildings in the world. Standing inside the Pantheon and looking upward, a visitor realizes that the dome is one of Rome's gifts to civilization.

The building shows genius in its conception and perfection in its execution. It also demonstrates the abundance of the emperor's finances, because a structure this splendid and enduring did not come cheap. Hadrian deserves credit for the idea of the building, although he was too amateurish an architect to have designed it in detail. We don't know the architect's name, but whoever it was succeeded in symbolizing the unity of the empire through brick, marble, and concrete. The rotunda recalls the "circle of lands," as the Romans called the world. The grid of the marble floor or the coffered ceiling brings to mind the regular pattern of a Roman military camp or town or landscape. The dome symbolizes the heavens, ruled over by Jupiter, just as the emperor rules the empire. The dome was a technological marvel, ranging from a massive thickness of 23 feet at its base to only 2 feet at the top. At a diameter of 142.4 feet, the Pantheon's dome was the world's widest vault for 1,300 years, until the Duomo (Cathedral) of Florence was built in 1436—and *that* span was not surpassed until the late nineteenth century.

Hadrian left his name off the Pantheon, labeling it simply "Agrippa son of Lucius built this in his third consulship." It was immodest modesty because it borrowed the prestige of one of the founding fathers of the empire.

Hadrian did give his name to Hadrianopolis, Hadrian City, founded on the site of an earlier village (today, Edirne, Turkey). It was one of eight places in the empire called Hadrian City and the only one still with an echo of the emperor in its name today. (*Edirne* comes from *Hadrianopolis*.) Located in European Turkey, close to the borders with Bulgaria and Greece, it sits on a historic crossroads. Beginning in the era of Constantine and continuing down to the twentieth century, it has been the site of no fewer than sixteen major battles, including the Roman Empire's most devastating defeat in 378. The late military historian John Keegan called this Hadrianopolis "the most frequently contested spot on the globe." The soldier-statesman Hadrian might have enjoyed that honor for the city in his name.

One of Hadrian's "constructions" involved the law. He empowered a brilliant young jurist to codify the praetor's edict, the annually issued declaration of the principles of Rome's laws. Although in theory a new praetor could start over each year, in practice, most praetors made few changes in the inherited tradition. But inconsistencies accreted over the years. Now, thanks to Hadrian, it was all consolidated and codified into a clear and rational whole. It would be known afterward as the perpetual edict. It marked a major reform for Rome and, indeed, for the history of law.

But law rarely excited Hadrian as much as construction did. Tiberius and Nero had their pleasure palaces, but Hadrian outdid them. What we know of today as Hadrian's villa was, in fact, a royal enclave, like Versailles. The "villa" contains thirty major buildings spread out more than three hundred acres—twice the size of Pompeii—in a lush river valley at Tibur (Tivoli), about eighteen miles from Rome, from where it was a three-hour ride on horseback.

Work began at Tibur probably at the start of Hadrian's reign and continued throughout. Materials were brought there from all over the empire to create a sense of the empire's variety and of Rome's power. The campus was filled with art and sculpture and with gardens, pools, canals, and fountains. Hadrian designed some of the structures himself. Not only were there his beloved "pumpkins"—domes—but also the first-known use of reverse curves in architecture; that is, the sinuous alternation of concave and convex walls. The overall plan of the campus was subtle, as complex and unusual as Hadrian himself. No other emperor did more to create a place where art and nature combined to provide inspiration. The villa also symbolized the imperial elites that Hadrian considered important. The architecture was overwhelmingly Roman, but it was filled with Greek art. Egyptian themes were prominent as well, for Egypt was to play a major role in Hadrian's life story. A multitude of slaves kept the villa going. Roman officials and soldiers were present throughout.

The villa had everything. Besides a palace, there were dining pavilions, libraries, baths, temples, a theater, and even an arena. There were heated buildings for winter use and cool northward exposures for summer. It was a retreat for Hadrian and a place for him to impress and entertain visitors, but it was also a place where he might lose touch with reality.

Tibur was Hadrian's Neverland. It was Alternate Rome; a Rome without the senate or the people; a combination of one of Hadrian's adored military bases and a Greek polis. From here he could govern Rome without having to enter the city and travel without having to leave home. Here Hadrian remained a wanderer.

HADRIAN'S TRAVELS

No emperor since Augustus traveled the provinces as much as Hadrian, and, in the end, he covered even more territory than his predecessor. Hadrian reigned for twenty-one years, making his the longest reign since Tiberius. He spent about half of those years on the road. During his prime years between ages forty-four and fifty-five, from 120 to 131, he was rarely in Rome. In the years 121 to 125, he made a great swing through Rome's northwestern provinces and then turned east to Greece and Asia Minor. A few years later, starting in 128, he visited Sicily, North Africa, Egypt, and other eastern Mediterranean lands, especially Greece. Then came a trip to Judea to deal with urgent business there.

It wasn't a hungry heart that made Hadrian travel but a desire to remake the empire from the ground up. It was also a way to escape Rome, with what he saw as a needy and insatiable Senate and people.

Hadrian's traveling entourage, complete with imperial secretaries, bureaucrats, hangers-on, servants, and his wife and her staff, was the second Rome; the government on the move. It was the Air Force One of the ancient world. It must have been quite a sight to see him and his train on the go, but not everyone was daunted. An old woman once tried to stop Hadrian as he passed by, to hand him a petition. When he said that he had no time for that, she said that in that case he should cease being emperor. He granted her a hearing.

Wherever Hadrian went, he headed for one of Rome's military bases. His policy of nonexpansion required maintaining the military in a state of absolute readiness. One ancient author comments, "Though more desirous of peace than of war, he kept the soldiers in training just as if war were imminent." Besides which, Hadrian loved the army.

Hadrian was a he-man whose heart beat for the military camp. When he visited a legionary garrison in North Africa, for example, he watched a series of maneuvers, and declared to the assembled troops afterward, "The outstanding manhood of that noble man, my deputy, Catullinus [that is, Quintus Fabius Catullinus, the legion's commander], shows itself in you, the men who are serving under him." Then there was the time that Hadrian's Horse Guards swam across the Danube fully armed under his admiring eyes.

In 121, after visiting Rome, Hadrian headed north to Germany, where he faced the harsh winter with aplomb. The empress Sabina and such important figures as the commander of the Praetorian Guard and the chief secretary accompanied him. The secretary is better known today as a writer: Suetonius, author of *The Twelve Caesars*, biographies of imperial rulers. Suetonius's access to the imperial archives provided unparalleled documentary riches. He began his work with Julius Caesar in 100 BC and ended it with the death of Domitian in the year 98. Anything more recent was too dangerous to touch.

Hadrian's motive in going to Germany was to erect a new border for the empire. It was a continuous wooden palisade replacing the network of forts and watchtowers established by his predecessors. It stood perhaps ten feet high and stretched approximately 350 miles across parts of what are today southwestern Germany, Alsace, and Switzerland.

This was the start of the famous Roman *limes*, or frontier. At its height in the second century, the *limes* extended more than 3,000 miles, from northern Britain to the Red Sea. It consisted of walls, towers, forts, ditches, and roads, but it was hardly systematic. If the *limes* represented fixed frontier defense, it also bore witness to the limits of Rome's power.

In Germany and elsewhere, the *limes* served as a checkpoint but not a serious obstacle to a concerted invasion effort. Its primary purpose was symbolic. The *limes* showed where the empire began and ended. It also showed that Rome was done expanding.

A case in point is Hadrian's next stop after Germany and the most famous part of the *limes* built in his reign: Hadrian's Wall, in Britain.

HADRIAN'S WALL

Hadrian's Wall undulates across the northern English landscape. Extending for a distance of seventy-three miles, from the River Tyne near the North Sea to Solway Firth on the Irish Sea, it is one of the world's icons of Roman imperialism and rightly attracts millions of visitors. Yet ancient reality belies the modern image.

Hadrian and his entourage traveled to Britain, probably for the ground-breaking for the wall. It served the emperor's glory, offering an effective engineering counterpart to Trajan's bridge over the Danube. At the eastern end was a bridge, named after Hadrian, and a network of towers and forts stretched westward across the island, much of the new work gleaming in the sun. It symbolized Rome's power, but, as in Germany, the wall served only a limited military purpose. Perhaps the most important one was to separate various British peoples who had earlier formed an alliance and risen against Rome. On Hadrian's accession in 117, there had been a rebellion in northern Britain. The details are obscure, but we know that it was serious, and it may have even destroyed a legion.

The wall represented a triple set of defenses, including a double dike to the north and a road to the south as well as the wall itself. It would keep large numbers of enemies from getting through, but the wall was too narrow to serve as a fighting rampart.

Although the wall looked imposing from a distance, up close it was sloppy and often of inferior quality, constructed by poorly trained men. It was built more for effect than utility and required large-scale rebuilding under a later emperor. The unimpressive turf wall built farther to the north by Hadrian's successor was much more practical. It's hard not to wonder if some of the funding for Hadrian's Wall found its way into private purses, skimmed off the top by Roman officials or local contractors.

And yet the people who built and manned the wall are a source of wonder even today. They lived in a series of fortified camps along the wall's length. Not long ago, archaeologists found an intact series of wooden tablets, preserved in the mud, that opens a window into camp life: from military maneuvers, to dealing with contractors, to an invitation to a birthday party—the latter possibly the oldest surviving document in Latin written by a woman. The letter states:

"I give you a warm invitation to make sure that you come to us, to make the day more enjoyable for me by your arrival . . . I shall expect you, sister."

The soldiers came from around the empire—from Batavia (the Netherlands) and Pannonia, from Syria and Arabia—and often married and had children with locals. They worshipped hybrid gods and no doubt spoke bastardized Latin. They formed the most multiethnic community that Britain would see until the late twentieth century.

Before Hadrian left Britain, he dealt with a scandal. He dismissed Suetonius, the commander of the Praetorians, and other officials because they were more familiar with Sabina than court etiquette allowed. As always, Caesar's wife had to be above suspicion. The sources, if they are to be believed, say that Hadrian was of half a mind to divorce Sabina. If only we had her side of the story!

So Hadrian behaved in regard to the empress. When it came to his own life, however, he tolerated a little sassiness. The poet and historian Publius Annius Florus, for instance, sent Hadrian a ditty, most of which has survived, mocking the emperor's travels:

> I don't want to be a Caesar,
> Stroll about among the Britons,
> Lurk about among the . . .
> And endure the Scythian winters

Hadrian responded with good humor:

> I don't want to be a Florus,
> Stroll about among the taverns,
> Lurk about among the cook-shops
> And endure the round fat insects.

THE POLITICS OF DEATH

Hadrian's mother-in-law, Matidia, died in 119, only two years after he became emperor. He honored her by giving the oration at her funeral. He put on gladiatorial games in her memory, had her deified, just as her mother, Marciana, Trajan's sister, had been, and built a temple to the two women in Rome—the first for any deified woman within Rome's city limits. Hadrian may have been the first man in history to deify his mother-in-law. But his motive was not simply family loyalty. He strengthened his legitimacy as emperor by making himself the son-in-law of a goddess, a fact recalled by every Roman who walked past Matidia's temple. The honors for her mother surely pleased Sabina too, but she knew that Hadrian had another woman.

His surrogate mother, Plotina, remained close to the man she helped put on the throne. She never asked too much of him, because she didn't have to. She was a wealthy woman with a comfortable life. She received respect from Hadrian, whose coins showed her with the legend "Plotina, Augusta of the Divine Trajan." And Plotina was nothing if not shrewd. On the rare occasions when she asked a favor, she aimed for something close to Hadrian's heart: for instance, appointing a new head for the Epicurean school in Athens, for which she sought and got the emperor's help. Hadrian appreciated her discretion and praised her for it after her death.

When Plotina died in 123, Hadrian wore black for nine days. He had her deified too, like Matidia, and rededicated the temple he had built for Trajan to the Divine Trajan and Divine Plotina. (One wonders if Plotina's name was in Trajan's original plan for the structure.) Hadrian arranged for Plotina's ashes to be placed next to Trajan's in the base of Trajan's Column. He also had a large public building built in her memory in her hometown of Nemausus. Men began referring to the late Plotina as Hadrian's *diva mater*: his "deified mother."

There's no reason to doubt Hadrian's attachment to Matidia and Plotina, but he was running a dynasty, not a fan magazine. "We are family" might have been his motto—but the family in question was Trajan's, leaving no doubt about Hadrian's right to the throne. In addition, by frequently referring to Augustus and Agrippa, Hadrian suggested that he was a rightful heir to the family of the first emperor too.

Hadrian's politics of death had taken a peculiar turn in 122, the year before Plotina's passing. It was then that he lost his favorite hunting horse. The steed was probably a gift from a barbarian king, a man with whom Hadrian negotiated a peace agreement in 117. It may have been then that he received the magnificent animal he named Borysthenes (another name for the Dnieper River) after its breeding grounds on the steppes. When Borysthenes died in southern Gaul, Hadrian gave him a proper tomb with a gravestone inscribed with verses that Hadrian probably wrote himself. It was over the top, but Borysthenes's tomb served a political purpose by reminding Hadrian's subjects that far-off barbarian tribes gave their emperor magnificent and manly gifts.

Hadrian was not always so generous when it came to posthumous honors. When his sister, Paulina, died in 130, for instance, he was notably stingy. That same year, however, a different death would have a profound effect on Hadrian.

THE YOUNG GREEK

In late October 130 a twenty-year-old drowned in the River Nile about 210 miles upstream of Cairo. Whether it was an accident or a suicide—and if a suicide, whether it was an act of love or of despair—remains uncertain. What followed, however, is perfectly clear. Suddenly and improbably, the youth was declared a god. He became the focus of a new religion that erected a city in the desert, that inspired devotion, temples, festivals, games, and masterworks of Greco-Roman art from the eastern Mediterranean to Italy, and that lasted for centuries before Christianity put an end to it. It was one of the final flowerings of classical art and of state-run Greco-Roman paganism. And in an eerie and unintended way, it pointed to the road ahead.

The young man in question was named Antinous. He came from Claudiopolis (Bolu, Turkey, about 150 miles east of Istanbul), a provincial city in the same Bithynia from which Pliny wrote to Trajan about the Christians. Antinous was very good-looking, and he shared Hadrian's love of hunting. Otherwise, nothing is known about him. We don't know how the two met, although the likeliest possibility has Hadrian passing through Claudiopolis in 123, when Antinous was thirteen. Nor do we know if Hadrian and Antinous had a physical relationship. But that the emperor loved the young man is beyond doubt.

Like Mark Antony, Hadrian fell in love with a Greek. Antony had Cleopatra, and Hadrian, Antinous. In both cases, the infatuation took them to Egypt. Hadrian arrived in Egypt around August 130. He was only the third emperor to visit the country, following Augustus and Vespasian. Hadrian planned to inspect Rome's wealthiest province and to strengthen the Greek presence by establishing a new Greek city in the mid–Nile Valley. It is possible that his health was another reason for the trip. A later and admittedly hostile source says that Hadrian went to Egypt because he was ill. Perhaps Hadrian had a respiratory illness; perhaps the early stage of the chronic illness that ultimately killed him. Egypt had a reputation as a place for respiratory cures. But this is speculation, and if the emperor had health problems, they were not serious enough to keep him off his feet in Egypt.

Upon reaching Egypt, Hadrian visited the tombs of Pompey and Alexander the Great. In Alexandria, he took part in debates in the Museum, the city's great institute of learning. Hadrian loved debating (read: beating) sophists; those oratorical, itinerant intellectuals of the age. One of them, Favorinus, explained neatly why he let Hadrian win their back-and-forth conversation: "Who could contradict the lord of thirty legions?"

It appears that Hadrian and Antinous enjoyed a getaway together in a resort outside Alexandria. It's certain, at any rate, that they both took part in a lion hunt in Egypt's Western Desert. Antinous was in the hunting party, and Hadrian supposedly saved him from the lion and killed the beast, if we believe official art and poetry.

Hadrian traveled with a large entourage of followers, including various officials, scholars, poets, hangers-on—perhaps as many as five thousand people. Records survive of the strain on Egyptian towns preparing food for their visit. Not only was Antinous with him but also Sabina. At least two years earlier, Hadrian had given her the honorific title of Augusta. This strengthened his legitimacy as emperor and also served as a gesture of respect to his spouse, perhaps even a gesture of love. The imperial party went on a cruise down the Nile. Along the way, as well as visiting the pyramids and other tourist attractions, Hadrian consulted priests and magicians about matters of life and death.

On October 22 Egypt celebrated the annual festival of the Nile. October 24 marked the anniversary of the death of the god Osiris in the Nile. According to Egyptian belief, Osiris triumphed over death and brought fertility and immortality to the land. It was around this time, possibly on the precise day, that Antinous drowned, and in the part of the Nile Valley where Hadrian planned to build his new city. Within a week, by October 30, Hadrian declared that the city would be laid out on the very place where Antinous's body had washed up to shore. No doubt he originally planned to call the town Hadrianopolis, but it now received a different name: Antinoopolis, or Antinous City.

Hadrian wrote, perhaps in his lost autobiography, that Antinous fell into the Nile, and that was that—an accident. But the emperor would have to deny suicide, because Egyptian practice denied immortality to suicides, and Hadrian and his spin doctors wanted nothing less than immortality for the dead lad. Other ancient writers disagreed. Some say that Antinous sacrificed himself nobly and unselfishly in order to guarantee Hadrian a long life, while others say that Antinous committed suicide in despair because Hadrian insisted on continuing their love affair past the age of seemliness. These are guesses, if not malicious gossip. Neither Greeks nor Romans were in the habit of giving up their lives as a magical way of extending someone else's life, but perhaps Antinous was just a mixed-up teenager. We will never know why he drowned.

Hadrian soldiered on, with the imperial party continuing down the Nile as if nothing had happened. They visited a famous colossal statue of an Egyptian pharaoh, whom the Greeks thought of as the legendary Ethiopian king Memnon. The statue was famous for emitting an unusual, high-pitched sound, especially at dawn, which was probably the result of evaporation of dew in the rock. There, Sabina's traveling partner, Julia Balbilla, a noblewoman of mixed Greek and Roman ancestry and a poet, recited four poems. The poems commemorate both Hadrian and Sabina as visitors to the statue. The poems were inscribed later on the statue's left foot and ankle, the prime position for viewing. Sabina herself left four lines of Greek prose on the same place. She wrote:

> *Sabina Augusta,*
> *wife of the Emperor Caesar*
> *Hadrian, heard Memnon*
> *twice within the hour . . .*

Short and formal as it is, it is invaluable, and the rarest of things. For once, the emperor's wife spoke. She proclaimed her rank and her achievement. If she felt any emotion over the death of Antinous, she kept it to herself.

No doubt Hadrian mourned Antinous, but no emperor would let a tragedy go to waste. Just as Augustus created a religious cult in memory of Caesar, so Hadrian created a religious cult in memory of Antinous. Augustus claimed that the sighting of a comet proved Caesar's immortality, and Hadrian claimed that the sighting of a new star did the same for Antinous.

The new god Antinous received temples and priests. Games were held in his honor in Greece, Asia Minor, Egypt, and Italy. His tomb in Antinoopolis was a shrine, and he had a temple at Tibur too. More than a hundred statues of Antinous have survived today, as well as coins and sculptural reliefs, and surely there were once others. It is said that more images of Antinous have been identified than of any other figure from classical antiquity except Augustus and Hadrian himself. Although people worshipped Antinous at first to please Hadrian, the new god was genuinely popular.

Paulina, Hadrian's sister, died around the same time as Antinous but had little to show for it in terms of honors. He commemorated her with the name of one of the ten tribes (or, roughly, wards) in Antinoopolis.

Some Romans ridiculed the new religious cult. They resented Hadrian's deification of a dead Greek youth more than they had his love affair with a living one. Some complained that Hadrian "cried like a woman" over Antinous.

But the new cult was no mere act of sentimentality on Hadrian's part. He understood that the world was changing and that the Greek East offered a cultural model for the future.

The self-confident Hadrian would not have been surprised that the Roman world eventually came to believe as he did in a new savior god offering the promise of resurrection. He would have been shocked, however, to learn that it chose the obscure, Jewish-inspired sect of Christianity rather than the reawakened glory of Greece. Jesus died almost exactly a century before Antinous, but, in the unlikely event that Hadrian or his theologians had Jesus in mind when they promoted the idea of Antinous's saving power, they might not have admitted it even to themselves. Hadrian did not hunt down Christians any more than Trajan had, but he remained willing to execute those who openly refused to worship the emperor.

Things didn't work out as planned. Hadrian offered Athens, but eventually the empire chose Jerusalem. Yet, as far as Hadrian was concerned, Jerusalem no longer existed. In fact, he was intent on giving it a decent burial.

THE JEWISH WAR

Hadrian incited a new, massive Jewish revolt against Rome, lasting from 132 to 135. The proximate cause was probably his decision to refound Jerusalem as a Roman city. Hadrian also banned circumcision, a fundamental Jewish practice, but maybe only as a punishment for rebellion; the chronology is unclear. We might think of Jerusalem as a wasteland after Titus destroyed the city in 70, but, in fact, it was still inhabited. In ancient times, a small number of people often continued to live in "destroyed" cities. So, not only was a legion based in Jerusalem, but also Jews continued to live there. Although the temple had been destroyed, there were seven synagogues.

Both Trajan and Hadrian hinted at first at friendlier policies toward Jews, even possibly allowing the temple to be rebuilt. But the plans for Aelia Capitolina, announced in 130, put an end to all that. The new city would be thoroughly Roman, laid out on a grid plan, and named after both Hadrian (Aelius) and Jupiter (Capitolinus, after Capitoline Jupiter).

The revolt, when it came, was violent and dramatic. The rebels prepared carefully by forging weapons and using caves as both fortresses and refuges. They declared independence and made it stick. They took a large part of Judea away from the Romans and governed it for three years. They passed laws, issued coins, and above all, ran a war.

Unlike in the revolt of 66 to 70, the Jews were united. Their leader was a charismatic, ruthless, and effective man who acquired the nom de guerre Simon Bar Kokhba, Simon, Son of a Star. This may refer to a biblical prophecy, to the new star that Hadrian's astrologers saw after Antinous's death, or to both. Bar Kokhba acquired the title of Prince of Israel, and his coins advertised liberty and redemption. Jews hoped that he was the Messiah. Romans saw a security challenge requiring a major response, especially when rebel attacks caused Roman losses leading to the disbandment of one and possibly two legions.

Hadrian might have considered the rebels ingrates who rejected his liberation from their backward beliefs. Before deciding to build Aelia, perhaps he spoke to Hellenized Jews who assured him that most Jews would embrace Hellenism with open arms. Alas, a very different reality lay ahead. Hadrian was neither the first nor the last Western statesman to underestimate the degree of resistance to outside reformers in the Middle East.

Hell hath no fury like an emperor scorned. Hadrian took emergency measures. He rushed troops to Judea from other provinces and levied soldiers in Italy, an unpopular policy that emperors tried to avoid. He sent in his best general, Sextus Julius Severus, the governor of far-off Britain. Hadrian probably even visited the front in person, which shows the seriousness of the situation. Roman strategy was a long, hard counterinsurgency campaign against the rebels in their caves. When the time was right, the Romans laid siege to Bar Kokhba's stronghold in the town of Betar, just southwest of Jerusalem. Its fall in late 135 marked the end of organized resistance, more than three years after the outbreak of the rebellion. Bar Kokhba lay dead, his head allegedly sent to Hadrian. Mopping-up operations in Judea continued.

Unlike Adolf Hitler, Hadrian did not set out to annihilate the Jews.

Yet the most civilized of Roman emperors unleashed perhaps the worst massacre in Jewish history until the Holocaust, with sources claiming that 580,000 Jews were killed. As usual, that number should be taken with a grain of salt, but the losses were surely great, with additional numbers sold into slavery.

After the revolt, Jews were a minority in Judea—now renamed Syria Palestina. Jews were prohibited access to Jerusalem and surrounding areas except for one day a year: the anniversary of the destruction of the temple, when they were allowed to come mourn.

And yet, by no means did Hadrian destroy the Jews' life in their country. Bolstered by refugees from Judea, Jewish numbers remained robust in Galilee and other northern areas, while even Judea continued to have a small number of Jews. Hadrian's persecution targeted leading rabbis, but it also made martyrs. The Talmud considered this martyrdom to be "sanctification of God's name," and hence it strengthened the people of Israel.

Meanwhile, Judaism as a religion thrived through synagogues and teachers. The Romans allowed Jews freedom of assembly, and Hadrian's successor eventually relaxed the ban on circumcision. But the new city of Aelia made it hard to think the temple would be rebuilt soon. No wonder that the rabbinic tradition cursed Hadrian, saying of him, "May his bones rot!"

DEATH COMES FOR THE EMPEROR

By 134, Hadrian was back in Rome—or, rather, in his Tibur villa. He was already a sick man. Besides consulting doctors, astrologers, and magicians, the emperor continued to take care of the empire's business, often lying on his couch. By 136, the most pressing item on his agenda was the succession. Hadrian did not intend to leave matters until his deathbed or to others after his death, as Trajan had done.

In 136, after he suffered a near-fatal hemorrhage, Hadrian named Lucius Ceionius Commodus as his successor and adopted him as his son. The elite expressed universal opposition to this move, as Ceionius, who was thirty-five, had little to recommend him other than being one of the good-looking young noblemen Hadrian liked to have around.

No one objected more than Hadrian's great-nephew Pedanius Fuscus, grandson of his sister, Paulina, who had expected to be named to the succession. Hadrian found Pedanius's displeasure threatening—so much, in fact, that he had Pedanius executed. Once again, Hadrian expressed his tendency to tyranny. In addition, Hadrian turned on Pedanius's grandfather for having supported the ambitious young man. This was none other than Servianus, Hadrian's old rival. Servianus was influential enough to serve as consul in 134 but not so powerful as to be able to defy the emperor with impunity. Although he was ninety years old, Servianus was forced to take his own life. Before dying, he uttered a curse that Hadrian be so sick that he would wish he could die but couldn't.

As it happened, it was Sabina who died next, late in 137. She was about fifty-two years old. Predictably, gossip says that Hadrian poisoned her or drove her to kill herself. His reaction to her death hardly suggests that he wanted her out of the way. Sabina's ascent to heaven—Hadrian had her deified—is recorded in a sensitive marble relief that shows him watching her brought above by a winged female. It is a polished and moving scene. Coins and a sculpted relief also record Sabina's deification and her ascent to heaven.

And all was not well with Hadrian's successor, Ceionius. In fact, he was dying of tuberculosis, and he passed away on New Year's Day 138. Now Hadrian chose a mature man to succeed him, fifty-one-year-old Aurelius Antoninus—later the emperor Antoninus Pius, who would rule from 138 to 161. But Hadrian did not want to leave the empire in the hands of a man who was nearly as old as he was. So he insisted that Antoninus adopt two young men. One was Lucius Verus, son of the late Ceionius Commodus. The other was Marcus Annius Verus, Antoninus's nephew by marriage and a distant relative of Hadrian. The sixteen-year-old was talented and promising and shared Hadrian's intellectual interests. It was an elaborate plan, but many think that the emperor had his eye on Marcus all along; that Ceionius and Antoninus were placeholders, with Lucius Verus a spare.

If Hadrian modestly left his name off the new Pantheon, he made up for it with his tomb, Hadrian's mausoleum. Augustus's mausoleum was closed, so, like the Flavians and Trajan, Hadrian found a new resting place, and he did it in style. He built a grandiose tomb across the Tiber River on the Vatican Fields, not far from where St. Peter's Basilica would rise one day. A new bridge led to the tomb, offering the traveler a marvel. The tomb was a vast and complex structure, with two stepped, cylindrical rings rising on a square base lined with the finest marble. Its form recalled the stepped shape of an imperial funeral pyre. The similarity may have called to a Roman's mind the funeral ceremony by which an emperor's soul rose to the gods. In its grandeur, Hadrian's mausoleum rivaled Augustus's, of which it had a direct view about a half mile across the Tiber. Hadrian's mausoleum still stands today. Now it is known as the museum of Castel Sant'Angelo, having been used for centuries by Popes and Roman nobles. The ancient core is still visible.

The mausoleum was ready for Hadrian's final illness in 138. Even in the comfort of his magnificent country estate, he had trouble breathing. The emperor was hemorrhaging blood from his nose and accumulating fluid in his legs and feet, the result of hardening of the arteries and heart disease. As his condition got worse, he tried magic and charms. When they came to nothing, Hadrian reached the conclusion that death would be a release. The man who described his soul as his body's "guest and comrade" was ready to let go. He begged his servants to kill him, but even though he promised money and immunity, they all refused. He was, after all, the Roman emperor—and who would be willing to kill the emperor?

At last, his hunting assistant, a barbarian prisoner of war and a slave known for his strength and bravery, agreed to do it. Hadrian drew a colored line on his skin under his nipple, at the spot where his doctor had advised the blow to be struck, but in the end, even the barbarian refused. Knowing that Hadrian was not done with suicide attempts, his heir, Antoninus, took his dagger from him. Now Hadrian asked his doctor for poison, but the physician refused. At sixty-two, Hadrian was old but not aged; "his old age was still fresh and strong," an ancient writer commented. But the emperor was wasting away.

Hadrian wished to die, but his desperate efforts to get someone to kill him all failed. So he fulfilled Servianus's curse. Finally, Hadrian saw the end coming. By now, he had reached a state of philosophical composure.

The failing emperor is said to have composed a short poem, thus:

> *O blithe little soul, thou, flitting away,*
> *Guest and comrade of this my clay,*
> *Whither now goest thou, to what place*
> *Bare and ghastly and without grace?*
> *Nor, as thy wont was, joke and play.*

Animula vagula blandula: the first line of the Latin original demonstrates the poem's singsong, nursery-rhyme quality, as if the great man were reverting to childhood—but in a carefully wrought way. He displays a certain wry realism; a philosophical detachment about what lay ahead. Or was he whistling in the dark?

On July 10, 138, Hadrian died.

When he passed on, it is said that the people hated him and that many had harsh words for Hadrian, remembering the murders of the ex-consul and of Pedanius and Servianus. He was not buried in his mausoleum in Rome but in a place on the Bay of Naples close to where he died. The new emperor, Antoninus, had to fight with the Senate to get it to agree to Hadrian's deification. The Senate did not have many powers left, but approving deification was one of them. A year after his death, Hadrian's ashes were finally laid to rest in his chosen burial place in Rome. In 139 his funeral procession solemnly climbed the spiral ramp through the center of the tomb in a stately march by torchlight and deposited his ashes in an urn in the heart of the complex. There he joined Sabina's ashes.

LEGACY

In some ways, Hadrian is an example of what not to do as emperor. He exhausted himself by too much travel, when he should have delegated some

Relief of Cleopatra and Caesarion. Temple of Hathor, Dendera, Egypt. Cleopatra and her son, allegedly fathered by Julius Caesar, are depicted here as Egyptians for an Egyptian audience. For Greek and Roman audiences, Cleopatra was usually depicted as a Greek.

Caligula. This gem in profile of the emperor Caligula (reigned 37–41), also known as Gaius, was carved in mother-of-pearl in the seventeen hundreds and possibly made in the Netherlands. The sculptor's name is not known.

Livia, wife of Augustus, mother of Tiberius. This life-size portrait of one of antiquity's most powerful women is carved in basalt, a dark stone that might have been meant to recall the color of bronze. It is now in the Louvre museum.

4

Claudius. This engraving of the emperor (reigned 41–54) on horseback features background scenes from his life: the construction of a new Tiber port (left) and the performance of a mock naval battle in Rome (right). The print by Adriaen Collaert was published in Antwerp in 1587–1589 as part of a series on Roman emperors.

5

Colosseum, Rome. These iconic ruins remain from what was originally known as the Flavian Amphitheater.

6

Nero and his mother, Agrippina the Younger. This gold coin minted in Rome, now in the British Museum, displays Agrippina's names and titles beside the heads, while Nero's appear in the less prestigious position on the reverse.

Pompeia Plotina. Wife of the emperor Trajan (reigned 98–117), Plotina was also a friend and supporter of Hadrian (reigned 117–138). The inscription, in French, praises her wisdom. This print is by Stefano della Bella (1610–1664), an Italian draftsman and printmaker.

Trajan's Column, Rome. The column depicts scenes from the Dacian Wars. Originally the column was topped by a statue of Trajan, but today there is a statue of Saint Peter.

Vibia Sabina. This marble head in the Vatican Museums conveys something of the beauty of the highborn wife of the emperor Hadrian.

Hadrian's Wall, England. Here it climbs the dramatic terrain of the Northumberland crags.

Pantheon, Rome. A view of the interior, with its regular, coffered panels and its soaring dome. Light pours through the circular opening at the dome's apex.

Hadrian's mausoleum, Rome. Later used by the Popes and much remodeled, it is also known as Castel Sant'Angelo.

Antinous, Hadrian's beloved. Detail of a statue, made of polychrome Parian marble, in the Delphi Archaeological Museum, Greece. Antinous was deified after his death in 130 and is today represented in many surviving statues.

Faustina the Younger. This gold coin of the wife of the emperor Marcus Aurelius proclaims her title as Augusta, an honor bestowed on her after the birth of her first child in 147.

15 Septimius Severus, his wife Julia Domna, his sons, Caracalla and Geta (erased). This remarkable work of art, tempera on wood from Egypt circa 200, shows the imperial family with Geta erased after his murder at his brother's order. Antikensammlung, Staatliche Museen zu Berlin, Germany.

16

Arch of Septimius Severus, Rome. Detail of a triumphal arch celebrating the emperor's Parthian victories.

17

Diocletian's Palace. A view of the partially restored peristyle or central court of the emperor's retirement residence and garrison fortress in Split (ancient Spalatum), Croatia.

Milvian Bridge, Rome. Much restored since antiquity, only the center is largely Roman. Constantine's victory here in 312 gave Rome its first Christian emperor.

Arch of Constantine, Rome. A triumphal arch celebrating the emperor's victory at the Milvian Bridge in 312.

Justinian. A detail of a mosaic showing the Eastern Roman, or Byzantine, emperor (reigned 527–565) with Bishop Maximian in the apse of the Church of San Vitale, Ravenna, Italy.

Theodora. A detail of a mosaic showing the Byzantine empress (reigned 527–548) with her retinue, in the apse of the same church.

Palace of Domitian. This great sunken garden in the imperial palace on the Palatine Hill, Rome, was nicknamed the hippodrome because of its resemblance to a racetrack. The circle of a private amphitheater, inserted centuries later, is visible in the background.

of it. He possibly made himself sick, either by travel or drinking, although genetic factors or mere chance may have been more important in causing his illness. He meddled in provincial affairs unnecessarily and stirred up a disastrous war in Judea.

Hadrian reached the throne in less-than-aboveboard circumstances and began his reign by murdering four very prominent men, thereby making the Senate hate and fear him. He was more gracious to ordinary people than to his peers, among which group he didn't suffer fools gladly. He had a tendency to be melancholy, volatile, and competitive.

His critics called him a know-it-all and a show-off who practiced every imaginable activity, from philosophy to painting, and couldn't stand those who outdid him. The historian Cassius Dio, who came from a provincial family that had risen to the Senate, passionately opposed that body's enemies, such as Hadrian. He wrote of the emperor: "For, inasmuch as he wished to surpass everybody in everything, he hated those who attained eminence in any direction." What some saw as attention to detail others considered meddling, what some considered discipline others thought of as rigidity, and what some applauded as generosity others decried as officiousness. Yet balanced against all this is a great set of achievements.

Hadrian called himself the new Augustus, a second founder of the empire, and in some ways he was right. Like Augustus, he built up the city of Rome. Both men rationalized, organized, and codified Roman laws and practices.

They both traveled around the provinces and promoted fundamental change. Both offered opportunity to provincial elites, but Hadrian opened the door even more widely than did Augustus. Hadrian promoted Hellenism, while Augustus was fundamentally Roman. Both founded cities, and both made their images ubiquitous around the empire to a degree that no other emperor matched.

In some ways, however, Hadrian was the opposite of Augustus—and to his credit, one might conclude. Although both promoted peace, Augustus advocated "empire without end" (*imperium sine fine*), and, in his continuing wars of conquest, he showed that he meant it. Like Tiberius, Hadrian considered Rome a satiated power: he withdrew from Trajan's conquests in the Middle East and eastern Dacia, and he built walls and trenches, signs of a policy of peace within fixed frontiers. Ironically, Augustus was not much of a soldier, while Hadrian loved the military life.

In politics, they displayed many differences. Hadrian, like Augustus, was a practical genius, but without the patience to conciliate the Senate. In him, one senses a Caligula or Nero waiting to break out. Maybe Trajan sensed it too and found yet another reason to hesitate before choosing Hadrian as his successor.

Hadrian had no alter ego or right-hand man; no one he trusted as Augustus trusted Agrippa, or Vespasian did Titus, or Trajan did Sura. But Hadrian promoted talent. He chose a philosopher as governor of Egypt, a scholar as his chief secretary, a jurist as a legal reformer, and a historian and military theorist as governor of Cappadocia in Asia Minor (today's Turkey). These were all intellectuals, but to head the Praetorian Guard, Hadrian chose a bruiser who had risen from the rank of centurion. Hadrian was open minded but not easy to work for: he fired the chief secretary and the Praetorian prefect.

Hadrian was vain and boastful about his multiple talents in culture and engineering (architecture, poetry, singing, playing the lyre, mathematics, military science, philosophy, sophistry), whereas Augustus was more discreet. In one of the few exceptions, Hadrian put the name of Agrippa on his rebuilt Pantheon and left off his own name, but the result accrued to Hadrian's credit because it associated him with the era of Augustus.

Augustus centered his personal life on his marriage and children and grandchildren, while Hadrian was primarily homosexual and had a love affair with a young Greek that would have scandalized Augustus, as it did some Romans of Hadrian's day. Both created a new religion, but Augustus put the focus on his adoptive father, his family, and himself, not a dead Greek young man.

Many observers see in the age of Hadrian the Roman Empire at its height. Hadrian largely succeeded in his goal of making the empire peaceful, prosperous, and more open. Under him, Rome and the Greek East were bursting with cultural production and artistic flowering. Some of the most famous surviving monuments of the ancient world date to his reign. Hovering above it all is Hadrian's visage. He is not only one of the most often illustrated emperors in ancient art but also the most engaging: handsome, intelligent, by turns sympathetic and terrifying, philosophical-looking with his beard, military in his bearing, enigmatic in his expression.

Hadrian left a rich legacy to his successor. Under Antoninus Pius, the empire was, if anything, more peaceful and prosperous than under Hadrian. Marcus Aurelius started out by continuing Hadrian's border policies, but events got in his way.

Perhaps that is not surprising, because Hadrian, for all his success, provokes a certain foreboding. He offered Greco-Roman elitism, border fortifications that were more show than substance, suppression of rebellion that left the survivors spiritually strong, and a new religion whose appeal was yet to be tested. Paganism's rebirth would prove short lived. The system of frontier defenses would not hold off the enemies who lived beyond them. Nor would Romans long display the self-control not to scratch the old itch of expansion without end.

Marcus Aurelius equestrian statue, detail.

7

MARCUS AURELIUS

THE PHILOSOPHER

This is a story about a statue and a book, for both explain what makes Marcus Aurelius different from every other Roman emperor.

The statue is known to millions of tourists who come to Rome every year and make their way to the Campidoglio, the ancient Capitoline Hill that rises above the Roman Forum. There they see the famous gilded bronze figure of a man on horseback: Marcus Aurelius. Dignified and upright, and a little larger than life-size, he sits calmly astride the beast. With his right arm outstretched over the plaza, itself a Renaissance masterpiece of harmonious design, the emperor projects a unique and palpable serenity. Although dressed in civilian clothes, he symbolizes victory. Originally he stood for military triumph over a now-obscure barbarian tribe. Today Marcus seems to represent a different sort of victory: one over the forces of disorder and darkness within every soul.

Look closely at the horseman's face—preferably by entering the adjacent museum where the original statue stands; the one on the plaza is a replica. Wide eyed, smooth skinned, and surrounded by curly locks and a long beard, Marcus's face has the stillness and otherworldliness of a Byzantine icon. There's nothing here of the world-weariness of another ancient portrait of him: no sagging flesh on the cheeks, no little lines and bags under the eyes. The man on horseback is in his prime and a master of self-control. Or maybe *master* is the wrong word. He seems at one with his horse, as much a part of nature as its lord. It was fitting for someone who wrote that we should "think of the universe as one living being, with one substance and one soul." In its expressiveness, the statue of Marcus offers a taste of the Rome that lay ahead: the eternal city whose power would reside in the spirit rather than the sword. And that brings us to the book.

Marcus is not the only Roman emperor to have published a book. Others did, starting with Augustus, or, if we count him as an emperor, Julius Caesar. But none of their books has survived except for Caesar's commentaries and the speeches, letters, and essays of the fourth-century emperor Julian. They are works of great interest, but none of them touches the heart the way Marcus's book does. No other ruler of the ancient world bares his soul like Marcus. In fact, very few rulers in history do anything of the kind—at least not until our tell-all age, and maybe not even then. Marcus lives as a person.

Marcus is the only emperor who wrote a self-help book. He didn't write it with that goal in mind or even with the intention of publication. He meant to keep it private. (More on that later.) Nonetheless, his *Meditations* remains a bestseller today, a book cherished by millions, and a favorite of presidents and generals and of Hollywood too. Of all the books written during the Roman Empire, it is second in readership today only to the New Testament.

He is as close to a philosopher-king as western history records. While Hadrian dabbled in Greek philosophy, Marcus lived and breathed it, particularly Stoicism. Yet like other Roman Stoics, Marcus viewed this Greek creed through a Roman lens. He saw it as a recipe for manliness, principle, and responsibility.

Marcus reaped what Hadrian sowed. He made Roman culture more Greek than ever before. He also represented a great turnaround. In the first century AD, Stoic philosophers provided a major source of elite opposition to the emperors. Seventy years after Domitian expelled philosophers from Rome, a philosopher ruled the empire.

In truth, it was a brief moment. With one later exception, Marcus was not only the first but also the last philosopher to rule Rome. Nor was Marcus simply a philosopher: he was an emperor. He could be harsh or capricious. He reinforced class distinctions. Persecution of Christians increased on the local level during his reign, and Marcus surely bears some responsibility. As a general, he was conscientious rather than outstanding. And yet Marcus was great because, more than any other emperor, he ruled through a commitment to justice and goodness. He aimed at humanity, steered clear of cruelty, and frequently sought compromise. He made duty his lodestar. Although he wanted to devote his reign to dispensing justice and putting into place reforms at home, Marcus spent most of it making war abroad. It pained him to do so, but he saved his complaints for his diary. In public, he was a rock.

He needed to be. Rome suffered unprecedented disaster under Marcus. In addition to war on two foreign fronts and the invasion of northern Italy and Greece, Rome witnessed a devastating epidemic and the manpower shortage that followed, as well as natural disaster and financial overstretch. Only a man of Marcus's strength of character could have coped with such threats—not that he did so perfectly.

Marcus Aurelius ruled Rome as emperor for nineteen years, but he is a figure for the ages.

THE CHOSEN

Marcus was born in Rome on April 26, 121. His family belonged to the "Spanish Mafia," like Trajan and Marcus's distant cousin Hadrian. His ancestors had moved to Rome, where Marcus was raised. His name at birth was Marcus Annius Verus. He took the name Marcus Aurelius later, when he was adopted into the imperial family.

Like many other Romans, Marcus lost his father early, when he was three. In principle, his paternal grandfather had the responsibility for his upbringing, with an assist from his maternal stepfather. In practice, his mother, Domitia Lucilla, played a large role. Marcus lived under her roof until his late teenage years.

Domitia Lucilla was noble and rich. Her property included a big brick-works outside Rome. Well educated, she could read Greek as well as Latin. Even when Marcus was a young man, she used to sit on his bed and hold conversations with him before dinner. Marcus thanks her in his *Meditations* for teaching him "the fear of God, and generosity; and abstention, not only from doing ill but even from the very thought of doing it; and furthermore to live the simple life, far removed from the habits of the rich." Although he thanks his grandfather first, for teaching him good morals and control of his temper, and his father second, for leaving him a reputation for modesty and manliness, Marcus has much more to say about his mother. Like so many Roman men, Marcus presented himself as someone shaped and molded in important ways by his mother.

In 138 Marcus's life changed when Hadrian adopted Antoninus as his son and successor and had Antoninus adopt both Lucius Verus and Marcus. After Antoninus became emperor later that year, Marcus moved into the palace on the Palatine.

Marcus had a series of tutors, many of them eminent and learned men. The best known is the greatest Latin orator of the age, Marcus Cornelius Fronto. A North African of Berber origin and a Roman citizen, Fronto made a fortune in Rome as a lawyer. Antoninus Pius appointed him as tutor to his two adopted sons, Marcus and Verus. Fronto's letters survive, including many between him and Marcus. They show the future emperor as a serious, talented, and sometimes carefree and even thoughtless young man who loved country life. He takes part in the grape harvest and, while on horseback, scatters a poor shepherd's flock just for fun. The letters tend to exaggerate Fronto's importance in Marcus's eyes. Other teachers had a greater influence on the young man, but no letters from or to them survive.

Marcus and Fronto write to each other in the stylized language of pederasty: love between man and boy. They said constantly how much they loved each other, sometimes in gushing terms. Some of this amounted to mutual flattery, and some of it showed off each writer's ability to imitate the homo-erotic language of the classical Greeks. It's unlikely that Marcus and Fronto really were in love, let alone that they had a physical relationship. If they did, they would hardly have expressed it in letters that could be read by Marcus's mother or by the educated slaves that formed part of the staff of a wealthy Roman household. Elite Romans frowned on homosexual relationships and could even prosecute relationships involving underage Roman citizens. In his *Meditations*, Marcus favored putting an end to the pursuit of boys.

Fronto wanted Marcus Aurelius to become a rhetorician. The equivalent does not quite exist in contemporary American culture. Think of an Ivy League lawyer, raised in Europe until college, whose speeches combine fancy rhetoric with literary erudition and an insufferable number of learned references and arcane words. After years of studying rhetoric, Marcus declined the honor. He decided to become a student of philosophy instead. In ancient Rome just as today a philosopher was an intellectual who engaged in profound argument, but he was something different as well. For the ancients, philosophy offered a guide to living. A philosopher was something between a guru and a clergyman.

To have a philosopher as heir to the throne might seem a paradox. In Rome, philosophy was best known for its opposition to the emperors, not for its support. Indeed, Marcus's main philosophy teacher was the descendant of a philosopher executed by Domitian. But after Nero, Vespasian, and Domitian, the emperors no longer persecuted philosophers. Romans now enjoyed, as Tacitus said, "the rare happiness of times, when we may think what we please, and express what we think."

Although Marcus's philosophy was eclectic, his main influence was Stoicism, which was in turn the most popular philosophy of the Roman elite. Stoicism taught that the world was governed by a rational principle, Logos, that guides all nature. By the pursuit of virtue, a good man would live according to nature. This austere doctrine was softened by a belief in the universe's goodness and its government by divine providence, as well as in the brotherhood of mankind.

Stoicism originated in Greece, but it appealed to the old Roman temperament because of its sternness and to Roman imperialism because of its universalism. Under the emperors, Stoicism gave men and women the courage to resist and the reason to do so too because it demonstrated the inner moral corruption that followed subjection to a higher power. And yet

Stoicism did not reject monarchy per se but only overbearing and corrupt monarchy. A good emperor, who was liberal, moderate, law abiding, public spirited, and respectful of his subjects, could be a philosopher.

So Marcus the philosopher was less an eccentric than a consummation. Enlightened by philosophy, he fulfilled the promise of the four Good Emperors who came before him.

Like Hadrian, Marcus admired the philosophy of Epictetus. The Greek Stoic had every reason to emphasize mind over matter, as both his body and his status taught him the limits of the flesh. He was lame. An ex-slave from Asia Minor, he had belonged to one of Nero's freedmen before eventually gaining his own freedom. After becoming a philosopher, Epictetus was exiled by Domitian—and chose to stay in exile even after that ruler's death, when it was safe to return to Rome. Evidently Epictetus preferred a quiet, provincial life. The philosopher emphasized the importance of achieving inner freedom. His teaching influenced Marcus greatly.

Looking back on Fronto in later years, Marcus considered him less influential than his teachers in philosophy; nor did he have a word to say about Fronto's lessons in rhetoric. In fact, Marcus criticized rhetoric as inferior to philosophy. Instead, he thanked Fronto for helping him learn about tyranny—its jealousy, duplicity, and hypocrisy—and about the lack of paternal affection in so-called patricians. Perhaps it was a gentle way of thanking Fronto for making Marcus an honest speaker rather than a trickster.

ANTONINUS PIUS

Antoninus had little experience of provincial administration or military service, but Hadrian did not expect his fifty-one-year-old successor to last long in power. It was Marcus whom the emperor really wanted, not only because Marcus was kin but also due to his exceptional strength of character. Hence Hadrian gave him the nickname Verissimus, "the Most Upright," a play on Marcus's family name before adoption, Verus. Marcus evidently did not return the compliment, since he leaves Hadrian out of the long list of friends and family whom he thanks in his *Meditations*.

Antoninus surprised everyone by reigning for twenty-three years, longer than Hadrian. In fact, Antoninus ruled longer than any emperor since Augustus. A wit once said to Antoninus after seeing Marcus's mother at prayer that she must have been asking for the emperor to die so that her son could replace him. The emperor's response is unknown. In any case, Marcus had to wait until the age of forty before ascending to power.

Antoninus came from a wealthy Roman family with roots in southern Gaul and political prominence founded on early support for Vespasian. He grew even richer by marrying the affluent Anna Galeria Faustina—Faustina the Elder. In spite of their combined fortunes, Antoninus began to worry about the expenses of his new position as soon as Hadrian adopted him. Shortly afterward, when Faustina the Elder complained about his stinginess to their household, Antoninus is said to have replied, "Foolish woman, now that we have gained an empire, we have lost even what we had before."

Antoninus took the nickname Pius, Latin for "faithful" or "loyal." On the one hand, it referred to his insistence on making a reluctant Senate give divine honors to his adoptive father, Hadrian. On the other hand, it announced his commitment to his family members and to family values more generally. Not only did he take the unusual step of naming his wife Augusta when he became emperor, but Antoninus greatly increased the number of coins depicting the empress.

In general, though, Antoninus was a conservative. Although not much of a builder, he did erect one structure that proclaimed him worthy of the country's past. He built a Temple of the Deified Hadrian in Rome next to the Temple of Matidia and Marciana, which in turn bordered the Pantheon. A walker in Rome would have seen the names of Agrippa (on the Pantheon), Matidia, Marciana, and Hadrian in rapid succession. The intended conclusion was that Antoninus, Hadrian's adopted and loyal son, had as legitimate a claim to rule as Augustus himself.

Antoninus prized the Senate, and, unlike the often vicious Hadrian, he had excellent relations with it. Nor did he continue Hadrian's travels. In fact, after becoming emperor, Antoninus never left Italy again. Although the frugal

Antoninus limited his building projects, unlike Hadrian, he was a realist and frequently distributed money to the Roman plebeians and to the army. In 148 he put on marvelous games in honor of the nine hundredth anniversary of the founding of Rome. It was commonly believed at the time that Rome was founded on April 21, 753 BC, although we do not know the real date of the city's foundation. As a result of these costly expenditures, Antoninus had temporarily to reduce the amount of silver in Roman coins.

The provincial elite did not feel neglected by the emperor's absence, not to judge from a famous speech of the era. Aelius Aristides, a wealthy Greek from northwestern Asia Minor and a Roman citizen, came to Rome and delivered an oration before Antoninus. He focused on the greatness of the Roman peace. Aristides praised the fair-mindedness that motivated Rome to share its citizenship with millions. "You conduct public business throughout the whole civilized world exactly as if it were one city-state," he stated. He glorified Romans for making war a thing of the past within the empire, and for fostering agriculture, trade, and public building. Meanwhile, they protected the borders with something better than a wall: the Roman army. "The entire earth," he stated, "has been made beautiful like a garden."

Antoninus probably rejoiced to hear it, as he had little interest in things military. His generals settled border problems in Dacia and Mauretania. The major effort came in Britain, where they put down a revolt and advanced into southern Scotland and built the Antonine Wall, a turf-wall companion to Hadrian's brick wall farther south. But Rome abandoned the wall less than ten years after it was completed, evidently concluding that the attempt to add territory was too ambitious.

Marcus praised Antoninus in the *Meditations*, calling him a man who was devoted to the empire's needs, energetic and hardworking, rational and reliable, modest, indifferent to honors and immune to flattery, tolerant and compassionate, and orderly but decisive. In a word, he was indomitable. Yet Marcus made no mention of military affairs, an extraordinary silence about a Roman emperor—and probably not a compliment. A storm was gathering across the border, and in retrospect, Antoninus did nothing to prepare Rome for it.

JUSTICE AT HOME

Antoninus died on March 7, 161, in his country villa. Supposedly his last word was *equanimity*—that is, keeping an even mind under stress. It was good advice for his successor.

In many ways, Marcus had superb preparation for the throne. His education gave him first-class training in rhetoric and philosophy, and he had as good a character as any man who ever ruled Rome. Before becoming emperor, he served in all the important public offices in Rome. Yet he suffered glaring deficiencies too. Antoninus kept Marcus on a tight leash and by his side in Italy. Marcus is said to have spent only two nights away from Antoninus during the latter's twenty-three-year-reign. By the time Marcus became emperor, he had never commanded an army or governed a province. Astonishingly, he had never left Italy. By contrast, Augustus had had considerable military and diplomatic experience by the age of twenty-one.

Although Hadrian made Antoninus adopt both Marcus and Lucius Verus, Antoninus clearly intended Marcus to be emperor. Yet Marcus surprised many by making Verus his coruler. Marcus served as senior partner. He was older, more respected, and the sole holder of the office of chief priest. Verus had a well-deserved reputation as a luxury-loving lightweight, although not a vicious man like Nero or Domitian. Still, there had never been co-emperors before.

Why Marcus chose a coruler is much debated. He might have wanted to respect Hadrian's wishes, or perhaps what Marcus really wanted was time to pursue philosophy. Even when emperor, he still attended philosophy lectures. Possibly Marcus feared Verus's powerful family and preferred to have them in the tent and happy than outside fighting to get in. But perhaps the real reason is that, as a philosopher, Marcus saw clearly that the emperor's job was too much for one man. If so, Marcus was ahead of his time. His immediate successors did not follow his practice, but, a little more than a century later, it became standard for Rome to have two emperors.

Another factor may have been Marcus's health, which worsened as he got older. Symptoms included chest and stomach pains, spitting blood, and dizziness. The emperor had the advice of one of the most famous doctors in history, Galen, a Greek who lived in Rome. Once, after Galen cured an aging Marcus, the emperor proclaimed him "first among physicians and unique among philosophers."

For the emperor's long-term care, Galen prescribed theriac, a drug consisting of various natural ingredients combined into a pill and taken with wine. The finishing touch, added by Galen to the pill, was opium. Whether the doctor added enough opium to addict Marcus is a distinct possibility, although we cannot be certain.

Marcus proved popular in his early years as emperor. Unlike Hadrian, he was no scheming courtier. He was straightforward and open, at least for a politician. Marcus was thoughtful but not, he wrote, quick witted. He tolerated dissent and even insult. He worked very hard. Early in his reign, Marcus wrote to Fronto that he found it difficult to relax, and it's not hard to understand why, with his conscientious approach to business.

Marcus proved exceptionally careful and judicious when it came to the law. He took special interest in the manumission of slaves, the appointment of guardians for minors and orphans, and the selection of town councilors for local governments in the provinces. He earned a reputation for being firm but reasonable. Like his predecessor, Marcus ruled in favor of a slave's freedom whenever possible.

Marcus went out of his way to show respect to the Senate. He extended that body's judicial powers and deferred to it even in cases that the emperor had the right to decide. He made a point of attending Senate meetings whenever he was in Rome. If any senator stood accused of a capital crime, he examined the evidence in secret before sharing it in public.

Marcus endeared himself to the people in other ways as well. He ignored professional informers. He improved welfare arrangements for poor children and paid careful attention to the grain supply. He kept the streets of Rome clean and in good repair. He made sure that town councils in Italy had full staffs and functioned effectively. However, one thing that Marcus did was probably not popular: he so disliked bloodshed that when he watched the games, he made gladiators use blunt swords. The public preferred blood.

Like his predecessor, Marcus practiced thrift. By the same token, he found quickly that military spending swamped other priorities. It's no surprise, then, that, like Antoninus but unlike Hadrian, he did little building. In Rome, Marcus raised a monumental column to mark Antoninus's deification and one or more triumphal arches. We don't know whether Marcus or his successor began the column that still stands in Rome and celebrates Marcus's military success; it wasn't completed until more than a decade after Marcus's death. The famous statue of Marcus on horseback, now so prominent, was modest compared with what certain other emperors erected. The statue celebrates a victory over the Germanic tribes and probably went up late in Marcus's reign or shortly afterward.

PORTRAIT OF A MARRIAGE

Like Hadrian, Marcus married into the emperor's family, but he stepped onto a higher level of nobility, so to speak. Hadrian married the emperor's grandniece, while Marcus married the emperor's daughter. Although Hadrian had named Marcus his eventual successor, Antoninus could have revoked the proclamation after Hadrian's death. Instead, he affirmed it by giving Marcus his daughter's hand. Marcus was his wife's nephew.

Anna Galeria Faustina, Marcus's bride, could hardly remember a time when she didn't live in a palace and enjoy its privileges, since her father became emperor when she was eight. Her mother, Faustina the Elder, was a very wealthy woman who was named Augusta when Antoninus became emperor. Two years later, when Faustina was ten, her mother died and was proclaimed a goddess. Antoninus set up a charitable institution for the daughters of the poor known in his wife's memory as Faustina's Girls. A temple in Faustina the Elder's honor would soon rise on the edge of the Roman Forum.

Five years later, Faustina married Marcus. He was twenty-four, she, fifteen. Two years after that, immediately following the birth of her first child, a girl, her father gave Faustina the title of Augusta. Marcus was only a Caesar, so Faustina outranked him. But Antoninus felt devoted to his daughter. He said he would rather live in exile on a bleak island with her than live in the palace at Rome without her. On his deathbed, Antoninus committed the state and his daughter to Marcus. He died on March 7, 161.

When Marcus became emperor, Faustina became the first Roman woman to follow her mother as empress. Six months after Marcus took power, she gave birth to twin boys, which made Faustina the first empress since Nero's wife Poppaea to give birth while her husband was emperor. Fourteen years after bearing her first child, Faustina was still having children. In the end, Faustina bore fourteen children. It was a remarkable record, and the palace's propaganda machine featured it prominently on coins. Fewer than half of the babies survived childhood, which is a bleak reminder of a world that knew high infant mortality rates.

Not only was the young Faustina noble, rich, and fertile, but she was also beautiful, as her portrait busts show. Coin images associated her with Venus, the goddess of love and sex and also victory. The austere Marcus probably limited his interest in things amatory to procreation. He had prided himself on having not lost his virginity any earlier than necessary. Nor was the heart the only organ in regard to which the two differed; they disagreed about the head as well. Faustina did not leave politics to her husband. She plotted and pushed against some of the very men in high office whom Marcus supported. Faustina wanted to have fun, and she wanted her way. Marcus was all business. It is doubtful that the two had an easy relationship.

The Roman rumor mill ground out gossip that an unhappy Faustina had a series of affairs, and not just with aristocrats but also with low-life characters. His friends told Marcus that while at her seaside villa, she slept with gladiators and sailors. The same friends encouraged him to divorce if not execute Faustina. He supposedly replied, "If we send our wife away, we must also return her dowry." That is, the empire, which he had inherited from his father-in-law.

Marcus presumably understood, if others did not, that the empire was a family business. Powerful people attracted malicious rumors, and that went double for powerful women, given the extent of Roman misogyny. Besides, if true, the rumors would cast into doubt the legitimacy of his children. So Marcus had every reason to deny stories about his wife's infidelity. In any case, the emperor felt real affection for Faustina. He described her in *Meditations* as obedient, affectionate, and straightforward.

Marcus was nothing if not a man who loved his children. He called his little daughter Faustina, for instance, "a cloudless sky, a holiday, hope close at hand, a wish come true, a total joy, an excellent and flawless source of pride." He makes several references in his book to the pain of losing a child.

VICIOUS CIRCLE

Foreign affairs soon turned Marcus's attention away from his family. Indeed, the cycle of war overshadowed everything else in his principate. It turned him from an enlightened reformer in the sunshine at home to an embattled warrior in a twilight struggle on the frontier. And it forced a man with almost no military background to become a field commander. Naturally, he made mistakes.

A two-front war was the empire's enduring security problem, and Rome confronted it for the first time during the reign of Marcus Aurelius. The first crisis came in the East, where the Parthians detected Roman weakness. No doubt they knew that it had been decades since a military man led. They attacked Armenia and drove out its pro-Roman ruler in favor of a pro-Parthian. When a Roman general counterattacked, the Parthians wiped out his legion, and the general committed suicide. The Parthians invaded Syria next and routed its governor.

This serious a situation required the emperor's presence in the war zone. Neither Marcus nor Verus had military experience, but Verus was younger and physically more robust, so Marcus sent him. No one would miss Verus in Rome, nor was he likely to threaten Marcus on his return. Verus would be more or less a figurehead in the east, where seasoned generals would serve as the real commanders.

To face the Parthians, Marcus withdrew three legions as well as other troops from Rome's western front. It was necessary but dangerous because it tempted a restive enemy that lay north of the Danube River. But Rome had no strategic reserve, a fundamental weakness that left the emperor with no choice but to move legions as needed.

Those legions proved effective. The war against Parthia took four years but resulted in complete victory. Rome reconquered Armenia and installed a highly appropriate man as the new king: a Roman senator who also had Parthian royal blood. The Romans then drove deep into Mesopotamia, where they burned a Parthian palace and, disgracefully, sacked a friendly city.

In 164 Marcus gave Verus his daughter Lucilla in marriage. She was fourteen at the time, while her husband was thirty-three. The girl had to make the long journey from Rome to the East, where the marriage took place. It was wartime, though, and everyone had to sacrifice. Perhaps as a consolation, Marcus made her an Augusta immediately, even before she gave birth to a child, which had not been the case for her mother, who received the title only after bearing a child.

Parthia would not challenge Rome again for thirty years. All was not quiet on the western front, however. In 166 and 167, Germans attacked Rome's provinces along the Danube. It marked a milestone in the empire's history. Rome had not faced a serious German threat in many decades, but now the Germans exploded into action. They would continue to threaten the empire on and off for centuries, until eventually they brought it down in the West. To make things worse, the invaders of 166–167 were themselves being pushed by other peoples on the move farther north. It was the beginning of a major migration of historic proportions.

The invaders took advantage of the reduced Roman military strength in the West. Marcus tried to compensate for the three legions that joined Verus in the East by raising two new legions. They lacked experience, however, and were insufficient in numbers.

Before Marcus could react to the invasion, a new problem assailed the empire in 167: plague. So the ancient sources call it, but the disease was probably smallpox. Modern historians call it the Antonine plague or the Great Pestilence. Antiquity witnessed many major epidemics. It's not clear whether this was one of the worst or just one of the best documented.

Accurate mortality figures are not available, but it's clear that nearly a million people or perhaps many millions died.

There is reason to think the disease began in Central Asia and first spread eastward to China before traveling the Silk Road, the trade route to the Middle East. Roman soldiers first caught the illness in Mesopotamia and brought it back with them to every part of the empire, with merchants spreading it as well. The same well-paved roads and safe seas that brought glory to the Roman peace now became the deadly vectors of infection. It was a universal epidemic for a universal empire, and it is the ancient epidemic of which we have the most knowledge. Reports survive of suffering and death in Egypt, Asia Minor, Gaul, Germany, Italy, and particularly in Rome—all roads led there, after all.

Conditions became so bad in Rome that the famous physician Galen left for his home in Asia Minor in fear of infection. Meanwhile, in the Greek cities of the East, people inscribed a verse above their doorways asking for Apollo's protection, but it tended to have the opposite effect—perhaps because people became overconfident and stopped taking precautions. A survivor of the disease remembered the sound of wailing and groans, the sight of the dead lying before their front doors, and the fact of doctors having to double as attendants because the illness had killed their slaves.

Marcus wanted to go north in 167, but he stayed in Rome to deal with the epidemic. In 168 he finally left for the front, joined by Verus. It was Marcus's first trip outside Italy, and it succeeded in restoring order temporarily. On their return, the two emperors stopped in northeastern Italy. Galen joined them there and discovered that the epidemic was rampant. Marcus and Verus went back to Rome with a small group of soldiers. Most of the army stayed in the north, and most of them died, as winter made it even more difficult to survive the disease. Galen barely escaped with his life. Verus proved unlucky. On the way back to Rome in early 169, he died, possibly of smallpox. Marcus accompanied the body back to Rome, where Verus was buried in Hadrian's mausoleum and declared a god.

Meanwhile, the crisis on the northern frontier continued. Rome had lacked soldiers before the epidemic; smallpox reduced its manpower even further. The government had to levy new troops, but paying them was expensive. So Rome resorted to unsatisfactory solutions. Once again, as under Antoninus Pius, Marcus reduced the amount of silver in his coins. Furthermore, the state turned to slaves, gladiators, so-called bandits (well, thugs at any rate), and police forces from the Greek cities and enrolled them in auxiliary units.

Marcus's daughter Lucilla was only twenty when her husband, Verus, died. Marcus wanted her to remarry Tiberius Claudius Pompeianus, a senior senator and ex-consul. He was fifty years old and from Syria. It seemed a big step down from her status as the co-emperor's wife, and both Lucilla and her mother, Faustina, opposed it. But Marcus prevailed. Lucilla gave her new husband a son who went on to a career in public life until, many years later, the son was executed by order of a later emperor.

In autumn 169 Marcus went back north. The next spring he launched a major offensive across the Danube. It began in farce, with the emperor agreeing to put two lions in the river to win the gods' support; the beasts just swam to the other side and were clubbed to death by the enemy. The battle ended in tears, with the Romans suffering a major defeat, with possibly twenty thousand casualties. Then enemy troops managed to outflank the remaining Roman army and burst into northern Italy. They burned one city there and besieged another. Other invaders raided Greece as far south as the outskirts of Athens, where they destroyed the shrine of the Mysteries.

For the first time in almost three hundred years, foreign forces had attacked Italy. Rome's defenses on the frontier had failed. In retrospect, it should not surprise. The Danube front had witnessed a decline in the number of soldiers. The Great Pestilence weakened Rome everywhere. Marcus himself had no experience as a military commander. Many of his troops were new and still raw, while even veteran soldiers on the frontier had experienced little fighting during the long years of peace.

The next year, 171, the situation began to improve. A Roman army under Marcus's new son-in-law, Pompeianus, drove the invaders out of Italy and destroyed them in a battle on the Danube. Meanwhile, Marcus stood on the frontier, negotiating with German ambassadors and trying to set enemy tribes against one another. In 172 he launched a new invasion across the river. He continued to campaign on the far side of the Danube through 175.

During these years, the Romans experienced two miracles, which they displayed prominently in propaganda. First, a lightning bolt destroyed an enemy siege engine. Then, one hot summer, a weary legion found itself surrounded by the enemy and almost had to surrender because it had no water. Suddenly the skies opened, and the rain saved the Romans. Pagans and Christians immediately engaged in a polemic about whose prayers had won the favor of heaven.

Marcus probably intended to create two new provinces across the Danube in what is today Hungary, the Czech Republic, and Slovakia. The purpose was both to contain the enemy and to shorten Rome's line of defense, as well as replace an easily crossed river boundary with a more defensible land boundary farther north, in the Carpathian Mountains. But new provinces would have taxed Rome's overstretched resources. Marcus's plan died with him.

Marcus had much greater success in his other plan for dealing with the barbarians: settling them on land in the empire. He scattered them across provinces from Roman Germany (today's southwestern Germany and Alsace), to Dacia (Romania), and including Italy. Although many attacked him for appeasement as well as for introducing dangerous barbarians within the boundaries of the empire, Marcus saw it differently. He believed that he had turned enemy soldiers into Roman farmers while also supplying a badly needed source of manpower.

In 175 Marcus reached a settlement with the German tribes that lived across the Danube. It was more of a truce than a peace, for by no means had Rome crushed its opponents. Still, they did return Roman prisoners. They also sent Marcus eight thousand cavalry to serve in the Roman army; most of them went to Britain to do frontier duty. To judge by a remarkable recent find, some of the cavalrymen were women. Archaeologists discovered near Hadrian's Wall a pair of female skeletons that seem to have been horsewomen in this force. Although Romans did not allow women to serve in the military, certain so-called barbarians did. The Greeks and Romans thought of them as Amazons.

Marcus was not a natural soldier, but he did his job. Doing so was his duty, and Marcus was nothing if not devoted. He wrote in the *Meditations*: "Every moment, think steadily as a Roman and a man to do what you have in hand with perfect and simple dignity, and feeling of affection, and freedom, and justice; and to give yourself relief from all other thoughts."

Marcus did his job, but he did not enjoy it. As he made clear in private, he had a low opinion of war and conquest. In fact, he compares victors to bandits: "A spider is proud when it has caught a fly, and another when he has caught a poor hare, and another when he has taken a little fish in a net, and another when he has taken wild boars, and another when he has taken bears, and another when he has taken Sarmatians [one of the German tribes]. Are not these robbers, if you examine their opinions?"

The wars brought sacrifice to Faustina as well as to Marcus. She had to sell some of her silk and jewelry in order to raise money for the Treasury. Worse, she spent years living with Marcus on the frontier. The cities of Carnuntum (in today's Austria) and Sirmium (in today's Serbia), where they made their base, might have both been provincial capitals and would know glory days in later years; but in this era, they were still garrison towns on the dark and chilly edge of the empire. It was a long way from the palace in Rome. Not since Agrippina the Elder served with her husband Germanicus in Germany and Syria 150 years earlier had an imperial woman lived in army headquarters on an active front. In 174 Marcus named Faustina Mother of the Camp (*Mater Castrorum*), making her the first empress to bear such a title. It boosted the public's morale during a time of crisis but probably offered Faustina poor recompense for the comforts that she gave up.

In any case, Faustina was not the last empress to be called Mother of the Camp. Emergency and invasion on the frontier would became all too common in the future.

REBELLION

Avidius Cassius was the most successful general of Verus's Parthian War. He was a man to watch, the son of an equestrian who outdid his father by becoming a senator. Under Verus, Avidius conquered the two great Parthian cities of Mesopotamia. Afterward, he served as suffect consul and governor of Egypt, his home province. Finally, he received a special command over all the provinces of the Roman East. Success like this might have gone to anyone's head, especially someone who considered himself descended from the kings of Syria who followed Alexander the Great, as Avidius did.

In 175 he claimed the throne. He launched a serious rebellion, supported by most of the East, including such important provinces as Egypt and Syria. It recalls every emperor's dilemma: entrust a glorious military task to someone else, and he might try to take your throne. But no emperor could do everything everywhere, and few emperors had sufficient military talent to serve competently as field commanders. Only rare ones, like Augustus, had a trusted friend to command the army while letting the emperor take the credit.

But in another way, Avidius's revolt was unique. The sources say that Faustina wrote to him and encouraged his rebellion. It sounds like just another scandalous, misogynistic charge among many in the sources, but for once, scholars find it plausible—although certainly not proven. After all, Marcus was in poor health. Faustina did have reason for concern about her future and that of her children. Her sole surviving son, Commodus, was only thirteen, and he risked being eclipsed by his sister Lucilla's husband. Perhaps Faustina wrote Avidius that she would support him if Marcus died, and he misunderstood, thinking it meant that Marcus was already dead.

So the revolt was on. Marcus's old Greek tutor, the wealthiest man in Athens, sent Avidius his opinion in a one-word letter: *emanēs*, Greek for "You are crazy!" In far-off Sirmium, meanwhile, Marcus gathered support and prepared to march eastward to put down the rebellion. Yet before he set off, a centurion brought the uprising to an end by killing Avidius, having probably heard that Marcus was still alive. The revolt lasted only three months and six days.

Marcus was fortunate, and he didn't want vengeance. He refused to look at Avidius's severed head, which was sent to him. No doubt he approved of—and perhaps personally ordered—the burning of Avidius's correspondence, which surely contained one if not many incriminating letters from Faustina.

The rebellion was over, but Marcus nonetheless decided to go east. It seemed prudent to show his subjects in the East their healthy emperor, in command of his household, and endowed with a strong son to succeed him.

GODDESS

In late 175 Marcus's imperial procession stopped in a small town on the southern edge of the central Anatolian plateau, at the foot of the mountains (in today's south central Turkey). About fifteen miles behind them lay the big, wealthy city of Tyana, graced only recently with splendid aqueducts under Trajan and Hadrian. Ahead of them lay the so-called Cilician Gates, a mountain pass that led to the Mediterranean. Alexander the Great's army took this route, centuries earlier, on the way to conquering the Persian Empire.

The traveling party was not small. In addition to his wife, his son, and at least one of his daughters, the emperor had with him his so-called Companions (his closest advisors) and a large contingent of soldiers, including a force of barbarians. The purpose of the expedition was to mend fences in the East, to show the emperor to his subjects, both trustworthy and not, and to punish rebels.

Nobody knows what goes on in a marriage except the two people in it. It seems clear, though, that Marcus had forgiven Faustina for her possible role in fomenting the revolt. And yet doom came calling in the dusty town along the Roman road. It was there and not in a villa that Faustina, the Augusta, Mother of the Camp, daughter of Antoninus Pius, wife of Marcus Aurelius, mother of Commodus, died.

The sources suggest the possibility that Faustina committed suicide, but that seems unlikely. At forty-five, she had borne fourteen children and was possibly pregnant again. She also suffered from gout. The aftermath of Avidius's revolt caused her stress. So natural causes seems likely.

In public, Marcus appeared grief stricken, and his private praise of Faustina in the *Meditations* confirms that state. The widower asked the

Senate to deify his late wife, and he had coins struck stating that she was now among the stars. Meanwhile, he closed the door on the plot in which she was incriminated, asking the Senate to spare anyone suspected of taking part. "May it never happen," he wrote to the senators, "that any one of you should be slain during my reign either by my vote or by yours." He had resolved to forgive and forget.

Faustina was no doubt cremated where she died, however humble the surroundings. They would not stay humble! The village received the highest status that a city could hold, a colony of Roman citizens. It acquired a new name, Faustinopolis—Faustina City—and also received a temple in honor of the new goddess.

Faustina would have liked that, but she probably would have preferred the honors in Rome that the Senate voted in her memory. Those included an altar where every bride and groom married in the city had to make a sacrifice in her memory. Like her mother, she too had a charity for poor girls founded in her memory: the beneficiaries were called the New Faustina's Girls. The Senate decreed silver images of Faustina and Marcus for the Temple of Venus and Rome, the great temple built by Hadrian. Best of all, a golden statue of Faustina had to be carried into the Colosseum when Marcus was present and placed in the special section where she used to watch the games, with all the most important women sitting around it.

Meanwhile, the cleanup after the Avidius Cassius revolt continued. A new law prohibited anyone from serving as governor of his native province.

On his way south toward Egypt, Marcus stopped in the Roman province of Palestine, which had supported the rebel Avidius. A Roman source said that the emperor found the Jews there so quarrelsome that he proclaimed them worse than the barbarians on the Danube frontier. The Talmud, on the other hand, suggests that Marcus gave an audience to Rabbi Judah I. He was not only patriarch but also editor of the Mishnah, the compilation of oral law that is still one of the most influential documents in the Jewish tradition. It is easy to imagine the philosophical Marcus in conversation with the erudite rabbi.

Before leaving the East, Marcus visited Athens, where he and

Commodus were initiated into the Mysteries, following in the footsteps of Hadrian. Marcus had the shrine rebuilt after its destruction in 170, making this in effect a celebration of the return to normalcy. Marcus made time in Athens to appoint four professors of philosophy.

CO-EMPEROR

In 176 Marcus returned to Rome. He decided to make Commodus co-emperor, occupying Verus's former position. Commodus was only fifteen, but an era of war and epidemic did not permit a prolonged adolescence. He had already accompanied his father on the northern front and in the East, so the boy had some experience of government. Besides, Marcus understood his responsibility to prepare for the succession. Yet he does not seem to have seriously considered the possibility that Commodus wasn't up to the job.

While in Rome, Marcus issued important rulings on slaves, giving them with one hand what he took away with another. He protected slaves who were granted freedom in their master's will from any third party who tried to keep them enslaved. By the same token, Marcus commanded governors and other public officials and security forces to help masters look for runaway slaves. The disorder of the era might have led to an increase in the number of such escaped slaves.

Christians ran the risk of being scapegoated for Rome's troubles and of paying the price for the shortage of gladiators, who were being drafted into the army. Because arenas now found it hard to find fighters, the Senate allowed local authorities to purchase condemned criminals to use as gladiators. And how did the Romans increase the supply of condemned criminals? It seems that accusations against Christians increased.

Rome's reality, therefore, consisted of the gloomy facts of disease, invasion, and persecution. On the Danube front, the enemy reopened its attack, adding to the empire's grim mood. Still, when Marcus left Rome again in August 178 to go back to war, he left to a shining scene out of Plato's Academy. A remarkable deputation thronged the emperor, as a later source reports:

Marcus possessed such wisdom, gentleness, integrity and learning that as he was about to march against the Marcomanni with his son Commodus, whom he had substituted as Caesar, he was surrounded by a throng of philosophers begging him not to commit himself to a campaign or to battle before he had explained some difficult and very obscure points of the philosophical systems.

Marcus also demonstrated his respect for the Senate and for traditional religion before leaving Rome. He swore an oath on the Capitoline Hill that he wasn't responsible for the death of any senator. He also engaged in the old ritual of throwing a bloody spear to symbolize the righteousness of Rome's attack on enemy territory.

However honorable Marcus's fight, it proved difficult and frustrating. During another year and a half at the front, he struggled without achieving final victory.

MEDITATIONS

A personal record of these difficult years survives. Marcus wrote the *Meditations* alone in his tent on the northern frontier, among other places, during the years 172 to 180. Book 2 is labeled "On The River Gran, Among the Quadi" and book 3 "In Carnuntum," while other books lack explicit locations.

He wrote the *Meditations* for himself, not for the public. These were private notebooks. An ancient editor called it *To Himself. Meditations* is a modern title. No one is sure just how the notebooks were eventually published. Possibly Marcus's friends or one of his freedmen preserved and circulated the manuscript. The sentimental favorite is his daughter Cornificia. Marcus's last surviving child, she was forced to commit suicide by a later emperor many years after Marcus's death. Her last words were worthy of her father: "My poor, unhappy soul, trapped in an unworthy body, go forth, be free, show them that you are the daughter of Marcus Aurelius!"

Marcus wrote the *Meditations* not in Latin but in Greek. Greek was the language of philosophy, but Latin had served well enough for many earlier Roman philosophers. The use of Greek was another index of the growing prestige of the eastern half of the empire.

The *Meditations* is the last major work of Stoic philosophy in ancient times and the most loved today. It is certainly not because the work is upbeat. The focus is often on the vanity of human life and on death. Our lives, says Marcus, are as fleeting as a passing sparrow. Even the great men of the past have vanished: Augustus and his court are all gone, Alexander the Great and the man who groomed his horse have both returned to dust.

Marcus's advice on how to face life's challenges is not for the faint of heart. He writes: "Be like a headland of rock on which the waves break incessantly; but it stands fast and around it the seething of the waters stands to rest."

Yet Marcus offers a recipe for dignity and for achievement. He expresses deep respect for the natural world and deep faith in divine Providence, writing:

> If you work at that which is before you, following right reason seriously, vigorously, calmly, without allowing anything else to distract you, but keeping thy divine part pure, as if you should be bound to give it back immediately; if you hold to this, expecting nothing, fearing nothing, but satisfied with your present activity according to nature, and with heroic truth in every word and sound which you utter, you will live happy. And there is no man who is able to prevent this.

Marcus also shows remarkable respect for the wider world, looking even beyond the boundaries of the empire that he ruled. Ancient Stoicism had a strong element of cosmopolitanism, and Marcus expresses it well: "But my nature is rational and social; and my city and country, so far as I am Antoninus that is, Aurelius, is Rome, but so far as I am a man, it is the world."

Perhaps as much as anything else, Marcus appeals to us because he is all too human. He speaks often of the need for courage and manliness, but he admits his own weaknesses. He doesn't want to get out of bed in the morning. He knew that he was tempted by the pomp, falseness, and flattery of court life, and he struggled against it constantly.

His biggest flaw, however, was anger. Marcus admits freely and repeatedly that he has trouble controlling his temper. He found the people he worked with an endless source of disappointment in their shallowness and failings. Yet he knew that he had to rise above his disappointment and suppress his rage.

In short, Marcus seems less a remote and lifeless statue than someone we might know and admire. He speaks to us not as an artwork in a museum but as a counselor and even a friend.

COMMODUS

Marcus's life ended where he had spent most of his last years: on Rome's Danube frontier, probably at or near Sirmium. He died on March 17, 180, just short of his fifty-ninth birthday. Marcus suffered an illness, perhaps smallpox or possibly cancer. One source claims that although Marcus was ailing, his doctors finished him off in order to win favor with Commodus, who was also at the front. He alleges to have heard this information from a reliable authority, but we cannot be sure. Marcus's body was cremated, and the ashes were returned to Rome and buried in Hadrian's mausoleum.

If creating two new provinces was his life's work, Marcus did not succeed. His son and successor preferred to make peace with the Germans and retreat to Rome. Yet Marcus hurt the enemy enough to buy Rome more than fifty years of peace on the northern frontier. Like others who enjoyed his leadership, he died, as one ancient admirer put it, "a beautiful death for the commonwealth."

Later ancient sources, representing the point of view of the Senate and the Roman elite, remembered Marcus very fondly. As one author writes: "He showed himself to be of all virtues and of celestial character, and was thrust before public calamities like a defender. For indeed, if he had not been born to those times, surely, as if with one fall, all of the Roman state would have collapsed."

Without question, Marcus was both the most humane of Rome's emperors and, thanks to his own writing, the most human. But he was not the most successful. He was a philosopher but must be judged as an emperor.

Marcus was fortunate neither in his times nor his preparation. He was singularly unlucky in the crises he faced. In fact, few emperors in Roman history saw deeper problems than he did. Marcus lacked the technical knowledge and experience needed in an emperor.

Yet he is a shining example of how a person of principle and intellectual discipline and a sense of duty can rise to the occasion. Marcus's reign marked a turning point for Rome. As one contemporary put it, with Marcus's death, an age of gold ended to be replaced by one of iron and rust. Strange to call an era of war and disease golden, but Marcus's benign character and his treatment of the Senate (always important to elite sources) shone, especially in comparison to what replaced them.

Marcus was the first emperor in eighty-two years not to be succeeded in power by an adoptive son. Instead, his birth son replaced him, making Commodus the first emperor in Roman history who was born to the throne. None of his predecessors learned that he was destined to rule before he was a teenager. Commodus took his power for granted—which may help explain why he abused it.

Only eighteen when he became emperor, Commodus behaved like a teenager who was suddenly freed from the burden of a father who had set a dauntingly high standard of austerity and responsibility. He gave up Marcus's war in the north and settled for a negotiated peace. He returned to Rome, where he turned over the reins of government to others and devoted himself to the opposite of philosophy: blood sport. Fit, handsome, and vain, Commodus identified with the god Hercules. He prided himself on his skills as a gladiator and actually fought in the arena.

Commodus remained popular with the army by paying generous bonuses and with the people by putting on frequent games, funding them by taxing senators and devaluing the currency. The Roman elite, however, was not about to stand for a decadent brute who threatened their lives and property and insulted their sense of dignity. Several conspiracies tried to assassinate him but failed, and they prompted brutal repression. Finally, a plot headed by his mistress and his closest officials succeeded. At their behest, Commodus's wrestling partner, a gladiator, strangled him to death in his bath on New Year's Eve, December 31, 192.

The rule of Marcus's family had reached an end. The age of the Five Good Emperors came to a close twelve years earlier, with Marcus's death, a reminder of the fragility of the imperial system. As Marcus discovered, forces beyond Rome's control offered constant danger: pressure from migrations by barbarian peoples hundreds of miles beyond the frontier and from epidemics with distant origins, as well as from the challenge of recurrent Parthian dynastic ambitions.

Marcus's reign also offered a reminder that, at its heart, the Roman Empire was a military monarchy. No matter how many wise edicts and enlightened laws an emperor might promulgate, no matter how good his relations with the Senate, in the end, he depended on the army. No emperor was ever safe from coup d'état or rebellion. No frontier was ever firm without a competent emperor in the lead and a fit and ready army to defend it.

Having a philosopher on the throne was a blessing, especially one who was versatile enough to turn himself into a good general. Yet the times also called for a man who was ruthless about his family. A more hard-nosed ruler might have pushed aside a son such as Commodus and chosen a better man as his successor—his son-in-law Pompeianus, say. Yet that might well have led to civil war. Rome's dynastic system was flexible only up to a point.

Indeed, the civil war came anyway after the farce of Commodus. It was long and bloody. It put another man of stature on the throne, but not someone of Marcus's breadth of vision. It took more than a century for such a great figure to reappear. During that time, a series of new disasters struck that made the good years between Nerva and Marcus seem a distant memory, if not a myth.

Bust of Septimius Severus.

8

SEPTIMIUS SEVERUS

THE AFRICAN

The year that followed Commodus's murder, 193, is sometimes known as the Year of Five Emperors. It marked Rome's first civil war in more than a century. For nearly 125 years, the succession to the throne had been relatively peaceful if not always proper. Yet not since the Year of the Four Emperors in 69 had anyone seized the throne by marching on Rome. But 69 was relatively mild compared with 193. While the change of dynasty after Nero's death was settled in eighteen months, it took four years to restore peace after the death of Commodus; fighting went on until 197.

Ultimately, Rome had a new ruler, Septimius Severus. His rule was a paradox. The man was egotistical, rude, and crude but also shrewd and fluent. Although not a professional soldier, he militarized the government as none of his predecessors had. He combined enlightened legal reform with autocracy and purges at home while launching Treasury-draining wars abroad. He also represented a new stage in Rome's ethnic history, and perhaps its racial history as well. Severus was Rome's first African emperor, and he founded a dynasty that also gave Rome its first emperors from the Middle East.

OUT OF AFRICA

Lucius Septimius Severus was born on April 11, 145, in the city of Lepcis Magna, on the Mediterranean coast of what is today western Libya, about eighty miles west of modern Tripoli. It was one of the great cities of Roman Africa. This was the height of the Roman peace under Antoninus Pius, and Africa shared in it fully.

Lepcis was an old city, a wealthy trading center founded by immigrants from Phoenicia (today, Lebanon) and also including native Libyan Berbers. Carthage took control of the city until Rome destroyed Carthage. Lepcis had been Roman for three hundred years when Severus was born.

A Latinized elite governed the town, but many of them, like Severus, had ancestors who spoke Punic, a Semitic language, related closely to Hebrew and Aramaic, and spoken in Carthage as well as Phoenicia. Severus spoke Punic as well as Greek and Latin. In Rome, they mocked his provincial accent. His father's family was wealthy, with strong connections to Rome, including two senators. Although they probably came from the native aristocracy, their status rose when Trajan declared Lepcis a *colonia*, which entitled all of its free citizens to Roman citizenship.

Severus's father, Publius Septimius Geta, did not pursue a political career. Unfortunately, his mother, Fulvia Pia, is little more than a name. She and her husband had two other children, another boy and a girl, both of whom rose high in Roman imperial circles, like Severus. Whether Fulvia Pia pushed her children toward their later success, like many Roman mothers, is a matter for speculation. Her ancestors were probably Italian colonists who intermarried with local people. She was likely related to Severus's boyhood friend Gaius Fulvius Plautianus. Severus and Plautianus established a relationship of trust. Gossip said they were once lovers, but Roman gossip *would* say that. Like Augustus and Agrippa, they became lifelong collaborators, although, unlike that earlier duo, their friendship did not end happily.

Severus was Rome's first African emperor. But was he Rome's first black emperor? We don't know, in spite of a variety of contemporary evidence. One written source makes him dark skinned, but it was written centuries later and is demonstrably wrong about other matters. One contemporary image shows him as dark skinned, but it is an outlier, and, besides, it comes from an Egyptian tradition that tended to depict men as dark skinned and women as light skinned. It is possible that Severus was of mixed descent—Italian, Middle Eastern, and perhaps native Libyan Berber—but that is speculation. As is often the case, the ancient sources don't tell us what we would like to know.

Roman Africa was in its heyday during Severus's lifetime, emerging to prominence like Hispania a century earlier. Africa provided roughly 15 percent of known knights and senators around 200. By this time, the Senate was no longer dominated by Italians but was representative of the empire as a whole.

No one symbolizes the change better than Cassius Dio, who lived from 155 to 235. A Roman senator and son of a Roman senator, he maintained a villa in Italy but was born and raised in the Greek-speaking city of Nicaea (near today's Istanbul). Yet Dio the Greek felt fully Roman, itself a sign of Rome's success in integrating provincial elites. Roman history fascinated Dio, who wrote a massive eighty-volume narrative of it, in Greek, over a period of twenty-two years. Parts concerning the late republic and early empire survive in full, but for the period from 41 to 229, we have only a later abridgement. Dio knew Severus personally and had mixed feelings about him. He admired Severus's intelligence, industry, judiciousness, and thrift, but he deplored his treatment of the Senate. Since Dio believed that that Rome had entered a period of decline, perhaps he was willing to overlook Severus's defects on balance.

Severus was educated in Greek and Latin as a boy in Lepcis. His schooling culminated in a public oration at age seventeen. Unlike Marcus Aurelius, Severus did not continue his formal education afterward, which he regretted. Dio describes him as a man of few words but many ideas.

Severus was thoughtful, cunning, and strategic. Although he wore a long beard, he was a man of action rather than a philosopher.

Yet Dio also claims that Severus took time off to study, first during a lull in his political career before becoming emperor, when he spent time in Athens, and then, while emperor, when he regularly spent afternoons in Greek and Latin debates. He was literate enough to publish an autobiography eventually. Apparently it was aimed at a broad audience and not merely at educated readers. Although not a word survives, indications elsewhere suggest the book included dreams and omens and chronicled wars. We shouldn't underestimate the importance of omens in the public mind as a way of legitimating a man who usurped the throne.

Severus had a special passion for the law. As a boy, he supposedly played at being judge. As emperor, he regularly held legal cases every peacetime morning. His jurists took a key part in codifying Roman law. Although Severus usually favored military men, he promoted one of his best jurists to the position of Praetorian prefect.

Physically, Severus was short but strong. He had curly hair and a short nose. He is said to have had a capacity for hard physical labor.

That young Severus was ambitious is certain. Other qualities would emerge in time. He was energetic, inquisitive, and blunt. He was quick witted and decisive. He had a temper, sometimes a violent one. His critics considered him ruthless and deceitful, but Severus did not suffer a low opinion of himself.

At eighteen, Severus went to Rome. One of his cousins was a senator, and he arranged for Severus and his brother to become senators too. Marcus Aurelius was on the throne, and he made an indelible impression on young Severus.

His career was in many ways typical of a young man on the make among Rome's elite. He held important political and administrative positions in Rome and the provinces, including a stint as legionary commander in Syria and governor of northwestern Gaul. He reached the position of consul in 190 at the age of forty-five. The next year, he became governor of Upper Pannonia, a strategic frontier province on the Danube. Marcus

Aurelius was based there during part of his frontier wars, and he wrote part of his *Meditations* there. As governor, Severus controlled three legions, or roughly eighteen thousand men. That made him a very important person when the central government collapsed. And he had the help of an intelligent, capable, and well-connected partner.

THE SYRIAN WOMAN

As a young man, Severus possibly sowed his wild oats. He stood trial for adultery but defended himself successfully. Then he married a woman from Roman Africa whose family were Roman citizens of Punic origin. She died, evidently without children, leaving Severus a widower. He looked eastward for a new bride.

In 185 Severus married Julia Domna. She was the daughter of a rich and powerful family in Emesa (today, Homs), a wealthy Syrian city whose population had Arab roots. She claimed to number among her ancestors the rulers of the city before Rome annexed it. Her father was priest of the local god, Elagabalus, literally "Mountain God." The god was worshipped in the form of a conical black stone in a temple in town. Family members were native speakers of Aramaic, with Greek as a second language, and they were Roman citizens.

Once upon a time, ambitious Roman men wanted to marry into the old republican nobility. Now they were happy to take brides from the prominent families of the East; families that provided imperial administrators and Roman senators, and who could give rich dowries to their daughters, as Domna's father surely did.

Domna was beautiful. According to one fairly speculative theory, she might even have served as the model for Venus de Milo, the famous Greek marble statue now displayed in Paris's Louvre museum. Meanwhile, we have many statues and coin images of Domna. They show that she had a broad face and rich, wavy hair, parted in the middle, drawn back on the sides, and sometimes gathered at the neck in braids. Various hairpieces were probably part of the coiffure.

Domna knew how power worked and liked wielding it. She was, as it turned out, fertile too. By bearing Severus two sons, she surely increased her stock in his eyes and her influence. Thanks to her, the Severans had a chance of a dynasty: Rome's first Libyo-Syrian ruling house.

She was a cultivated woman. In addition to Aramaic and Greek, she also spoke Latin, although probably not as well. As empress, Domna gathered a loose circle of intellectuals around her, probably including philosophers, mathematicians, and jurists. One of them, a Greek man of letters who settled in Rome, gave Domna the title of the Wise or the Philosopher. At Domna's urging, he wrote a book about a first-century Greek philosopher and miracle worker. Conservative in outlook, it serves as a kind of guide to princes—or, in this case, to princesses.

In short, Domna was a very good catch, and it wouldn't be surprising if Severus were in love with her. Her talents could only have been an asset to him in the struggle that lay ahead.

THE YEAR OF THE FIVE EMPERORS

The year 193, the Year of Five Emperors, was Rome's first civil war in 124 years and its longest and most violent civil war in more than 225 years. But for all its drama, 193 did not settle things. It took four years before a new emperor ruled without challenge.

The story begins on December 31, 192, the day Commodus was murdered. Tipped off about the plot, Publius Helvidius Pertinax was ready to be named emperor by the Senate that very night. He was a man of impeccable professional qualifications and distinctly nonaristocratic background. It would be hard to find a better example than Pertinax of the opportunity society that the empire represented occasionally. And like many a social climber, Pertinax adapted impeccably to the ways of the ruling class—in his case, the Senate.

Pertinax was born the son of a freed slave in northwestern Italy. After starting out as a schoolteacher and trying and failing to get a commission as captain in the army, he finally attained an officer's position on the eve of Marcus Aurelius's wars. He went on to distinguish himself on the Rhine and Danube frontiers and as governor of Britain. To his credit, he earned both Marcus Aurelius's praise and the enmity of one of Commodus's henchmen.

A mature man, Pertinax was nearly seventy when he became emperor. He was bearded, and, in coin portraits, he has the wrinkles and sunken cheeks that come with age.

With Pertinax as emperor, many in the Senate thought that good government had returned to Rome. But he proved to be too ambitious and immediately ran afoul of the Praetorian Guard. Commodus had given the Guard free rein; now Pertinax tried to restore discipline. Strapped for cash, he offered the Guard a smaller bonus on his rise to the throne than his predecessors had done. The Guard responded by murdering Pertinax. He had served barely three months in office.

Violence now gave way to farce. In a moment of great unseemliness, two senators next competed for the favor of the Guard by each offering a juicy bonus. The higher bidder got the nod as emperor. He was Didius Julianus, the first emperor imposed by the Praetorian Guard since they had put Claudius on the throne 150 years earlier. Julianus was an experienced provincial governor, but the circumstances of his "appointment" denied him any credibility, even with the Praetorians themselves.

The action now switched to the provinces, where suddenly imperial power was within reach. Three provincial governors each eyed the throne. Pescennius Niger, governor of Syria, had notched a small military success on the Danube frontier. An Italian, he had strong support from the common people of Rome, but otherwise his base was in the East. After being proclaimed emperor, he had ten legions ready to march for him and support from the Parthians as well.

Clodius Albinus was governor of Britain. He had only three legions in Britain, but they were battle-hardened veterans, and he had followers in Gaul. Like Severus, he came from Africa (from modern Tunisia), and, like Niger, he won military success in the Danube region. But he decided in the end to support Severus. The shrewd Severus gave Albinus the title of Caesar, thereby naming Albinus his successor and dividing him from Niger.

Severus had once served under Pertinax in Syria, and he considered himself that martyred emperor's avenger. Twelve days after Pertinax's murder, Severus was proclaimed emperor by his troops on the Danube. Along with the troops on the Rhine, he had the loyalty of sixteen legions. As he approached the capital, the Senate voted Severus its support. Didius Julianus was duly murdered. The new ruler entered Rome on June 9, two months to the day after being proclaimed emperor, a distance of up to 735 miles away from Severus's province. One of Severus's strengths was his speed.

Severus was now Augustus, and it is probably now that he had Domna proclaimed Augusta. He swore an oath to the Senate that he would never execute any senator. Yet he also marched into Rome with his army, making the military basis of his rule obvious. In a memorable passage, Dio describes Severus's entry into the city:

> The spectacle proved the most brilliant of any that I have witnessed; for the whole city had been decked with garlands of flowers and laurel and adorned with richly colored stuffs, and it was ablaze with torches and burning incense; the citizens, wearing white robes and with radiant countenances, uttered many shouts of good omen; the soldiers, too, stood out conspicuous in their armor as they moved about like participants in some holiday procession; and finally, we senators were walking about in state. The crowd chafed in its eagerness to see him and to hear him say something, as if he had been somehow changed by his good fortune; and some of them held one another aloft, that from a higher position they might catch sight of him.

How could someone with as little connection to Italy as Severus become emperor? The answer is: sixteen legions, and they had even less of a tie to Italy than their commander did. Most of them came from northern

Europe. The Italians had grown accustomed to a long peace. One contemporary puts it well: "The men of Italy, long unused to arms and war, were devoted to farming and peaceful pursuits."

Severus did not stay long in Rome because he had a war to fight against Pescennius Niger. He also knew how to play dirty and made a point of capturing Niger's children as hostages while keeping his own safe. There followed two years of armed struggle against Niger in the East, ending in a complete victory and Niger's death. Severus then attacked Parthian territory and created a new province by annexing a border state that today straddles the Syrian-Turkish border. By doing so, he took revenge on Niger's supporters there, added a wealthy area to the empire, and balanced the criticism of his killing fellow Romans in a civil war. But he did not hesitate to execute his long-held hostages, Niger's children.

It was inevitable that so ruthless a man as Severus would fall out with his supporter Clodius Albinus. The two rivals went to war, climaxing in a battle in Gaul that almost cost Severus his life. His troops prevailed in the end and killed Clodius, whose head Severus sent to Rome to be displayed on a pike. He also executed Clodius's wife and sons. In early 197 the civil war was over at last.

Severus finally returned to Rome, aware both of the price he had paid to rule and the support that not a few senators had shown his rivals. Although he pardoned thirty-five senators, he ordered the execution of twenty-nine others, despite his oath several years earlier not to execute any senators. We know of at least ten other senators whom he killed on other occasions. A contemporary compared his reign to bloody Tiberius's, while Severus openly compared himself to the brutal soldier-statesmen of the late Roman Republic, Gaius Marius and the dictator Sulla (Lucius Cornelius Sulla Felix). Yet a better comparison is probably Augustus, whom Severus also cited, and who had more than a hundred senators killed before settling down to respectability. Like Augustus, Severus fought a long and bloody civil war.

To punish the Praetorian Guard for its role in murdering Pertinax and auctioning off the throne, Severus executed several hundred guardsmen and fired the rest. Traditionally the Guard was recruited from Italy, but Severus replaced them with his own foreign-born legionaries, many of them probably from the Danube region. In Roman eyes, especially to nobles, the new guardsmen were savages.

To top things off, Severus doubled the size of the Praetorian Guard. He also doubled the size of Rome's firemen and tripled the size of its police, both of which were paramilitary forces. He may have also increased the number of specialist troops—archers and spies, among others—located in a garrison in the southeast part of the city. In addition, Severus built a permanent garrison for one of his legions south of Rome in the Alban Hills, in a town along the Appian Way. Built to last, the camp's ruins still lie scattered through the little town of Albano Laziale, just down the road from the summer residence of the Popes.

Altogether, Severus increased the number of troops in and around Rome from approximately 11,500 to roughly 30,000. His purpose was partly military, as the new forces provided the nucleus of a mobile reserve that Rome needed badly to respond rapidly to challenges at various points on the frontier. Later emperors would do much more along these lines. But Severus's changes had a political effect, too, making the capital feel as if it were in a military vise.

To Severus, a strong army and a strong state went together. He raised three new legions, increasing the total from thirty to thirty-three, or about a half million men. Soldiers from the Danube region and the Balkans loomed large in importance among his troops.

More generally, Severus favored the military. He gave the legions their first pay raise in over a century. He allowed soldiers to marry, as many of them had done over the years anyhow, in violation of regulations. A bigger, better-paid army was expensive, and the emperor debased the currency to pay for it. So had Marcus and Commodus, but Severus lowered its value even more. In the short run, Rome was strong enough to absorb the stress, but a later generation paid for it with runaway inflation.

Severus became the greatest military expansionist emperor since

Trajan. In this, too, he followed in Marcus Aurelius's footsteps, although Marcus did not succeed in creating new provinces, and Marcus attempted to expand the empire only in response to aggression against Rome. Severus had less of an excuse. He created two new provinces in the east beyond the Euphrates River. In Africa, he extended the boundaries of Rome's provinces southward. In Britain, he tried to conquer the entire island. He was indeed someone who enlarged the empire, as the inscription of his triumphal arch in Rome proclaims.

Ironically, Severus did not have a strong military background. His was almost entirely a civilian career before 193. He commanded armies but only in peacetime roles—he did not fight in any war. He was more bureaucrat than warrior. Yet, like Marcus Aurelius, Severus found himself forced by circumstances into a combat role, and he took to it with gusto. Unlike Marcus, Severus first tasted blood in a civil rather than foreign war. The outcome was that Severus became a kind of Roman caudillo, the sort of military strongman who has plagued modern Latin America. Or perhaps the better analogy is a new CEO, brought in to effect a restructuring, and who ruthlessly reshapes a corporation to save it.

Violent as they are, civil wars allow people to break through social boundaries. Around 195, for example, a school principal from Gaul impersonated a Roman senator, raised a small army in support of Severus, won a real victory, and lived the rest of his life on an imperial pension. It was brash, to put it mildly, but Severus liked brash.

In April 195 Severus did something that not even his most outrageous predecessors had done: he adopted himself! He made himself son of Marcus Aurelius, and he did it on his own, never mind the Senate nor, obviously, the long-dead Marcus. Severus changed his oldest son's name from Caracalla to Marcus Aurelius Antoninus and also made him Caesar, thereby making Caracalla (we will stick to that name) his successor. At the same time, Severus announced the deification of Marcus's son Commodus, which outraged the late, unlamented rogue emperor's enemies in the Senate. But the soldiers had adored Commodus, who paid them well, and they surely loved the move.

One Roman wit congratulated Severus for finding a father in Marcus Aurelius, which was a backhanded compliment and a nice piece of snobbery, since it called attention to the obscurity of Severus's birth father. Yet Severus's move was serious business and not just a wink-nod ploy. Romans wanted to believe in hereditary succession, in one continuous imperial family. They preferred blood descent, but they did not require it. Romans were nothing if not pragmatic, and they accepted adoption readily. Severus's "adoption" was a bald lie and too hard to swallow for some, but most considered it worth the price to pay for peace in a civil war.

Severus offered constant reminders of the military basis of his rule. To take one index, he gave his wife Domna the title of Mother of the Camp, recalling the only previous holder of that title, Faustina, wife of Marcus Aurelius and mother of Commodus. The house of Severus was the Roman army, and the army was the house of Severus—so the title said. Some legionaries even met Domna personally, as, over the years, she constantly joined Severus on his wars and travels from Britain to Iraq.

Severus had an impact on Roman government. He promoted fellow Africans to the Senate and to provincial governorships and legionary commands. He also shifted the balance of new administrative positions away from the Senate and to the knights.

WAR, POLITICS, AND MURDER

Domna was valuable to Severus in Rome as a liaison to elites from the eastern Mediterranean. She was equally valuable, because she had eastern connections, when her husband left Rome in 197 to renew the war on Parthia. Once again, she joined him in his travels.

Severus had three reasons to attack Parthia. He needed to retaliate for a Parthian invasion of Roman territory during his absence in the west to fight Clodius. He wanted glory for himself. And he surely found fewer headaches dealing with the army than with the Senate. It was Rome's first major foreign war of conquest since Trajan, and Severus constantly reminded people that he followed in distinguished footsteps.

Severus invaded Iraq, sacked the capital city (near modern Baghdad) and annexed the northern part of the country, which he named the province of Mesopotamia. He thereby re-created Trajan's lost province. Like Trajan, though, Severus failed to capture an important fortress city even after two sieges. Nonetheless, he declared victory and took the title Parthicus Maximus, which roughly means the Great Victor in Parthia.

Severus turned the capture of the Parthian capital into a propaganda coup. He timed the event for January 28, 198, the hundredth anniversary of Trajan's becoming emperor. Severus also made that the official day of Caracalla being named Augustus, or, co-emperor. In short, the emperor squeezed the maximum political advantage he could from his military success.

He should have been careful in what he wished for. The new province of Mesopotamia was an overextension of the empire and not in Rome's interests. A contemporary critic complained about its expense and tendency to embroil Rome in new and dangerous conflicts. But when Severus finally returned to Rome in 202, after several more years in Syria and a long trip to Egypt, he was voted a triumph. He declined to celebrate it, though, because he was too sick with gout to stand in a triumphal chariot.

Severus's health did not stop him from traveling with his family to North Africa in 202 and 203, including a proud homecoming in Lepcis. Severus sponsored a magnificent program of urban renewal in his native town, with marble monuments still visible today. In 203 Severus and his family returned to Rome, where they dedicated themselves to a big program of buildings and festivals. That same year, they dedicated the new Arch of Severus and Caracalla, celebrating their victories over Parthia.

Triumphal arches were squarely in the Roman tradition, but Severus erected his arch in an unconventional spot, near monuments celebrating Augustus, thereby basking in his predecessor's glory. As for the sculpted reliefs carved on the new arch, they are unusually blunt and brutal scenes of military victory and unlike earlier Roman triumphal arches. As he did so often, Severus had one foot in the genteel past and the other in a violent present. Just as victory in a civil war won him the empire, so, he claimed, victory in a foreign war justified the continuation of his dynasty. He prided himself on having expanded the empire.

Other construction projects in Rome included rebuilding temples destroyed in an earlier fire, adding a massive addition to the imperial palace, and constructing a freestanding façade near the palace. This monument displayed members of the imperial family among the seven planets then known, as if to say that the heavens themselves approved of the new dynasty.

There would be other celebrations, most notably the Secular Games of 204, marking the completion of roughly another century of Rome's history. It was another echo of Augustus, the first emperor to hold the games. A new touch, though, was the term Holy City to refer to Rome, which came into use at this time. The title Eternal City went back to the Augustan Age, and the adjective "most holy" had already been used to describe several emperors. Calling the city itself holy was a logical next step. Although today the designation of Rome as Holy City refers to Christianity, originally the term was pagan.

But it was Tiberius rather than Augustus whom Severus resembled in his willingness to let much of his power devolve to his prefect of the Guard, Plautianus. He was an intimate second in command, a boyhood friend who traveled everywhere with the emperor, but he was not to be trusted.

Like Sejanus, the unscrupulous Praetorian prefect under Tiberius, Plautianus aimed at building up his own base and eventually gaining supreme power. An assiduous networker with soldiers and civilians alike, Plautianus also became rich, which brought new friends in turn and the clout to execute enemies. He badmouthed Domna constantly. Plautianus reached a peak of power in 202, when he married his daughter to Caracalla, then fourteen. The hope was that, at a minimum, Plautianus's grandson would be emperor one day but, if he played his cards right, Plautianus might get rid of Caracalla and succeed Severus on the throne. Both Caracalla and his mother feared and hated Plautianus and his family, so it was not a happy marriage.

But Plautianus overplayed his hand. Crowds at the races in Rome complained loudly about his ambition. He allowed more bronze statues of him to go up than of Severus. The emperor noticed and had some of the offending statues melted down. When Severus's brother lay dying in 205, he delivered a deathbed warning against Plautianus. Finally, that same year, Caracalla, sixteen, successfully accused Plautianus of plotting to kill Severus.

On January 22, 205, Caracalla had the arrogant prefect executed in the imperial palace in Rome. Then he had a tuft of Plautianus's beard brought into another room, where Caracalla's wife—Plautianus's daughter—and his mother, Domna, were waiting. "Here's your Plautianus!" the messenger said, which horrified one woman and cheered the other. Caracalla then divorced his wife and sent her into exile on a remote island.

There is a trace of this squalid vendetta in an often-overlooked monument on a quiet street in Rome. There stands a marble arch, dedicated in 204 by the cattle merchants and their bankers, as a tribute to Severus on the tenth anniversary of his reign. It was the Roman equivalent of a campaign donation—a gift by a business group in honor of the imperial family—no doubt in the hope of a return favor such as a tax break.

The stone is thickly chiseled with an ornate but appropriate combination of themes. Legionary emblems, imperial eagles, prisoners of war, Hercules—the god of the cattle market, with his club and lion skin—cattle being driven by their herders, and knives and axes for the sacrifice all decorate the monument. The biggest images belong to the imperial family: Severus and Domna stare down in a blunt and frontal pose in a relief on one inner wall. The emperor, dressed in a toga, is carrying out a sacrifice, while Domna holds a symbol of her role as Mother of the Camp. Opposite them is their older son, Caracalla, also engaged in a sacrifice to the gods.

Upon closer look, the signs of violent erasure are visible. Caracalla's wife and his father-in-law, Plautianus, were once depicted, as was Caracalla's younger brother, Geta, but all three were later chiseled out after they were disgraced, exiled, or murdered.

CARACALLA

In 208 Severus, Domna, their sons, and much of the rest of their entourage left for Britain and the hope of one last campaign of conquest and one chance of reconciling the two feuding heirs to the throne. The two boys were so competitive that Caracalla once fell and broke his leg in a chariot race with his younger brother. He threatened to murder Geta.

Apparently, Severus considered the threat credible. At least some thought that the emperor chose to undertake a distant military campaign, despite such poor health that he had to be carried to war on a covered litter, in hope of distracting the boys. It was a vain hope: not only did Caracalla continue to threaten Geta but also once, while riding on horseback beside Severus to a parley with the enemy in Caledonia (Scotland), Caracalla raised a sword against Severus himself. The emperor's men saw him, and they shouted loud enough to stop Caracalla. Later, back at headquarters, the emperor chewed out his son, but he did nothing to punish him. Severus often blamed Marcus Aurelius for not getting rid of Commodus; but despite often angrily threatening to kill Caracalla, love or pragmatism stopped Severus.

The emperor launched his British campaign with dreams of laurels. He waged war for two seasons in Scotland with the hope of conquering all Britain, only to see the army stall against an elusive enemy and inhospitable terrain. Then illness forced him to quarters for months. For a decade now, disease and hard living had worn him out, and at sixty-six, he was losing the battle. Gone were the days when Severus thought nothing of riding bareheaded through the rain and snow on campaign in the mountains in order to encourage his men. Yet this short man still had a big appetite for work. Even now he gasped to his aides, "Come, give it here, if we have anything to do."

Caracalla and Geta attended him. Julia Domna was nearby. Even though they were on the frontier, hundreds of miles from home, she carried on. Not for nothing did she bear the title Mother of the Camp. No less determined than her husband, Domna was his constant companion on campaign.

Gout-ridden, immobile, saddened, the emperor lay on his deathbed. Now, with the end finally near, Severus addressed his sons. Supposedly, his exact words were, "Be harmonious, enrich the soldiers, and scorn all other men." The thoughts bear the mark of the man: terse, blunt, wise, and at once both cynical and hopeful.

And then Severus was dead, on February 4, 211. A man born amid the marble colonnades of a rich city on North Africa's sunny Mediterranean coast ended his life in far-off Eboracum (today's York), a spartan military town in northern Britain. The rituals of an imperial funeral—the procession at double-time around the pyre that was adorned with gifts from the soldiers, the corpse in armor, the two boys lighting the fire—dissipated the winter gloom. So did the final touch: a purple urn in which Severus's bones were deposited. It was later brought back to Rome and laid to rest in Hadrian's tomb. The story went that Severus sent for the urn before dying. After feeling it, he is supposed to have said, "You shall hold the bones of a man that the world could not hold."

Although Severus failed to conquer Scotland, he succeeded in establishing a dynasty. Caracalla succeeded him as emperor, sharing the rule at first with Geta.

"Caracalla" is actually a nickname. It comes from the heavy woolen military cloak or *caracallus*, which the emperor discovered in use by Roman soldiers in northern Europe and which he brought to the armies of the East. Caracalla was born Julius Bassianus and, as mentioned, became Marcus Aurelius Antoninus after his father "adopted" himself into Marcus Aurelius's family.

Coins and sculpture alike show Caracalla as a strong-looking man with blunt features. He has curly hair, a close-cropped beard, a prominent nose, and a thick neck. The word *gentle* does not come to mind.

Domna was now also the mother of the emperors. She played an important role as a sign of continuity and a source of advice. Eventually Caracalla put her in charge of his correspondence and replies to petitions. No imperial woman ever held such an office before, and it certainly attests to Domna's literacy and perhaps even more to how few other people Caracalla could trust with important jobs.

But he didn't listen to his mother's pleas. Less than a year after their father's death, Caracalla sent a team of soldiers to kill his brother. Geta was in the palace and ran for safety to his mother's arms, but he was killed there. She was wounded in the hand. Domna was no doubt distraught, but she continued as one of Caracalla's advisors, whether out of duty or love or love of power, or all of these reasons. Caracalla, meanwhile, won over the Praetorian Guard with a big bonus, then purged his enemies. More generally, he carried out his father's advice and increased spending on the soldiers.

Caracalla was shrewd, articulate, and ambitious but also emotional, impulsive, and violent. He loved physical activity. He had many enemies, which is no surprise. Who could trust a man who ordered the murder of his brother?

Caracalla spent most of the rest of his reign on military campaigns, first in northern Europe and then in the East. Seeing himself as a new Alexander the Great, he negotiated to marry the daughter of the Parthian king and, when that failed, prepared a war of conquest. He is remembered mostly, though, for two nonmilitary acts.

Seen from today, Caracalla's great achievement was extending Roman citizenship to every free inhabitant of the empire in a law, promulgated in 212, known as the *Constitutio Antoniana*, or, the Antonine constitution (after Caracalla's official name). Earlier, Rome had extended its citizenship, as a reward to favored communities and to prominent local officials, but probably only a minority of free people were citizens. Now, all free Romans were citizens. Never in human history had citizenship been shared so widely.

But Rome's elite focused more on the big tax increases that Caracalla put into effect to fund his increased military spending. According to a contemporary, the purpose of extending the citizenship was to raise revenue from the citizens-only inheritance tax. Over the decades, the citizen-noncitizen divide had faded in importance. The more important division in the Roman world was between the rich and privileged, officially called *honestiores*, and the poor and humble, called *humiliores*. The former group, whether citizen or not, enjoyed various privileges in law and practice, while the latter suffered. In short, Rome extended the citizenship only when it started not to matter.

Meanwhile, Caracalla undertook a massive building project to win support from the urban poor. The Baths of Caracalla, whose massive ruins still delight tourists today, were one of imperial Rome's largest construction projects. Severus planned the work, and Caracalla completed it. The great complex included gyms, a swimming pool, and libraries (one Latin, one Greek). High-quality works of art decorated it. The complex was free and open to the public. Enormous engineering challenges faced the builders, from removing around 17.7 million cubic feet of clay for the foundation, to erecting columns that stood 40 feet tall and weighed about 100 tons. Yet the project was completed within six years, using an estimated 12,000 to 20,000 workers.

Domna accompanied Caracalla to the east and based herself in Syria while he advanced farther eastward. Then, in April 217 he was assassinated. The prefect of the Praetorian Guard, Marcus Opellius Macrinus, discovered that he was next on the emperor's hit list, so he struck first. At his prompting, a soldier whom Caracalla had insulted stabbed the emperor to death. Macrinus arranged for the assassin to be killed and then disavowed any knowledge of the deed.

Distraught at the news and possibly ill herself, Domna committed suicide. Macrinus, proclaimed emperor by his troops, lasted in power for only a year.

Domna's elder sister, Julia Maesa, was determined to put their family back on the throne. Coin portraits show her as attractive and dignified. She has wavy hair like her sister, but fastened in a small bun at the back of her neck. In some portraits, she wears a diadem, the symbol of royalty.

Maesa's candidate was her grandson, Varius Avitus Bassianus, son of her daughter. Bassianus was only fourteen. Although raised in Rome, he lived now in Emesa, Syria, and was priest of the local god Elagabalus. (And Elagabalus is the name by which Bassianus is known to history.) On the face of it, not promising material for an emperor, but the determined Maesa spent her own money to buy the support of soldiers. Claiming that Elagabalus was Caracalla's love child, she had the soldiers proclaim him as emperor in 218. After a brief civil war, Macrinus was defeated and killed, clearing the path for Elagabalus to reign in Rome.

No television epic boasts any female powers-behind-the-throne to rival those who now stepped across the Roman stage. Maesa and her daughter Julia Soaemias, Elagabalus's mother, went with the new emperor to the capital. It was a good thing, too, because they ran the government while Elagabalus devoted his time to establishing his religious cult in Rome. In coin portraits, Elagabalus appears to be a hale and hearty young man with a thick neck, a laurel wreath or a diadem, and a breastplate. He looks ahead vigorously like a military commander. Wishful thinking! A marble bust depicts a slim, curly headed teenager with a mustache and an ethereal look.

Elagabalus rebranded his exotic deity as a sun god, a familiar guise in the Roman pantheon, now calling him the Unconquered God of the Sun. That raised eyebrows, but Elagabalus's wish to replace Jupiter, Rome's chief deity, with his god aroused fury. Nor was Elagabalus shy about it. He gave the new god a temple on the Palatine Hill, paraded through town the black conical stone representing his god, and danced around an altar. Public opinion objected to all this. It is best to be skeptical about the other deeds that hostile ancient sources attribute to him, such as his alleged marriage to a Vestal Virgin and his alleged homosexual affairs, in which he supposedly flouted convention by being the passive partner.

In any case, Elagabalus was unpopular. Not one to let sentiment get in the way, Maesa decided that she had to replace him in order to save the dynasty. She turned to her other daughter, Julia Avita Mamaea and to Mamaea's thirteen-year-old son, Severus Alexander. After agreeing to adopt him as heir, Elagabalus thought better of it but it was too late. In 222, the Praetorian Guard murdered Elagabalus and Soaemias, decapitated their bodies, and threw Elagabalus's corpse in the Tiber. He'd ruled for four years.

Official Rome was relieved to have a more conventional man on the throne, even if he was just a thirteen-year-old boy and even if his mother probably held more power over him than even Agrippina had held over Nero, who was seventeen when he became emperor. A coin from early in the new reign shows Alexander in military and royal garb, as it did Elagabalus, except that Alexander looks like his very young age. In some later coins, he is bearded. A marble bust shows him in a toga, his face poised between youth and maturity. Mamaea is depicted with her family's characteristic wavy hair, in some coins, very elaborately coiffed in rows. Sometimes she wears a diadem. She looks royal and dignified.

Mamaea had the official title of Augusta, Mother of the Augustus, the Camp, the Senate, and the Fatherland. Unofficially, she ran the empire. It was hardly conventional, yet mother and son both remained popular until Rome started losing wars. The unmilitary Alexander made little headway in the East against the new Sasanian Persian dynasty. Compared with their predecessors, the Sasanians were better organized, more threatening, savvier at military technology, and more resilient. In the West, Alexander decided to buy off aggressive Germans on the Rhine rather than fight them. Mortified, the soldiers on the Rhine named one of their commanders as emperor. Then they murdered both Mamaea and Severus Alexander in 235.

CONCLUSION

The dynasty founded by Septimius Severus lasted forty-two years to the death of Severus Alexander minus a year's interruption by another North African, Macrinus. It was far less than the ninety-nine years of the

Julio-Claudians and less than the fifty-four years of the Antonines (Antoninus Pius, Marcus Aurelius, Lucius Verus, and Commodus) but almost double the twenty-seven years of the Flavians. Not for another seventy years after 235 would anyone found a longer-reigning Roman dynasty. Hence it marked a real achievement.

Septimius Severus himself ruled for nearly eighteen years. His was the longest reign of any emperor in the century after the death of Marcus Aurelius. He restored stability to the empire after Commodus's tyranny and the civil war that followed it. Modeling himself on Marcus, Severus supported the study of philosophy and initiated a golden age for Roman law. Yet when it comes to his historical reputation, the military man overshadows the reformer. As much by circumstance as by design, Severus was the first true soldier-emperor. He came to power by the sword, spent much of his reign on campaign, showed the Senate the back of his hand, and went out of his way to exalt the military. And he was a harbinger of things to come.

To Edward Gibbon, Severus's lack of respect for the Senate made him "the principal author of the decline and fall." Gibbon was a snob, writing in the Age of Enlightenment, with little sympathy for upstarts and outsiders. Other scholars, writing during the nineteenth- and twentieth-century heyday of European Western imperialism, are even more scathing toward the so-called barbarian, surely betraying a certain bigotry toward the African emperor.

The western empire would last 250 years after Severus's death. Many of his acts, although jarring to tradition, were necessary. Rome became less civilian, true, but military crisis had made civilian rule a luxury. Besides, Severus paid as much attention to public relations as he did to the army because he insisted on making his family legitimate and popular. Finally, by opening the elite to new people, Severus made Rome stronger, not weaker.

Severus did not merely seize the throne; he founded a dynasty. The Severans became Rome's first family of militaristic mayhem but also of multicultural enlightenment.

Severus was Rome's first African emperor and his wife Julia Domna was Syrian and definitely of non-Roman descent. Severus filled Rome's highest offices and its legions with men of new blood from the provinces, thereby writing a new chapter in the history of Rome's ethnic and racial diversity.

True, violence began to spiral out of control in Severan Rome. Severus combined the civil wars of Augustus or Vespasian with the expansionist policies of Trajan and the police-state apparatus of Tiberius. Yet it was the moment for ambitious men and women who knew how to hustle.

Like many of his predecessors, Severus was no friend of the Senate. He purged the body and executed more senators than either Commodus or Domitian did. He filled his top administrative and military positions with knights, the wealthy and elite order that stood just below the Senate in rank and prestige. Yet this may reflect less hostility to senators than a shortage of qualified senators or an unwillingness of some senators to serve. By doubling the size of the Praetorian Guard and stationing a legion in a permanent camp outside Rome, as Severus did, he put a severe chill on freedom of speech.

Yet this same militarist—a lawyer early in his career—took a great interest in Roman law. He appointed excellent jurists whose work codified the law for centuries. One of the legal principles enunciated during Severus's reign was "the emperor is not bound by the laws." It was more honest than novel, as this rule had marked every reign starting with Augustus. For what it's worth, Severus and Caracalla promised to live in accordance with the laws, although they didn't have to.

With the Severans, magnificent multiculturalism and enlightened despotism met the morals of a crime family. Perhaps it was ever thus, and perhaps this dynasty's sole mistake was not working harder to disguise the harsh truth. Although some cried foul at his comparing himself to Augustus, Severus was no more ambitious or ruthless than Rome's first emperor. He was just less polished.

Severus made his biggest mark in the military sphere or, rather, in the conjunction of the military and politics. Under Severus, a series of long-simmering trends coalesced that made the Roman government less civilian and more military. The army obtained more power and became more expensive, which strained Roman finances and laid the groundwork for major instability. By raising army pay, making war, and engaging in a big public building program, Severus strained Rome's budget. Instead of levying taxes to pay for it, he and his successors inflated the currency, which eventually had disastrous effects on the Roman economy. By the same token, both army and imperial administration at the top became more diverse. The result was a rougher and cruder Rome, with plain folk from the margins pouring into the center, but it was a more democratic Rome as well.

Although imperial women wielded great influence in all periods of Roman history, no dynasty since the Julio-Claudians saw such powerful women as the Severans. Domna was probably the most powerful empress since Livia. Her sister, Maesa, was a kingmaker to rival the Praetorian Guard, her niece Soaemias was the power behind the throne, and her niece Mamaea was as close to a regent as the Roman system allowed.

The Severans liked to think big, whether it was a new bath complex, the renovation of the city of Rome, a rebuilding of their home city of Lepcis Magna, a military campaign against Parthia, a purge in the Senate, the introduction of a new god to Rome, or the extension of the Roman citizenship (backhanded compliment though that was).

Septimius Severus pointed to the shape of things to come. He was only the first of a series of military men who came from distant parts of the empire. Nor was he the last emperor to have a woman in the family who worshipped a nontraditional god. More than most of his predecessors, he based his power on continuing military success, but soldier-emperors would become the rule in Rome. He was a man of violence with a troubled family and with an incongruous taste for the rule of law. It might not have seemed so contradictory to the Romans, with their legalistic frame of mind, emphasizing as it did the legal aspects even of war. Severus combined a strong army with a strong state. Diocletian and Constantine would be cut from the same cloth.

They would also be men of brutality who banged heads together to save the system but at the cost of changing it enormously.

Diocletian Antonianus coin.

9

DIOCLETIAN

THE GREAT DIVIDER

The emperor Diocletian was a career soldier. No aristocrat he, Diocletian came up from poverty in the Balkans, and he had the rugged manners to prove it. He once stabbed a rival to death in front of the assembled troops. On another occasion, he threatened to drown a rebellious city in rivers of blood up to the knees of his horse. Yet the most famous thing that he ever said was a tribute to vegetables.

"If only you could see at Salona the cabbages raised by our hands," said Diocletian, "you surely would never judge *that* a temptation." *That* was a request that he return to power as emperor after three years of retirement outside the provincial city of Salona, on the lovely coast of today's Croatia. It was an unusual request, but then, it was an unprecedented retirement. Diocletian was the first and only emperor to abdicate by choice. He relinquished his throne in front of his army and then lived as a private citizen.

Although Diocletian set aside his sword, the reference to cabbages seems like a case of protesting too much. You wonder if, like an elderly Don Corleone tending his tomatoes in *The Godfather*, Diocletian in his garden offered shrewd advice to his hand-picked successor, his son-in-law and father of Diocletian's only grandchild, who faced tough political opposition. It's hard to imagine the retired emperor indifferent to current events. Like Lewis Carroll's Walrus, Diocletian surely talked not only of cabbages but also of kings.

Diocletian was one of the longest-reigning Roman emperors and one of the most consequential. He ruled for twenty-one years. Along with his more famous successor, Constantine, Diocletian ended the crisis that had nearly destroyed Rome. He laid the foundations for a new course that allowed the empire to survive, if in a much-changed form. Yet we have few good sources of evidence for this great man.

Diocletian was big, bold, brutal, and orderly. Finesse was not his way, but the times did not call for finesse. They demanded military muscle, a steel-trap mind, an iron will, and absolute self-confidence. Diocletian fit the bill.

Portrait sculpture shows a strong-featured, bearded man with a wrinkled brow and a watchful expression. One marble bust depicts a rough-hewn thug, but with eyes turned upward for divine inspiration. Another striking bust in black basalt, thought to be Diocletian, shows an aging but vigorous man. His tense mouth projects resolution, while his eyes portray intensity that you would not like to meet head on.

Diocletian reorganized the Roman Empire and, in a real sense, saved it. Yet he proceeded by division: by shaking things out before putting them back together. He divided East and West, giving each a separate emperor and subemperor, but with all of them answering to one man: him. He divided Roman and barbarian, soldier and civilian, buyer and seller, and, most notably, pagan and Christian. He achieved a real measure of success, if neither perfect harmony nor the results he most wanted. But he left a realm that was stronger and better able to survive than it had been in several generations.

FROM DIOCLES TO DIOCLETIAN

Diocletian was born on December 22 around 245. He came from Dalmatia—modern Croatia—possibly from the city of Salona, near

Spalatum (the modern Split, Croatia). He was born Diocles, Greek for "Glory of Zeus," the god called Jupiter by the Romans. His family was poor. His father was a scribe or perhaps the freedman of a senator. His mother was supposedly named Dioclea.

Diocles, a career soldier, had a talent for leadership. He rose in the ranks to hold command as a general on the Danube. Then in 283 he served with the emperor Marcus Aurelius Carus on his eastern campaign. Just under age forty, Diocles was now commander of the imperial bodyguard, an elite force created a generation earlier and separate from the Praetorian Guard.

Carus died in 283 after ruling for only a year. But it was an immensely successful year in which he captured the Sasanian capital in Iraq. In his tent after a severe storm, the emperor died either of natural causes, the after-effects of a battle wound, or a lightning strike. Earlier, Carus had wisely named his sons corulers. It was unusual to have co-emperors but not un-precedented. Marcus Aurelius and Septimius Severus both named corulers, while Augustus and Vespasian each delegated power to his son and succes-sor. In no case was there a formal division of the empire between East and West. One of Carus's sons, Numerian (Marcus Aurelius Numerianus), was with the army in Mesopotamia and was proclaimed emperor there. His brother, Marcus Aurelius Carinus, was already recognized as emperor in the west, where he won a battle against a German tribe.

Although victorious against the Sasanians, the Roman army decided not to risk further fighting under an untested new ruler. So it marched back westward. Numerian stayed in a closed coach, because, according to his staff, he had an eye infection. They said that he needed to protect his ailing eyes from the wind and the sun. But after a few days, his soldiers smelled a foul odor. They opened the coach and discovered Numerian dead. His staff attributed the death to natural causes, but many people suspected foul play.

Who would replace him? The obvious choice was the prefect of the Praetorian Guard, a man named Arrius Aper, who was also Numerian's father-in-law. But another, more impressive candidate emerged: a tough, ruthless, and experienced commander who knew how to wield power. Aper was passed over by a council of Numerian's senior officers on November 20, 284, who chose Diocles instead. The man born plain Diocles now claimed the more Latinate sounding name Diocletianus—our Diocletian.

The new emperor took the army's salute on a hill outside the prosperous city of Nicomedia, which lies at the head of a gulf off the Propontis (today's Sea of Marmara), not far from modern Istanbul. (Today Nicomedia is known as Izmit.) After swearing an oath that he had not betrayed Numerian or killed him, Diocletian proclaimed Aper's guilt for Numerian's death, drew his sword, and executed the man in full view of the army. There is speculation that Diocletian was lying and that he was really part of a plot to murder Numerian. In that case, he killed Aper in order to silence him.

If Diocletian was lying, that was all the more reason for him to lay it on thick. One source, claiming to cite an eyewitness, says that Diocletian quoted a line from Virgil's *The Aeneid*, that classic epic poem, as he ran Aper through—a rather literary turn for a soldier. The same source says that Diocletian once received a prophecy that he would become emperor after killing a boar. *Aper* means "boar" in Latin, as Diocletian supposedly noted after killing the man.

Rome had just acquired an outstanding new leader. Diocletian was not merely hard-nosed and violent, but also a man of energy, ambition, and vision. As little as he knew Rome, he was thoroughly Roman, because Rome was now less a city than an army, and the Roman army was his home. By the same token, Diocletian was no narrow-minded soldier but a shrewd political strategist. We often underestimate the intelligence of great soldiers. Doing so with Diocletian would be a fatal mistake because he was a political practitioner of the first order.

His full title was the high-flown Imperator Caesar Gaius Aurelius Valerius Diocletianus Augustus. Yet a realist like Diocletian understood that being acclaimed emperor by his troops was just a hunting license. He would have to earn the title by fighting and politicking. Numerian's brother, Carinus, ruled the western part of the empire and claimed to be the only legitimate emperor. Diocletian quickly marched against him. They fought in a battle in Serbia in spring 285 that Carinus won—and then lost. According to one account, an officer whose wife Carinus had seduced murdered him. Equally likely, the officer was a traitor working for Diocletian. Carinus's troops now accepted Diocletian as emperor. After securing control of the region, he then turned to the next phase of his campaign for legitimacy: politics. He crossed the Alps to Italy and visited Rome, probably for the first time.

The Roman Senate of that era exercised little direct political or military power, with one big exception: the Senate's support was still needed to pass legislation recognizing the army's choice of emperor. Besides, the Senate still held enormous indirect power. Senators could plot or promote behind the scenes. More important, the Senate represented wealth and the power of money in politics, since senators were rich on a grand scale. The Senate then was like Wall Street or Silicon Valley today but with the added advantage of being tax-exempt like a modern foundation or university. By opening or closing their moneybags, senators could make or break an ambitious politician.

Diocletian knew all that, and so he went to Rome. During a brief visit there, he traded favors and made friends; for example, by appointing key senators to consulships that in recent years had gone to military men instead. For the time being, at any rate, he had the Senate on his side.

Diocletian did not dawdle in Rome. Enormous challenges faced the empire, starting with military tests, and Diocletian now turned to these. He spent most of the next decade on campaign on the Danube and in the east.

THIRD-CENTURY CRISIS

Diocletian's first and greatest accomplishment was to restore stability to an empire trapped in a cycle of violence. To get a sense of his achievement, we need to glance at the half century that came before him.

The fifty years between the murder of Alexander Severus and the accession of Diocletian marked a period of crisis and then slow recovery. Rome had faced emergencies before but nothing on this scale.

From around 240 on, Rome's enemies kept pushing across the frontiers both east and west. Both Gaul and what is today Jordan declared independence. Decius (Gaius Messius Quintus Decius), an ambitious mid-third-century emperor, fell in a battle against German invaders in today's Bulgaria. Decius's son and coruler died first, which supposedly led Decius to say bravely that the loss of one soldier hardly mattered. The biggest shock came a few years later with the capture of the emperor Valerian (Publius Licinius Valerianus) by the Sasanian king in 260. That king had a stone relief carved on a cliff in Iran that showed him on horseback, triumphing over Valerian. An inscription on a stone structure nearby bragged that the king had captured Valerian and his officers with his own hands and deported them to Iran, where they died later. It was an enormous humiliation for the Romans.

Coping with invasion and revolt at opposite fronts stretched Rome to the breaking point. Defeats abounded, and most of the province of Dacia was abandoned for good. To pay for defense, the emperors devalued the currency, but the result was massive inflation. As if this wasn't bad enough, another major epidemic broke out again at midcentury and raged through the empire for fifteen years, compounding Rome's military manpower problems. Then too, a drought in the 240s brought an end to the favorable climate that had blessed agriculture.

The population shrank, especially in cities. Meanwhile, the danger of invasion led many cities to build new fortifications or expand old ones. Rome itself was the prime example. The thick city walls seen by visitors today were first built by the emperor Aurelian (Lucius Domitius Aurelianus) who ruled from 270 to 275, and were later renovated in medieval and early modern times.

Rome's signature problem was political instability. Assassinations and civil wars shook government stability. Between 235, when Severus Alexander was murdered, and 284, twenty men were emperor, however briefly in some cases. The average reign was less than three years.

Yet the empire rebounded, which is a tribute to Roman resilience as well as a sign of the disunity and weaknesses among the empire's enemies.

Recovery began during the reign of Valerian's son and coruler Gallienus (Publius Licinius Egnetius Gallienus), who instituted a series of reforms during his unusually long fifteen years in power, from 253 to 268. Gallienus excluded senators from high military commands and replaced them with professionals. Moreover, he began a new, more modest policy of border defense. The Romans now conceded much of the frontier to the enemy and shifted to a defensive mode: fortified cities near the frontier served as bases from which to prevent deeper enemy penetration into Roman territory. Rome also concentrated mobile armies at strategic points in the rear, moving them where needed.

Thanks to his new policies, Gallienus inflicted defeats on invading Germans. His successors checked the invaders decisively and reconquered both Gaul and the East. They won sweet revenge against the Sasanian Empire by conquering its capital and reestablishing the Roman province of Mesopotamia (which, in this case, refers not to Iraq but instead to a relatively small region that today is in southeastern Turkey).

Gallienus came from the senatorial nobility, but his successors were all self-made military men; products of the professional army that Gallienus himself created. None of these emperors was able to reestablish political stability. In fact, the most successful of them died suddenly and often violently.

Only Diocletian was able to restore order.

THE WARRIOR BAND THAT RULED ROME

As Diocletian understood, in order to hold power, you need to share power. So he did it on a grand scale. Within a year of being named emperor, he chose a fellow professional soldier from the Balkans to work with: a man named Maximian (Marcus Aurelius Valerius Maximianus), who was a few years younger than him. The son of a grocer from what is today Serbia, Maximian rose in the ranks like Diocletian. The two of them served together in the army, and Maximian was probably outside Nicomedia the day Diocletian was proclaimed emperor. First Diocletian named him

Caesar—his deputy and successor—and sent him to Gaul. Then Diocletian named Maximian Augustus, or co-emperor, and put him in charge of the West. Diocletian mostly kept to the East, the wealthiest and most populous part of the empire.

A surviving marble portrait bust that might be Maximian shows him as strong featured and bearded, with deep-set eyes, sunken cheeks, and a shrewd, even skeptical expression. His critics during his lifetime called him fierce, wild, and uncivilized.

Although Diocletian was not the first emperor to take a coruler, what was extraordinary was his decision to add two more men as Caesars. He did this on March 1, 293, a little more than eight years after taking power.

During those years, the drumbeat of war went on and on, and Diocletian followed a punishing schedule of fighting, negotiating, and traveling. In just one year, for example, 290, it is estimated that he traveled ten miles a day. Over the years, he led military campaigns on the Danube, in Egypt, and on the eastern border, going back and forth from one theater of operations to another. He supervised the building of a new series of forts on the eastern front from the Euphrates River to the Arabian Desert. He negotiated a truce with the Sasanians. Diocletian met with Maximian to coordinate policy in the face of a revolt by the rebel commander of northwestern Gaul, who also led a breakaway movement in Britain. Meanwhile, he still had domestic reforms that he wanted to implement.

With so much to do, no wonder Diocletian called for help. Besides, sharing power with talented men was a way of discouraging them from revolting. It was a fine example of the principle of keeping your friends close but your enemies closer.

The two Caesars served the two Augusti and mostly played a military role. In the West, Flavius Valerius Constantius became Caesar to the Augustus, Maximian. Constantius was a former provincial governor and Maximian's prefect of the Guard. In the East, Galerius (Gaius Galerius Valerius Maximianus), possibly prefect of the Guard to Diocletian, now became Caesar. All four men were poor boys from the Balkans who rose in the Roman army. And none of the four lived in Rome. Rather, they chose residences closer to the front. They lived in northwestern Turkey, Germany, northern Italy, Syria, and northern Greece. They were constantly on the move, coping with war and revolt, but rarely meeting one another except for occasional summit conferences. They communicated mostly by letter or messenger.

The rulers are sometimes called tetrarchs (literally, "four rulers") and the system, tetrarchy ("rule by four"), but this is a modern term: the ancients did not use it. Nor were the four rulers equals. Diocletian was in charge. He showed this by inventing two new titles. Diocletian called himself Iovius—that is, Jupiter, the king of the gods. He gave Maximian the title of Herculius or Hercules, the son of Jupiter. While imperial coins of this period stress harmony and agreement, it's clear that loyalty to Diocletian came first. As one ancient orator put it, the empire remained "an undivided inheritance."

In practice and for day-to-day affairs, Maximian and Constantius ran the West while Diocletian and Galerius ran the East, but there was no official division of the empire. Diocletian controlled its overall strategy, and he made the final decisions. Yet in a real sense, the Roman Empire was divided. Diocletian recognized that Rome's problems were too big for one man to handle. For the rest of its history, the empire usually had two emperors.

MOTHER COURAGE AND THE MATE OF MARS: IMPERIAL WOMEN OF THE TETRARCHY

Following standard Roman procedure going back to Augustus, Diocletian used marriage to cement political relations. He had Maximian marry his daughter to the Caesar Constantius, who was required to divorce his wife, and then also had Maximian adopt Constantius as his son. A soldier-statesman, Constantius spent a large part of his career on military campaigns, with little noticeable desire to leave the field as he got older.

Meanwhile, Diocletian married his only child, Valeria, to the Caesar Galerius, whom he also adopted as his son. Coins show Valeria as a pretty young woman with a somewhat masculine face and elaborately plaited hair raised above the forehead. She wears a small diadem. She and Galerius had a baby girl, who was promised in marriage to Maximian's son.

A shepherd as a boy, Galerius joined the army and rose in the ranks. He was tall and rugged. One ancient source, admittedly hostile, calls him intimidating and coarse. He supposedly kept pet bears and fed criminals to them while he ate dinner.

In spite of the importance of imperial marriage in Diocletian's policies, we know frustratingly little about the wives of the four rulers. Diocletian was married to Aurelia Prisca. As later events would show, she was a loyal and courageous mother, but her role as a wife is largely undocumented. She had the title of Most Noble Woman, and Diocletian put her statue in a temple of Jupiter, in Salona, but he didn't give her the title of Augusta. We are not sure why not—perhaps to avoid offending the wives of his three fellow rulers.

Galerius's mother, by contrast, stands out as an intriguing character. Romula, as she was called, was one of those Roman mothers such as Atia or Agrippina who loomed large in their sons' lives and public image. Even Galerius's retirement villa, an enormous estate built on the site of Galerius's boyhood home in what is now Serbia, was named after her.

Romula was supposedly a very religious pagan. Galerius claimed that she had mated with Mars, the god of war, in the form of a snake, and he was their child. The claim harks back to Augustus's propaganda that his mother had mated with the god Apollo in the form of a snake. No doubt Galerius was honoring his mother when he built temples to the mother goddess and to Jupiter within his retirement villa.

Diocletian and his three fellow rulers were already a band of brothers from the army. Now they were a family (or at least two families), joined by marriage. A famous statue group of the four rulers, originally in the Roman East but now on the exterior of St. Mark's Basilica in Venice, shows the image they projected. They stand in two groups, in each of which the senior man is bearded and the junior smooth shaven. They all wear heavy armor and Danube-region-style woolen caps. Their sword handles have barbarian-looking eagle-head pommels. Each man has one hand around the shoulder of his fellow ruler and the other hand on the hilt of his own sword, suggesting that they are ready to fight outsiders while protecting each other.

The statues are made of porphyry, a precious stone from Egypt used to represent emperors. The style is anything but classical. Stubby and heavy, the figures look like something from the early Middle Ages. But they are typical of the big changes in Roman sculpture during the third century, a period when art became simpler.

"A PEACE WHICH WAS EARNED
WITH MUCH SWEAT"

With his three colleagues in place in spring 293, it was time for Diocletian to advance on all fronts. All the while, he increased troop deployments on the frontier and beefed up border forts. Compared with earlier Roman forts, Diocletian's were smaller, thicker, and harder to access. Networks of them have been found in various border and coastal regions, east and west.

The number of legions shot up from thirty-three under Septimius Severus to fifty under Diocletian, but with fewer men per legion. Whether Diocletian increased the size of the army is unclear, but he certainly made it easier to reach recruitment goals; he reinstated an annual draft for the first time since the days of the republic. He also required the sons of serving soldiers or veterans to join up.

Diocletian was a warrior, but Galerius was his workhorse. After defending the Danube frontier and putting down a rebellion in Egypt, Galerius was sent eastward to deal with a Sasanian invasion of Armenia. Meanwhile, in 297 Diocletian had to go to Egypt to respond to another rebellion there. After a long siege, he took Alexandria by cutting off its water supply.

That same year, Galerius suffered a big defeat against the Sasanian Empire. An angry Diocletian humiliated him. Having left Egypt for Syria, Diocletian now made Galerius, in his scarlet robes, run beside the emperor's chariot for a mile as they both entered the city of Antioch.

Yet Galerius's shame was short lived. After gathering new troops from the Balkans, he defeated the Sasanians battle in 298. He even captured the Sasanian royal harem, complete with the king's wives, sisters, and children. While Galerius marched south into what is now Iraq, Diocletian reoccupied former Roman territory in southern Turkey. Using the return of the harem as a bargaining chip, Diocletian negotiated with the Sasanian king and won recognition of Rome's sovereignty over its regained territory. This great Roman victory led to a peace treaty that would last for nearly forty years. Now Diocletian welcomed back Galerius with open arms. Afterward, he sent Galerius to the Danube frontier, where heavy fighting awaited. Indeed, Galerius would spend much of the following ten years campaigning there.

In the West, meanwhile, Maximian worked hard. He put down rebels in Gaul, Spain, and Africa, and pushed back various German invaders on land and pirates by sea. He failed, though, to retake unruly Britain. That job fell to Constantius, who crossed the British Sea (today's English Channel) in 296 and finally crushed that island's long-running rebellion. A gold medallion survives that commemorates his entry into London on horseback. The medallion's legend hails Constantius as Restorer of the Everlasting Light.

By 298, after fourteen years of continual warfare, Diocletian and his corulers finally settled the frontiers. They took the credit for defeating and slaughtering barbarians, as they called them, and so establishing "a peace which was earned with much sweat." It was time to turn to reform at home and to refine and expand a program that was already well under way.

BIG GOVERNMENT

Diocletian's plans were expensive. The military, with its endless series of wars, was the biggest-ticket item, but there was also a massive building campaign. In addition to the border forts and roads, every tetrarch needed at least one palace and often several. Nor did Diocletian neglect the city of Rome. He rebuilt the Senate House after a devastating fire (that rebuilt Senate House still stands in the Roman Forum today), erected a triumphal arch (no longer standing), and built the massive Baths of Diocletian, the largest baths ever built in Rome. Since then, the various parts of the sprawling, ten-plus-acre ruins of those baths have been converted into two Renaissance churches (one designed by Michelangelo), a major archaeological museum, an exhibition hall and former planetarium, and, last but not least, one of the main squares of modern Rome.

Another expense was the new and expanded administrative structure that Diocletian imposed on the empire, doubling the number of provinces from about fifty to roughly a hundred. He also grouped the provinces into twelve new regions, which he called dioceses (a term still used in the Christian Church for a territorial administrative unit), each with its own administrator. Senators were virtually closed out of provincial governance, as nearly all the jobs went to knights. The purpose of the new system was to make it easier to collect taxes and to enforce laws and rules.

Throughout the empire's history, Italy was exempt from taxes. No longer. Diocletian treated the peninsula like any other province. Even the city of Rome had to pay taxes and—unkindest cut of all—so did senators. A reservoir of resentment began filling up.

To meet the needs of a bigger army, the government established arms factories at various places around the empire. This in turn imposed duties on local populations. The administration had a very long reach. For example, records show that in September 298 an Egyptian blacksmith failed to show up for work in the local arsenal. The governor ordered the police to find and detain him and bring the man and his tools into his presence.

However, it all played out against the background of a nearly worthless currency. Already, under Septimius Severus, Roman silver coins were only 50 percent precious metal. By the 260s, some coins contained only 2 percent to 3 percent precious metal. Not surprisingly, this led to a financial crisis. As usual, Diocletian had a response—actually several responses.

As background, consider that during the uncertain times of the crisis years, farmers in various parts of the empire gave up their independence for protection by a local landlord. Formerly freeholders, they became tenants. Now Diocletian codified the situation and tried to tie them permanently to the land as tenants because fixed laborers were easier to tax than mobile ones. A new tax system paid in kind rather than currency was established.

Soldiers, however, needed to be paid in coin, so the problem of inflation had to be faced. Around 294, Diocletian increased the weight of the gold coin, established a new and reliable silver coin, and reformed the bronze coinage. Despite this noble attempt, bronze coins remained overvalued, and inflation ran rampant. So in 301 the government stepped in, issuing a decree that in effect cut the value of bronze coins in half.

A few months later, Diocletian and his colleagues made a massive attempt to impose wage and price controls, issuing their famous Edict on Maximum Prices. The preface is revealing. After decrying greed and profiteering, the four rulers set maximum wages and prices. They pronounced the punishment for violating price ceilings as death.

They expressed special concern about the army, citing cases of soldiers who lost their whole salary plus their bonus in a single transaction. The villains, they said, were cheating not only individuals but also society as a whole, since tax money paid the military.

The edict sets prices on more than a thousand goods and services ranging from chickpeas to mustard, goat to pheasant, compensation for marble workers to camel drivers, and veterinarians to schoolteachers. The goal was ambitious but doomed. In the end, goods were withheld from the market while a thriving black market developed.

STANDING ON CEREMONY

As the statue group of Diocletian and his three corulers suggests, the emperor paid a great deal of attention to self-presentation. In fact, under Diocletian, the imperial court lost all pretense of republicanism and became a place where the haughtiest of monarchs might feel at home. Several of his predecessors had already increased court ceremony, but Diocletian went much further.

Diocletian often wore a purple robe with gold threads accessorized with jewels and silk shoes. To the ancients, purple was the color of kings. The first emperors avoided wearing purple, and although Hadrian and his successors made ever more use of it, no one had adopted the color with as much gusto as Diocletian. He also insisted on being called master (*dominus*) in public. Imperial palaces built during his reign all have grand audience chambers, organized so that the ruler would make a stunning impression on visitors. Often he was surrounded by figures that classical writers looked down on as a sign of despotism: eunuchs.

Eunuchs had played a role in imperial government from early days, but it was generally a small role. Romans associated them with foreign autocracy but under Diocletian, they came into their own in Roman government. They were freed slaves, often from Armenia or Persia. They now held key positions in the emperor's household, and they often controlled access to him.

One point of access was the emperor's entry into town, usually a grand ceremonial occasion. That, along with presentation at court, could be the time for a panegyric, or speech of praise. Never less than fulsome in earlier reigns, these speeches reached new levels of sycophancy under Diocletian. In 301, for example, Diocletian and Maximian held a meeting in the palace in Mediolanum (now Milan). A speechwriter exclaimed: "What a vision your piety granted when those who had been admitted into the palace at Milan to adore your sacred faces caught sight of you both, and your twinned godhead suddenly threw into confusion the customary practice of single veneration."

The same writer says that when the two rulers exited the palace and were carried on litters through town, the buildings themselves almost moved because of the throngs that poured out onto the streets or leaned out the upper-story windows to catch a view. He writes that people cried out joyfully and without fear: "Do you see Diocletian? Do you see Maximian? They are both here! They are together! How closely they sit! How they chat in harmony! How quickly they pass by!"

The empire had come a long way from the days when Livia conspicuously wove her husband Augustus's woolen toga on her own loom or when the Senate under Tiberius outlawed silk clothes for men. But the hard military men from the Balkans who now ruled came from a different world. Now that they had wealth and power, they liked to show off.

THE GREAT PERSECUTION

It might seem odd that Diocletian devoted time and energy to religious persecution. In fact, a military man like him might have been expected to exclaim as Soviet dictator Joseph Stalin did, "How many divisions does the Pope have?"

But the Romans, unlike modern people, did not grow up in the shadow of the belief that God is dead. On the contrary, most Romans saw in the empire's misfortunes a clear sign of divine disapproval. The gods were angry at Rome. They needed to be appeased, and the state had to restore what the Romans called "the peace of the gods." But how?

To some the answer was "with new gods." The crisis of the third century, with its many miseries, encouraged conversion from the old gods to new ones.

A variety of foreign and in some cases new religions had been coming to Rome from the east during the empire's first centuries. The religious marketplace of third-century Rome was like a multicolored mosaic. Worshipers could choose from among Greek mystery cults offering the secret of eternal life; the worship of the Egyptian goddess Isis, whose priests paraded through the streets chanting in robes like today's Hare Krishna but with the addition of self-flagellation; the men-only worship of Mithras, a combination of sun god and machismo symbol whose members took part in bull sacrifices in underground rooms that call to mind the chapter houses of some American college fraternities; or the Persian-imported egghead's religion of Manichaeism, which saw the world in dualistic terms as a struggle between light and darkness. Judaism attracted many converts and probably more sympathizers who liked its theology and time-honored holy book more than its strict laws.

Finally, there was Christianity, which offered salvation, ritual, community, and Judaism's benefits without its restrictions. Official hostility did not keep the church from spreading. In fact, the Roman government largely left Christianity alone. Persecution was sporadic, local, and relatively rare, with the exception of the 250s, when the emperors, reeling from a series of disasters, began a short-lived persecution of Christians who didn't sacrifice to the gods. The previous situation of de facto toleration soon returned.

Christianity won followers by its emphasis on charity and community. The church was open to women and slaves. In spite of apocalyptic and revolutionary strains, Christianity largely became mainstream. Wealthy people, intellectuals, and even Romans soldiers began converting.

Christians were a minority and concentrated in the east and North Africa. But they made up perhaps 10 percent of the empire's population overall, which is no small number, especially because most Christians lived in cities, the nerve centers of Roman civilization. By the same token, Christians generally looked and acted like everyone else. They didn't wear special clothes, live in ghettos, bury their dead separately, or speak a different language. They were the neighbor, the woman who ran the household or engaged in business, the teacher, the lawyer, or the soldier in the next tent. The only thing that made them different from other Romans was their absence from temple and festival ceremonies, their worship in churches (mostly rooms in private houses), and their disinclination to sacrifice to the gods on behalf of the emperor.

Diocletian noticed that disinclination, and he considered it a dereliction of duty. He was not someone to seek the peace of the gods with a new religion. On the contrary, the man born to humble circumstances in Dalmatia doubled down on the old Roman deities with the fervor of an outsider. In addition to sacrificing to the old gods himself, he decided to persecute those who did not. Maybe the idea had been brewing in his mind for some time, but, if so, he couldn't act until after 298, when the war with Persia was finally over. Perhaps he acted because he was thinking of his legacy as he grew older and wanted to win the favor of the gods before his time in office came to an end. At any rate, in 303 he made his move.

First Diocletian turned on the Manichaeans, who were suspect not only for being new and different but also for their origin in Persia. Manichaeans were, the emperor said, like poisonous and evil snakes. Then he turned on the Christians.

Diocletian feared and disliked the growing power of the church, especially in the army. His instinct was to smash it. In this, he had the strong support of his colleague Galerius. Indeed, some sources say that persecution was Galerius's idea. One intriguing possibility is that the driving force behind Galerius was his mother, Romula, moved by her strong faith in the pagan gods. It is at least possible that behind the worst persecution that the Christian Church faced in ancient times stood a woman from the rolling hills of rural Serbia.

A series of orders proclaimed in 303 and 304 formed what Christians called the Great Persecution. The first orders targeted clergy as well as Christians in high office. Then the regime turned on ordinary Christians as well and demanded that they sacrifice to the pagan gods. Churches were torn down and holy books confiscated. Diocletian was particularly interested in driving Christians from the army.

According to a Christian source, the persecution began in winter 303 with the destruction of a Christian church in Nicomedia near Diocletian's palace. The writer accuses Galerius of then setting fire to Diocletian's palace and blaming Christians, in order to inflame the emperor's enthusiasm for persecution. Diocletian seemingly took the bait and had his servants tortured in the hope of extracting a confession, but he failed.

Diocletian supposedly even suspected his wife and his daughter. That, at any rate, is probably why he ordered them to sacrifice to the gods. They were surely not Christians, but maybe they had expressed sympathy for Christians.

Christians reacted to persecution in various ways. Some went into hiding, some bribed officials, some agreed to sacrifice, and some refused and were executed for their faith. Martyrs there were, as Christian literature recounts. A veteran named Julius with twenty-seven years of military service and seven campaigns behind him preferred to be executed rather than offer incense to the gods. Crispina, a wealthy mother with children who lived in what is today Algeria, also accepted execution rather than sacrifice. Bishop Felix, in what is now Tunisia, refused to turn over his holy books and so was executed at the age of fifty-six.

These were terrible times for Christians. The persecutions lasted on and off for ten years and caused great suffering, but ultimately they failed. Steadfastness on the part of martyrs is one reason, while another is the unwillingness of certain non-Christian authorities to take part. How many Romans were ready to condemn to death fellow citizens who had committed no real crime? In Britain and Gaul, Constantius limited himself to tearing down churches but otherwise left Christians alone. He was surely not the only official who tempered Diocletian's order.

There were not many martyrs, but martyrdom loomed large in Christian consciousness and probably won non-Christian admirers, so that Christianity emerged stronger from the persecution.

As for Romula, after she died, she was buried in a specially built mausoleum at Galerius's estate named for her. She was then declared a goddess. You could hardly guess from her fate that the pagan religion that she championed would soon itself be persecuted.

CABBAGES AND KINGS

Diocletian was the first and only Roman emperor to retire. Even more remarkable, he lived unmolested for nearly a decade after stepping down.

Why did he leave office? The sources say that Diocletian's health failed him, but other emperors clung to power in spite of strokes, heart disease, and gout. No Roman strongman had given up power voluntarily since the dictator Sulla stepped down from office nearly four hundred years earlier, which Julius Caesar called an act of political illiteracy, arguing that dictators can't retire. But Diocletian was not unschooled. He knew that his loyal fellow rulers would stop being loyal the minute they smelled blood. Each of them coveted the purple and would fight for it, but Diocletian wanted to choose his own successor, and couldn't do that from the grave. He probably thought it was better to hand over power, to step down, and then pull strings as needed from the wings while he was still alive.

Maximian and Constantius were both able and ambitious men, but Diocletian preferred Galerius. For over a decade, Galerius had been

Diocletian's faithful servant and his military enforcer. He was also the husband of Diocletian's daughter, Valeria, and father of Diocletian's grandchild. So the emperor prepared for the big day.

Around 300, Diocletian began building his retirement home at Spalatum in Dalmatia, near his birthplace in Salona. The ruins, which still stand in considerable splendor, are usually called Diocletian's Palace, but it was more than just a palace. It was to retirement homes what Fort Knox is to the corner bank.

Diocletian's Palace covered an area approximately 705 by 590 feet and housed thousands of people. The palace was walled, fortified, divided into four parts like a Roman military camp, and included a small arms factory. There was also a temple and a mausoleum. Unlike previous emperors, Diocletian did not build his mausoleum in Rome.

The palace was also an ideological statement in stone. The four parts of the palace represent the four tetrarchs, who were practically gods walking the earth. The most important of them was Diocletian, the son of Jupiter.

Maximian did not share Diocletian's eagerness for retirement. He wanted to stay in power, and he also wanted to provide for his son, Maxentius, to succeed him. But Diocletian refused. He forced Maximian to retire and to leave out Maxentius. The two new Augusti would be Galerius in the East and Constantius in the West. The two new Caesars would be Flavius Valerius Severus and Maximinus Daia, both soldiers from the Balkans and both associated with Galerius. Daia was his nephew.

In carefully coordinated and formal ceremonies, Diocletian and Maximian each stepped down from power on the same day, May 1, 305, Diocletian in Nicomedia and Maximian in Mediolanum. They turned over their purple robes and put on the clothes of private citizens.

Each man had a new title: Senior Augustus. It was an attempt to maintain authority even from retirement, but it didn't work.

Band of Brothers quickly turned into *Game of Thrones* as the four men fought. It took twenty years for a result to finally shake out, but when it did, it led to one of the biggest and most dramatic changes in the history of Western civilization.

On July 25, 306, a little more than a year after Diocletian stepped down, the western Augustus, Constantius, died. Coincidentally, he met his end in Eboracum, Britain, like Septimius Severus. Constantius's troops immediately launched a coup d'état, one surely long in the making. Instead of accepting Diocletian's choice of Caesar as the new ruler, they acclaimed Constantius's son, Constantine, as Augustus. Constantine treated the acclamation as a bargaining chip. After a deal with Galerius, he accepted the lesser title of Caesar instead of Augustus, but it was still a big step up for him.

The next problem for Diocletian's succession plans came a few months later. On October 28 the city of Rome effectively rose in revolt, fueled in large part by anger over an attempt to tax ordinary people. The Praetorian Guard, in a move reminiscent of bygone days, roared again and chose an emperor. They declared Maxentius, son of the retired Augustus Maximian, as new emperor. They gave him the now-antiquated title of Princeps (First Citizen). Maxentius called his father out of retirement and declared him Augustus once more.

To widen his son's circle of supporters, Maximian arranged a strategic marriage. He gave the hand of his daughter to Constantine and recognized him as Augustus. In return, Constantine recognized Maximian as Augustus and also recognized Maxentius as Caesar.

What followed would confuse even the most dedicated observer. Maxentius was married to Galerius's daughter, but Galerius violently opposed the young man's power play. From his base in the East, Galerius sent Severus to Italy to fight Maxentius, but Severus lost and was captured, imprisoned, and eventually executed. Galerius attacked next and also failed, but at least he escaped. Meanwhile, Maximian fell out with Maxentius. This ugly quarrel led to a failed attempt by the father to remove his son from office in 308.

At this point, Maximian made the appeal to Diocletian with which this chapter began. In November 308 they both attended a conference at Carnuntum. There Maximian tried to convince Diocletian to return to power. The former emperor wisely declined. He referred to his vegetables as a reason for returning to safety in the walls of his fortified palace, where he could influence events from behind the scenes. Maximian had to abdicate as Augustus for a second time, but he still itched for power. Now he quarreled with his son-in-law Constantine and even tried to assassinate him. That was enough for Constantine, and in 310 he forced Maximian to take his own life.

Meanwhile, Galerius wasn't idle. He tried to improve his position both through propaganda and dynastic maneuvering. Although Diocletian never gave his wife, Aurelia Prisca, the title of Augusta, Galerius now bestowed it on his wife, Valeria, Diocletian's daughter. He also named a province after her. Galerius wanted to flaunt his superiority over his fellow rulers, but they, of course, didn't agree.

That same year, 308, Galerius appointed yet another Balkan soldier as Augustus in the West, in the hope that he could finally pry power from Maxentius in Rome. A longtime army comrade of Galerius and one of his generals in the war against Persia, his name was Valerius Licinianus Licinius. He was, as usual, a poor boy from the Balkans who had climbed the military ranks. But not even an experienced commander could breach Rome's mighty walls, and he did not succeed in removing Maxentius.

Galerius, however, would die of cancer by the end of 311. Before he died, he canceled his measures against Christians, though others would continue them. Why Galerius yielded is unclear, but some said that his illness made him rethink his certainty that the Christian god lacked power.

Four men now claimed to rule part of the Roman Empire: Constantine, Maxentius, Licinius, and Daia. Their struggles will be resolved in the next chapter. In the meantime, consider the fate of Diocletian and his family.

How and when Diocletian died is unclear. His life ended sometime between 311 and 313, either by illness or suicide. Following his death, both his widow and his daughter—the widow of Galerius—were murdered. Diocletian was unable to ensure his family's safety, but he had saved the empire and reorganized the government.

Not since Augustus had anyone changed the Roman government so dramatically. Diocletian laid down a precedent for dividing the government of the empire. True, the tetrarchy, or rule by four, did not long survive his retirement. By the same token, for most of the fourth century, two men at a time ruled the empire rather than one, which concedes Diocletian's point that Rome's problems were too big for one man to handle.

Diocletian also ended the power of the city of Rome. Never again would it serve as the empire's capital. Like Diocletian, most emperors would now come from the Balkans and from the military, further weakening ties to the Eternal City.

Thanks to Diocletian, Rome's army was better funded and more thoroughly deployed on the borders, with a new network of roads and forts. He also bought two generations of peace with Persia in the East. Also thanks to Diocletian, imperial administration was bigger and more intrusive than ever. To finance all of this, Diocletian increased the burden of taxation. He strengthened and codified a process that tied peasants to the land.

So much for his successes; there were failures, too. Despite his violent efforts, Diocletian did not stop the growth of Christianity. Nor did he succeeded in putting the empire in the hands of his son-in-law and his family. Enemies were on the rise, and not even the solid walls of his palace would save his family from them.

The man who would ultimately triumph as Diocletian's successor, Constantine, marked less of a break than it might seem. As the first Christian emperor, it is true, Constantine represents a stark change. But he behaved much like Diocletian with respect to government, the military, and the economy. Constantine founded a dynasty that was descended from two of Diocletian's closest comrades: Constantius and Maximian. In retrospect, the reigns of Diocletian and Constantine amounted to one common enterprise to reform and thus save the Roman Empire.

Bust of Constantine.

10

CONSTANTINE

THE CHRISTIAN

In the courtyard of Rome's Capitoline Museums, located, ironically, almost precisely on the site of the city's holiest pagan site, there stands a colossal marble bust of Constantine, Rome's first Christian emperor. We can't overestimate the significance of Constantine's conversion. In ways big and small, it changed the world. It gave us Christ as the Lord of Rome, Sunday as the day of rest, and Istanbul as Europe's most populous city—a city that would put Rome in the shadow. In fact, the conversion is such an important moment in the next 1,700 years of European history that it is almost easier to think of Constantine as a man of the Middle Ages—the Age of Faith—than as a Roman emperor, the successor of Caesar and Augustus. But the bust reminds you that he was.

It is an impressive monument, fit for a ruler and well known to all students of ancient history. The bust once belonged to a larger-than-life-size statue. The head alone is ten feet tall. A few other parts survive, including a veined and muscular right arm, a right hand with pointed finger, and a foot. But it is the bust that grabs our attention. Constantine looks as radically different from his predecessors as the first bearded emperor, Hadrian, once did from his.

Constantine is beardless with a dimpled chin, handsome and young, but also massive and strong. He has a full head of hair. His neck is thickly muscled. His eyes gaze upward, in search of divine inspiration. Yet, novel as these features are, they hearken back to models centuries earlier.

Constantine was every inch a Roman. He was a soldier, a statesman, and a builder. He was ruthless and single-minded, but so were most successful emperors. He was ambitious, power hungry, brilliant, subtle, spiritual, and violent. He was a warrior, an administrator, a public relations genius, and a visionary. If he had a healthy ego, that, too, was nothing new.

He compared himself to Augustus, but Augustus compared himself to Romulus, and both emperors thought of Alexander the Great as their forerunner. Like Augustus, Constantine embraced change while trying to preserve the best of the old. Like Augustus, Constantine began by employing violence and then switched mainly to peaceful and gradual methods. He paid the soldiers, but he also paid attention to women, and he followed a familiar imperial pattern in having a close relationship with his mother. He aspired to starting a dynasty, and in this, he succeeded more than most.

Constantine was both Roman and Christian. We see this in his description of his achievements in a way that combined the one Christian God and the promise of salvation with the traditional imperialism of a Roman pagan: "With the power of this God as ally, beginning from the shores of Ocean I have raised up the whole world step by step with sure hopes of salvation."

Constantine was a man of blood and a man of God. In making it a priority to readjust Rome's relationship with the gods there too, Constantine followed precedent. But the consequences of his policy proved revolutionary.

Constantine was one of history's great success stories. That might have been the most Roman thing of all.

RISE TO POWER

Constantine was born at Naissus (today's Niš, Serbia) on February 27, 273. Nobody could guess at Constantine's birth that the child of this provincial capital would one day found what would become the most important city in the world, as Constantinople long was, about 450 miles southeast of his birthplace. Nor could they guess that he would begin an epochal change in the religion and culture of the empire.

At the time of his birth, Constantine's father, Constantius, who came from what is now Bulgaria, was a junior officer in the Roman army. Constantine's mother, Helena, was the respectable but humble daughter of the owner of a small hotel on the main military highway in northwestern Turkey. Constantius met her there in 272 when he was on a military campaign with the emperor Aurelian. They fell in love and married. Nine months later, Constantine was born.

Constantius rose quickly in the military ranks, and by the time Constantine was ten, Constantius was already a provincial governor. Constantius now had the resources to give the boy a superb education, especially in Latin literature, but it included Greek too, as well as philosophy. Constantine was also trained to be a soldier like his father.

Constantine was probably in his early teens when his father divorced Helena to marry a princess, the daughter of the ruler of the western empire, the Augustus Maximian. Constantius remained close to Constantine and groomed him for an illustrious great future. Still, the divorce was surely a blow. We can only imagine how great an effort Helena made to protect and nourish her son.

She was one of the most important figures in his life and remained so for the next three decades. Like many a previous Roman mother, such as Livia, Agrippina, and Julia Domna, for example, Helena play a big role in the adult life of an emperor.

Around the time Constantius was appointed Caesar in 293, Constantine was sent east. Now twenty years old, he served in the armies that invaded Persia and put down revolt in Egypt. Then Constantine joined Diocletian's court in Nicomedia. As the oldest son of the Caesar Constantius, he was expected to succeed his father one day.

Naturally, he made a good marriage. Not long before 300, Constantine married a woman named Minervina. She has been plausibly identified as Diocletian's niece. They had a son named Crispus.

When the Great Persecution began in 303, Constantine was still at the imperial court in Nicomedia. Like his father, he opposed intolerance toward Christians, but he kept quiet, no doubt in order to keep his career on track.

The court of Diocletian was a school of power politics. Among the other lessons it offered was that anything was possible for a man who was ambitious and talented enough. After all, Diocletian himself rose from obscurity to supreme power. Constantine had much greater advantages of birth and education. Still, there was one major caveat: anything was possible *if* a man had the favor of heaven. That needed to be taken into consideration. Some historians think he had the help of his mother, who might have moved nearby to be with her talented son and might have shaped his view of the gods.

THE MAN OF DESTINY

In 305 Galerius upended young Constantine's calculations by convincing Diocletian to change his plans. When Diocletian and Maximian stepped down from office as Augusti, Galerius took over in the East and Constantius in the West, just as was long planned. But instead of appointing Constantine (Constantius's son) and Maxentius (Maximian's son) as Caesars, Diocletian appointed Maximinus Daia (Galerius's nephew) and Severus (Galerius's army crony). This was a complete change of plan, done at Galerius's behest. Neither of the rejected men took it lying down; each being too ambitious.

Constantine left Nicomedia and headed west to join his father in Britain. As mentioned in the previous chapter, when Constantius died there the next year, Constantine accepted the acclamation of the troops as his father's replacement as the new Augustus and ruler of the West. Soldiers tended to approve of the hereditary principle, so Constantine was the natural choice, and, besides, before he died, Constantius had given his support to his son. On top of that, Constantine earned the men's respect by campaigning with them in northern Britain beyond Hadrian's Wall in the last year of his father's life. No doubt Constantine displayed his combat experience already gained in Eastern Europe and the Near East. He also had one other advantage: the support of a German king who served as Constantius's loyal military lieutenant in Britain.

A few months later, Maxentius in Rome declared himself to be the successor of his father. Galerius tried to stop them, but after two failed military campaigns in Italy, he was forced to accept both Constantine and Maxentius, although as Caesars, not Augusti. He appointed another army friend, Licinius, as Augustus and ruler of the West.

Constantine, meanwhile, consolidated his power. Like his father, he made his capital at Augusta Treverorum (modern Trier), in what is today southwestern Germany. A prosperous city in the early empire, Trier had been destroyed by Germanic tribes in 275, but Constantius and Constantine raised the city to new heights. Constantine built a palace there whose audience hall still stands because it was later used as a church. The building is a long, large, lofty hall with an apse at the far end, where the emperor's throne once stood. Light pours in through a double row of large, rounded windows. Originally decorated with colored marbles, the building's interior was not as austere as it now appears. Yet it was simpler than earlier imperial audience halls because it lacked columns. In its stark dignity, it set a precedent for early church architecture.

From Augusta Treverorum, Constantine governed his father's provinces of Britain, Gaul, and Hispania while also winning a series of campaigns against German invaders on the Rhine frontier. Although the empire remained on the strategic defensive throughout Constantine's lifetime, emperors often crossed into foreign territory to raid, plunder, and show the locals who was boss. As emperor, Constantine led his armies in person, like any successful Roman ruler. He was proud of his titles won on campaign such as Germanicus Maximus IIII, indicating that he'd defeated the Germans four times.

Meanwhile, back inside the empire, Constantine advanced his position by making a deal with his rivals. A widower after the death of Minervina, Constantine now arranged to marry Fausta (Flavia Maxima Fausta), sister of Maxentius. Fausta was more than twenty years younger than Constantine, and, to judge by coins, pretty enough that she could be considered a trophy wife, but she served the interests of dynasty by bearing children.

Maximian and Maxentius now recognized Constantine as Augustus, while Constantine acknowledged his new brother-in-law as Caesar and his father-in-law as a senior Augustus. Both Constantine and Maxentius proclaimed religious tolerance in the lands they controlled, stretching from Britain to North Africa, as well as the restoration of Christian property confiscated during the Great Persecution.

But Maximian quarreled with Constantine and tried to assassinate him. In 310 a frustrated Constantine forced Maximian to take his own life. We can only imagine how uncomfortable this made Fausta feel.

Meanwhile, another imperial death the next year further shifted the play of power: Galerius died from cancer. Four men now shared the rule of the empire, but there was little trust among them. In the East, Licinius and Daia were locked in a power struggle, while in the West, Constantine and Maxentius eyed each other warily. In 312 a new set of alliances emerged: Constantine joined Licinius against Maxentius and Daia, and then made his move, invading Italy. Constatine was a warrior in command of veteran troops, while the much weaker Maxentius prepared to withstand a siege behind the strong walls of Rome. All that remained was the ultimate prize: Rome.

THE MILVIAN BRIDGE

The Milvian Bridge spans the Tiber River north of Rome. First built in 206 BC and often reconstructed, the modern bridge still contains some ancient stones. As long ago as Nero's youth, it was a place for nighttime escapades, and today it remains a magnet for lovers. But it is best known for the Battle of the Milvian Bridge on October 28, 312, when Constantine defeated Maxentius and conquered Rome. It was the empire's most decisive military engagement since the naval victory at Actium sealed Augustus's power on September 2, 31 BC.

The battle actually took place not on the bridge but north of it, on land. By coincidence, Constantine's army marshaled just under the hill on which Livia's suburban villa had stood. By that point, Constantine had enjoyed a string of victories, and Maxentius was so worried that he buried his regalia of office on the Palatine Hill, where archaeologists discovered them in 2006. The prize find was Maxentius's scepter, the only imperial scepter ever uncovered. Imperial scepters often were two-to-three-foot ivory rods holding a globe or eagle. Maxentius's scepter features a blue orb representing the earth and held in place by a gold-colored brass alloy grip.

In order to keep Constantine away from the city, Maxentius tore down enough of the Milvian Bridge to make it impassable. Then he changed his mind and decided to march out and fight Constantine, so he had a pontoon bridge put up as a replacement. Maxentius led his troops into battle and suffered a crushing defeat. Afterward, he tried to find safety back within the city's walls, but he fell off the bridge in the crush of refugees and was drowned in his armor. Maxentius's body later washed up to shore.

Maxentius and Constantine were brothers-in-law, but the two men did not hesitate to fight to the death. Nor did Constantine protest when Maxentius's severed head was paraded through Rome on a pike. Later, it went to North Africa in order to prove Maxentius's death to his supporters there. It was another blow to Fausta, whose brother and father had been killed at her husband's command.

More important than his conquest of Rome was what Constantine did with it. He announced to the world that he was now a friend of the Christian Church. In fact, he was a Christian himself.

How Constantine reached this position and just what being a Christian meant to him makes a fascinating story, debated among scholars.

THE CONVERSION OF CONSTANTINE

Several years before 312, Constantine declined to enforce persecution de-
crees against Christians. In this, he followed his father, who was no Christian. But Helena possibly was a Christian. Our most important source for
the life of Constantine says otherwise and maintains that the emperor converted his mother to Christianity. Yet later church historians say that Helena raised him as a Christian. All of these authors had their own agendas,
and it is hard to say where the truth lies.

At a minimum, it is clear that Christianity meant a great deal to Constantine if he wanted his mother to convert, and his mother meant a great
deal to him (emotionally as well as politically) if he cared about her religious affiliation. Helena went on, later in Constantine's reign, to play a key
role in Christianizing the Roman world.

Two years before the Battle of the Milvian Bridge in 310, Constantine
and his army saw a dramatic sight in the afternoon sky: a solar halo, or ring
around the sun. It happened near a temple of Apollo in Gaul. Apollo is the
sun god, but the temple was also understood to praise another Roman deity,
the Unconquered Sun (*Sol Invictus* in Latin). This was the favorite deity
of Constantine's father, Constantius, although it had come to Rome only
fairly recently during a military campaign in the east, when the emperor
Aurelian saw a local sun god promising him victory in a battle in Syria.

Young Constantine believed that he had a special relationship with the
sun god, yet he was not sure what to make of the remarkable sight in the
sky over Gaul. He consulted various wise men, including Christian bishops.
They assured him that the vision was a sign not from the sun god but from
Christ. Christians already associated Christ with the sun. In the Gospels,
Jesus describes himself as "the light of the world," and Matthew says that
Jesus's face shone like the sun. Early Christians saw Christ as a source of
spiritual illumination.

The final persuader for Constantine was a dream in which Christ
showed him a sign to use as protection against the enemy. Constantine

now put a well-known early Christian symbol on (or above) his personal banner: the Greek letters *chi* and *rho*, the equivalent of the Latin *CHR* for Christ. This took place probably while Constantine was still in Gaul and before he crossed into Italy. It was now that Constantine declared himself a Christian. Later, before the Battle of the Milvian Bridge, he made his men put the *chi-rho* symbol on their shields. And he reiterated his Christian faith after entering Rome.

Was Constantine a sincere convert? Although the words *sincerity* and *politician* don't usually go together, there is reason to think that he was. Ancient people took dreams and omens seriously. Previous emperors certainly did, and they consulted astrologers as well. Modern Westerners always look for the "real motive," but we are often blind to the reality of religious motivation.

It is possible that Constantine was a cynic from start to finish who manipulated religion to gain power. But was converting to Christianity the smart move in 312? Only in hindsight does it seem so. Nothing guaranteed that a pagan-majority empire would tolerate a Christian emperor. Only a man with a high capacity for risk—or a man who believed that God had chosen him for a mission—would behave as Constantine did. As early as 314, Constantine stated that God Himself had entrusted him with the direction of human affairs, provided that Constantine handled them well, and he would return to the theme of his mission in later years.

Constantine continued to behave as a pagan in various ways for years after converting. For example, he still had to work out the relationship between his new god, Christ, and his old god, the Unconquered Sun. He saw no reason at first why he couldn't worship both. For years, his coins continued to bear the image of the sun god, often stating the legend TO THE INVINCIBLE SUN, COMPANION OF THE EMPEROR UNCONQUERED CONSTANTINE.

But Constantine was the ruler of an empire in which the vast majority of people were pagans, particularly in the military, where Christians were a distinct minority. During the Great Persecution, individual Christians died as martyrs for their principles. Yet when it came to reaching a wider pagan audience, it could be useful to blur the difference between the old gods and the new one.

For a dozen years after the Milvian Bridge, Constantine faced Licinius, the ruler of the East, a dangerous rival who tolerated Christianity without embracing it himself. The pagan Licinius could use the majority's religion against Constantine. After becoming sole emperor by defeating Licinius in 324, Constantine had more flexibility, but he still faced formidable anti-Christian odds. Rulers who don't do the math don't survive, and Constantine was always a good student.

Even after 312, Constantine engaged in murder and bloodshed that would make even a pagan blush. But conversion does not make someone perfect. Constantine undoubtedly spread the gospel and made the church splendid and safer. Surely that made him a Christian.

CHRISTIANIZING THE CITY OF ROME

When Constantine entered Rome in late October 312, it was his first visit to the city. He was nearly forty years old, a seasoned military veteran, and the ruler of much of the western empire before ever visiting the Eternal City. It says quite a bit about the decline in Rome's status that Constantine could reach such heights without having seen it.

Constantine stayed only two months, long enough to win over the city's pagan elite and to shower favor on its Christian community. Maxentius was an avid builder, and Constantine took over and finished his projects, including a massive basilica used for public administration and for shopping. Nowadays we think of a basilica as a church, but basilicas were originally public buildings.

Constantine destroyed the basis of the defeated regime's military power by abolishing its elite cavalry units and by finally dissolving the Praetorian Guard—or what was left it, since the Guard had suffered heavy casualties at the Milvian Bridge. The Guard had begun with Augustus, but Diocletian had reduced its role, and now Constantine ended its long run. Pause for a moment to consider the impact of the Praetorians on Roman history, from the power of the Praetorian prefect Sejanus to the Guard's part in choosing Claudius and Nero as emperors, to its murder of Pertinax and selling off the throne to the highest bidder.

Constantine replaced the Praetorians with other elite units to protect the emperor. He created new select cavalry regiments—2,500 men by the end of his reign—to accompany him and keep away trouble. Of these, 40 men were picked to serve as the emperor's bodyguard. They were known as *candidati* from the white tunics they wore, just as centuries earlier, office seekers in the Roman Republic wore white togas, which gives us our word *candidates.*

Constantine began immediately the process of making Rome a more Christian city, but in a careful and diplomatic manner. Except for setting up a cross in his new basilica—an unpopular measure with Rome's old guard—he kept all Christian-themed building projects away from downtown. Instead, he placed a series of new churches on the edge of town and on imperial property. The largest of them, Saint John in the Lateran, still stands. It was the first great Christian church. Before Constantine, Christians usually met in simple structures, often private houses. Although the sources speak of some separate churches, we know nothing about their appearance. Whatever they looked like, Constantine surely built something grander.

The Lateran was a great building, about three hundred feet long from the entrance to the original end of the apse. Like all of Constantine's Roman churches, it was magnificent only on the inside; the outside was plain and modest, almost as if not to cause offense. Despite later renovations to the Lateran, a visitor today can still make out its heavy, five-aisled structure, typical of a Late Roman public building. The basilica church resembled the basilica government office building. Seeing the architectural similarity, a Roman visitor in Constantine's day took away the clear lesson that church and state were now connected. One other detail stands out: Constantine built the new church on the site of the demolished headquarters of Maxentius's elite cavalry troops. The message was unmistakable: a new day had dawned.

Next to the Lateran basilica stood a wealthy person's house, owned by Constantine. He presented it to Pope Miltiades, and it became the official residence of the Popes for centuries to come. The Pope was bishop of Rome. He already claimed a special status as the successor to Peter and Paul. Constantine showed respect to Miltiades and his successor, Pope Sylvester I, but the emperor did not hesitate to exercise supreme authority in the church. The Popes of Constantine's day were important, but they had nothing like the power of later Popes.

Constantine also put energy into building shrines to saints and martyrs on the outskirts of the city. The best known is the Church of Old St. Peter's, which rose over the traditional site of Peter's tomb in the Vatican region west of the Tiber River. It stood for more than a thousand years but eventually fell into disrepair. Between 1506 and 1626, the magnificent Renaissance basilica that we see today was built, replacing Constantine's church.

At first, Constantine acted more like a friend of the church than its supreme governor. His Christian construction projects were essentially private acts of charity and not state policy. The official face of Constantine in Rome, as it were, was inoffensive to pagans.

The best official example is also Constantine's most famous Roman monument, at least to today's tourists: the triumphal arch that bears his name and rises up beside the Colosseum. It was built by the Senate to commemorate the victory at the Milvian Bridge three years before. There was nothing openly Christian about the arch. In fact, a contemporary visitor saw a pagan symbol—a colossal statue of the sun god, Constantine's original patron—looming up in the distance through its central arch.

The artwork is a series of sculpted reliefs. Some of them, specially commissioned for the arch, show Constantine's military victories in Italy, his entrance into Rome, and his distribution of money to the Roman people. The other reliefs were plundered from earlier imperial monuments. Works of Trajan, Hadrian, and Marcus Aurelius display scenes of war, hunting, and pagan sacrifice, and even Antinous makes a cameo appearance. The presence of old art works placed Constantine in Rome's imperial tradition although it might indicate that the arch was built under time pressure, forcing the reuse of earlier works.

Only the dedicatory inscription lends itself to Christian interpretation—but it also lends itself to pagan interpretation. It says that the Senate and people of Rome dedicated the arch to the emperor Constantine and his triumphs because he was moved by greatness of spirit and "divine inspiration." The latter term could refer to Jupiter or the Unconquered Sun as well as to Christ. Both this inscription and two shorter ones refer to Constantine as a liberator from tyranny and the founder of peace, both traditional Roman designations.

CONQUERING THE EAST

In 313 Constantine held a summit conference with Licinius in Mediolanum. They agreed to divide the empire. Constantine sealed the deal with Licinius the traditional Roman way by giving him his half sister, Constantia (Flavia Julia Constantia), in marriage. But the meeting is best known for the famous Edict of Milan. The title is a misnomer. It was neither an edict nor from Milan but, rather, a letter issued later by Licinius from his base in the East.

The letter was important but not as much as historians sometimes make it. The western empire already enjoyed religious freedom and the restoration of property confiscated from Christians during the Great Persecution. Before his death in 311, the persecutor Galerius gave in and restored toleration. Only Daia continued persecuting Christians in the eastern empire, most of which he controlled until 313. Now Licinius promised to extend those policies to Daia's realm.

He was soon able to make good on his promises because he defeated Daia in battle and took control of the East. Daia committed suicide. Two men, not four, now ruled the empire, but it wasn't big enough for Constantine and Licinius. They were each too ambitious and too suspicious of the other. They struggled in a series of civil wars between 316 and 324. Ever a man to lead from the front, Constantine was wounded in one of his civil war battles.

In spite of having also to deal with fighting on the Rhine and Danube frontiers and of a tactical misstep, Constantine defeated Licinius at Hadrianopolis. Then Constantine's son, Crispus, won a victory over Licinius's fleet in the Hellespont, the narrow strait dividing Europe from Asia at the entrance to the Aegean Sea. The final battle took place on September 18, 324, at Chrysopolis (modern Üsküdar, Turkey), in what is today the Asian part of Istanbul. The religious contrast was stark. On one side, Licinius displayed images of the pagan gods, while on the other side, Constantine brandished a military flag with the *chi-rho* Christian image. Constantine felt confident enough to launch a frontal attack and won complete success. With large numbers of his troops slaughtered, Licinius took the rest of his army and fled.

Constantia now acted as a go-between between her defeated husband and her half brother. They agreed that Licinius and their son, Licinius Junior, would lose their power but keep their lives. They were sent into internal exile. Constantia was welcomed back into Constantine's house and became a power at court.

Constantia was not the only formidable woman in Constantine's family. His wife, Fausta, received the title of Augusta in 324. At the same time, so did Helena. With two powerful women attached to the emperor, rivalry was inevitable and conflict a constant danger.

Coin portraits show Helena as a handsome and dignified woman. She wears a diadem, the sign of royalty, and a modest mantle. Fausta too bespeaks self-possession and noble bearing in her coin portraits. She sometimes has the lovely profile of a classical Greek statue. Her hair is elaborately coiffed, and she sometimes wears a diadem too. Each woman stands on the reverse of her coins. Helena's coins show a robed female figure holding a lowered olive branch, with the legend SAFETY. Fausta's coins show a woman holding two children and the legend HOPE, a reference to Fausta's motherhood.

TOWARD A CHRISTIAN EMPIRE

After the defeat of Licinius, Constantine became more openly Christian. In 326, when he visited Rome to celebrate the twentieth anniversary of becoming emperor, for the first time he refused to sacrifice to Jupiter, which led to protest.

The emperor had a sense of mission. He believed that God had chosen him to convert the empire to Christianity. In a speech delivered to a Christian audience in 325, Constantine said:

> We strive to the best of our ability to fill those who are uninitiated in such teachings with good hope, having summoned God to assist us in the endeavor. For it is no mean task for us to turn the minds of our subjects to piety if they happen to be good or, if they are wicked and unfeeling, to lead them to the opposite, making them useful instead of good-for-nothings.

Roman religion always depended on government support. Constantine diverted subsidies from pagans and gave them to the Christian Church. It was a huge boon.

Constantine had promised toleration in the West before 324, but he had a free hand in the East now. Although he allowed the East's pagan temples to continue to stand, he confiscated their wealth, from gold to bronze. He also prohibited sacrifice, which rendered temples all but empty shells.

One purpose for these funds was to build churches, and many new churches rose thanks to Constantine's generosity. A pagan author criticized this as a waste of public money, but Christians surely thought differently. Another purpose was to distribute charity to the poor. Roman emperors had helped the poor before, but not on the scale that they did now, under a Christian emperor. It would mark a permanent change in Roman government.

The emperor also elevated the status of bishops. Like all Christian clergy, they were freed from having to perform expensive and time-consuming duties that other prosperous Romans owed to local government. Bishops had certain other privileges, most notably the right of trial by their peers, something no other Romans enjoyed. They served as agents for distributing imperial funds to their churches and to the poor. They were even able to preside in church over the freeing of slaves by their owners. All in all, bishops became very important people.

Several other changes in Roman law affecting Christians came into effect under Constantine. The punishment of celibacy, which became law centuries ago under Augustus, was now abolished, since Christians, unlike pagans, considered celibacy a virtue. Crucifixion, the death penalty imposed on Jesus (and many others), was abolished as a form of capital punishment. Divorce was made more difficult, although not abolished, probably under the influence of the New Testament and its opposition to divorce.

Like Jews, Christians recognized a day of rest, or Sabbath. Jews celebrate the Sabbath on Saturday (actually, roughly from sundown Friday to nightfall Saturday). Early Christians followed one of two paths: some celebrated the Jewish Sabbath, while others celebrated the Sabbath on Sunday, the day when Jesus rose from the dead. Meanwhile, pagans recognized Sunday as a day holy to the sun, although not as a day of rest. Constantine decreed that Sunday, "the venerable day of the sun," be a day of rest for all city activities. (Farmers were allowed to take care of the crops on Sunday.) It took another generation or two for Constantine's rule to become universal among Christians.

Constantine's patronage elevated the church but also changed it. The ultimate outsider movement was now the establishment. Jesus said to render unto Caesar the things that are Caesar's and unto God the things that are God's. Constantine was a man of God but was also Caesar, and he insisted on the final say about how and what to owe to God. He might have acted from the best of motives, out of the belief that a godly king has the responsibility to promote true religion. But act he did, and Christians had to decide how to respond.

Constantine became the ruler of the Christian Church, or, to be more accurate, of the Christian *Churches*. Christianity as Constantine knew it was a diverse religion, an umbrella sheltering a great deal of regional variation and doctrinal choice. After nearly twenty years of hard-fought war and politics, Constantine had finally unified all Romans under the rule of one man. He equally insisted on unifying all Christians, but it was no easy task.

While still ruler of only the West, Constantine intervened in a split in the church of North Africa, which was divided on the question of how much forgiveness to show Christians who had made deals to survive the Great Persecution. Having put his career on the line for the church, Constantine insisted that Christians display a united front against their opponents. He wrote in 314 to the Roman official in charge of North Africa, describing him as "a fellow worshipper of the most high God," and declared his goal of achieving Christian unity. But years of negotiation, bribery, exile, and even execution failed to bring together the two factions of the African church.

In 325 Constantine waded into an even bigger controversy raging through the eastern church. The fundamental question was just *how* Jesus was God. Most Christians believed that Jesus was both man and God at the same time, a mystery that could be reconciled only by faith. The Arians, named after their leader, an Egyptian Christian named Arius, believed that God the Father created his son Jesus, who was greater than other humans but not equal to God Himself. Constantine tried to get both sides to agree by holding a great meeting of bishops in the city of Nicaea. It was the church's first ecumenical—in Greek, "world"—council. Two hundred fifty bishops attended, and the emperor himself presided. One of those bishops, Eusebius of Caesarea, in Syria Palestina, was a major Christian writer and thinker. He is our most important contemporary source for Constantine.

The stakes were high at Nicaea, and the disagreement reached the highest levels of the court. Constantia advised the pro-Arian faction at the council. Later, even on her deathbed, she still lobbied her brother on behalf of the Arians. But she didn't get her way.

The council agreed on a statement reaffirming the traditional belief that Jesus was both man and God. With some later changes, that statement is still recited by Christians today as the Nicene Creed. Although this put the state-sponsored church on record against the Arians, Arian Christianity survived for centuries.

Constantine wanted to impose an official or orthodox Christianity and to oppose other beliefs, which were labeled as heresy. But *heresy* comes from *hairesis*, a Greek word for "choice," and Christianity had a long tradition of freedom and decentralization. It proved resistant to central control.

Still, with Christianity now the imperial religion, the image of Jesus in Christian art began to change. Earlier, artists depicted Jesus as an ordinary person engaged, for instance, in healing the sick. They also commonly showed him as a simple shepherd, recalling Jesus's description of himself as the good shepherd. Now Jesus began to sit on a throne in a very fine toga, like the emperor himself, surrounded by male disciples who look like senators and by females who look like Roman nobles. It was an imperial Christ for an imperial religion. To be sure, Christianity was not yet the official state religion and wouldn't be until 395. Paganism was still practiced. Yet with his lavish funding and imperial patronage, Constantine put the Church on the road to success.

THE SORROW AND THE GLORY

Having killed one brother-in-law to conquer Rome, Constantine killed another to add the Roman East to his portfolio. After promising Constantia to spare Licinius and their son, he changed his mind. He accused the two men of plotting against him and had them both executed. Licinius was killed first, in 325, and his son a year later.

That, however, was only the beginning of woes for Constantine's family. In 326 the emperor put his oldest son, Crispus, on trial. The young man was found guilty and the punishment was execution by poisoning. This was a shocking development considering Crispus's status as well as his success as a commander against German tribes in the West and against Licinius in the East. Elevated to the rank of Caesar, Crispus, it seemed, was being groomed to be emperor someday. But suddenly, around the age of twenty-six, he was gone. His name was expunged from all public records and documents.

The reasons for Crispus's execution are much debated, but the most likely explanation is that Fausta accused him of having sexual relations with her. Fausta was closer in age to her stepson than to Constantine. Did the two really sleep together, or did Fausta, like a character in Greek myth, proposition Crispus and then turn on him with a false accusation after he rejected her advance? Was there another factor: Did Fausta resent her husband for killing her father and brother? We can only guess.

Later, Constantine came to the conclusion that Crispus was innocent and Fausta had lied. His mother, Helena, convinced him of this and persuaded him that her grandson had been killed unjustly. Fearing vengeance, Fausta committed suicide in an overheated bath.

A woman who was daughter of one emperor (Maximian), sister of another (Maxentius), and wife of a third (Constantine), a woman with the exalted rank of Augusta, Fausta had spent most of her life in palaces. She could never have expected such a sordid end. She left behind five young children and a ruined reputation. Like Crispus, Fausta was banned from official records. Meanwhile, the imperial family suffered disgrace.

THE HOLY LAND

The following year, Constantine sent Helena on a pilgrimage to Syria Palestina. It was part piety and part public relations in order to repair the damage done to the imperial house by the events of the previous year.

During her time there, Helena located the key sites where Jesus had lived, particularly in Jerusalem. She was on an official mission with access to unlimited government funds, which she used to build new churches and beautify existing ones and to help the poor. She founded beautiful churches in Bethlehem and on the Mount of Olives in Jerusalem.

Also in Jerusalem, Constantine sponsored the building of the Church of the Holy Sepulcher on the site of the Resurrection. Part of that church, much renovated, still exists. Originally, there stood next to it a magnificent basilica, now gone.

After the Romans destroyed Jerusalem as punishment for the Jewish revolt, they rebuilt it under Hadrian but as a pagan city rather than a Jewish city; Aelia Capitolina instead of Jerusalem. Now they rebuilt it as Jerusalem but, again, not as a Jewish city; Jerusalem was now a Christian city.

Constantine rebranded Syria Palestina as the Christian Holy Land. A backwater province became the center of Christian pilgrimage. This had long-lasting historical consequences. On the one hand, it led, centuries later, to the Christian clash with Muslims known as the Crusades. On the other hand, it tended to undercut the right of Jews to live in their historic homeland. Just who the land belongs to is still fought over today.

Constantine was no friend to the Jews. Yet by Roman standards, he was not the worst of enemies, either. He didn't destroy the temple like Vespasian and Titus or bathe Judea in blood like Hadrian. Nor did he destroy Jewish communal life, which continued to thrive both in the land of Israel and in the Diaspora. But Constantine did make Judaism inferior to Christianity. He was not the first emperor to insult Jews, although his branding Jews as "murderers of the Lord" proved particularly harmful. He made it illegal for Jews to accept Christian converts and illegal to prevent Jews from converting to Christianity. Yet he did Jews an unintended favor by freeing their slaves if the slaves converted to Christianity, thereby removing at least part of what we now consider a moral stain—slavery—from the Jewish community.

When a prominent rabbinical scholar converted to Christianity, Constantine gave him high rank and the funding to build the first churches in Galilee, an area of heavily Jewish cities. Decades later, one of these cities was the center of a Jewish revolt against Rome.

CONSTANTINOPLE

Like Diocletian, Constantine recognized the reality that the empire was now too big and complicated to be governed from any one city, and that it needed an eastern capital as well as a western one. Constantine did not rule from Rome. For most of his reign, he governed the empire either from Augusta Treverorum in the west or from either Sirmium or Serdica (modern Sofia, Bulgaria) in the east. After defeating Licinius, he wanted a new capital in Licinius's former lands. Nicomedia, where Diocletian and Galerius ruled in the East, no longer seemed suitable because it had been the center of the Great Persecution. Constantine wanted a new Christian eastern capital for a Christian empire. Besides, he had his eye on a site with both strategic and propaganda advantages.

Few cities have a better location than Constantinople, but Constantine was the first to exploit its full potential. It's no exaggeration to say that by refounding Byzantium, as it was then known, as Constantinople, Constantine created one of the most important cities in history, not to mention one of the liveliest.

The site came to his attention during his battle for the East, when Licinius used Byzantium as a fortified base. Byzantium was a Greek city founded in the six hundreds BC. It had its ups and downs over the years, most recently when it was destroyed by Septimius Severus as punishment for supporting his rival and then rebuilt probably by Licinius. Constantine rebuilt Byzantium again. He called the city Constantinople, that is, "Constantine's City," after himself. It is possible that he also called it New Rome, but that name might not have come until fifty years after Constantine. We don't know.

Constantinople is located on a peninsula on the southern end of the Bosporus, a narrow strait that runs between the Euxine Sea and the Propontis, and from there to the Hellespont, the Aegean Sea, and the Mediterranean. On one side of the Bosporus lies Europe; on the other, Asia. The Bosporus was and still is one of the most strategic bodies of water on earth.

Constantinople lies on the European side of the Bosporus. A peninsula surrounded by water on three sides, it is accessible by land only on one side and so is easily defended. Constantine gave the city new walls, extending its area nearly two miles to the west. The result was a large and well-protected fortress located where two continents meet. The city is close to the Danube River and equidistant from two other Roman frontiers, the Rhine River in the West and the Euphrates River in the East.

Constantinople was also a victory monument. It lies across the Bosporus Strait from the site of Constantine's final battle against Licinius, on the Asian shore. By building a city near his victory over a fellow Roman, Constantine followed in the footsteps of Augustus. That emperor, too, built a city across the water from his victory over a rival: Antony at Actium. Augustus called his new city Nicopolis, Greek for "Victory City." Yet there the analogy ends. Neither Augustus nor any other emperor ever built a city as great as Constantinople.

The new city was dedicated on May 11, 330. The emperor built on a grand scale. Constantinople had a new palace, a circus (that is, horse-racing venue), a forum surrounded by porticoes, a senate, and a series of churches. In the center of the forum stood a tall porphyry column, part of which still stands. On the top was a large, nude statue of Constantine himself wearing a crown with rays coming out of it. It could be interpreted as a Christian symbol, a symbol of the sun god, or both. Christian though he was, a politician such as Constantine was capable of calculated ambiguity in order to widen his appeal.

REORGANIZING THE GOVERNMENT

Constantine reorganized Rome's governmental institutions. He made them more specialized and flexible but also, above all, more likely to bend to his will, starting with the military. He needed no reminder of Severus's warning to pay the soldiers. Like emperors since Gallienus, Constantine separated military from civilian careers. Freed from the constraint of having to promote senators to army commands, Constantine increased the number of non-Roman officers, men the Romans considered barbarians. For example, a German king, no less, was in charge of the troops at Eboracum when Constantine's father died. Although most soldiers were native born, a fair numbers of foreigners crossed the frontier to join the Roman army, which they considered a good way to make a living. Moors, Armenians, and Persians but especially Germans served.

Constantine increased the separation, already begun under Diocletian, between field army soldiers and border troops. The first group was fitter, better paid, and required to serve a shorter term than the second. The enhanced field army served directly under the emperor's command. It provided mobility, allowing the emperor to move troops rapidly to wherever they were needed.

Constantine beefed up the palace bureaucracy. He created a set of powerful officials who were directly responsible to him. They were new and more specialized administrators with new bureaus to run. There was an even a new corps, staffed by legionaries, to carry confidential messages between the center and the provinces. All this consolidation and centralization made government more efficient but not more pure. All those administrators expected "tips," to put it mildly. In fact, the bigger Roman government grew, the more corruption became a problem.

Constantine understood that exchanging gifts and favors in return for services was no small part of government. So, in order to forge ties with powerful people in the provinces, he created new titles and distinctions and even, as mentioned, a new Senate for Constantinople. He was also lavish in his generosity to individuals and cities. This was good for politics but not for the Treasury. As a result, taxes went up.

What was, in fact, good for the Treasury was the new gold coin that Constantine minted: the solidus, which replaced an older gold coin whose value had been shattered by inflation. Good quality solidi continued to be issued by Constantine's successors. In fact, the coin was destined to become so reliable and well regarded that some call it "the dollar of the Middle Ages." But bronze and silver coins continued to lose value.

CHURCH AND MOSQUE

Helena died in Constantinople around 328, not long after her return from the Holy Land. Her son was with her at the end. He sent his mother's body to Rome, where she had lived since 312. There the body was laid to rest in an elaborate porphyry sarcophagus in a mausoleum with a dome rotunda, standing beside a martyrs' church outside the city. The sarcophagus is still seen today by millions of visitors every year in the Vatican Museums. The ruins of the mausoleum still stand in a park on the edge of Rome, but they are ill publicized and get few visitors.

Constantine's remaining years proved relatively peaceful. With trouble brewing again on the eastern frontier, however, he planned a new military campaign against Persia. He would lead it himself. Shortly after departing from Constantinople, he fell ill and stopped near Nicomedia. With the end approaching, he was baptized. It was common at the time to postpone baptism to near death, in order to minimize the danger of sinning after baptism. He died on May 22, 337.

Constantine had three surviving sons by Fausta. In his later years, he had named each of them Caesar, along with his nephew, and gave each responsibility for governing a part of the empire. He kept the four Caesars on a tight leash but hoped they would succeed him in a cordial joint rule of the empire. It did not work out. The nephew and his father, Constantine's half brother, were both killed immediately after Constantine's death.

The three siblings divided up the empire, but not for long. One brother wanted more territory, so he attacked another's land, but lost both the battle and his life. A second brother suffered a coup d'état and was murdered. That left the third brother, Constantius II, who ruled for twenty-four years after his father's death, from 337 to 361. Yet he had to fight a very bloody civil war against the man who had usurped his brother's power. Nor did Constantius II prosper when he appointed two of his cousins to serve as his Caesars. He had to execute one for disobedience and was about to march on the other for raising a rebellion, but that plan was not to be. Constantius II died of natural causes before he could implement it, and the rebel reigned.

As was customary for many emperors, Constantine planned his burial place long before his death. Like Diocletian and Galerius, he turned his back on the city of Rome. Instead, Constantine chose a site on a hill in the western part of Constantinople, a place with views of the sea. There his remains would rest in a building that was both a mausoleum and a church. Called the Church of the Holy Apostles, it contained Constantine's sarcophagus lying near memorials for the twelve apostles. The church housed the remains of apostles and other church fathers as well as relics from the Holy Land. There was also an altar, so that Constantine's soul would enjoy the benefit of people worshipping the apostles.

It was a magnificent building: tall, domed, and decorated with marble, bronze, and gold. Although no longer extant, it was fit for a king from what we know of it. More than a millennium after Constantine, in 1453, the Ottoman Turks conquered Constantinople. By then, the Church of the Holy Apostles was already falling down. The city's new Ottoman ruler, Sultan Mehmed II the Conqueror, ordered that the remaining church be demolished and replaced by a mosque. The result was a splendid structure, the Conqueror's Mosque (Fatih Camii), designed by the leading architect of the day. Damaged by a series of earthquakes, it was rebuilt several hundred years later according to a different design and still stands. Outside of the mosque is the tomb of Mehmed, the conqueror who made Constantinople a Muslim governed city. By associating himself with Constantine's resting place, Mehmed strengthened his claim to be *Kayser-i-Rum*—that is, Caesar of Rome. So potent was the reputation of the man who remade the Roman Empire in a new image.

LEGACY

If another man rose from a minor position and defeated powerful opponents to conquer the empire, reform the military, overhaul administration, and create a dynasty, all the while displaying a remarkable energy that saw him fight in battles from northern Britain to the Rhineland, from Rome to the Danube, and from the Hellespont to the Euphrates, we would consider him a major figure. Yet Constantine is such a historical giant that these feats, all of which he achieved, seem minor. Instead, Christianity and Constantinople mark him. Like other emperors, Constantine left many

monuments but none greater than the city that bears his name. Nor was he
the only emperor to intervene in religion, but not even Augustus made as
fateful a change as he did.

Orthodox Christians recognize Constantine as a saint. Helena is a
saint not only for Orthodox Christians but also for Roman Catholics and
Anglicans. If Constantine was the father of Christianity as *the* Roman religion, then Helena was the mother.

The triumph of Christianity was one of the most remarkable turn-
arounds in history. The preaching of an executed holy man in a corner of
the empire became the favored religion of the Roman state and, indeed, by
the end of the fourth century, the official state religion.

The church was already a powerful force in Roman society when Diocletian unleashed the state against it, and its ability to survive the Great
Persecution only made it stronger. It was necessary to find some way to
reconcile the Roman state with what was, in a sense, a state within the state.
Constantine was the way.

Not since Augustus, had any emperor been so strikingly both insider
and outsider before his rise to power as was Constantine. Both Augustus
and Constantine made key allies of men in their own images; men with
power and influence but not quite in the inner circle. For Augustus, it was
the Roman knights of Italy and the surviving senatorial elite, while for
Constantine, it was bishops, bureaucrats, and even barbarian kings. Both
men courted provincial elites and, of course, the army.

History offers few examples of men who understood power better than
Constantine. His staggering ambition was matched only by his genius at
self-presentation. We needn't doubt his possession of a genuine strain of
spirituality, but it was equaled by a taste for violence and a lust for power.

He was one of history's most creative and original statesmen. He
changed Christianity from a minority religion to the dominant cultural
force of the western world. He founded one of the greatest cities in history
and shifted Rome's strategic balance.

Christianity's change from victim of the Great Persecution to imperial
religion seems dizzying, if not miraculous. Yet it follows a familiar Roman

pattern. Whatever else they were, the emperors were pragmatists. Starting with Augustus, they survived by embracing change while maintaining what they could of the past. Sometimes change was relatively minor, like the uplifting of the Greek East under Hadrian. Sometimes it was radical, like the destruction of free, republican institutions under Caesar and Augustus and their replacement with monarchy. Often, change was violent, entailing civil war, confiscation of property, and execution.

In retrospect, the Great Persecution and Constantine's civil wars can be compared with the proscriptions under Augustus and his civil wars. In both cases, the result was a new regime but one rooted in the old one. In both cases, conservatives groaned and resisted, sometimes violently. Yet both times, the empire adjusted and survived. One big difference between the two cases, however, was geographical.

Like many of his predecessors, Constantine looked to the East. The East gave Augustus his richest conquest, Egypt, but Augustus remained rooted in the West. The East propelled Vespasian to the throne—in Rome. It gave Hadrian his ideal, Marcus Aurelius his philosophy, and Septimius Severus his wife, but they too all focused on the Eternal City. Then Diocletian made the East his base. Constantine went further: he moved the axis of the empire eastward, both with a new capital city and with the new spiritual capital of Christianity, which was still rooted in the East.

No one could see at the time of Constantine's death that he had opened the door for the eclipse of Rome. Without meaning to, Constantine created the conditions for a Roman Empire without Rome, without Italy, and even without most of Europe. Constantine laid the foundation for three great eastern empires: the Muslim Caliphate, Russia, and the Eastern Roman Empire or, as it is better known today, the Byzantine Empire.

At the same time, he unwittingly weakened the props that held up the Western Roman Empire. In the three generations after Constantine, no one man ruled the entire empire for more than fifteen years. Finally, in 395, within sixty years of Constantine's death, the empire was officially divided into eastern and western halves. Never again did a single emperor rule from Britain to (northern) Iraq.

The Roman West had always been poorer than the Roman East. Now it became less powerful as well. In the fifth century, Rome was sacked twice. Constantinople, meanwhile, was so well fortified that no adversary took the city for nine hundred years after Constantine founded it.

Perhaps with better leadership and wiser use of resources, the Western Empire could have survived. But 139 years after Constantine died, the Roman Empire in the West ceased to exist. Invaders had already conquered most of its provinces, then they forced the emperor to abdicate. Young Romulus Augustulus gave up his power in the Italian city that had served for three generations as the capital of the Roman West, Ravenna, on September 4, 476.

It was a sad end to the saga of the Roman West but not to the Roman Empire. The pragmatic Romans had simply moved eastward. The successors of Augustus continued to rule but not from Rome. The grandeur that was Constantinople had only just begun in 476.

EPILOGUE

THE GHOSTS OF
RAVENNA

Ravenna sits in northern Italy a few miles from the coast of the Adriatic Sea. For centuries, it was a seaport, but its harbor eventually silted over, and now the sea lies several miles away, connected to Ravenna by a canal. These days the town is a sleepy place, often overlooked among its famous neighbors, spectacular Venice and seaside Rimini. Yet Ravenna acquired a series of exquisite attractions long ago, in particular an alluring set of mosaics. They quietly recall the forgotten time when the Roman Empire fell in the West and rose in the East. More than any place else, Ravenna evokes Rome's imperial twilight.

Today a visitor there confronts a set of ghosts. The first ghost is the imperial palace that once dominated the town. In the years after Constantine, the usual capital of the Western Roman Empire was Mediolanum, rather than Rome or Augusta Treverorum. But over the course of the fourth century, the empire lost the ability to defend Italy from attack. After a Germanic tribe laid siege to Mediolanum, it was apparent that the city was too exposed on the northern Italian plain to continue to serve as the capital. Ravenna was safer. It enjoyed the protection of a ring of marshes, breeding grounds for malaria until recent times. Ravenna also had a good harbor in those days, allowing for reinforcements by sea—or for escape. Augustus had recognized Ravenna's strategic advantages and made it the eastern Italian homeport of the Roman imperial fleet.

So in the fifth century, Ravenna became the capital of the Western Roman Empire. A dozen men ruled as emperor from Ravenna, and their palace was grand. At least, it must have been grand, but we don't know for sure because nothing remains of it.

The last of the Ravenna Roman emperors lived there. His name was Romulus Augustus, and he came to power in 475. He had two famous names: that of Rome's legendary founder and its first king, Romulus, as well as its first emperor, Augustus, but they belied the new emperor's feebleness. His nickname, Augustulus, "Little Augustus," is closer to the truth. He was only fifteen when he came to the throne. His father, a general, was the real power. He had conquered Ravenna and deposed the previous emperor. For some reason, he preferred putting his son in power rather than rule himself. Romulus Augustulus governed an empire that had shrunk to Italy and southern Gaul. He lacked legitimacy, as the Eastern Roman emperor did not recognize his rule.

The real power in Italy was Flavius Odoacer. He was the foreign chieftain—perhaps a German, although that is uncertain—who led the Germanic mercenaries of Italy. Like many earlier Roman soldiers, those mercenaries wanted land of their own. Romulus Augustulus's father refused them, so they revolted. The mercenaries killed both Romulus Augustulus's father and uncle, and then took Ravenna.

They spared the young emperor's life, but they forced him to leave the palace. They gave Romulus Augustulus a generous pension and exiled him to a seaside villa overlooking the Bay of Naples. Along with him went his relatives, possibly including his mother. Odoacer was proclaimed king of Italy. Meanwhile, the Senate in Rome—that body still existed—took the symbols of imperial power, including the diadem and cloak, and sent them to the emperor in Constantinople, as if to say that the western emperor no longer existed.

The date of Romulus Augustulus's abdication, September 4, 476, came a little more than five hundred years since Octavian was proclaimed Augustus in Rome, and 139 years after Constantine died. The Roman Empire in the West ceased to exist, although Odoacer and the other Germanic rulers who came after him considered themselves worthy successors to the purple. They supported Italy's Roman art and literature, just as earlier emperors had. They continued to sponsor gorgeous mosaics and monuments in Ravenna, for example.

But Germans now ruled the Western empire. Roman citizens of the West would hold very high governmental office, but none of them would be emperor again.

Writing about a century later, an author described Romulus Augustulus as the last ruler of "the Western Empire of the Roman race," noting that from "then on, kings of the Goths, a Germanic people, held Rome and Italy." A rival Western emperor, Julius Nepos, claimed to rule as late as 480, but not from Italy; he lived in exile in Dalmatia, where the father of Romulus Augustulus had forced him to flee in 475. Nepos was eventually murdered.

What went wrong? Why did men "of the Roman race" cease ruling in the West? Suffice it to say that, one by one, the provinces of the Western empire fell into the hands of various non-Roman invaders. Here are some dates of note: By 410, the Romans had pulled out of Britain. In 418 they settled Goths, a Germanic people, in southwestern Gaul. In 435 they conceded much of North Africa to Vandals, another Germanic invader.

Then there were attacks that terrified Romans without depriving the empire of land. In the 440s and 450s, Attila and the Huns, a nomadic Mongolian people who were fierce cavalrymen, invaded the Balkans, Gaul, and Italy. Although they plundered several cities and extorted gold, they did not conquer any Roman territory. Meanwhile, barbarians sacked the city of Rome itself in 410 and again in 455.

By conquering Rome's vital grain-producing provinces in North Africa, the Vandals cut Italy's food lifeline. Only the Eastern Roman Empire, based in Constantinople, had the resources to raise a military expedition to try to reopen it. Yet when the Eastern Roman fleet tried to land in what is now Tunisia, the Vandals destroyed it in a fire-ship attack launched at night. The Battle of Cap Bon in 468 spelled doom for the Roman Empire in the West.

Gibbon suggested long ago that Christianity played a big role in the fall of Rome because it sapped the fighting spirit of its people. This is nonsense.

The eastern half of the Roman Empire was more passionately Christian than the west, and it did not fall in 476. In fact, it remained as an empire for another 150 years, until the Islamic conquest of most of it. Afterward, it survived as a regional power for another 800 years, finally coming to an end only in 1453, nearly 1,000 years after the fall of the West. Nor did Christianity stop European states from fighting one another and conquering much of the world for the better part of two millennia.

The Roman Empire in the West fell because of bad leadership as well as poorly deployed military resources, internal division, strong enemies, unfavorable geography, and a decline of resources. The empire would have other great leaders before the West fell, but most of them would be in the East.

The money, the talent, and the power flowed eastward. The great capital city of Constantinople had no western equivalent. Nor was there any comparable fortress in the West.

Constantine fortified his new city well, both on land and sea. Within a century, the town expanded far beyond his land walls. So, early in the fifth century, the Romans built a new and even stronger set of walls about a mile farther west, which doubled the area of the city. The mighty set of land walls—an inner and outer wall protected by a moat—stretched for three and a half miles. They were connected to sea walls that guarded the city from attack by sea.

While Rome reeled from its sacks, Constantinople rose higher. And that will bring us, by a roundabout way, to the second set of Ravenna's ghosts. They are found, at the outset, in Constantinople, which reached one of its peaks during the reign of Justinian (527–565) and Theodora (527–548), the emperor and empress. They dominate the early history of the Byzantine Empire, as it is known today. (Ironically, the term *Byzantine* did not come into use until after the Eastern Empire fell.)

In the tradition of Augustus and Constantine, Justinian was a great conqueror, legislator, administrator, and builder who presided over an era of great literature and art. In the East, he maintained Byzantine rule against a powerful Persian offensive. In the West, his generals conquered Italy and part of North Africa. He was unable to stop attacks in the Balkans and incapable of preventing the settlement of Slavs and Bulgars in Byzantine territory.

As a legislator, Justinian was one of the most influential in history. He sponsored an initiative to codify Roman law that led to the Justinian Code, a magisterial reference work that had a major influence on the Western legal tradition. As an administrator, he promoted good government, attacked corruption, and promoted trade.

As a builder, Justinian sponsored a grand program of public works including bridges, forts, aqueducts, orphanages, and even whole cities. His most famous project was the Church of the Holy Wisdom, or Hagia Sophia, in Constantinople, which still stands today, now as a museum. Like Nero and Hadrian, Justinian built a domed structure as his architectural masterpiece. Decorated lavishly inside by mosaics, it was the world's largest cathedral for a thousand years. Justinian was so stunned by the magnificence of the building when he first saw it completed that he exclaimed, "Solomon, I have outdone thee!" referring to the Jewish king who built the First Temple in Jerusalem.

As head of the Orthodox Christian Church, Justinian turned the screws on heretics, pagans, Jews, and Samaritans (who followed a different version of Judaism than the rabbinical tradition observed by most Jews). He expelled pagan teachers from the Platonic Academy in Athens and alienated many Christians in Egypt and Syria, who followed a non-Orthodox theology. He prohibited an essential part of Judaism, rabbinical interpretations of the Hebrew Bible. Many of Justinian's prohibitions were honored only in the breach, but he did stir up riot and revolt.

Theodora came from a humble background and worked as an actress, a disreputable profession. But she was shrewd and brilliant as well as beautiful. She earned Justinian's love. He married her and named her Augusta. She had great influence in his regime. Theodora is remembered for bucking up Justinian's courage in the face of riots in Constantinople that almost drove him from his throne. "Royal purple is the noblest shroud," she told him and convinced a shaky emperor to stand and fight. Soon afterward, one of his generals crushed the rioters. Theodora is also remembered for sponsoring legislation to help women by stopping forced prostitution and giving women greater rights in divorce and in owning property.

There would be many great Byzantine emperors and empresses after

Justinian and Theodora, but, in a sense, they represented a final flowering for Rome, for they were the last great rulers of the Eastern Empire to speak Latin. Afterward, Greek became the language of the rulers and their government, as it was of the eastern Mediterranean. Yet they continued to call themselves Roman.

And so did the people of Ravenna. They too were part of Justinian's empire. His greatest general captured Ravenna from the Germanic people who had seized it earlier. He "reclaimed" Italy for the Roman Empire, although Italy had not been ruled from Constantinople since 395. But now the Byzantines were in Italy, and they stayed for two hundred years, with Ravenna serving as their seat. The city experienced a long cultural Renaissance, but its iconic moment came at the start. Shortly after the Byzantine conquest, a fabulous set of mosaics was executed in the city's Church of San Vitale. Twin mosaic panels flanking the apse depict Justinian and Theodora. Each ruler appears in a halo against a shimmering gold background, surrounded by a splendid set of lords and ladies and by clergymen and armed soldiers, as if they and their retinues were right there in the church. These gorgeous images are the iconic portraits of the two rulers. They hold a place of honor in the history of medieval art.

But what are the monarchs of the Roman East doing in Ravenna? Neither Justinian nor Theodora ever set foot in the city that is forever associated with their names. They ruled from Constantinople. Like Ravenna's lost imperial palace, they are ghosts.

Yet one other thing remains of the presence of the Roman emperor in Ravenna. That is the name of the region where Ravenna sits: Romagna, "the land of the Romans," as it is still called today. The term was first used in the four hundreds and then again when the area was under Byzantine rule. It is understandable that people would be proud of their connection to that empire. Under Justinian, the Roman Empire was one of the greatest powers in the world, and Constantinople was one of the greatest cities.

Yet when Augustus created the Roman Empire, he could never have guessed that it would be in little Ravenna, a port city far from Rome, that the empire's last afterglow in the west would linger.

ACKNOWLEDGMENTS

Gratitude, says Cicero, contains the memory of friendships and of kindness on the part of others, and the desire to repay them (Cicero, *On Invention*, 2.161). If so, then my memory is sweet, my desire is ardent, but my ability to repay is poor. What follows is inadequate as a way of saying thank you for the friendship and generosity shown to me in the course of writing this book.

I'm deeply grateful to the colleagues, friends, and students who read all or part of the manuscript in draft. They made it much better. The faults, of course, remain my own. Thank you to Maia Aron, Kathleen Breitman, Serhan Güngör, Adam Mogelonsky, Jacob Nabel, and Tim Sorg.

Dr. Francesco M. Galassi, University of Zurich, shared his expertise on ancient medicine. Mary McHugh shared her work and thoughts on the two Agrippinas. Waller Newell offered many stimulating conversations on ancient tyranny. Walter Scheidel shared ideas from his forthcoming project on Roman emperors. Barry Weingast offered insights on institutions and paradigms, ancient and modern. Kevin Bloomfield and Jonathan Warner provided expert research assistance. Lieutenant Colonel (ret.) Timothy Wilson, Royal Artillery, proved a generous guide to Hadrian's Wall Country.

Four institutions generously offered support for this project: the American Academy of Rome, where I was a visiting scholar; the Bogliasco Foundation, where I was a fellow; the Hoover Institution, where I was a visiting scholar; and Cornell University, which was kind enough to grant me leave to research and write. At the American Academy in Rome, there are too many people to thank, but I would like especially to mention current and former directors John Ochsendorfer and Kim Bowes. At the Bogliasco Foundation, I would like to thank

Laura Harrison as well as many others. At the Hoover Institution, I would like to thank Victor Davis Hanson for his friendship and hospitality as well as for the example he sets as a historian. I would also like to thank David Berkey and Eric Wakin. At Cornell, I would like to thank my colleagues and the staffs of the Departments of History and of Classics. I would also like to express my gratitude to Cornell's wonderful John M. Olin Library.

A long list of people shared expertise, displayed hospitality, offered guidance around ancient sites, served as sounding boards, offered encouragement, and provided the most important service of all: they were there when needed. Thank you to Benjamin Anderson, Darius Arya, Jed Atkins, Ernst Baltrusch, Elizabeth Bartman, Colin Behrens, Leo Belli, Sandra Bernstein, Lisa Blaydes, Nikki Bonanni, Philippe Bohström, Dorian Borbonus, Elizabeth Bradley, Mary Brown, Judith Byfield, Holly Case, Christopher Celenza, Giordano Conti, Bill Crawley, Craig Davis, Angelo De Gennaro, Megan Drinkwater, Ertürk Durmus, Radcliffe Edmonds, Gary Evans, Michael Fontaine, Bernard Frischer, Adam Friedman, Lorenzo Gasperoni, Rick Geddes, Genevieve Gessert, Giovanni Giorgini, Stephen Greenblatt, Meyer Gross, Stephen Haber, John Hyland, Isabel Hull, Brian Jay Jones, Eleanor Leach, Susann Lusnia, Craig Lyons, Sturt Manning, Harvey Mansfield, Brook Manville, Adrienne Mayor, Kelly McClinton, J. Kimball McKnight, Alison McQueen, Ian Morris, Thomas J. Morton, Josiah Ober, Grant Parker, Piergiorgio Pellicioni, Verity Platt, Danielle Pletka, Sergio Poeta, David Pollio, Eric Rebillard, Claudia Rosett, Lukasz Rzycki, Aaron Sachs, Daniel Szpiro, Ramie Targoff, Robert Travers, Christian Wendt, Greg Woolf, and M. Theodora Zemek.

At Simon & Schuster, my editor, Bob Bender, outdid himself as far as the care and attention he devoted to this manuscript and the wisdom and good judgment that he was always ready to share. His assistant, Johanna Li, was helpful and patient. I would like to thank them as well as Marketing Director Stephen Bedford. My literary agent, Cathy Hemming, is an author's best friend.

Adjectives don't begin to express my gratitude to my wife, Marcia, and to my children, Sylvie and Michael, for their continuing support and affection.

I dedicate this book to my students, past and present. I can think of no better way to express my appreciation for their energy, their insights, and their friendship than the statement of the Talmud: "I have learned much from my teachers, more from my colleagues, and the most from my students."

CAST OF CHARACTERS

AUGUSTUS

Octavian, later Augustus	Rome's first emperor, 27 BC–AD 14
Atia	Augustus's mother
Octavia	Augustus's sister
Julius Caesar	Dictator, Augustus's great-uncle and adoptive father
Marcus Agrippa	Augustus's second in command and eventually his son-in-law
Cicero	Rome's greatest orator
Mark Antony	Octavian's greatest rival
Cleopatra	Queen of Egypt
Livia	Augustus's wife
Julia	Augustus's daughter
Tiberius	Livia's son, eventually Augustus's adopted son and successor

TIBERIUS

Tiberius	Augustus's successor, emperor 14–37
Livia	Tiberius's mother, Augustus's widow, honored with title of Julia Augusta

Vipsania	Tiberius's wife, later divorced
Julia	Tiberius's wife, later divorced
Germanicus	Tiberius's nephew, named by Augustus as Tiberius's successor
Agrippina the Elder	Augustus's granddaughter, married to Germanicus
Sejanus	Praetorian prefect, Tiberius's second in command and a threat to his power
Antonia	Augustus's niece
Gaius, also known as Caligula	Son of Germanicus and Agrippina the Elder, later Tiberius's successor

NERO

Gaius, also known as Caligula	Emperor, 37–41
Claudius	Emperor, 41–54
Nero	Emperor, 54–68
Messalina	Claudius's wife, later executed
Agrippina the Younger	Nero's mother, Claudius's wife
Seneca	Nero's tutor and advisor; philosopher, man of letters
Poppaea Sabina	Nero's greatest love, later his wife

VESPASIAN

Galba	Emperor, 68–69
Otho	Emperor, 69
Vitellius	Emperor, 69
Vespasian	Emperor, 69–79
Caenis	Vespasian's mistress
Titus	Vespasian's older son, emperor 79–81
Mucianus	Governor of Syria, ally of Vespasian

Berenice	Jewish princess, Titus's mistress
Antonius Primus	General, politician, ally of Vespasian

TRAJAN

Domitian	Emperor, 81–96
Nerva	Emperor, 96–98
Trajan	Emperor, 98–117
Plotina	Trajan's wife, later Augusta
Marciana	Trajan's sister, later Augusta
Sura	Trajan's second in command
Pliny the Younger	Intellectual, imperial propagandist, provincial governor

HADRIAN

Hadrian	Emperor, 117–138
Sabina	Hadrian's wife, later Augusta
Plotina	Augusta, Hadrian's patron and promoter
Suetonius	Hadrian's chief secretary, imperial biographer
Antinous	Hadrian's boyfriend, divinized after death

MARCUS AURELIUS

Antoninus Pius	Emperor, 138–161
Marcus Aurelius	Emperor, 161–180
Domitia Lucilla	Marcus Aurelius's mother
Fronto	Tutor to Marcus Aurelius
Lucius Verus	Co-emperor with Marcus Aurelius, 161–169

Faustina the Younger   Antoninus Pius's daughter, Marcus
                       Aurelius's wife, Augusta and Mother
                       of the Camp

Galen   Physician to Marcus Aurelius

Commodus   Marcus Aurelius's son, emperor
           180–192

SEPTIMIUS SEVERUS

Pertinax   Emperor, 192–193

Julianus   Emperor, 193

Pescennius Niger   Emperor, 193–195

Clodius Albinus   Emperor, 193–197

Septimius Severus   Emperor, 193–211

Julia Domna   Severus's wife

Caracalla   Severus's older son, emperor, 211–217

Geta   Caracalla's younger brother,
       co-emperor, 211

Elagabalus   Emperor, 218–222

Julia Mamaea   Mother of Alexander Severus, virtual
               regent

Alexander Severus   Emperor, 222–235

DIOCLETIAN

Aurelian   Emperor, 270–275

Numerian   Emperor, 283–284

Diocletian   Emperor, 284–305

Aurelia Prisca   Diocletian's wife

Valeria   Diocletian's daughter, Galerius's wife

Maximian   Western Augustus

Maxentius   Son of Maximian

Galerius	Eastern Caesar
Romula	Galerius's mother
Constantius	Western Caesar
Constantine	Son of Constantius

CONSTANTINE

Constantius	Constantine's father, Caesar and Augustus
Helena	Constantine's mother, later a saint
Constantine	Emperor, 306–337
Fausta	Constantine's second wife
Crispus	Constantine's oldest son
Maximinus Daia	Emperor, 305–314
Maxentius	Emperor, 306–312
Licinius	Emperor, 308–324
Eusebius	Bishop of Caesarea

RAVENNA

Romulus Augustulus	Emperor, 475–476
Justinian	Emperor, 527–565
Theodora	Empress, 527–548

THE FAMILY OF AUGUSTUS/

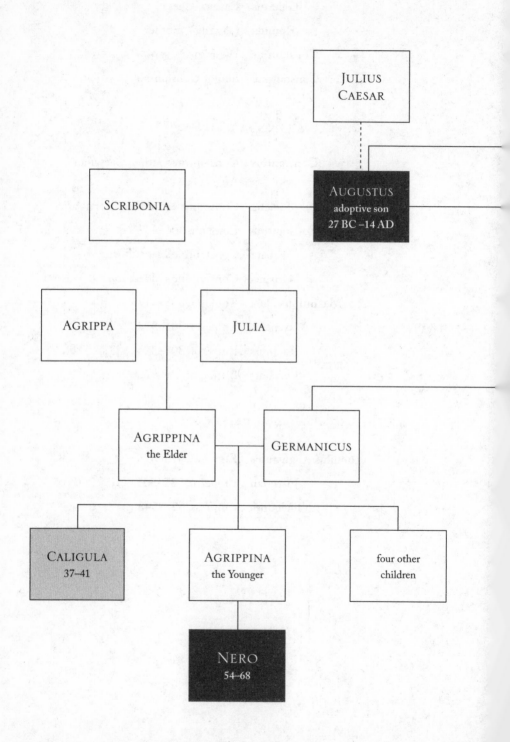

THE JULIO-CLAUDIAN DYNASTY

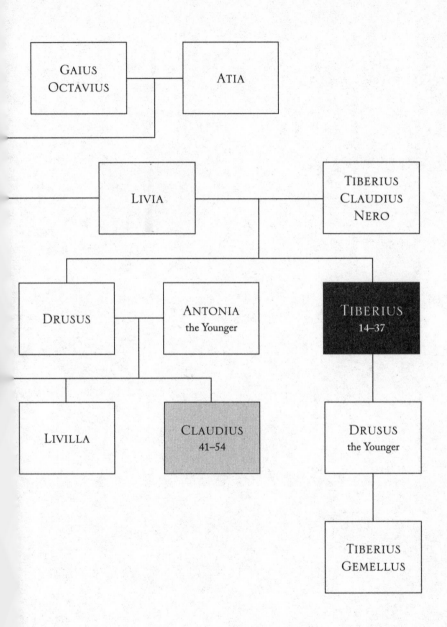

THE FLAVIAN FAMILY TREE

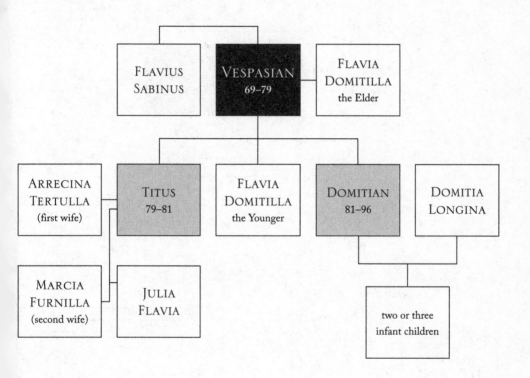

THE FAMILY OF TRAJAN AND HADRIAN/

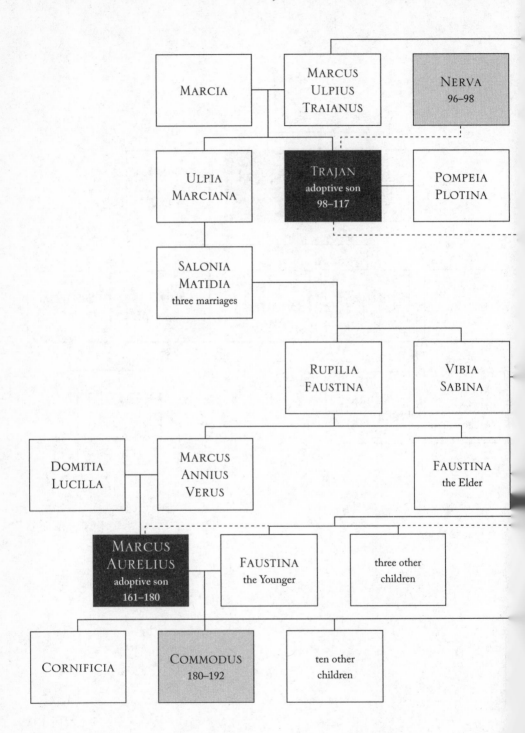

THE FIVE GOOD EMPERORS

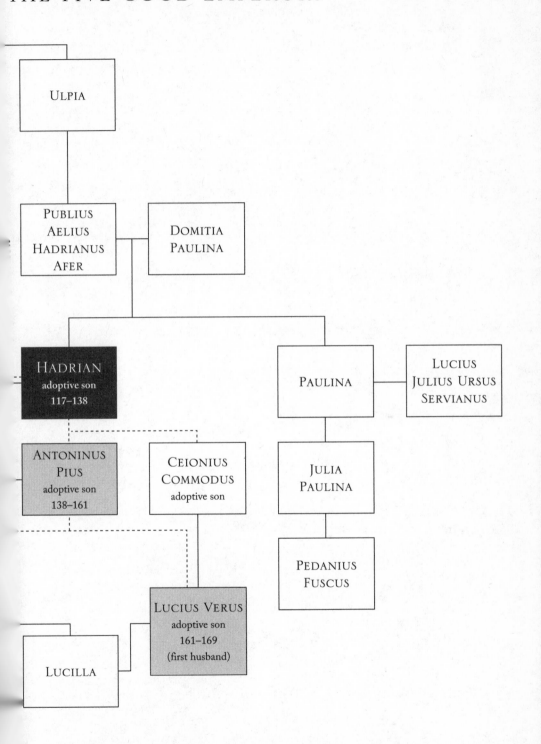

ULPIA

PUBLIUS
AELIUS
HADRIANUS
AFER

DOMITIA
PAULINA

HADRIAN
adoptive son
117–138

PAULINA

LUCIUS
JULIUS URSUS
SERVIANUS

ANTONINUS
PIUS
adoptive son
138–161

CEIONIUS
COMMODUS
adoptive son

JULIA
PAULINA

PEDANIUS
FUSCUS

LUCIUS VERUS
adoptive son
161–169
(first husband)

LUCILLA

THE SEVERANS

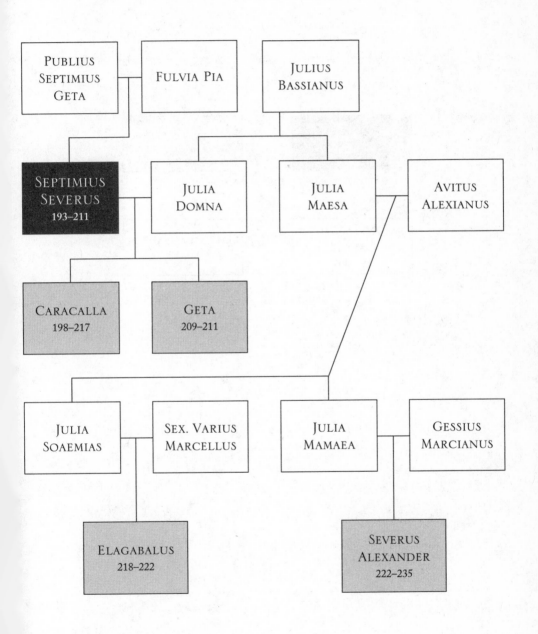

THE FIRST TETRARCHY

DIOCLETIAN	MAXIMIAN
284–305	286–305

CONSTANTIUS CAESAR	GALERIUS CAESAR
293–305	293–305

THE FAMILY OF CONSTANTINE

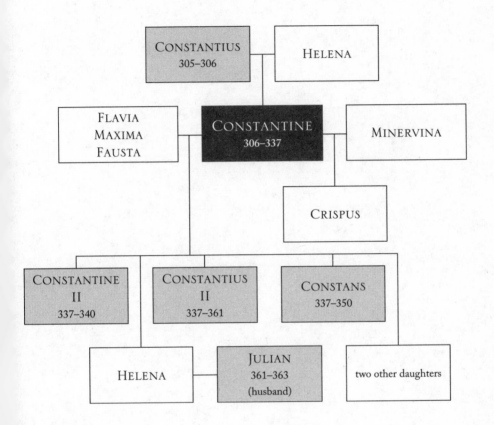

NOTES

PROLOGUE: A NIGHT ON THE PALATINE

2 *Circus Maximus*: A Roman *circus* was an oblong-shaped space used for horse and chariot races and other events. The Circus Maximus or Greatest Circus was the largest of several circuses in the city.

2 *dining with Jupiter in midheaven*: Statius, *Silvae*, 4.2.18.

2 *the emperor had the walls painted black*: Cassius Dio, *Roman History*, 67.9.3.

2 *another emperor turned the palace into a brothel*: Suetonius, *Caligula*, 41.1.

2 *the palace steps*: Suetonius, *Nero*, 8.1; Suetonius, *Vitellius*, 15.2.

2 *the grand entrance*: Cassius Dio, *Roman History*, 68.5.5.

2 *the back door*: Suetonius, *Claudius*, 18.2.

5 *"money has no smell"*: Suetonius, *Vespasian*, 23.3; Cassius Dio, *Roman History*, 66.14.5.

CHAPTER 1: AUGUSTUS, THE FOUNDER

8 *"When I had extinguished the flames of civil war"*: Res Gestae Divi Augusti, 34, trans. Loeb Classical Library, here and throughout.

8 *By "nobility," the Romans meant a very small group*: See Ronald Syme, "The Nobilitas" in *The Augustan Aristocracy* (Oxford: Clarendon Press, 1986), 1–14.

8 *Her name was Atia*: On Atia, see Ilse Becher, "Atia, die Mutter des Augustus—Legende und Politik," Ernst Günther Schmidt, ed.,

Griechenland und Rom, Vergleichende Untersuchungen zu Entwicklungs-tendenzen und-höhepunkten der antiken Geschichte, Kunst und Literatur (Tbilissi: Universitätsverlag Tbilissi in Verbindung mit der Palm & Enke, Erlangen und Jena, 1996), 95–116.

9   *chaste, old-school mother*: One of the characters in Tacitus's *Dialogue on Orators*, 28, esp. 28.6 (ca. 102) describes her thus, perhaps harkening back to Augustus's autobiography.

9   *Venus, who drives her son, Aeneas, forward*: Virgil, *Aeneid*, here and there. See the discussion in Susan Dixon, *The Roman Mother* (Norman: University of Oklahoma Press, 1968), 74.

9   *Atia remarried, this time to another prominent public figure*: He was Lucius Marcius Philippus, consul in 56 BC.

9   *Octavian was eager to join Caesar at the front in 46 BC*: Nicolaus of Damascus, *Life of Caesar Augustus*, 157.14.

10   *Burning with ambition, Octavian was a natural politician*: Jürgen Malitz offers an excellent discussion of young Octavius's career in " 'O puer qui omnia nomini debes,' Zur Biographie Octavius bis zum Antritt seines Erbes," *Gymnasium* 111 (2004): 381–409.

10   *her son's father was not really Gaius Octavius but the god Apollo*: Perhaps the tale comes from a later period, when Augustus's divinity was commonly spoken of, but it might just be early. Suetonius, *Augustus*, 94.4 and D. Wardle, *Suetonius: Life of Augustus = Vita Divi Augusti* (Oxford: Oxford University Press, 2014), 512–15; Cassius Dio, *Roman History*, 45.1.2; Domitius Marsus Hollis, *Fragments of Roman Poetry, ca. 60 BC–AD 20* (Oxford: Oxford University Press, 2007), 313n181.

11   *Caesar supposedly even visited his bedside before departing Rome*: Nicolaus of Damascus, *Life of Caesar Augustus*, 158.20.

11   *Mark Antony later accused*: Suetonius, *Augustus*, 68.

11   *Caesar himself had gone to bed with a powerful older man*: Suetonius, *Julius Caesar*, 2.1, 22.2, 49.1–4.

12   *he is supposed to have given up sex for a year*: Nicolaus of Damascus, *Life of Caesar Augustus*, 159.36.

12   *"now he had to be a man"*: Ibid., 91.38.

13   *Octavian gave a speech that he later proudly circulated*: Cicero, *Letters to Atticus*, 16.15.3.

13 *swore by his hopes of attaining his father's honors*: Ibid., trans. Shackleton Bailey.

14 *His mother was the first person to address him as Caesar*: Nicolaus of Damascus, *Life of Caesar Augustus*, 93.54. Appian, *Civil Wars*, 3.11, says that the army at Brundisium accepted the name first. Toher thinks that it was only later that Atia called her son by the name of Caesar. See Nicolaus, *The Life of Augustus and the Autobiography*, ed. Mark Toher (Cambridge: Cambridge University Press, 2016), 258.

14 *But she advised cunning and patience*: Appian, *Civil Wars*, 3.14.

14 *he sealed documents with the image of a sphinx*: Cassius Dio, *Roman History*, 51.3.

14 *"chameleon"*: Julian, *The Caesars*, 309.

14 *Octavian got his sphinx seal from Atia*: Pliny, *Natural History*, 37.4.10.

15 "At the age of nineteen at my own initiative": Augustus, *Res Gestae*, 1.1–3.

15 *Antony . . . hurled a charge of cowardice at Octavian*: Suetonius, *Augustus*, 10.4.

15 *he drank no more than three glasses of wine at dinner*: Suetonius, *Augustus*, 77; See the commentary by Wardle, *Suetonius: Life of Augustus*, 468.

16 *"The young man should be honored and lifted up—and out"*: Cicero, *Letters to Friends*, 11.20.1.

16 "Here, stranger, the ashes of Atia": Hic Atiae cinis est, genetrix hic Caesaris, hospes,/condita; Romani sic voluere patres. *Epigrammata Bobiensia* 40; A. S. Hollis, *Fragments of Roman Poetry c. 60 BC–AD 20* (Oxford: Oxford University Press, 2007), 313n182.

17 *probably around three hundred were killed*: On the numbers, see Josiah Osgood, *Caesar's Legacy: Civil War and the Emergence of the Roman Empire* (Cambridge: Cambridge University Press, 2006), 63n6.

18 *"the victorious general Caesar son of a god"*: IMPERATOR CAESAR DIVI FILIUS, Frederik Juliaan Vervaet, "The Secret History: The Official Position of Imperator Caesar Divi Filius from 31 to 27 BCE," *Ancient Society* 40 (2010): 79–152, esp. 130–31.

18 *He said later that he was ill*: Suetonius, *Augustus*, 91.1; compare Appian, *Civil Wars*, 4.110; Cassius Dio, *Roman History*, 41.3.

19 *"It's time to die"*: Suetonius, *Augustus*, 15.

21 *"The lucky have children in three months"*: Cassius Dio, *Roman History*, 48.44.5, trans. Loeb Classical Library, here and throughout.

21 *"He loved and esteemed her to the end"*: Suetonius, *Augustus*, 62.2.

23 *"Poor Antony," he said in effect. "An alien queen had unmanned him."* See, for example, Plutarch, *Antony*, 60.1; Appian, *Civil Wars*, 5.1, 8, 9; Cassius Dio, *Roman History*, 50.4.3–4.

24 *He said that he would spare them for three reasons: the memory of Alexander the Great, the size and beauty of the city, and as a favor to his teacher*: Plutarch, *Antony*, 80.1–3; *Moralia*, 207A–B; compare Cassius Dio, *Roman History*, 51.16.3–4.

24 *"Too many Caesars is not a good thing"*: Plutarch, *Antony*, 81.2.

24 *"I wished to see a king, not corpses"*: Cassius Dio, *Roman History*, 51.16.

25 *Cassius of Parma*: Not to be confused with the famous assassin Cassius (Velleius Paterculus, *History of Rome*, 2.87.3; Valerius Maximus, *Memorable Deeds and Sayings* 1.7.7).

25 *Augustus was unique*: Cassius Dio, *Roman History*, 53.16; Suetonius, *Augustus*, 7.2.

25 *Coins issued in 27 and 26 BC*: for instance RIC I (second edition) *Augustus*, 277, 488–91, 493–94, http://numismatics.org/ocre/results?q=Augustus%20 AND%20year_num%3A%5B-27%20TO%20-27%5D&start=0.

26 *The personal decadence of the elite bothered him*: You can take the erotic temperature of the wicked old days of the Late Republic—the world that Augustus enjoyed as a young man and then legislated against as emperor—in Daisy Dunn, *Catullus' Bedspread: the Life of Rome's Most Erotic Poet*, 1st US ed. (New York: Harper), 2016.

27 *"a cunning fox imitating a noble lion"*: Horace, *Satires*, 2.3.186.

27 *Augustus himself would eulogize Agrippa*: P. Köln, 4701, lines 12–14, in Köln et al., *Kölner Papyri* (Wiesbaden: VS Verlag für Sozialwissenschaften, 1987), 113–14.

28 *who advised usurpers*: Machiavelli, *The Prince*, bk. 8.

28 *Augustus did not start soft*: see Seneca, *On Clemency*, 1.9.1 and 1.11.1.

28 *he killed more than a hundred senators*: see, for example, Suetonius, *Augustus*, 15, and Appian, *Civil Wars*, 4.5.

28 *He satisfied his troops*: See Tacitus, *Annals*, 1.2.

28 *"empire without end"*: Virgil, *Aeneid*, 1.278–79.

28 *"Make haste slowly"*: Suetonius, *Augustus*, 25.4; Aulus Gellius, *Attic Nights*, 10.11.5; Macrobius, *Saturnalia*, 6.8.8; Polyaenus, *Stratagems*, 8.24.4.

29 *"Quinctilius Varus, give me back my legions!"*: Suetonius, *Augustus*, 23.

30 auctoritas: *Res Gestae Divi Augusti*, 34.3.

30 *a mere "semblance of the republic"*: Tacitus, *Annals*, 13.8.

30 *Augustus spent another decade outside Italy*: Suetonius, *Augustus*, 47; D. Wardle, *Suetonius*, 351.

32 *he made sure to greet every member by name, without a prompter*: Suetonius, *Augustus*, 53.3.

32 *"Lord"*: (*Dominus*) Ibid., 53.1.

32 *"the transfer of the state to the free disposal of the senate and the people"*: Augustus, *Res Gestae*, 34.14–15.

32 *He used language that suggested that he had restored the republic*: res publicam restituit. E.g. the Praenestine Fasti ad January 13, 27 BC: Victor Ehrenberg and A. H. M. Jones, *Documents Illustrating the Reigns of Augustus and Tiberius* (Oxford: Oxford University Press, 1949), 45. Compare E. T. Salmon, "The Evolution of Augustus' Principate," *Historia* 5.4 (1956): 456–78, esp. 457; Karl Galinsky, *Augustan Culture: An Interpretive Introduction* (Princeton, NJ: Princeton University Press, 1996) 42–79.

33 *Augustus paid for the new forum with the spoils of war*: Augustus, *Res Gestae*, 21.

33 *"I found a Rome of bricks; I leave to you one of marble"*: Cassius Dio, *Roman History*, 56.30.3.

33 *Rome as the Eternal City*: Stephanie Malia Hom, "Consuming the View: Tourism, Rome, and the Topos of the Eternal City," *Annali d'Italianistica*, "Capital City: Rome 1870–2010," 28 (2010): 91–116.

34 *he made sure the crowd saw him*: Suetonius, *Augustus*, 43–46.

34 *he wore lifts in his shoes to look taller*: Ibid., 73.

35 *pouring wine as an offering to the emperor at every banquet*: Cassius Dio, *Roman History*, 51.19.7.

36 *Heloise once defiantly wrote*: "The Personal Letters: Letter 1. Heloise to Abelard," in Abelard, Peter, Héloïse, Betty Radice, and M. T. Clanchy, *The Letters of Abelard and Heloise*, rev. ed. (London: Penguin Books, 2003), 51.

36 *"Ulysses in a stola"*: Ulixes stolatus, Suetonius, *Caligula*, 23.

37 *young and ageless, with a sweet face*: Compare Augustus of Prima Porta, Vatican Museums, Cat. 2290.

37 *Livia saved her husband's letters*: Suetonius, *Augustus*, 84.2, and *Tiberius*, 54.1.

37 *Hostile and sometimes brilliant literary tradition*: Tacitus, *Annals*, here and there. Compare Robert Graves's novel *I Claudius*.

37 *"the first woman in the history of the West to be depicted systematically in portraits."* Elizabeth Bartman, *Portraits of Livia: Imaging the Imperial Woman in Augustan Rome* (Cambridge: Cambridge University Press, 1999), xxi.

38 *"the Hen Roost"*: *Ad Gallinas* in Latin (Suetonius, *Galba*, 1; Pliny the Elder, *Natural History*, 15.136–37; Cassius Dio, *Roman History*, 48.52.3–4).

38 *"Livia was destined to hold in her lap even Caesar's power"*: Cassius Dio, *Roman History*, 48.52.3–4.

39 *Julia grew up to be bright and witty*: Macrobius, *Saturnalia*, 2.5.

39 *soon make old men of them*: Ibid., 2.5.6.

40 *that she only took on passengers when the ship was full*: Ibid., 2.5.9–10.

40 *Father of his Country*: Res Gestae, 35.1.

40 *a small and barren island off the Italian coast*: The ancient island of Pandateria, today, Ventotene.

42 *"A copy of the military exploits of the deified Augustus"*: Res Gestae, 1.1.

43 in one version of the story, he reached his adoptive father in time: Suetonius, *Tiberius*, 21.1.

44 the "mime" of life: Suetonius, *Augustus*, 99.1.

44 *"If the play has anything of merit, clap and send us out joyfully"*: Ibid.

44 *"Livia, live mindful of our marriage and farewell"*: Ibid.; trans. Wardle, *Suetonius: Life of Augustus*, 77.

44 *People noticed the irony that Augustus died in the very same room*: Suetonius, *Augustus*, 100.1.

45 *as she began a year of mourning*: Cassius Dio, *Roman History*, 56.42.

CHAPTER 2: TIBERIUS, THE TYRANT

48 *"Is it really you that we see, Commander?"*: Velleius Paterculus, *The Roman History*, 2.104.3.

48 *rose and addressed the senators*: On this senate meeting, see Tacitus, *Annals*,

1.5–13; Suetonius, *Tiberius*, 23–25, and *Augustus*, 100–101; Cassius Dio, *Roman History*, 57.2–7.

48   *He was good at hiding what he felt*: Tacitus, *Annals*, 4.71; compare Cassius Dio, *Roman History*, 57.1.1–6.

48   *(Tiberius remembered the man's slight)*: The man in question was Gaius Asinius Gallus, who married Vipsania after Tiberius divorced her (Tacitus, *Annals*, 1.2, 6.23; Cassius Dio, *Roman History*, 58.23).

48   *"Until I reach the point that it seems fair"*: Suetonius, *Tiberius*, 24.2, in what Suetonius claims to be Tiberius's own words and not a paraphrase or invention.

48   *"holding a wolf by the ears"*: Ibid., 25.1.

50   *"just as a father would"*: Cassius Dio, *Roman History*, 48.44.3.

51   *"considered an exalted rank for a woman to be a diminution of his own"*: Tacitus, *Annals*, 1.14. See also Suetonius, *Tiberius*, 50.3.

52   *so stiff and stern that he came off as unpleasant*: Suetonius, *Tiberius*, 68.

52   *tough and obstinate jaws*: Ibid., 21.2.

52   *overbearing mother*: Tacitus, *Annals*, 5.1.

53   *Tiberius was so upset when he once happened to see Vipsania*: Suetonius, *Tiberius*, 7.2–3.

53   *He said that he was exhausted*: On Tiberius's motives for going to Rhodes, see Velleius Paterculus, *The Roman History*, 2.99; Tacitus, *Annals*, 1.4.4, 1.53.1–2, 2.42–43, 4.57; Suetonius, *Tiberius*, 10.1–2; Cassius Dio, *Roman History*, 55.9.

55   *praises Tiberius as a wise, prudent*: Velleius Paterculus, *The Roman History*, 2.111.3.

55   *A coin of the year 13*: e.g., RIC I (2nd ed.) Augustus 225, http://numismatics.org/ocre/id/ric.1(2).aug.225.

56   *"too many Caesars is not a good thing"*: Plutarch, *Antony*, 81.2.

58   *It was said that Julia gave up*: Tacitus, *Annals*, 1.53.

58   *He acknowledged the senators' freedom of speech*: Cassius Dio, *Roman History*, 57.7.4.

58   *"I am master of the slaves"*: Ibid., 57.8.2.

58   *"kind, just, and indulgent masters"*: Suetonius, *Tiberius*, 29.

59   *"the body of the republic is one"*: Tacitus, *Annals*, 1.12.

59   *"Men fit to be slaves!"*: Ibid., 3.65.

59   *the affability and thoughtfulness*: Suetonius, *Julius Caesar*, 72.1.

59   *as such only in his fluency in Greek*: Suetonius, *Tiberius*, 71.1.

59   *his real temples would be in people's hearts*: Tacitus, *Annals*, 4.38.

59   *"Tiberius possessed a great many virtues"*: Cassius Dio, *Roman History*, 58.28.5.

60   *dishonest and cruel*: Ibid., 57.6.3, compare 57.1–2; Suetonius, *Tiberius eius diritatem* 21.2, *saeva ac lenta natura* 57.1.

60   *an elderly noble widow died at the end of the year 22*: Tacitus, *Annals*, 3.76.

61   *Germanicus was easygoing*: Josephus, *Jewish Antiquities*, 18.207–208; Tacitus, *Annals*, 1.33.

61   *Portraits show his wife, Agrippina the Elder*: e.g. RIC I (2nd ed.) Gaius/Caligula 55, http://numismatics.org/ocre/id/ric.1(2).gai.55.

61   *an epic poem trumpeting his boldness*: Albinovanus Pedo in Seneca the Elder, *Suasoriae*, 1.15; see Tacitus, *Annals*, 2.23–24.

62   *Germanicus had to ask the Alexandrians to tone it down*: M. G. L. Cooley, ed., *Tiberius to Nero* (Cambridge: London Association of Classical Teachers, 2011), 163.

62   *allegedly suspected Piso and Plancina*: Tacitus, *Annals*, 2.71; Cassius Dio, *Roman History*, 57.18.9.

62   *universal outpouring of grief*: Josephus, *Jewish Antiquities*, 18.209.

62   *"I, Hades, declare"*: Bassus 5, On the Death of Germanicus = Palatine Anthology 7.39, translation in Cooley, *Tiberius to Nero*, 164.

65   *"A Prince Uninterested in Extending the Empire"*: Tacitus, *Annals*, 4.32.

65   *typically accounting for more than half the annual budget*: E. Cascio, "The Early Roman Empire: The State and the Economy," in *The Cambridge Economic History of the Greco-Roman World*, ed. W. Scheidel, I. Morris, and R. Saller (Cambridge: Cambridge University Press, 2007), 624n26.

65   *devotes less of its budget to the military*: www.cbo.gov/topics/defense-and-national-security.

66   *Rome had already conquered the best part of the world*: Strabo, *Geography*, 17.839; compare William V. Harris, *Roman Power: A Thousand Years of Empire* (Cambridge: Cambridge University Press, 2016), 129.

67   *daring, wicked, and crafty*: Tacitus, *Annals*, 4.1–2.

69   *"Rome is where the emperor is"*: Herodian, *History of the Roman Empire Since the Death of Marcus Aurelius*, 1.6.5.

69   *a ruler 150 years later*: Commodus ruled from 180 to 193.

70   *It seems unlikely that Tiberius left Rome to escape his mother, Livia, as some said*: Cassius Dio, *Roman History*, 57.12. See also Tacitus, *Annals*, 4.57; Suetonius, *Tiberius*, 51.

70   *pulling out old letters from Augustus*: Suetonius, *Tiberius*, 51.1.

70   *The senate also voted to honor Livia with a triumphal arch*: Cassius Dio, *Roman History*, 58.2.3–6.

71   *"A good shepherd shears his flock"*: Suetonius, *Tiberius*, 32.2.

71   *The "old goat"*: Ibid., 45.

71   *"minnows"*: Ibid., 44.1.

71   *"the last of the Romans"*: Ibid., 61.3.

71   *forced to commit suicide*: Tacitus, *Annals*, 4.34–35.

71   *so eager to rule that*: Ibid., 6.25.

72   *he accused her of adultery*: Ibid., 6.25.

72   *as if to imply that he wanted to poison her*: Suetonius, *Tiberius*, 53.

72   *a rumor that she was starved to death*: Tacitus, *Annals*, 6.25.

72   *"Let them hate me"*: Suetonius, *Tiberius*, 5.

73   *If the sources can be trusted*: Josephus, *Jewish Antiquities*, 18.6.6.

73   *said to be as beautiful as Venus*: Nikos Kokkinos, *Antonia Augusta, Portrait of a Great Roman Lady* (London and New York: Routledge, 1992), 15–119.

73   *she wouldn't so much as spit*: Pliny the Elder, *Natural History*, 7.80.

74   *viper*: Suetonius, *Caligula*, 11.

74   *"When I am dead"*: Cassius Dio, *Roman History*, 58.23.2.

75   *Some said that Gaius had Tiberius poisoned*: Tacitus, *Annals*, 6.50; Suetonius, *Tiberius*, 73.2; Cassius Dio, *Roman History*, 58.28.3.

75   *"To the Tiber with Tiberius!"*: Suetonius, *Tiberius*, 75.1.

76   *"riveted the fetters of his country"*: Edward Gibbon, *The History of the Decline and Fall of the Roman Empire*, vol. 1, ed. David Womersley (Harmondsworth, UK: Penguin Press, 1994), 128.

CHAPTER 3: NERO, THE ENTERTAINER

80   *"A rumor had gone forth everywhere"*: Tacitus, *Annals*, 15.39. Many other similar accounts are found in the ancient sources except that they all treat Nero's behavior as a fact and not as merely a rumor. See Suetonius, *Nero*, 38; Cassius Dio, *Roman History*, 62.18.1; Pliny the Elder, *Natural History*, 17.1.5.

80   *lyre*: technically, a cithara, a two-stringed instrument played by professional musicians.

82   *a short-lived marriage to one of his sisters and incest*: Suetonius, *Caligula*, 24.1.

82   *stabling his favorite horse in marble and ivory*: Ibid., 55.3.

82   *boast to his horrified, aristocratic grandmother*: Ibid., 29.

82   *a man ought either to be frugal or be Caesar*: Ibid., 37.

83   *"If only the Roman people had but one neck!"*: Ibid., 30.2.

84   *A statue shows her in a formal robe*: Louvre Museum, MR 280.

84   *"Augusta the whore"*: Juvenal, *Satires*, 6.118.

85   *Female Wolf-Dog*: Ibid., 6.123.

85   *all-night sex competition*: Pliny the Elder, *Natural History*, 10.83.

85   *A statue of Agrippina*: Centrale Montemartini, Rome, inv. MC 1882; Copenhagen, Ny Carlsberg Glyptotek inv. 753.

86   *extra canine tooth*: Pliny the Elder, *Natural History*, 7.71.

86   *"It is impossible for any good man to be sprung"*: Cassius Dio, *Roman History*, 61.2.

87   *"sand without lime"*: Suetonius, *Caligula*, 53.2.

87   *change a free state into a Persian despotism*: Seneca, *On Benefits*, 2.12.

87   *judged Caligula to be bloodthirsty*: Ibid., 4.31.

87   *She accused him of committing adultery with Caligula's youngest sister*: Cassius Dio, *Roman History*, 60.80.5.

88   *He had blue-gray eyes . . . regular but not especially pleasing features*: Suetonius, *Nero*, 51.1.

89   *He was carried away above all by popularity*: Ibid., 53.

89   *"the Best Mother"* (optima mater): Tacitus, *Annals*, 13.2; Suetonius, *Nero*, 9.

89   *On coins, she was depicted facing Nero*, e.g. RIC I (2nd ed.) Nero, 1, http://numismatics.org/ocre/id/ric.1(2).ner.1.

89   *she could give her son the empire*: Tacitus, *Annals*, 12.64.

89   *"pumpkinification"*: The joke sounds better in Greek where deification is *apotheosis* and pumpkinification is *apocolocyntosis*, but even in Greek the meaning is unclear.

90   *mushrooms are the food of the gods*: Cassius Dio, *Roman History*, 60.35.

90   That the two actually committed incest, as rumor had it: Tacitus, *Annals*, 14.2; Suetonius, *Nero*, 28.2; Cassius Dio, *Roman History*, 61.11.3–4.

91   *poem about Poppaea's amber hair*: Pliny the Elder, *Natural History*, 37.12.

91   *bathed daily*: Ibid., 28.182–183, 11; Cassius Dio, *Roman History*, 62.28.1.

91   *line of cosmetics*: Juvenal, *Satires*, 6.462.

92   *So the story goes*: Tacitus, *Annals*, 14.3–7; Cassius Dio, *Roman History*, 62.12–13, Suetonius, *Nero*, 34.2–3; compare Anthony Barrett, *Agrippina: Sex, Power, and Politics in the Early Empire* (New Haven, CT: Yale University Press, 1996), 187–88.

92   *told the men to strike there*: Tacitus, *Annals*, 14.8; Cassius Dio, *Roman History*, 62.13.5.

92   *this day had given him rule of the empire*: Tacitus, *Annals*, 14.7.

92   *"we look on accomplices"*: Ibid., 14.62.

92   *The choice might indicate, as the sources claim*: See Edward Champlin, *Nero* (Cambridge, MA: Belknap Press of Harvard University Press, 2003), 96–103.

94   *Copies of his poetry*: Suetonius, *Nero*, 52.

94   *As for singing, the sources differ*: See Champlin, *Nero*, 283n11.

96   *Civilis Princeps*: On the concept of the *civilis princeps*, see Andrew Wallace-Hadrill, *"Civilis Princeps*: Between Citizen and King," *Journal of Roman Studies* 72 (1982): 32–48.

96   *only the goodness of the ruler protected liberty*: Seneca, *On Clemency*, 1.1.

97   *"Why, Nero, did you fear a man with such a big nose?"* Tacitus, *Annals*, 14.57, 59; Cassius Dio, *Roman History*, 62.14.1.

97   *Her wedding day had been her funeral*: Tacitus, *Annals*, 14.63.3.

97   *It is said that he kicked her*: Tacitus, *Annals*, 16.6; Suetonius, *Nero*, 35.3; Cassius Dio, *Roman History*, 62.28.1.

97   *she had prayed to die young*: Cassius Dio, *Roman History*, 62.28.1.

97   *a vast quantity of Arabian incense*: Pliny the Elder, *Natural History*, 12.83.

97   *stuffed with spices and embalmed*: Tacitus, *Annals*, 16.6.

98   *"No soldier was more loyal"*: Ibid., 15.67, which claims to be a verbatim account. Translation modified from Tacitus, *Complete Works of Tacitus*. Alfred John Church, William Jackson Brodribb, Sara Bryant, edited for Perseus (New York: Random House, rprnt., 1942), www.perseus.tufts.edu/hopper/text?doc=Perseus%3Atext%3A1999.02.0078%3Abook%3D15%3Achapter%3D67.

99   *silence, not words*: Musonius Rufus, frag. 49, Cora Elizabeth Lutz, *Rufonius Musus: "The Roman Socrates"* (New Haven, CT: Yale University Press, 1947), 143.

99   *"You deserved it!"*: Cassius Dio, *Roman History*, 63.17.5–6.

100   *he accused an unpopular and relatively new religious sect: Christians*: Recently
      there has been a scholarly debate on the historicity of Nero's persecution of
      Christians. Brent Shaw makes a strong case against it but, in my judgment,
      Christopher Jones argues convincingly for the historicity of the persecu-
      tion. See Brent Shaw, "The Myth of the Neronian Persecution," *Journal of
      Roman Studies* 105 (2015): 73–100; Christopher P. Jones, "The Historicity
      of the Neronian Persecution: A Response to Brent Shaw," *New Testament
      Studies* 63 (2017): 146–52.

100   *"new and pernicious superstition"*: Suetonius, *Nero*, 16.2.

100   *"hated for their disgraceful acts"*: Tacitus, *Annals*, 15.44.

100   *"hatred of the human race"*: Ibid.

101   *sympathy for the victims*: Ibid.

102   *inanimate, porous looks*: Joseph Brodsky, "Ode to Concrete," *So Forth: Poems*
      (New York: Farrar, Straus and Giroux, 1996), 116.

103   *now at last he could live like a human being*: Suetonius, *Nero*, 31.

103   *Nero treated the whole city as if it were his house*: Tacitus, *Annals*, 15.37.1.

105   *"What an artist perishes in me!"*: Suetonius, *Nero*, 49; Cassius Dio, *Roman
      History*, 63.29.2; compare Champlin, *Nero*, 49–51.

CHAPTER 4: VESPASIAN, THE COMMONER

109   *just a flesh wound*: Josephus, *Jewish War*, 3.236.

109   *equal of the great generals of old*: Tacitus, *Histories*, 2.5.

110   *Ordering his men to link shields in a protective formation*: Josephus, *Jewish
      War*, 4.33.

111   *"the secret of empire was now divulged"*: Tacitus, *Histories*, 1.4.

111   *he would rather that the officer smelled of garlic*: Suetonius, *Vespasian*, 8.3.

111   *"the navel of Italy"*: Varro in Pliny the Elder, *Natural History*, 3.10.

112   *his brother's anteambulo*: Suetonius, *Vespasian*, 2.2.

113   *to cover Vespasian's toga with mud*: Cassius Dio, *Roman History*, 59.12.3.

113   *Seated Agrippina*: Naples Archaeological Museum Inv. No. 6029.

114   *If later tradition is accurate*: Cassius Dio, *Roman History*, 65.14.1–4.

115   *"fate came to know Vespasian"*: Tacitus, *Agricola*, 13.3.

115   *the pride of the family*: Tacitus, *Histories*, 3.75.

117   *"kingdom of arrogance"*: Jewish liturgy, weekly *Amidah* prayer, twelfth bene-
diction.

118   *"By common consent, he would have been a capable ruler"*: Tacitus, *Histories*,
1.49.

118   *In Roman eyes, he lacked authority*: Ibid., 4.11; Suetonius, *Vespasian*, 7.2.

118   *Vespasian's soldiers came up with the idea of naming him emperor*: Josephus,
Jewish War, 4.603.

119   *gay man*: Strictly speaking "gay" and "homosexual" are unhistorical, since
the ancients did not think about sex in terms of modern categories. Yet
they do evoke for the modern reader that Mucianus preferred same-sex
relationships.

119   *"his private life had a bad reputation"*: Tacitus, *Histories*, 1.10.

119   *"notorious unchastity," grumbling, "I at least am a man"*: Suetonius, *Vespasian*,
13.1.

119   *Mucianus himself made these points*: Tacitus, *Histories*, 2.76–77.

119   *he added to his reputation for manliness*: Ibid., 3.13.

119   *exercising enormous power behind the scenes*: Cassius Dio, *Roman History*,
65.8.

119   *"a man who would find it easier to transfer the imperial power to another"*:
Tacitus, *Histories*, 1.10.

120   *"the darling and delight of the human race"*: Suetonius, *Titus*, 1.

120   *"Titus was qualified for attracting even a man of Mucianus's habits"*: Tacitus,
Histories, 2.5.

120   *No need to bother becoming emperor, said Mucianus*: Ibid., 2.77.

120   *Romanized Jews*: Like "gay," "Romanized" is another problematic term for
ancient history but it will have to do; it evokes the notion of assimilation to
the conquerors' ways.

120   *"an evil man"*: Babylonian Talmud, *Gittin* 56B.

122   *she was, says Tacitus, in the prime of her beauty*: Tacitus, *Histories*, 2.2, 81.

123   *he supposedly healed two members of the common people*: Ibid., 4.81; Suetonius,
Vespasian, 7.2; Cassius Dio, *Roman History*, 66.8.2, who says the second
man had a withered hand.

123   *"He was brave in battle, ready of speech"*: Trans. Tacitus, *Complete Works of
Tacitus*. Alfred John Church, William Jackson Brodribb, Sara Bryant, edited for Perseus (New York: Random House, Inc. 1873. reprinted 1942),

www.perseus.tufts.edu/hopper/text?doc=Perseus%3Atext%3A1999.02.00
80%3Abook%3D2%3Achapter%3D86.

124   *"more like the emperor's colleague than his agent,"* Tacitus, *Histories*, 2.77.

125   *For the first time*, Caesar *was used to designate an heir*: Tacitus, *Histories*, 4.39; see Angela Pabst, *Divisio regni: der Zerfall des Imperium Romanum in der Sicht der Zeitgenossen* (Bonn, Ger.: Dr. Rudolf Habelt GMBH, 1986), 46–48, 68.

125   *He died around the year 75.* Mucianus was alive in 74 (Tacitus, *Dialogus*, 37.2) and was dead by 77 (Pliny the Elder, *Natural History*, 32.62).

125   *most Roman emperors enjoyed only short tenures in office*: I owe this insight to Walter Scheidel, who is working on a book on this subject.

125   *as if, as one wit put it, he suffered from constipation*: Cassius Dio, *Roman History*, 66.17.1; Suetonius, *Vespasian*, 20; compare Martial, *Epigrams*, 3.89, 11.52–56.

126   *Lucius Mestrius Florus*: Suetonius, *Vespasian*, 22.1; *Suetonius, Vespasian*, ed. Brian W. Jones, with intro., commentary, and biblio. (London: Bristol Classical Press/Duckworth, 2000), ad loc., 8.

126   REDEMPTION OF ZION: Ran Shapira, "Hoard of Bronze Coins from Jewish Revolt Found Near Jerusalem," *Haaretz*, August 17, 2014, www.haaretz .com/jewish/archaeology/1.610916.

127   *The coins show Judea as a mourning woman seated beneath a palm tree*: e.g. RIC II, Part 1 (2nd ed.) Vespasian 3, http://numismatics.org/ocre/id /ric.2_1(2).ves.3.

127   *Now a tribunal had been erected before the Portico of Octavia*: Josephus, *Jewish War*, in *The Works of Flavius Josephus*, trans. William Whiston (Auburn and Buffalo: John E. Beardsley, 1895), 126–29, www.perseus.tufts.edu/hopper /text?doc=Perseus%3Atext%3A1999.01.0148%3Abook%3D7%3Awhis ton%20chapter%3D5%3Awhiston%20section%3D4.

128   *The emperor carried out a load of soil from the site on his head*: Suetonius, *Vespasian*, 8.5; Cassius Dio, *Roman History*, 66.10.2.

128   *it was originally painted a rich yellow*: Elisabetta Polvoledo, "Technology Identifies Lost Color at Roman Forum," *New York Times*, June 24, 2012, www.nytimes.com/2012/06/25/arts/design/menorah-on-arch-of-titus -in-roman-forum-was-rich-yellow.html, and www.yu.edu/cis/activities/ar ch-of-titus.

128 *Archaeologists recently discovered parts of this second arch*: Ariel David, "Second Monumental Arch of Titus Celebrating Victory over Jews Found in Rome," *Haaretz* March 21, 2017, www.haaretz.com/archaeology/1.778103.

129 *"the general's share of the booty"*: G. Alföldy, ed., *Corpus Inscriptionum Latinarum* VI. *Inscriptiones Urbis Romae Latinae* VIII. Fasc. 2. (Berlin: 1976), no. 40454a. See G. Alföldy, "Ein Bauinschrift aus dem Colosseum," *Zeitschrift für Papyrologie und Epigrafik* 109 (1995): 195–226.

129 *rising an estimated 115 feet*: Herbert W. Benario, *A Commentary on the Vita Hadriani in the Historia Augusta* (Chico, CA: Scholars Press, 1980), 118.

130 *"While the Colosseum stands"*: Beda Venerabilis and Jacques-Paul Migne, *Patrologia Latina* 94: 453.

130 *Vespasian did not like gladiatorial shows*: Cassius Dio, *Roman History*, 65.15.2; Barbara Levick, *Vespasian*, 2nd ed. (London: Routledge, 2017), 202.

130 *"No man can be an orator unless he is a good man"*: Quintilian, *The Institutions of Oratory*, trans. Butler, 12.1.3, 10.7.15.

130 *the purpose of history is to tell a good story*: Ibid., 10.1.31–34; historia . . . scribitur ad narrandum, non ad probandum, 10.1.31.

131 *"Either my son will succeed me or no one at all will"*: Cassius Dio, *Roman History*, 66.12.1.

133 *"prudence rather than avarice"*: Aurelius Victor, *De Caesaribus*, 9.9.

133 *"the sinews of sovereignty"*: Cassius Dio, *Roman History*, 66.2.5.

133 *money has no smell*: Suetonius, *Vespasian*, 23.3; Cassius Dio, *Roman History*, 66.14.5.

134 *"the good fortune and good discipline of eight hundred years"*: Tacitus, *Histories*, 4.74.3.

135 *Vespasian replied that, in the future, they should go barefoot*: Suetonius, *Vespasian*, 8.3.

136 *Caenis is said to have sold access and offices*: Cassius Dio, *Roman History*, 65.14.3–4.

136 *She had a villa and extensive grounds in the suburbs*: The estate was located on the via Nomentana.

136 *Caenis's funerary monument*: Florence, Museo Storico della Caccia e del Territorio, Palazzo Bardini, inv. A231. See Mauro Cristofani, "L'ara funeraria di Antonia Caenis concubina di Vespasiano," *Prospettiva* 13 (April 1978): 2–7.

136 *"Antonia Caenis, Freedwoman of the Augusta, the best of patrons"*: Corpus Inscriptionum Latinarum VI 12037.

137 *People said that she expected to marry him*: Suetonius, *Titus*, 7.1.

137 *the great Quintilian as her lawyer*: Quintilian, *Institutes of Oratory*, 4.1.19, with Michael R. Young-Widmaieir, "Quintilian's Legal Representation of Julia Berenice," *Historia* 51.1 (2002): 124–29.

137 *To some, she was another Cleopatra*: Suetonius, *Titus*, 7.1; Cassius Dio, *Roman History*, 65.15.3–4.

137 *daily regimen*: See Suetonius, *Vespasian*, 21–22.

138 *"Methinks I'm becoming a god"*: Ibid., 23.4; Cassius Dio, *Roman History*, 66.17.2.

138 *"An emperor should die on his feet"*: Suetonius, *Vespasian*, 24–25; Cassius Dio, *Roman History*, 66.17.2; Pseudo-Aurelius Victor, *Epitome de Caesaribus*, 9.18.

138 *"Give me a hundred thousand"*: Suetonius, *Vespasian*, 19.2.

139 *Vespasian alone changed for the better*: Tacitus, *Histories*, 1.50.

140 *1.1 million Jews died in the siege of Jerusalem, and 97,000 Jews were taken prisoner*: Josephus, *Jewish War*, 6.240.

140 *"against his will and hers"*: invitus invitam, Suetonius, *Titus*, 7.2; Compare Cassius Dio, *Roman History*, 66.18.1; Pseudo-Aurelius Victor, *Epitome de Caesaribus*, 10.7.

140 *October 79*: "Pompeii: Vesuvius Eruption May Have Been Later Than Thought," https://www.bbc.com/news/world-europe-45874858.

CHAPTER 5: TRAJAN, THE BEST PRINCE

143 *an earthquake struck Antioch*: Cassius Dio, *Roman History*, 68.24–25.

143 *an estimated magnitude of a ferocious 7.3 or 7.5*: Mustapha Meghraoui et al., "Evidence for 830 Years of Seismic Quiescence from Palaeoseismology, Archaeoseismology and Historical Seismicity Along the Dead Sea Fault in Syria," *Earth and Planetary Science Letters* 210 (2003): 35–52.

144 *the Best Prince*: Pliny the Younger, *Panegyricus*, 88.4.

144 *"luckier than Augustus, better than Trajan"*: Eutropius, *Abridgment of Roman History*, 8.2, 8.5; Julian Bennett, *Trajan, Optimus Princeps: A Life and Times* (Bloomington: Indiana University Press, 1997), 107.

145 *"Our Master and Our God orders that this be done"*: Suetonius, *Domitian*, 13.2.

145 *catching flies and stabbing them with a stylus*: Ibid., 3.

146 *Tall and handsome*: Ibid., 18.

146 *Portrait busts give him a full head of curly hair*: for example, Capitoline Museums, inv. MC 1156; Louvre Museum, inv. Ma 1264.

146 *She looks serenely lovely in a portrait bust*: Louvre Museum, inv. Ma 1193.

147 *Trajan was never much of a student*: Cassius Dio, *Roman History*, 68.74; Pseudo-Aurelius Victor, *Epitome de Caesaribus*, 13.8.

147 *an obsequious source*: Pliny the Younger, *Panegyricus*, 15.1–3.

148 *no one believes in a conspiracy*: Suetonius, *Domitian*, 21.

148 *the rumor that she helped the men who killed him*: Cassius Dio, *Roman History*, 67.15.2–4.

149 *Nerva managed to combine what had seemed incompatible*: Tacitus, *Agricola*, 3.

149 *"May good success"*: Cassius Dio, *Roman History*, 68.3.4; Pliny the Younger, *Panegyricus* 8.6, 7.6–7, 8.1.

150 *"I enter here as the same kind of woman"*: Cassius Dio, *Roman History*, 68.5.5.

150 *His portrait busts*: for example, Glyptothek, Munich inv. 336.

150 *looked stupid and was believed to be honest*: Ronald Syme, *Tacitus* (Oxford: Clarendon Press, 1958), 39.

151 *"Everything is under the authority of one man"*: Pliny the Younger, *Letters*, 3.20.12.

151 *A flattering speech claims that unlike the tyrant Domitian*: Pliny the Younger, *Panegyricus*, 20.

151 *into his carriage and even of entering citizens' houses*: Cassius Dio, *Roman History*, 68.7.3.

152 *When friends accused him of being too accessible*: Eutropius, *Abridgement of Roman History*, 8.5.1.

152 *A senator describes being charmed*: Pliny the Younger, *Letters*, 5.6.36.

152 *"grain and spectacles"*: Fronto, *Principles of History*, 20 (A 259).

152 *"bread and circuses"*: Juvenal, *Satire*, 10.81.

152 *"plenty of bread and a seat at the chariot races"*: Dio Chrysostom, *Oration*, 31.31.

152 *"the camps, bugles, and trumpets"*: Pliny the Younger, *Letters*, 9.2 LCL translation, 83, www.loebclassics.com/view/pliny_younger-letters/1969/pb_LCL 059.83.xml?readMode=recto.

152   *Trajan was styled a military man of the old school*: Pliny the Younger, *Panegy-ricus*, 44.

152   *"my excellent and most loyal fellow soldiers"*: *Digest*, 29.1.

153   *marching on foot and fording rivers with the rank and file*: Cassius Dio, *Roman History*, 68.23.1.

153   *had his own clothing cut into strips to serve*: Ibid., 68.8.2.

153   *"If Sura had desired to kill me"*: Ibid., 68.5.6, Loeb translation.

155   *"as much as her gender allows"*: Pliny the Younger, *Panegyricus*, 83.8.

155   *he praises the two imperial ladies*: Ibid., 83–84.

156   *Ambitious writers*: Pliny, *Letters*, 9.28.1.

156   *a student of music and math*: Nicomachus of Gerasa, Encheiridion Harmon-icum, in Karl von Jan, *Musici Scriptores Graeci. Aristoteles, Euclides, Nicoma-chus, Bacchius, Gaudentius, Alypius et Melodiarum Veterum Quidquid Exstat* (Stuttgart, Ger.: Teubner, 1995 [1895]), 242, line 14.

156   *philosophical school in Athens*: E. M. Smallwood, *Documents Illustrating the Principates of Nerva, Trajan and Hadrian* (Cambridge: Cambridge Univer-sity Press, 1966), no. 442, 152.

156   *Trajan called the Treasury the spleen*: Pseudo-Aurelius Victor, *Epitome de Caesaribus*, 42.21.

156   *"I have no idea what you are talking about, but I love you as myself"*: Philostra-tus, *Lives of the Sophists*, 488.

156   *"not merely as the partner of his bed and affections, but also as his helpmate"*: Dio Chrysostom, *On Kingship*, 3.119.

157   *Later generations looked back fondly on Plotina*: Pseudo-Aurelius Victor, *Epitome de Caesaribus*, 42.20–21; Cassius Dio, *Roman History*, 68.5.5.

157   *"woman of the highest moral integrity"*: E. Bormann, ed. *Corpus Inscriptio-num Latinarum* vol. XI, Inscriptiones Aemiliae, Etruriae, Umbriae Latinae, Pars II, fasc. 1, Inscriptiones Umbriae, viarum publicarum, instrumenti do-mestici (Berlin: Brandenburg Academy of Sciences and Humanities, 1901, impr. iter. 1968): 6520, p. 981; compare Pliny the Younger, *Letters*, 9.28.1.

158   *Hercules was popular in Trajan's hometown*: Gaditanus—the cult of Hercules of Gades (modern Cádiz), the city facing the island where Hercules was supposed to have labored.

158   *he often had the demigod depicted on his coins*: for example, RIC II Trajan 49, http://numismatics.org/ocre/id/ric.2.tr.49_denarius.

158   *Pliny says that like Hercules, Trajan*: Pliny the Younger, *Panegyricus*, 14.5, 82.7; Dio Chrysostom also compares Trajan to Hercules, *Oration*, 1.56–84.

158   *Then he compares Trajan to Jupiter*: Pliny the Younger, *Panegyricus*, 80.3–5.

159   *A sculpted relief on the Arch of Trajan in central Italy*: Located in Benevento, ancient Beneventum.

159   *Trajan's coins recognized him as "the best prince"*: e.g. RIC II Trajan 128, http://numismatics.org/ocre/id/ric.2.tr.128.

161   *"who were called deaconesses"*: Pliny the Younger, *Letters*, 10.96.8.

161   *"depraved and immoderate superstition"*: Ibid.

161   *"by worshipping our gods"*: Ibid., 10.97.2.

161   "not in the spirit of our era": Ibid.

161   *The sources refer to King Decebalus*: Cassius Dio, *Roman History*, 67.6.1.

162   *In the course of the campaign, he himself performed many deeds*: Ibid., 68.14.1.

162   *A sculpted relief shows the emperor*: panel depicting the emperor in battle on horseback, one of reliefs of the Great Trajanic Frieze removed from an earlier monument in order to adorn the central archway of the Arch of Constantine, Rome.

163   *"From Berzobim, we then proceeded to Azi"*: Priscian, *Institutiones Grammaticae* 6.13.

163   *"a creeper that grows on walls"*: Constantine, Pseudo-Aurelius Victor, *Epitome de Caesaribus*, 41.13.

164   *War spoils from Dacia financed the new forum*: Aulus Gellius, *Attic Nights*, 13.25.

165   *demolished part of the Quirinal Hill*: Domitian began the demolition of the Quirinal, but Trajan designed and carried out the rest of the project.

166   *because he wanted glory*: Cassius Dio, *Roman History*, 68.17.1.

166   *"I should certainly have crossed over to the Indi"*: Ibid., 68.29.1.

167   *"the enemy, seeing his majestic gray head"*: Ibid., 68.31.2.

168   *"If a man were called upon to fix that period in the history of the world"*: Gibbon, *Decline and Fall of the Roman Empire*, vol. 1, 103.

168   *the empire's gross domestic product*: For these estimates and for Rome's market economy more generally, see Peter Temin, *The Roman Market Economy* (Princeton, NJ: Princeton University Press, 2013).

168   *Roman Climate Optimum*: Kyle Harper, *The Fate of Rome: Climate, Disease*

and the End of an Empire (Princeton, NJ: Princeton University Press, 2017), 14–15, 39–55.

169   *Nonetheless, all was not rosy*: See the discussion in Frank McLynn, *Marcus Aurelius: A Life* (Cambridge, MA: Da Capo Press, 2009), 2–13.

171   *bronze bust that some identify as Trajan*: Museum of Anatolian Civilizations, Ankara, Turkey, Inventory Number 10345; but for skepticism about the identification, see Stephen Mitchell, "The Trajanic Tondo from Roman Ankara: In Search of the Identity of a Roman Masterpiece," *Journal of Ankara Studies* 2.1 (2014): 1–10.

171   *he is reported to have suffered a stroke*: See Cassius Dio, *Roman History*, 75.32–33.

171   *"coast is narrow"*: H. L. Jones, trans., *The Geography of Strabo*, vol. 6, Loeb Classical Library 223 (Cambridge, MA: Harvard University Press, 1929), 327.

CHAPTER 6: HADRIAN, THE GREEK

175   *Plotina signed Trajan's letters to the Senate naming Hadrian*: Cassius Dio, *Roman History*, 69.1.2–4.

175   *Plotina smuggled in an actor to impersonate Trajan*: "Hadrian," in *Historia Augusta*, 4.10.

176   *a young freedman*: ILS 1792.

176   *"full of light and bright"*: Polemon, see Simon Swain, "Polemon's Physiognomy," in *Seeing the Face, Seeing the Soul: Polemon's Physiognomy from Classical Antiquity to Medieval Islam*, ed. Simon Swain and G. R. Boys-Stones (Oxford; New York: Oxford University Press, 2007), 167–68.

176   *large number of images of him that survive—more than of any other emperor*: Alan K. Bowman, Peter Garnsey, and Dominic Rathbone, eds., *The Cambridge Ancient History*, 2nd ed. v. 11. *The high empire, A.D. 70–192* (Cambridge: Cambridge University Press, 2000), 975.

176   *visiting more places*: Cassius Dio, *Roman History*, 69.5.3.

176   *"alike amid German snows"*: Ibid., 69.9.4; compare *Historia Augusta*, 17.9, 23.1.

176   *killing a boar with a single blow*: Cassius Dio, *Roman History* 69.10.3[2].

177   *"He was, in the same person, austere and genial"*: "Hadrian," in *Historia Augusta*, 14.11, Loeb Classical Library translation modified.

177   *Hadria*: modern Adria, located in the Po River Delta, between Ravenna and Venice.

178   *It all earned him the nickname of* Graeculus: *"the little Greek"*: "Hadrian," in *Historia Augusta*, 1.5.

178   *"little Greeks are fond of their gymnasia"*: Pliny the Younger, *Letters*, 10.40.2.

179   *"Live unknown"*: Plutarch, "Is 'Live Unknown' a Wise Precept?," *Moralia* 1128B–1130D.

179   *"conquered Greece took captive"*: Horace, *Epistles*, 2.1.156–57.

181   *various busts and full-length statues of Sabina*: for example, portrait bust in the Prado, Madrid, inv. E00210.

181   *Rumor said the couple disliked each other*: "Hadrian," in *Historia Augusta*, 11.3; Pseudo-Aurelius-Victor, *Epitome de Caesaribus*, 14.8.

182   *Hadrian came to share Trajan's hard-drinking*: "Hadrian," in *Historia Augusta*, 3.2.

182   *diamond*: Ibid., 3.7.

182   *the emperor was going to adopt him*: Ibid., 3.10.

183   *reports that Plotina used her influence to get Hadrian a position*: Ibid., 4.1.

183   *Rumor said that Hadrian was bribing*: Ibid., 4.5.

183   *a rumor that Trajan planned to name another man his heir*: Ibid., 4.3–5, 8–10.

184   *"He was by turns an excellent prince"*: Gibbon, *Decline and Fall of the Roman Empire*, vol. 1, 100.

185   *"within my own time the emperor Hadrian"*: Pausanias notes one exception to Hadrian's abjuring of war, the suppression of the Jewish revolt. Pausanias, *Description of Greece*, 1.5.5, trans. Loeb Classical Library—modified, Pausanias, *Description of Greece* with an English Translation by W. H. S. Jones, LittD, and H. A. Ormerod, MA, in 4 Volumes. (Cambridge, MA: Harvard University Press, 1918).

187   *Apollodorus*: Cassius Dio, *Roman History*, 69.4.1–5, compare Birley, loc. 6316.

188   *one of eight places in the empire called "Hadrian City"*: Numerous other places added "Hadrian" to their name, and there was also "Hadrian's Hunt," named after a spot where the emperor had gone hunting.

188   *"the most frequently contested spot on the globe"*: John Keegan, *A History of Warfare* (London: Hutchinson, 1993), 70.

189   *"pumpkins"*: The scornful characterization by Trajan's architect Apollodorus (Cassius Dio, *Roman History*, 69.4.2).

190   *An old woman once*: Ibid., 69.6.3.

190   *"Though more desirous of peace than of war"*: "Hadrian," in *Historia Augusta*, 10.1, Loeb translation.

190   *"The outstanding manhood of that noble man"*: Michael Speidel, *Emperor Hadrian's Speeches to the African Army: A New Text* (Mainz, Ger.: Verlag des Römisch-Germanischen Zentralmuseums, 2006), 15, translation modified.

191   *Hadrian's Horse Guards swam across the Danube*: Cassius Dio, *Roman History*, 69.9.6.

192   *"I give you a warm invitation to make sure that you come"*: Vindolanda Tablet, 291, Vindolanda Inventory 85.057, translated, http://vindolanda.csad .ox.ac.uk/4DLink2/4DACTION/WebRequestTablet?thisLeafNum=1&s earchTerm=Families,%20pleasures%20and%20ceremonies&searchType= browse&searchField=highlights&thisListPosition=3&displayImage=1&d isplayLatin=1&displayEnglish=1.

193   *Hadrian was of half a mind to divorce Sabina*: "Hadrian," in *Historia Augusta*, 11.3.

193   *I don't want to be a Caesar*: Ibid., 16.3.

194   *"Plotina, Augusta of the Divine Trajan"*: for example, RIC II Hadrian 29, http://numismatics.org/ocre/id/ric.2.hdn.29.

194   *"deified mother"*: So Plotina was honored on a gold coin, Kunsthistorisches Museum, Vienna, MK 8622, 134–38.

195   *Hadrian gave him a proper tomb with a gravestone and inscription*, Cassius Dio, *Roman History*, 69.10.2; compare "Hadrian," in *Historia Augusta*, 20.12.

196   *A later and admittedly hostile source*: Epiphanius, *On Weights and Measures*, 14.

196   *"Who could contradict the lord of thirty legions?"*: "Hadrian," in *Historia Augusta*, 15.13.

196   *official art and poetry*: For the details, see Anthony Birley, *Hadrian: The Restless Emperor* (New York: Routledge, 1997), 240–43.

196   *Records survive of the strain on Egyptian towns*: For the details, see ibid.

197   *Hadrian wrote, perhaps in his lost autobiography*: Cassius Dio, *Roman History*, 69.11.2.

197   *Antinous fell into the Nile*: Ibid.

197   *Other ancient writers disagreed.* Ibid., 69.11.2–3; "Hadrian," in *Historia Augusta*, 14.6; Aurelius Victor, *de Caesaribus*, 14.7–9.

198   *Sabina Augusta, wife of the Emperor Caesar*: Patricia Rosenmeyer, "Greek
      Verse Inscriptions in Roman Egypt: Julia Balbilla's Sapphic Voice," *Classi-
      cal Antiquity* 27.2 (2008): 337.

198   *more images of Antinous have been identified*: C. Vout, "Antinous, Archaeol-
      ogy and History," *Journal of Roman Studies* 95 (2005): 82.

198   *Some Romans ridiculed*: Cassius Dio, *Roman History*, 69.11.4; "Hadrian," in
      Historia Augusta, 14.7.

198   *"cried like a woman"*: "Hadrian," in *Historia Augusta*, 13.5.

201   *580,000 Jews were killed*: Cassius Dio, *Roman History*, 69.14.1.

201   *"sanctification of God's name"*: Bavli Berachot, 20a; *Midrash Tehillim*.

201   *"May his bones rot!"*: for example, *Deuteronomy Rabbah*, 3:13; *Pesikta Rab-
      bati*, 21.

201   *the emperor continued to take care of the empire's business*: Dio, *Roman History*,
      69.20.1.

201   *universal opposition*: "Hadrian," in *Historia Augusta*, 23.10.

202   *Predictably, gossip says that Hadrian poisoned her*: "Hadrian," in *Historia Au-
      gusta*, 23.9; Pseudo-Aurelius Victor, *Epitome de Caesaribus*, 14.8.

202   *Sabina's ascent to heaven*: For the coin evidence, see, for example, RIC II
      Hadrian 1051A, http://numismatics.org/ocre/id/ric.2.hdn.1051A; H. A.
      Mattingly and E. A. Sydenham, eds., *Roman Imperial Coinage*, vol. 2 (Lon-
      don: Spink & Son, 1926), 386 and 399. For the sculpture, see W. Helbig,
      *Die vatikanische Skulpturensammlung. Die kapitolinischen und das latera-
      nische Museum*, vol. 1, *Führer durch die öffentlichen Sammlungen klassischer
      Altertümer in Rom* (Leipzig, Ger.: Teubner, 1891), 357; G. M. Koeppel,
      "Die historischen Reliefs der römischen Kaiserzeit IV," *Bonner Jahrbücher
      des Rheinischen Landesmuseums in Bonn und des Vereins von Altertumsfreun-
      den im Rheinlande* 186 (1986), 1–90.

203   *"guest and comrade"*: Ibid., 25.9, trans. A. O'Brien-Moore.

203   *physician refused*: Ibid., 24.13, says the physician killed himself instead, but
      that sounds like a rumor, perhaps planted by Hadrian's enemies.

203   *"his old age"*: Aurelius Victor, *de Caesaribus*, 14.12, with an echo of Virgil,
      The Aeneid, 6.304.

204   *Servianus's curse*: Cassius Dio, *Roman History*, 69.17.1–3.

204   *O blithe little soul*: "Hadrian," in *Historia Augusta*, 25.9, trans. A. O'Brien-
      Moore.

204   *the people hated him*: Ibid., 27.1; Cassius Dio, *Roman History*, 69. 23.2.

205   *"For, inasmuch as he wished to surpass everybody in everything"*: Cassius Dio, *Roman History*, 69.5.1–3. Dio's father, Apronianus, was no admirer of Hadrian: Ibid., 69.1.12.

CHAPTER 7: MARCUS AURELIUS, THE PHILOSOPHER

210   *another ancient portrait*: the gold bust of Marcus Aurelius found at Aventicum (today's Avenches, Switzerland). Römermuseum Avenches inv. no. 39/134, P. Schazmann, "Buste en or représentant l'empereur Marc-Aurèle trouvé à Avenches en 1939," *Zeitschrift für schweizerische Archäologie und Kunstgeschichte* 2 (1940): 69–93.

210   *"think of the universe as one living being"*: Marcus Aurelius, *Meditations* 4.40, in Marcus Aurelius, and Charles Reginald Haines. *The Communings with Himself of Marcus Aurelius Antoninus, Emperor of Rome: Together with His Speeches and Sayings: a Revised Text and a Translation into English* (Cambridge, MA: Harvard University Press, 1953), 91.

211   *With one later exception*: The emperor Julian, who reigned from 361 to 363.

212   *"the fear of God, and generosity"*: Marcus Aurelius, *Meditations*, 1.3, trans. Haines, *Communings with Himself*, 3.

212   *Marcus has much more to say about his mother*: Marcus Aurelius, *Meditations*, 1.3.

212   *He takes part in the grape harvest*: Marcus Cornelius Fronto, *The Correspondence of Marcus Cornelius Fronto: with Marcus Aurelius Antoninus, Lucius Verus, Antoninus Pius, and Various Friends*. Edited by Marcus Aurelius, Antoninus Pius, Lucius Aurelius Verus, and Charles Reginald Haines (Cambridge, MA: Harvard University Press, 1919), letter 2.12.

212   *They said constantly how much they loved each other*: *Marcus Aurelius in Love*. Edited by Marcus Aurelius, Marcus Cornelius Fronto, and Amy Richlin (Chicago: University of Chicago Press, 2006), 5–9.

213   *an end to the pursuit of boys*: Marcus Aurelius, *Meditations*, 1.16.2.

213   *"the rare happiness of times"*: Tacitus, *Histories*, 1.1. Tacitus was referring to Nerva and Trajan, but the verdict suits Hadrian, Antoninus Pius, and Marcus Aurelius as well.

214   *Instead he thanked Fronto for helping him learn about tyranny*: Marcus Aurelius, *Meditations*, 1.11.

215   *A wit once said to Antoninus after seeing Marcus's mother*: "Marcus Aurelius," in *Historia Augusta*, 6.8–9.

215   *"Foolish woman"*: "Antoninus Pius," in *Historia Augusta*, 4.8, trans LCL.

216   *"You conduct public business throughout the whole civilized world exactly as if it were one city-state"*: http://coursesa.matrix.msu.edu/~fisher/hst205/read ings/RomanOration.html.

216   *"The entire earth," he stated, "has been made beautiful like a garden"*: http:// coursesa.matrix.msu.edu/~fisher/hst205/readings/RomanOration.html.

216   *Marcus praised Antoninus in the* Meditations: Marcus Aurelius, *Meditations*, 1.16, 17.3, 4.33, 6.30, 8.25, 9.21, 10.27.

217   *Supposedly his last word was* equanimity: "Antoninus Pius," in *Historia Augusta*, 12.6.

217   *Marcus is said to have spent only two nights away from Antoninus*: "Marcus Aurelius," in *Historia Augusta*, 7.3.

218   *"first among physicians"*: Galen, *On Prognosis*, 11.8, 129.

218   *Marcus was thoughtful but not, he wrote, quick witted*: Marcus Aurelius, *Meditations*, 5.5.

218   *he made gladiators use blunt swords*: Cassius Dio, *History of Rome*, 71.29.4.

219   *He said he would rather live in exile on a bleak island with her*: Fronto, *Ad Pium* 2 (Haines, *Correspondence of Fronto* 1.128; AD 143). Some think that the "Faustina" referred to here is Faustina the Elder, Antoninus's wife.

220   *the palace's propaganda machine featured it prominently on coins*: For example, RIC III Marcus Aurelius 1635, http://numismatics.org/ocre/id/ric.3.m _aur.1635.

220   *high infant mortality rates*: Recent research shows that Roman infant mortality rates tended to range between 20 percent and 35 percent. See Nathan Pilkington, "Growing Up Roman: Infant Mortality and Reproductive Development," *Journal of Interdisciplinary History* 44, no. 1 (Summer 2013): 1–35.

220   *as her portrait busts show*: For example, Rome, Capitoline Museum inv. 449; Louvre Museum, Ma 1176.

220   *Coin images associated her with Venus*: For example, RIC III Marcus Aurelius 1681, http://numismatics.org/ocre/id/ric.3.m_aur.1681.

220   *"If we send our wife away, we must also return her dowry"*: "Marcus Aurelius,"
       in *Historia Augusta*, 19.8–9.

221   *as obedient, affectionate, and straightforward*: Marcus Aurelius, *Meditations*,
       1.17.7.

221   *"a cloudless sky"*: trans. Richlin, *Marcus Aurelius in Love*, letter 44, 143.

221   *several references in his book to the pain of losing a child*: Marcus Aurelius,
       Meditations, 8.49, 9.40, 10.34, 11.34. Compare McLynn, *Marcus Aurelius*,
       93.

223   *Galen left for his home in Asia Minor*: Galen, *On His Own Books*, 19.15.

223   *inscribed a verse above their doorways*: Lucian, *Alexander*, 36.

223   *A survivor of the disease remembered the sound*: Aelius Aristides, *Oration*,
       43.38–44.

223   *Galen joined them*: Galen, *On Prognosis to Posthumus*, 9.

224   *both Lucilla and her mother, Faustina, opposed it*: "Marcus Aurelius," in *His-
       toria Augusta*, 20.7.

225   *the Romans experienced two miracles, which they displayed prominently in pro-
       paganda*: Ibid., 24.2; Cassius Dio, *Roman History*, 74.8–10; RIC III Mar-
       cus Aurelius, 264–66, http://numismatics.org/ocre/id/ric.3.m_aur.264,
       http://numismatics.org/ocre/id/ric.3.m_aur.265, http://numismatics.org
       /ocre/id/ric.3.m_aur.266.

225   *Pagans and Christians immediately engaged in a polemic about whose prayers
       had won the favor of heaven*: Xiphilinus in Cassius Dio, *Roman History*,
       72.9.

225   *a pair of female skeletons*: see Adrienne Mayor, *The Amazons: Lives and Leg-
       ends of Warrior Women Across the Ancient World* (Princeton, NJ: Princeton
       University Press, 2014), 81–82.

226   *"Every moment, think steadily"*: Marcus Aurelius, *Meditations*, 2.5, trans.
       George Long, Internet Classics Archive, http://classics.mit.edu//Antoni
       nus/meditations.html, modified.

226   *"A spider is proud when it has caught a fly"*: Ibid., 10.10, trans. Long, modi-
       fied.

226   *Mother of the Camp (Mater Castrorum)*: "Marcus Aurelius," in *Historia Au-
       gusta*, 26.8; Cassius Dio, *Roman History*, 71.10.5.

227   *"You are crazy!"*: Philostratus, *Lives of the Sophists*, 2.1.13.

228   *The sources suggest*: Cassius Dio, *Roman History*, 72.29.

228   *private praise of Faustina*: Marcus Aurelius, *Meditations*, 1.14.

229   *coins struck stating that she was now among the stars*: For example, RIC
      III Marcus Aurelius 1717, http://numismatics.org/ocre/id/ric.3.m_aur
      .1717.

229   *"May it never happen," he wrote to the senators*: Cassius Dio, *Roman History*,
      72.30.

229   *the honors in Rome that the Senate voted in her memory*: Ibid., 72.31.1–2.

229   *prohibited anyone from serving as governor of his native province*: Ibid.,
      72.31.1.

229   *worse than the barbarians on the Danube frontier*: Ammianus Marcellinus,
      History of Rome, 22.5.

229   *Marcus gave an audience to Rabbi Judah I*: For the sources, see Maria Laura
      Atarista, *Avidio Cassio* (Rome: Edizioni di Storia e Letteratura: 1983),
      119–23.

231   *Marcus possessed such wisdom, gentleness, integrity*: Aurelius Victor, *De Cae-
      saribus* 16.9–10, in Sextus Aurelius Victor, *Liber de Caesaribus of Sextus
      Aurelius Victor*, trans. H. W. Bird, Translated Texts for Historians, v. 17
      (Liverpool: Liverpool University Press, 1994), 19.

231   *"My poor, unhappy soul"*: Cassius Dio, *Roman History*, 78.16.6.

232   *"Be like a headland of rock on which the waves break incessantly"*: *Meditations*
      4.49, Marcus Aurelius, *The Meditations*, trans. Long.

232   *If you work at that which is before you*: Marcus Aurelius, *Meditations*, 3.12,
      Marcus Aurelius, *The Meditations*, trans. Long, modified.

232   *"But my nature is rational and social"*: Marcus Aurelius, *Meditations*, 6.44,
      Marcus Aurelius, *The Meditations*, trans. Long.

233   *One source claims*: Cassius Dio, *History of Rome*, 72.33.

233   *"a beautiful death for the commonwealth"*: Ammianus Marcellinus, *History of
      Rome*, 31.5.14.

233   *"He showed himself to be of all virtues"*: Pseudo-Aurelius Victor, *Epitome de
      Caesaribus*, 16.2, trans. Thomas M. Banchich, www.roman-emperors.org
      /epitome.htm.

234   *an age of gold ended to be replaced by one of rust and iron*: Cassius Dio, *History
      of Rome*, 71.36.4.

CHAPTER 8: SEPTIMIUS SEVERUS, THE AFRICAN

238   *Lepcis Magna*: Also known as Leptis Magna.

239   *dark skinned*: John Malalas, *Chronicle*, 12.18.

239   *One contemporary image*: Severan Tondo, Staatliche Museen, Berlin, Antikenmuseum, Inv. No. 31329.

239   *Dio knew Severus personally and had mixed feelings*: Cassius Dio, *Roman History*, 77.16–17; compare 75.2 and 72.36.4.

239   *a man of few words but many ideas*: Cassius Dio, *Roman History*, 77.12.

240   *As a boy, he supposedly played at being judge*: "Septimius Severus," in *Historia Augusta*, 1.4.

240   *energetic*: Herodian, *History of the Roman Empire Since the Death of Marcus Aurelius*, 2.9.2.

240   *inquisitive*: Cassius Dio, *Roman History*, 76.13.

240   *blunt*: Ibid., 75.8.1, 76.8.1.

240   *quick witted and decisive*: Herodian, *History of the Roman Empire Since the Death of Marcus Aurelius*, 2.9.2.

240   *He had a temper*: "Septimius Severus," in *Historia Augusta*, 2.6.

240   *ruthless and deceitful*: Cassius Dio, *Roman History*, 75.2.1–2; Herodian, *History of the Roman Empire Since the Death of Marcus Aurelius*, 2.14.4.

240   *Severus did not suffer a low opinion*: Cassius Dio, *Roman History*, 77.15.3.

241   *served as the model for Venus de Milo*: See Barbara Levick, *Julia Domna, Syrian Empress* (London: Routledge, 2007), 3.

241   *images of Domna*: For example, bust in Glyptothek, Munich Inv. 354; coins, for example, RIC IV Septimius Severus 540, http://numismatics.org/ocre/id/ric.4.ss.540_aureus; RIC IV Septimius Severus 857, http://numismatics.org/ocre/id/ric.4.ss.857.

242   *Greek man of letters who settled in Rome*: Philostratus of Athens.

242   *the Wise or the Philosopher*: Philostratus, *Lives of the Sophists*, 622.

243   *coin portraits*: For example, RIC IV Pertinax 1, http://numismatics.org/ocre/id/ric.4.pert.1.

244   *The spectacle proved the most brilliant of any that I have witnessed*: LCL translation 1927 modified, http://penelope.uchicago.edu/Thayer/E/Roman/Texts/Cassius_Dio/75*.html.

245   *"The men of Italy, long unused to arms and war"*: Herodian, *History of the Roman*

Empire Since the Death of Marcus Aurelius, trans. Edward C. Echols (Herodian of Antioch's History of the Roman Empire, 1961 Berkeley and Los Angeles), www.livius.org/sources/content/herodian-s-roman-history/herodian-2.11.

245   *compared his reign to bloody Tiberius's*: Cassius Dio, *Roman History*, 58.14.1.

245   *Marius and Sulla*: Ibid., 76.8.1.

245   *Augustus, whom Severus also cited*: Ibid.

248   *One Roman wit congratulated Severus for finding a father*: Ibid., 76.9.4.

249   *A contemporary critic complained about its expense*: Ibid., 75.3.3.

250   *"most holy" had already been used to describe several emperors*: Hermann Dessau, *Inscriptiones Latinae Selectae*. Berlin, vol. 2, pt. 1 (1902), nos. 6472, 6988. Hadrian and Antonius Pius were both "most holy" princes.

251   *"Here's your Plautianus!"*: Cassius Dio, *Roman History*, 77.4.4.

251   *an often-overlooked monument on a quiet street in Rome*: Arch of the Argentarii.

252   *"Come, give it here"*: Cassius Dio, *Roman History*, 77.17.4.

253   *Mother of the Camp*: CIL XII 4345; XIV 120.

253   *"Be harmonious, enrich the soldiers"*: Cassius Dio, *Roman History*, 77.15.2.

253   *"You shall hold the bones of a man"*: Ibid., 77.15.3.

253   *a strong-looking man with blunt features*: For example, bust in the National Archaeological Museum, Naples inv. 6603.

254   *According to a contemporary, the purpose*: Cassius Dio, *Roman History*, 77.9.5.

255   *Coin portraits show Maesa*: For example, RIC IV Elagabalus 256, http://numismatics.org/ocre/id/ric.4.el.256.

256   *In coin portraits, Elagabalus*: For example, ibid., 25, http://numismatics.org/ocre/id/ric.4.el.25.

256   *A marble bust depicts a slim, curly headed teenager*: Rome, Capitoline Museums, Inv. MC 470.

257   *A coin from early in the new reign*: RIC IV Severus Alexander 7d, http://numismatics.org/ocre/id/ric.4.sa.7d.

257   *In some later coins, he is bearded*: For example, ibid., 648a http://numismatics.org/ocre/id/ric.4.sa.648a.

257   *A marble bust shows him in a toga*: Rome, Capitoline Museums Inv. MC 471.

257   *Mamaea is depicted with her family's characteristic wavy hair*: For example, RIC IV Severus Alexander 670, http://numismatics.org/ocre/id/ric.4.sa.670.

258   *"the principal author of the decline and fall"*: Gibbon, *Decline and Fall of the Roman Empire*, vol. 1, 148.

259   *"the emperor is not bound by the laws"*: *princeps legibus solutus est*, Justinian, *Institutes*, 2.17.8.

CHAPTER 9: DIOCLETIAN, THE GREAT DIVIDER

263   *"If only you could see at Salona"*: Pseudo-Aurelius Victor, *Epitome de Caesaribus*, 39.6, trans. Thomas M. Banchich modified, www.roman-emperors .org/epitome.htm.

264   *One marble bust shows a rough-hewn thug*: J. Paul Getty Museum, Villa Collection, Malibu, CA 78.AA.8.

264   *Another striking bust in black basalt*: Worcester Art Museum, "Head of a Man (possibly Diocletian)," 1974.297.

266   *quoted a line from Virgil's The Aeneid*: "Carus, Carinus and Numerianus," in *Historia Augusta*, 13.3–5.

266   *Aper means "boar" in Latin*: Ibid., 14.1–15.6.

267   *an officer whose wife Carinus had seduced*: Pseudo-Aurelius Victor, *Epitome de Caesaribus*, 38.8.

267   *the loss of one soldier hardly mattered*: Ibid., 29.5; Jordanes, *Getica*, 18.

267   *another major epidemic*: Harper, *Fate of Rome*, 136–45.

267   *brought an end to the favorable climate*: Ibid., 129–36, 167–75.

270   *A surviving portrait bust that might be Maximian*: Civico Museo Archeologico, Milan, www.comune.milano.it/wps/portal/luogo/museoarcheolo gico/lecollezioni/milanoromana/ritratto_massimiano/lut/p/a0/04_ Sj9CPykssy0xPLMnMz0vMAfGjzOItLL3NjDz9Dbz9Az3NDBx9 DIMt_UxMjc28DfQLsh0VAba4yro!. For a coin image, see RIC V Diocletian 342, http://numismatics.org/ocre/id/ric.5.dio.342.

270   *fierce, wild, and uncivilized*: Eutropius, *Abridgment of Roman History*, 2.9.27.

270   *estimated that he traveled ten miles a day*: Timothy D. Barnes, *The New Empire of Diocletian and Constantine* (Boston: Harvard University Press, 1982), 51–52.

271   *"an undivided inheritance"*: "Genathliacus of Maximian Augustus," Panegyrici Latini 11.6.3, trans. C. E. V. Nixon and Barbara Saylor Rodgers, *In*

Praise of Later Roman Emperors: The Panegyrici Latini: Introduction, Translation, and Historical Commentary, with the Latin Text of R.A.B. Mynors (Berkeley: University of California Press, 1994), 91.

271 *Coins show Valeria as a pretty young woman*: For example, RIC VI Serdica 34, http://numismatics.org/ocre/id/ric.6.serd.34.

272 *One ancient source, admittedly hostile*: Lactantius, *On the Death of Persecutors*, 9.

272 *temple of Jupiter*: Jasna Jeličić-Radonić, "Aurelia Prisca," *Prilozi povijesti umjetnosti u Dalmaciji* (*Contributions to Art History in Dalmatia*), 41, no. 1 (August 2008): 5–25, http://hrcak.srce.hr/109683.

272 *Galerius claimed that she had mated with Mars*: Pseudo-Aurelius Victor, *Epitome de Caesaribus* 40.17; Lactantius, *On the Death of Persecutors*, 11.21.

272 *statue group of the four rulers*: www.basilicasanmarco.it/basilica/scultura /la-decorazione-delle-facciate/la-facciata-orientale/?lang=en and https:// en.wikipedia.org/wiki/Portrait_of_the_Four_Tetrarchs. Found on the south façade of the Basilica of San Marco, Venice, Italy.

273 *Diocletian humiliated him*: Ammianus Marcellinus, *History*, 14.11.10; 22.7.1; Eutropius, *Abridgment of Roman History*, 9.24; Festus, *Breviarum*, 25.

274 RESTORER OF THE EVERLASTING LIGHT: The Arras Medallion, British Museum B.1147.

274 *"a peace which was earned with much sweat"*: Diocletian, Edict of Maximal Prices, as cited in Roger Rees, *Diocletian and the Tetrarchy* (Edinburgh: Edinburgh University Press, 2004), 139.

275 *in September 298 an Egyptian blacksmith failed to show up for work*: P. Beatty Panop. 1.213–16 (September 17, 298); Rees, *Diocletian and the Tetrarchy*, II.21, 149.

277 *"What a vision your piety granted"*: *Panegyrici Latini* 11(3) (July 21, 291, Trier) (I Chapter 4.2), 11.1.1, Roger Rees, *Diocletian and the Tetrarchy*, 132.

277 *"Do you see Diocletian?"*: *Panegyrici Latini* 11(3) (July 21, 291, Trier) (I Chapter 4.2), 11.11.4, Roger Rees, *Diocletian and the Tetrarchy*, 132.

278 *"How many divisions does the Pope have?"*: Winston Churchill, *The Second World War*, vol. 1 (London: Houghton Mifflin, 1948), 105.

278 *"the peace of the gods"*: For example, Cicero, *For Marcus Fonteius*, 30; Livy, *History of Rome*, 1.31.7.

279 *like poisonous and evil snakes*: Manichaean rescript. Collation of the Laws of Moses and Rome 15.3 (March 31, 302(?), Alexandria) as cited in Rees, *Diocletian and the Tetrarchy*, 174.

280 *the driving force behind Galerius was his mother*: Lactantius, *On the Deaths of the Persecutors*, 11.1–3.

280 *According to a Christian source*: Lactantius, *On the Deaths of the Persecutors*, 12–14.

280 *he ordered them to sacrifice to the gods*: Ibid., 15.1.

280 *Christians reacted to persecution in various ways*: Herbert Musurillo, *The Acts of the Christian Martyrs*, Oxford Early Christian Texts (Oxford: Clarendon Press, 1972), 260–65, 266–71, 302–9.

281 *As for Romula, after she died*: See Dragoslav Srejovic and Cedomir Vasic, *Imperial Mausolea and Consecration Memorials in Felix Romuliana* (Gamzigrad, East Serbia) (Belgrade: Centre for Archaeological Research, Faculty of Philosophy, The University of Belgrad, 1994), 149–51. Cited in Bill Leadbetter, "Galerius, Gamzigrad and the Politics of Abdication," *ASCS* [*Australasian Society for Classical Studies*] 31 (2010): 8–9. These at least are plausible conclusions from the archaeological evidence.

281 *Julius Caesar called an act of political illiteracy*: Suetonius, *Julius Caesar*, 77.

CHAPTER 10: CONSTANTINE, THE CHRISTIAN

287 *In the courtyard of Rome's Capitoline Museums*: In ancient times, the statue stood not here but in the Basilica of Maxentius, on the far side of the Roman Forum.

287 *colossal marble bust of Constantine*: Rome, Capitoline Museums, Inv. MC0757.

287 *a right hand with pointed finger*: Actually, two versions of the hand survive.

288 *"With the power of this God as ally"*: Constantine, Letter to Shapur II, in Eusebius, *Life of Constantine* 4.9, trans. by Averil Cameron, and Stuart George Hall, *Eusebius, Life of Constantine* (Oxford: Clarendon Press, 1999), 153.

289 *born at Naissus (today's Niš, Serbia) on February 27, 273*: T. D. Barnes, *The New Empire of Diocletian and Constantine* (Cambridge, MA: Harvard University Press, 1982), 36, 39–42.

289 *They fell in love and married*: As reconstructed by Barnes, *New Empire of*

Diocletian and Constantine, 36–37, 39–42. Possible, but less likely, they never married, making Constantine a bastard.

294 *Our most important source for the life of Constantine says otherwise*: Eusebius, *Life of Constantine*, 3.47.2, a text completed shortly after the emperor's death in 337. T. D. Barnes, *Constantine: Dynasty, Religion and Power in the Later Roman Empire* (Chichester, UK: Wiley-Blackwell, 2011), 44–45, rejects Eusebius's statement as mere flattery of the emperor.

294 *later church historians say that Helena*: For example, Theodoret, *Ecclesiastical History*, 1.18. See Cameron and Hall, *Eusebius, Life of Constantine*, 395.

294 *"the light of the world"*: John 8:12.

294 *Jesus's face shone like the sun*: Matthew 17:2.

295 *God Himself had entrusted him with the direction of human affairs*: Letter of Constantine to Ablavius (or Aelafius). Found in the third appendix of Optatus of Milevis, *Against the Donatists*. See *Optatus: Against the Donatists*, trans. Mark Edwards, Translated Texts for Historians 27 (Liverpool: Liverpool University Press, 1997), 183–84.

295 TO THE INVINCIBLE SUN, COMPANION OF THE EMPEROR: For example, RIC VII Treveri 135, http://numismatics.org/ocre/id/ric.7.tri.135.

299 *"divine inspiration"*: *instinctu divinitatis*, CIL VI.1139.

300 *Helena's coins*: See for example, RIC VII Treveri 481, http://numismatics .org/ocre/id/ric.7.tri.481.

300 *Fausta's coins*: See, for example, RIC VII Treveri 484. 1944.100.13272, http://numismatics.org/ocre/id/ric.7.tri.484.

301 *We strive to the best of our ability*: Constantine, *Speech to the Assembly of the Saints 11.1*, trans. T. D. Barnes, *Constantine*, 119.

301 *a waste of public money*: Zosimus, *New History*, 2.32.

302 *"the venerable day of the sun"*: *Theodosian Code*, 2.8.1.

302 *render unto Caesar*: Matthew 22:21.

303 *"a fellow worshipper of the most high God"*: Letter of Constantine to Ablavius (or Aelafius) Found in the third appendix of Optatus of Milevis, *Against the Donatists*. See *Optatus: Against the Donatists*, trans. Edwards, 183–84.

304 *good shepherd*: John 10:11.

305 *the most likely explanation*: Zosimus, *New History*, 2.29.2; *Epitome de Caesaribus* 42.11–12; Barnes, *Constantine*, 144–50.

306 *"murderers of the Lord"*: Eusebius, *Life of Constantine*, 4.27.1, compare 3.18.2; Theodoret, *Ecclesiastical History*, 1.9.

309 *"the dollar of the Middle Ages"*: Robert Sabatino Lopez, "The Dollar of the Middle Ages," *Journal of Economic History* 11, no. 3 (1951): 209–34.

EPILOGUE: THE GHOSTS OF RAVENNA

317 *the last ruler of "the Western Empire of the Roman race"*: Jordanes, *Getica*, 46.243.

317 *Gibbon suggested long ago that Christianity played a big role in the fall of Rome*: Gibbon, *Decline and Fall of the Roman Empire*, vol. 3 (1994): cp. LXXI.II, 1068–70.

319 *"Solomon, I have outdone thee!"*: *Narratio de Aedificatione Templi S. Sophiae* 27, in *Scriptores Originum Constantinopolitanarum*, ed. Theodor Preger (Leipzig, Ger.: B. G. Teubner, 1901), 105.

319 *"Royal purple is the noblest shroud"*: Procopius, *History of the Wars*, 1.24.37.

A NOTE ON SOURCES

The bibliography on the Roman emperors is vast. Here I emphasize accessible books in English that might provide the basis of further reading.

GENERAL AND REFERENCE

Cancik, Hubert, Helmuth Schneider, Christine F. Salazar, and David E. Orton, eds. *Brill's New Pauly: Encyclopaedia of the Ancient World*. English ed. Leiden, Ned.: Brill, 2002.

Hornblower, Simon, Anthony Spawforth, and Esther Eidinow. *The Oxford Classical Dictionary*. 4th ed. Oxford: Oxford University Press, 2012.

OCRE, "Online Coins of the Roman Empire," http://numismatics.org/ocre/.

"Orbis, The Stanford Geospatial Network of the Ancient World," http://orbis.stanford.edu.

Talbert, Richard J. A., ed. *The Barrington Atlas of the Ancient Greco-Roman World*. Princeton, NJ: Princeton University Press, 2000.

ANCIENT SOURCES

Many ancient sources are available online both in translation and in the original languages. Several good websites are Lacus Curtius: Into the Roman World, http://penelope.uchicago.edu/Thayer/E/Roman/home.html; Perseus Digital Library, www.perseus.tufts.edu; and Livius.org, Articles on Ancient History, www.livius.org, which offers both texts and encyclopedia articles.

Most of the ancient sources referred to in this book are available in bilingual editions in the Loeb Classical Library (Harvard University Press). Here, in addition, are some readily available English-language translations of important sources:

Birley, Anthony. *Lives of the Later Caesars: The First Part of the Augustan History, with Newly Compiled Lives of Nerva and Trajan.* Harmondsworth, UK: Penguin Books, 1976.

Cocceianus, Cassius Dio. *The Roman History: the Reign of Augustus.* Translated by Ian Scott-Kilvert. Harmondsworth, UK: Penguin Books, 1987.

Josephus. *The Jewish War.* Edited by Martin Goodman. Translated by Martin Hammond. Oxford: Oxford University Press, 2017.

Marcus Aurelius. *Meditations.* Translated by and with a foreword by Gregory Hays. Modern Library ed. New York: Modern Library, 2002.

Pliny the Younger. *Complete Letters.* Translated by P. G. Walsh. Oxford: Oxford University Press, 2009.

Suetonius. *Lives of the Caesars.* Translated by Catherine Edwards. Oxford: Oxford University Press, 2000.

Tacitus. *The Annals.* Translated by A. J. Woodman. Indianapolis: Hackett, 2004.

———. *The Histories.* Rev. ed. Edited by Rhiannon Ash. Translated by Kenneth Wellesley. London: Penguin Classics, 2009.

THE ROMAN EMPIRE

Beard, Mary. *SPQR: A History of Ancient Rome.* New York: Liveright, 2015.

Bowman, Alan K. et al. *The Cambridge Ancient History*, 2nd ed., vol. 10: The Augustan Empire, 43 B.C.–A. D. 69; vol. 11: The High Empire, A.D. 70–192; vol. 12: The Crisis of Empire, A. D. 193–337. Cambridge: Cambridge University Press, 1996–2005.

Gibbon, Edward. *The History of the Decline and Fall of the Roman Empire.* 3 vols. Edited by David Womersley. Harmondsworth, UK: Penguin, 1994.

———, *The History of the Decline and Fall of the Roman Empire.* Abbr. ed. Edited by David Womersley. Harmondsworth, UK: Penguin, 2001.

Harris, William V. *Roman Power: A Thousand Years of Empire.* Cambridge: Cambridge University Press, 2016.

Potter, D. S. *Ancient Rome: A New History, with 200 Illustrations, 149 in Color.* 2nd ed. New York: Thames & Hudson, 2014.

Scheidel, Walter, ed. *State Power in Ancient China and Rome.* Oxford: Oxford University Press, 2015.

Woolf, Greg. *Rome: An Empire's Story*. Oxford: Oxford University Press, 2012.

ROMAN EMPERORS

INTRODUCTION AND REFERENCE

Barrett, Anthony, ed. *Lives of the Caesars*. Malden, MA: Blackwell, 2008.

"De Imperatoribus Romanis: An Online Encyclopedia of Roman Rulers and their Families," www.roman-emperors.org/impindex.htm.

Grant, Michael. *The Roman Emperors: A Biographical Guide to the Rulers of Imperial Rome, 31 BC–AD 476*. New York: Scribner, 1985.

Meijer, Fik. *Emperors Don't Die in Bed*. Translated by S. J. Leinbach. London: Routledge, 2004.

Potter, David. *The Emperors of Rome: The Story of Imperial Rome from Julius Caesar to the Last Emperor*. London: Quercus Publishing, 2016.

Scarre, Chris. *Chronicle of the Roman Emperors: The Reign-by-Reign Record of the Rulers of Imperial Rome*. New York: Thames & Hudson, 1995.

Sommer, Michael. *The Complete Roman Emperor: Imperial Life at Court and on Campaign*. New York: Thames & Hudson, 2010.

DYNASTIES AND ERAS

Ando, Clifford. *Imperial Rome AD 193 to 284: The Critical Century*. Edinburgh: Edinburgh University Press, 2012.

Brown, Peter. *The World of Late Antiquity: From Marcus Aurelius to Muhammad*. London: Thames & Hudson, 1971.

Holland, Tom. *Dynasty: The Rise and Fall of the House of Caesar*. 1st US ed. New York: Doubleday, 2015.

Mitchell, Stephen. *A History of the Later Roman Empire, AD 284–641*. 2nd ed. Chichester, UK: Wiley Blackwell, 2015.

Potter, David. *The Roman Empire at Bay, AD 180–395*. 2nd ed. Abingdon, UK: Routledge, 2014.

WHAT EMPERORS DID

Ando, Clifford. *Imperial Ideology and Provincial Loyalty in the Roman Empire.* Berkeley: University of California Press, 2000.

Campbell, Brian. *The Emperor and the Roman Army, 31 BC–AD 235.* Oxford: Clarendon Press, 1984.

Hekster, Oliver. *Emperors and Ancestors: Roman Rulers and the Constraints of Tradition.* Oxford Studies in Ancient Culture & Representation. Oxford: Oxford University Press, 2015.

Lendon, J. E. *Empire of Honour: The Art of Government in the Roman World.* Oxford: Clarendon Press, 1997.

Millar, Fergus. *The Emperor in the Roman World, 31 BC–AD 337.* Ithaca, NY: Cornell University Press, 1977.

Noreña, Carlos. *Imperial Ideals in the Roman West: Representation, Circulation, Power.* Cambridge: Cambridge University Press, 2011.

Saller, Richard. *Personal Patronage Under the Early Empire.* Cambridge: Cambridge University Press, 1982.

IMPERIAL WOMEN

D'Ambra, Eve. *Roman Women.* Cambridge: Cambridge University Press, 2007.

De la Bédoyère, Guy. *Domina: The Women Who Made Imperial Rome.* New Haven, CT: Yale University Press, 2018.

Freisenbruch, Annelise. *Caesars' Wives: Sex, Power, and Politics in the Roman Empire.* New York: Free Press, 2010.

Hemelrijk, Emily Ann, and Greg Woolf. *Women and the Roman City in the Latin West.* Leiden, Ned.: Brill, 2013.

Kleiner, Diana E., and Susan B. Matheson, eds. *I Claudia: Women in Ancient Rome.* New Haven, CT: Yale University Art Gallery, 1996.

———. *I, Claudia II: Women in Roman Art and Society.* Austin: University of Texas Press, 2000.

ROMAN IMPERIAL SOCIETY,
ECONOMY, CULTURE, MILITARY

Beard, Mary, John North, and S. R. F Price. *Religions of Rome.* Cambridge: Cambridge University Press, 1998.

Campbell, J. B. *The Roman Army, 31 BC–AD 337: A Sourcebook.* London: Routledge, 1994.

Claridge, Amanda, Judith Toms, and Tony Cubberley. *Rome: An Oxford Archaeological Guide.* 2nd ed., rev. and expanded. Oxford: Oxford University Press, 2010.

Dench, Emma. *Romulus's Asylum: Roman Identities from the Age of Alexander to the Age of Hadrian.* Oxford: Oxford University Press, 2005.

Flower, Harriet. *The Art of Forgetting: Disgrace & Oblivion in Roman Political Culture.* Chapel Hill: University of North Carolina Press, 2006.

Goldsworthy, Adrian. *The Complete Roman Army.* New York: Thames & Hudson, 2003.

Harl, Kenneth W. *Coinage in the Roman Economy, 300 B.C. to A.D. 700.* Baltimore: Johns Hopkins University Press, 1996.

Luttwak, Edward. *The Grand Strategy of the Roman Empire: From the First Century CE to the Third.* Rev. and updated ed. Baltimore: Johns Hopkins University Press, 2016.

MacDonald, William L. *The Architecture of the Roman Empire.* Rev. ed. New Haven, CT: Yale University Press, 1982.

Mattern, Susan. *Rome and the Enemy: Imperial Strategy in the Principate.* Berkeley: University of California Press, 1999.

Peachin, Michael, ed. *The Oxford Handbook of Social Relations in the Roman World.* Oxford: Oxford University Press, 2011.

Ramage, Nancy H. and Andrew Ramage. *Roman Art.* 6th ed. Upper Saddle River, NJ: Pearson, 2014.

Rebillard, Éric. *Christians and Their Many Identities in Late Antiquity, North Africa, 200–450 CE.* Ithaca NY: Cornell University Press, 2012.

Rüpke, Jörg. *Pantheon: A New History of Roman Religion.* Translated by David Richardson. Princeton, NJ: Princeton University Press, 2018.

Scheidel, Walter, Ian Morris, and Richard P. Saller, eds. *The Cambridge Economic History of the Greco-Roman World.* Cambridge: Cambridge University Press, 2007.

Sherwin-White. A. N. *The Roman Citizenship.* 2nd ed. Oxford: Clarendon Press, 1973.

Temin, Peter. *The Roman Market Economy.* Princeton, NJ: Princeton University Press, 2013.

AUGUSTUS

ANCIENT SOURCES

Cooley, Alison. *Res Gestae Divi Augusti: Text, Translation, and Commentary.* Cambridge: Cambridge University Press, 2009.

Nicolaus. *The Life of Augustus and the Autobiography.* Edited by Mark Toher. Cambridge: Cambridge University Press, 2016.

Wardle, D. *Suetonius: Life of Augustus = Vita Divi Augusti.* 1st ed. Oxford: Oxford University Press, 2014.

BIOGRAPHIES

Everitt, Anthony. *Augustus: The Life of Rome's First Emperor.* New York: Random House, 2006.

Galinsky, Karl. *Augustus: Introduction to the Life of an Emperor.* New York: Cambridge University Press, 2012.

Goldsworthy, Adrian. *Augustus, First Emperor of Rome.* New Haven, CT: Yale University Press, 2014.

Southern, Patricia. *Augustus.* 2nd ed. London: Routledge, 2014.

SPECIALIZED STUDIES

Angelova, Diliana. *Sacred Founders: Women, Men, and Gods in the Discourse of Imperial Founding, Rome Through Early Byzantium.* Oakland: University of California Press, 2015.

Barrett, Anthony. *Livia: First Lady of Imperial Rome.* New Haven, CT: Yale University Press, 2002.

Bartman, Elizabeth. *Portraits of Livia: Imaging the Imperial Woman in Augustan Rome.* Cambridge: Cambridge University Press, 1999.

Everitt, Anthony. *Cicero: the Life and Times of Rome's Greatest Politician.* 1st US ed. New York: Random House, 2002.

Fantham, Elaine. *Julia Augusti: The Emperor's Daughter.* London: Routledge, 2006.

Galinsky, Karl. *Augustan Culture: An Interpretive Introduction.* Princeton, NJ: Princeton University Press, 1996.

Goldsworthy, Adrian. *Antony and Cleopatra.* New Haven, CT: Yale University Press, 2010.

Milnor, Kristina. *Gender, Domesticity, and the Age of Augustus: Inventing Private Life.* Oxford: Oxford University Press, 2005.

Osgood, Josiah. *Caesar's Legacy: Civil War and the Emergence of the Roman Empire.* Cambridge: Cambridge University Press, 2006.

Powell, Lindsay. *Marcus Agrippa: Right-Hand Man of Caesar Augustus.* Barnsley, UK: Pen & Sword Books, 2015.

Severy, Beth. *Augustus and the Family at the Birth of the Roman Empire.* New York: Routledge, 2003.

Strauss, Barry. *The Death of Caesar: The Story of History's Most Famous Assassination.* New York: Simon & Schuster, 2015.

Syme, Sir Ronald. *The Roman Revolution.* Oxford: Oxford University Press, 1939.

Welch, Kathryn. *Magnus Pompeius: Sextus Pompeius and the Transformation of the Roman Republic.* Swansea, UK: Classical Press of Wales, 2012.

Zanker, Paul. *The Power of Images in the Age of Augustus.* Ann Arbor: University of Michigan Press, 1988.

TIBERIUS

ANCIENT SOURCES

London Association of Classical Teachers. *Tiberius to Nero.* Edited by M. G. L. Cooley and Alison Cooley. London: LACTORs, 2011.

BIOGRAPHIES

Levick, Barbara. *Tiberius the Politician.* Rev. ed. London: Routledge, 1999.

Seager, Robin. *Tiberius.* 2nd ed. Malden, MA: Blackwell, 2005.

Winterling, Aloys. *Caligula.* Berkeley: University of California Press, 2011.

SPECIALIZED STUDIES

De la Bédoyère, Guy. *Praetorian: The Rise and Fall of Rome's Imperial Bodyguard.* New Haven, CT: Yale University Press, 2017.

Kokkinos, Nikos. *Antonia Augusta: Portrait of a Great Roman Lady.* London: Libri, 2002.

MacMullen, Ramsay. *Enemies of the Roman Order: Treason, Unrest and Alienation in the Empire.* London: Routledge, 1992.

Wilkinson, Sam. *Republicanism During the Early Roman Empire.* London: Continuum, 2012.

NERO

ANCIENT SOURCES

Barrett, Anthony A., Elaine Fantham, and John C. Yardley, eds. *The Emperor Nero: A Guide to the Ancient Sources.* Princeton, NJ: Princeton University Press, 2016.

Smallwood, E. Mary. *Documents Illustrating the Principates of Gaius, Claudius and Nero.* London: Cambridge University Press, 1967.

BIOGRAPHIES

Champlin, Edward. *Nero.* Cambridge, MA: Belknap Press of Harvard University Press, 2003.

Griffin, Miriam T. *Nero: The End of a Dynasty.* New Haven, CT: Yale University Press, 1985.

Malitz, Jürgen. *Nero.* Translated by Allison Brown. Malden, MA: Blackwell, 2005.

SPECIALIZED STUDIES

Ball, Larry F. *The Domus Aurea and the Roman Architectural Revolution.* Cambridge: Cambridge University Press, 2003.

Barrett, Anthony. *Agrippina: Sex, Power, and Politics in the Early Empire.* New Haven, CT: Yale University Press, 1996.

Bartsch, Shadi, Kirk Freudenburg, and C. A. J. Littlewood, eds. *The Cambridge Companion to the Age of Nero*. Cambridge: Cambridge University Press, 2017.

Donovan Ginsberg, Lauren. *Staging Memory, Staging Strife: Empire and Civil War in the Octavia*. New York: Oxford University Press, 2017.

Ginsburg, Judith. *Representing Agrippina: Constructions of Female Power in the Early Roman Empire*. Oxford: Oxford University Press, 2006.

Lancaster, Lynne C. *Concrete Vaulted Construction in Imperial Rome*. Cambridge: Cambridge University Press, 1985.

Romm, James. *Dying Every Day: Seneca at the Court of Nero*. New York: Alfred A. Knopf, 2014.

Rudich, Vasily. *Political Dissidence Under Nero: The Price of Dissimulation*. London: Routledge, 1993.

Wallace-Hadrill, Andrew. "*Civilis Princeps*: Between Citizen and King," *Journal of Roman Studies* 72 (1982): 32–48.

Wilson, Emily. *The Greatest Empire: A Life of Seneca*. New York: Oxford University Press, 2014.

VESPASIAN

ANCIENT SOURCES

Suetonius. *Vespasian*. Edited by Brian W. Jones. London: Bristol Classical Press, 2000.

BIOGRAPHY

Levick, Barbara. *Vespasian*. 2nd ed. London: Routledge, 2017.

SPECIALIZED STUDIES

Goodman, Martin. *Rome and Jerusalem: The Clash of Ancient Civilizations*. London: Allen Lane, 2007.

Hopkins, Keith, and Mary Beard. *The Colosseum*. Cambridge, MA: Harvard University Press, 2005.

Morgan, Gwyn. *69 A.D.: The Year of the Four Emperors.* Oxford: Oxford University Press, 2007.

TRAJAN

ANCIENT SOURCES

Smallwood, Mary E. *Documents Illustrating the Principates of Nerva, Trajan and Hadrian.* Cambridge: Cambridge University Press, 1966.

BIOGRAPHIES

Bennett, Julian. *Trajan, Optimus Princeps: A Life and Times.* Bloomington: Indiana University Press, 1997.

Everitt, Anthony. *Hadrian and the Triumph of Rome.* New York: Random House, 2009.

Grainger, John D. *Nerva and the Succession Crisis of AD 96–99.* London: Routledge, 2003.

Southern, Pat. *Domitian, Tragic Tyrant.* Bloomington: Indiana University Press, 1997.

SPECIALIZED STUDIES

Keltanen, M. "The Public Image of the Four Empresses: Ideal Wives, Mothers and Regents?," in Päivi Setälä. *Women, Wealth and Power in the Roman Empire* (Rome: Institutum romanum Finlandiae, 2002), 105–46.

Lepper, Frank A. *Trajan's Parthian War.* London: Oxford University Press, 1948.

Packer, James E. *The Forum of Trajan in Rome: A Study of the Monuments in Brief.* Berkeley: University of California Press, 2001.

Setälä, Päivi. "Women and Brick Production—Some New Aspects," in *Women, Wealth and Power,* 181–202.

HADRIAN

ANCIENT SOURCES

Benario, Herbert W. *A Commentary on the Vita Hadriani in the Historia Augusta.* Chico, CA: Scholars Press, 1980.

Smallwood, Mary E. *Documents Illustrating Principates of Nerva, Trajan and Hadrian.*

Speidel, Michael. *Emperor Hadrian's Speeches to the African Army: A New Text.* Mainz, Ger.: Verlag des Römisch-Germanischen Zentralmuseums, 2006.

BIOGRAPHIES

Birley, Anthony. *Hadrian: The Restless Emperor.* London: Routledge, 1997.

Everitt, Anthony. *Hadrian and the Triumph of Rome.*

SPECIALIZED STUDIES

Boatwright, Mary Taliaferro. *Hadrian and the Cities of the Roman Empire.* Princeton, NJ: Princeton University Press, 2002.

Goldsworthy, Adrian. *Hadrian's Wall.* New York: Basic Books, 2018.

Horbury, William. *Jewish War Under Trajan and Hadrian.* New York: Cambridge University Press, 2014.

Keltanen. "Public Image of the Four Empresses," 117–25.

Lambert, Royston. *Beloved and God: The Story of Hadrian and Antinous.* 1st US ed. New York: Viking, 1984.

MacDonald, William L. *The Architecture of the Roman Empire.* Rev. ed. New Haven, CT: Yale University Press, 1982.

———. *Hadrian's Villa and Its Legacy.* New Haven, CT: Yale University Press, 1995.

Speller, Elizabeth. *Following Hadrian: A Second Century Journey Through the Roman Empire.* Oxford: Oxford University Press, 2003.

MARCUS AURELIUS

SOURCES

Marcus Aurelius in Love. Edited by Marcus Aurelius, Marcus Cornelius Fronto, and Amy Richlin. Chicago: University of Chicago Press, 2006.

BIOGRAPHIES

Birley, Anthony. *Marcus Aurelius: A Biography.* London: B. T. Batsford, 1993.
Hekster, Oliver. *Commodus: An Emperor at the Crossroads.* Amsterdam: J. C. Gieben, 2002.
McLynn, Frank. *Marcus Aurelius: A Life.* 1st Da Capo Press Ed. Cambridge, MA: Da Capo Press, 2009.

SPECIALIZED STUDIES

Harper, Kyle. *The Fate of Rome: Climate, Disease and the End of an Empire.* Princeton, NJ: Princeton University Press, 2017, 64–118.
Keltanen, "Public Image of the Four Empresses," 125–141.
Levick, Barbara. *Faustina I and II: Imperial Women of the Golden Age.* New York: Oxford University Press, 2014.

SEPTIMIUS SEVERUS

ANCIENT SOURCES

Sidebottom, Harry. "Severan Historiography: Evidence, Patterns, and Arguments," in Swain, Simon, S. J. Harrison, and Jaś. Elsner, eds. *Severan Culture.* Cambridge: Cambridge University Press, 2007, 52–82.

BIOGRAPHIES

Arrizabalaga y Prado, Leonardo de. *The Emperor Elagabalus: Fact or Fiction?* Cambridge: Cambridge University Press, 2010.
Birley, Anthony. *Septimius Severus, the African Emperor.* Rev. ed. New Haven, CT: Yale University Press, 1989.

SPECIALIZED STUDIES

Levick, Barbara. *Julia Domna, Syrian Empress.* London: Routledge, 2007.
Swain, Harrison, and Elsner, eds. *Severan Culture.*

DIOCLETIAN

SOURCES

Aurelius Victor: De Caesaribus. Translated by H. W. Bird. Liverpool: Liverpool
   University Press, 1994.
Bowen, Anthony, ed., trans. *Lactantius: Divine Institutes.* Translated Texts for
   Historians. Liverpool: Liverpool University Press, 2003.
Corcoran, Simon. *The Empire of the Tetrarchs: Imperial Pronouncements and Gov-*
   ernment, AD 284–324. Rev. ed. Oxford: Clarendon Press, 2000.
Eutropius: Breviarium. Translated by H. W. Bird. Liverpool: Liverpool University
   Press, 1993.
Nixon, C. E. V, and Barbara Saylor Rodgers. *In Praise of Later Roman Emperors:*
   The Panegyrici Latini: Introduction, Translation, and Historical Commentary,
   with the Latin Text of R. A. B. Mynors. Berkeley: University of California
   Press, 1994.
Rees, Roger. *Diocletian and the Tetrarchy.* Edinburgh: Edinburgh University
   Press, 2004.

BIOGRAPHIES

Leadbetter, Bill. *Galerius and the Will of Diocletian.* London: Routledge, 2009.
Rees. *Diocletian and the Tetrarchy.*
Williams, Stephen. *Diocletian and the Roman Recovery.* New York: Routledge,
   1997.

SPECIALIZED STUDIES

Barnes, Timothy David. *The New Empire of Diocletian and Constantine.* Cambridge, MA: Harvard University Press, 1982.

Jeličić-Radonić, Jasna. "Aurelia Prisca," *Contributions to Art History in Dalmatia*, vol. 41. No. 1 (August, 2008): 5–25 (English summary, 23–25).

Wilkes, J. J. *Diocletian's Palace of Split: Residence of a Retired Roman Emperor.* Oxford: Oxbow Books, 1993.

CONSTANTINE

SOURCES

Bleckmann, Bruno. "Sources for the History of Constantine." In Lenski, Noel Emmanuel, ed. *The Cambridge Companion to the Age of Constantine.* Cambridge: Cambridge University Press, 2006, 14–32.

Eusebius, Averil Cameron, and Stuart George Hall. *Life of Constantine.* Oxford: Clarendon Press, 1999.

Nixon and Rodgers. *In Praise of Later Roman Emperors: The Panegyrici Latini.*

BIOGRAPHIES

Barnes, Timothy David. *Constantine: Dynasty, Religion and Power in the Later Roman Empire.* Chichester, UK: Wiley-Blackwell, 2011.

Potter, D. S. *Constantine the Emperor.* New York: Oxford University Press, 2013.

Van Dam, Raymond. *The Roman Revolution of Constantine.* New York: Cambridge University Press, 2007.

SPECIALIZED STUDIES

Barnes. *New Empire of Diocletian and Constantine.*

Hughes, Bettany. *Istanbul: A Tale of Three Cities.* Boston: Da Capo Press, 2017.

Lenski, ed. *Cambridge Companion to the Age of Constantine.*

Nixey, Catherine. *The Darkening Age: The Christian Destruction of the Classical World.* New York: Houghton Mifflin Harcourt, 2018.

THE GHOSTS OF RAVENNA

SOURCES

Mathisen, Ralph W. "Romulus Augustulus (475–476 A.D.)—Two Views." "De Imperatoribus Romanis," www.roman-emperors-org/auggiero.htm.

BIOGRAPHY

Kos, Marjeta Šašel. "The Family of Romulus Augustulus." In Ingomar Weiler and Peter Mauritsch. *Antike Lebenswelten: Konstanz, Wandel, Wirkungsmacht: Festschrift Für Ingomar Weiler Zum 70. Geburtstag.* Wiesbaden, Ger.: Harrassowitz Verlag, 2008, 446–49.

Moorhead, John. *Justinian.* London: Longman, 1994.

Potter, David. *Theodora: Actress, Empress, Saint.* New York: Oxford University Press, 2015.

SPECIALIZED STUDIES

Bowersock, Glen W. "The Vanishing Paradigm of the Fall of Rome." *Bulletin of the American Academy of Arts and Sciences* 49. No. 8 (May, 1996): 29–43.

Goldsworthy, Adrian. *How Rome Fell: Death of a Superpower.* New Haven, CT: Yale University Press, 2009.

Heather, Peter. *The Fall of the Roman Empire: A New History of Rome and the Barbarians.* New York: Oxford University Press, 2007.

Traina, Giusto. *428 AD: an Ordinary Year at the End of the Roman Empire.* Princeton: Princeton University Press, 2009.

Ward-Perkins, Bryan. *The Fall of Rome and the End of Civilization.* Oxford: Oxford University Press, 2005.

ILLUSTRATION CREDITS

INTERIOR

INSERT

9. © Vanni Archive/Art Resource, NY
10. Barry Strauss
11. Barry Strauss
12. Barry Strauss
13. stamkar/Shutterstock.com
14. HIP/Art Resource, NY
15. bpk Bildagentur/Art Resource, NY
16. Marco Rubino/Shutterstock.com
17. carol.anne/Shutterstock.com
18. Barry Strauss
19. Barry Strauss
20. mountainpix/Shutterstock.com
21. mountainpix/Shutterstock.com
22. Barry Strauss

INDEX

ALSO BY BARRY STRAUSS

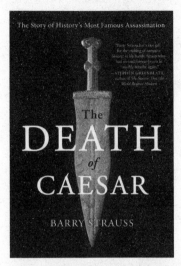

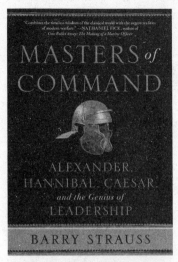

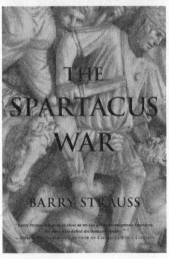

"**Barry Strauss has a rare gift** for the crafting of narrative history: in his hands, figures who had seemed forever frozen in marble breathe again."

—**Stephen Greenblatt**, author of
The Swerve: How the World Became Modern